DICTIONARY
OF
ACCOUNTING
TERMS

DICTIONARY
OF
ACCOUNTING
TERMS

Derek French

First published in Great Britain 1985 by Financial Training Publications
Limited, Avenue House, 131 Holland Park Avenue, London W11 4UT

ISBN: 0 906322 67 7

Typeset by Kerrypress Limited, Luton, Beds
Printed by Redwood Burn Limited, Trowbridge, Wilts

Introduction

Dictionary of Accounting Terms provides definitions of over 3,400 words and expressions used with a special meaning in accounting. The dictionary has been written primarily for people who are studying, or have studied, accounting, and the definitions may be used either as a reminder of what has already been learned or as a basis for study of a new topic. Accounting cannot be learned or practised without understanding its technical terms, especially where the meaning of a word has legal significance, as in company accounting or trusteeship. However, it is impossible actually to learn accounting merely by learning the meanings of its technical terms: accounting must be learned step by step in a logical sequence of topics and with a great deal of practical experience. Accordingly the entries in this dictionary are concise statements of the meanings of terms, without detailed explanations of how accounting techniques are used, and the terms are arranged in a simple alphabetical sequence rather than grouped by subject.

The terms have been chosen so as to provide a good coverage of the topics that have to be studied for professional accountancy examinations. I was concerned for some years in writing and editing the Financial Training Study Packs for accountancy and banking students. It was necessary to ensure that in these students' texts each new technical term is explained when it is first mentioned. In each Study Pack explanations are drawn together and printed as a glossary at the end of the Pack, and I have paid particular attention to those glossaries in compiling this dictionary.

I have included all terms that are specially defined in Statements of Standard Accounting Practice and in Exposure Drafts issued up to May 1985. I have also included a selection of terms that are given statutory definitions in legislation on companies and taxation.

The definitions in this dictionary have been written in accordance with the law and practice of England and Wales. Information has been given about different usages in Scotland and America so as to point to restrictions on where a term may be used. I have also occasionally labelled a term 'informal', meaning that, at present, it would be inappropriate to use it in careful writing except for special effect, or 'colloquial', meaning that the term is used much more in spoken than in written English.

Order in which entries appear
Each entry begins with the word or expression defined, which is the entry title printed in **bold type**. These words and phrases occur in letter-by-letter alphabetical order, disregarding spaces, hyphens, apostrophes and punctuation marks. So, for example, entries appear in the following order:

capital gain
capital gains tax

v

capitalisation issue
capitalise
capital issue

Numerals and the ampersand ('&') are arranged as if they were spelled out as words.

Grammatical description
As is usually the case with technical dictionaries, nearly all the terms defined in this dictionary are nouns or are strings which, if they were part of a sentence would be noun phrases. In this dictionary, if a term is not a noun or a noun phrase, then a brief grammatical description has been given as a warning that the form of the definition will be different from most other definitions in the dictionary. The system of grammatical description used is based on the principles stated in: Rodney Huddleston, *Introduction to the Grammar of English* (Cambridge: Cambridge University Press, 1984).

Homonymy and polysemy
This is almost entirely a dictionary of the written language. Therefore, the only reason for having separate entries for terms is if the terms are written differently (disregarding the use of capital and lower-case letters, italics and typefaces of different weights). (Throughout this dictionary, 'writing' includes handwriting, typing, typesetting for printing or any other visual presentation of English using the alphabet.) If a single written form represents two or more words that are different parts of speech, or one or more words with different meanings, then the entry is divided into numbered paragraphs to deal with the various aspects. The order in which the aspects are dealt with is determined only by my own view of what will make the entry most readable and does not reflect, for example, the history of the use of the term.

As is usual with technical dictionaries, meanings that do not concern accounting are ignored—though it is often difficult to draw the line.

Spelling
There is considerable variation in the way in which English is spelled. When taking care over the presentation of written English, people usually refer to some reference book—usually a dictionary—that they consider authoritative, and most people are unaware that different dictionaries prefer different spellings of the same word or that dictionaries sometimes give alternative spellings without indicating a preference. For convenience, publishing houses adopt arbitrary rules about which alternative is preferred in every case that they have to consider. In choosing how to spell the words and expressions defined in this dictionary I have been guided by the rules adopted by its publisher.

Subject to what is said below about the treatment of abbreviations and designatory letters, hyphenation and '-ise' spelling, I use the spelling preferred in the *Concise Oxford Dictionary*, 7th ed., edited by J.B. Sykes (Oxford: Clarendon Press, 1982) or, where that dictionary gives no clear choice, the spelling preferred in the *Oxford Dictionary for Writers and Editors* (Oxford: Clarendon Press, 1981, reprinted with corrections 1983). If a term does not appear in either of these books I have chosen a spelling myself, influenced, no doubt, by the Oxford style. If, in addition to the spelling chosen for a term when it appears—as the entry title—in the entry in which it is defined, there is an alternative spelling that is often used then the alternative is given after the entry title and there is a separate entry for the alternative, in its correct alphabetical position, referring back to the main entry.

For some words there is a clear difference between British and American spelling—for example, cheque/check, labour/labor. The American spelling of a term is given after the entry title in this dictionary and there is a separate entry for each American spelling referring to the British form unless the two would be next to each other. I have used as authority on American spellings, *Webster's Ninth New Collegiate Dictionary* (Springfield, Mass: Merriam-Webster, 1983).

The suffix '-ise' in a word such as 'capitalise' may be spelled either '-ise' ('s' spelling) or '-ize' ('z' spelling), with some exceptions noted in the next paragraph. Similarly the inflected forms, '-ises', '-ised', '-ising', and the derived forms '-isable' and '-isation' may be spelled with s or z. In America 's' spelling is very rare. In Britain, 's' spelling is quite common, especially in newspapers, and is used in all government publications and by the publishers of this dictionary.

Verbs with infinitives that end '-ise' which can only be spelled with an 's' (both in Britain and America) include: advise, arise, compromise, demise, devise, enterprise, excise, exercise, promise, supervise. The verb 'practise' is spelled only with an 's' in Britain but the word is spelled 'practice' in America. 'Advertise' is spelled with a 'z' by a few people.

Hyphenation and compounding

Sometimes there is an alternative way of writing a term which does not involve using different letters (so in this dictionary the alternative would have the same alphabetical position as the preferred spelling) but involves using or not using a hyphen or space between parts of the term (as with 'flow chart', 'flow-chart' and 'flowchart'). Where such variation occurs for a term defined in this dictionary, I give the entry title in the form preferred by the Oxford dictionaries mentioned under 'spelling' (with some exceptions) followed by any other forms that seem to be in widespread use.

Variation of this kind is quite common and it is often difficult to choose a preferred form. For some terms the form that, in my opinion, is in most common use in accounting is not the one preferred by the *Concise Oxford Dictionary* (COD). I prefer 'changeover' to COD's 'change-over', 'database' to COD's 'data base', 'dividend warrant' to COD's 'dividend-warrant', 'flowchart' to COD's 'flow chart', 'payoff' to COD's 'pay-off'. Also, though the words do not occur in entry titles, I prefer 'cooperate' to COD's 'co-operate' and 'cooperative' to 'co-operative'.

If a phrase written as two or more separate words is put before a noun to modify it (in the manner of an adjective) then the fact that the whole phrase is being used as a unit to modify the noun is emphasised by linking its component words with hyphens—for example 'a winding-up order' as opposed to 'an order for winding up a company'. The possibility that a hyphen may be put in place of a space in a term for this reason is not specially noted in this dictionary. See also under 'Italics' below.

Abbreviations and designatory letters

If a word or expression for which there is an entry has a commonly used abbreviation then the abbreviation is given after the entry title. These abbreviations are also given entries of their own. In this dictionary, abbreviations, and letters designating membership of professional bodies, are set entirely in capitals without internal punctuation unless some other style (as with B/L, Cr, p.a.) is usual. In practice, abbreviations are sometimes written with spaces or full points after each letter (or group of letters) that represents a separate word (for example, 'M.I.C.M.(Grad.)') though this is less common now than in the past. Sometimes, abbreviations (though not designatory letters) are written entirely in lower-case letters (except for a capital first letter when occurring at the beginning of a sentence). The solidus '/' (also called an 'oblique' or a 'diagonal slash') is optional in many abbreviations.

Use of capital letters

In this dictionary, normally, all the letters of an entry title are lower-case (except as noted under 'Abbreviations and designatory letters'). If a letter of an entry title has been set as a capital it is because that letter would normally be written as a capital regardless of the position of the word in a sentence (assuming both capital and lower-case letters are being used). The dictionaries mentioned under 'Spelling' have been relied on as authorities in this respect.

Italics

An entry title is set in **bold italic** if it is usual, when the term occurs in a text in English, to write the term in some way different from the rest of the text. In printing, for example, such a term may be set in *italics* when the rest of the text is not in italic (or vice versa) or may be in a different weight of typeface from the rest of the text. Where different weights of typeface or italic letters are not available (for example, in handwriting and typewriting), such a term may be underlined or put in capitals. This form of distinction is used: (a) for terms that are traditionally regarded as being in a foreign language (for example, *'ab initio'* and many other Latin terms defined in this dictionary), (b) for the titles of books, newspapers, journals, films, plays, etc. and, (c) in the name of a law case, for the name of a party to that case (other uses are not relevant to this dictionary).

The two Oxford dictionaries mentioned under 'Spelling' have been regarded by me as authorities on whether terms are distinguished for reason (a). *Webster's* gives no information on this.

If a phrase written as two or more separate words is written in a distinctive fashion and is put before a noun to modify it then some people consider it unnecessary to put hyphens between the component words (see 'Hyphenation and compounding' above).

Sources and style of definitions

'All definitions are essentially *ad hoc*. They are relevant to some purpose or situation, and consequently are applicable only over a restricted field or "universe of discourse"' (C.K. Ogden and I.A. Richards, *The Meaning of Meaning*, 10th ed. (London: Routledge & Kegan Paul, 1949), p. 111).

In this dictionary the definition of a term is a description of the way in which the term is usually used in accounting, stating what is commonly understood to be the essential part of the meaning of the term. It is in the nature of language that when a word is actually used by a person it is given a special meaning by the context of its use. It is a particular feature of English that words are occasionally used with a variety of grammatical functions with associated changes of meaning. For example, it may be that any English noun is capable of being used to modify other nouns, in the manner of an adjective, and that any English noun can be converted into a verb. A definition of a term in this dictionary should provide enough information to elucidate any non-eccentric current use of the term in accounting, but I do not think it possible to provide a definition in the form of words that can be substituted for the defined term wherever it occurs. Accordingly I have not thought it necessary to word a definition so that it has exactly the same grammatical function as the term defined. I start a definition of a noun with an article, and a definition of the infinitive of a verb with the word 'to', even though these are not present in the entry title. Many of the definitions of adjectives, preposition phrases etc. are introduced with the phrase 'used to describe'. In my opinion this makes the definitions easier to read.

My aim has been to express the definition of each term in my own words so as to achieve a consistent style in the dictionary. However, if a term is given a special meaning for the purposes of an accounting standard or statute, it is important to state the definition of that meaning as nearly as possible in the words used in the document concerned. Wherever this is done, a reference is made to the source of the definition. If a definition in this dictionary is within quotation marks then it has been reproduced unaltered from the source document (apart from any material in square brackets or any omission indicated by three ellipsis points '. . .').

A definition in an accounting standard or a statute is intended to apply only for the purposes of the particular document in which the definition is given. It is intended to delimit the application of the standard or statute rather than to describe how the term is used by people generally. Sometimes, however, the definition given in such a document is also an accurate description of the way the term is used generally; sometimes the importance of the document may have influenced usage; and sometimes a term is devised specially for a document and has no other uses. Where I have taken a definition from a standard or statute but the same term is also used in other ways in accounting then descriptions of those other uses are given in the entry.

The function of British Standard glossaries is to specify the terms that should be used for particular concepts in a subject so as to facilitate information interchange and translation. This naturally involves giving a careful description of the concept to which each term is attached and I have often found it difficult to improve upon those descriptions, especially for the terminology of work study and production planning and control. References to British Standards and quotation marks are used in the same way as for accounting standards and statutes.

I hope that the definitions in quotation marks and the definitions accompanied by a note of a source are the only ones that I have deliberately copied from other writers. Permission for this use of other people's work is noted under 'Acknowledgements'. I have also taken some material from the *Dictionary of Management* which I wrote with Heather Saward (2nd ed., Aldershot: Gower, 1983/London: Pan, 1984). However, it is inevitable that, without quoting a significant number of consecutive words precisely, I have, consciously or unconsciously, taken ways of expressing definitions from books I have consulted. This is partly because there is often very little choice of ways of expressing a definition and partly because it often seems a shame to discard an existing good idea. I am not convinced that a lexicographer, like a poet, has to express every single idea anew (but see Robert Burchfield, 'Dictionaries, new and old', *Encounter*, vol. 43, No. 3 (Sep/Oct 1984), p. 10).

'Person' and 'he'

In definitions in this dictionary, the word 'person' is used where what is referred to could be either an individual human being or an association, either incorporated (such as a limited company) or unincorporated (such as a partnership). The word 'individual' is used where what is referred to can be only an individual human being.

In definitions quoted from statutes the pronoun 'he' is used for an antecedent that could be a male or female individual, or even an association of persons. The Interpretation Act 1979 provides that in any Act of Parliament passed after the year 1850, and in any subordinate legislation made after 1 January 1979, 'unless the contrary intention appears, . . . words importing the masculine gender include the feminine; . . . words in the singular include the plural'.

Citations of law reports

Occasionally definitions refer to a court decision on the meaning of a term and cite a report of the decision in the style usually used by lawyers. Explanations of citations of law reports will be found, e.g., in: Terence Ingman, *The English Legal Process* (London: Financial Training, 1983), pp. 182–6; Glanville Williams, *Learning the Law*, 11th ed. (London: Stevens, 1972), pp. 34–40.

Pending legislation

Some of the information in this dictionary is based on Bills introduced into Parliament in the 1984/85 session which had not been enacted when this dictionary went to press. If enacted they will all be 1985 Acts.

Acknowledgements

This book would not have been written without assistance. The idea for it came from Alan Davidson and Jonathan Sykes of Parks bookshop, High Holborn, London, and they provided me with library and office facilities. The idea was passed to me by Alistair MacQueen of Financial Training Publications Ltd.

Mandy Jones, principally, entered the material into a word processor, and Eric Smith copy-edited the result. Uschi Gubser did much additional word-processing, copy-editing and proof-reading. These and subsequent stages of the production of the book were organised and managed with valued friendliness and customary vigour by Heather Saward. Geoffrey Little questioned many definitions and caused them to be rewritten (as did Eric Smith) and suggested many extra entries.

The following granted permission for the use of copyright material: the Accounting Standards Committee, Addison-Wesley Publishing Co., American Accounting Association, British Standards Institution, Butterworth Scientific Ltd, Institute of Cost and Management Accountants, McGraw-Hill Book Co.

Secretaries and other officials of accountancy bodies provided information on which the entries for the bodies have been based.

The presence of Sylvester and Miranda has always been cheering especially when it became clear that putting together a dictionary to a standard that would satisfy me and people who are to buy it and use it was going to be much more difficult than I had expected.

Si quem dura manet sententia iudicus olim,
   Damnatum aerumnis suppliciisque caput:
Hunc neque fabrili lassent ergastula massa,
   Nec rigidas vexent fossa metalla manus.
Lexica contexat, nam cetera quid moror? omnes
   Poenarum facies hic labor unus habet.

Joseph Juste Scaliger

Abbreviations

The following abbreviations are used in the definitions.

BS	British Standard
c.	chapter
Cmnd	command paper
ED	exposure draft of a proposed Statement of Standard Accounting Practice or Statement of Recommended Practice issued by the Accounting Standards Committee
ed.	edition
FASB	Financial Accounting Standards Board
HMSO	Her Majesty's Stationery Office
IAS	International Accounting Standard
ICMA official terminology	The book, *Management Accounting: Official Terminology of the ICMA* (London: Institute of Cost and Management Accountants, 1982)
ISO	used as part of the reference number of an International Standard
p.	page
para.	paragraph
paras	paragraphs
pp.	pages
r.	rule
reg.	regulation
s.	section
SI	statutory instrument
SR&O	statutory rules and orders
ss.	sections
SSAP	Statement of Standard Accounting Practice

A

A. Abbreviation of 'adverse variance'.

AAAI. Designation of an Associate of the Institute of Administrative Accountants.

AAIA. Designation of an Associate of the Association of International Accountants.

AAPA. Designation of an Associate of the Association of Authorised Public Accountants.

AAT. Abbreviation of 'Association of Accounting Technicians'.

ABC analysis. Arrangement of items in order of value of some quantitative characteristic, putting them into three classes, those with the highest values in class A, those with medium values in class B and those with the lowest values in class C. Also called 'Pareto analysis' because it is reminiscent of work by Vilfredo Pareto (1848-1923), an Italian economist, who studied the distribution of wealth in various countries by considering, for various values of x, the number of individuals within a country whose income exceeded x. Pareto suggested that the distribution of wealth is the same in every country and users of ABC analysis claim that the distribution of the quantitative characteristic among items is the same in many situations, in particular, that 20% of the items will account for 80% of the total value of a quantitative characteristic.

ab initio. *Preposition phrase.* Latin for 'from the beginning'.

abnormal loss. General term for abnormal shrinkage, abnormal spoilage and abnormal waste.

abnormal shrinkage. The difference between actual shrinkage and normal shrinkage.

abnormal spoilage. The difference between actual spoilage and normal spoilage.

abnormal waste. The difference between actual waste and normal waste.

above par. *Preposition phrase.* In relation to a security, at a price greater than its nominal value.

abridged accounts. Any balance sheet or profit and loss account relating to a financial year of a British registered company (or purporting to deal with any such financial year) otherwise than as part of full accounts (Companies Act 1985, s. 255(1)).

absolute bill of sale. A bill of sale of goods in which no provision is made for return of ownership of the goods to the grantor.

absolute difference. The absolute value of the difference between two numbers.

absolute error. The absolute difference between a quantity and an approximation to that quantity.

absolute insolvency. State of having liabilities greater than assets.

absolute value. The absolute value of a number a is a if the number is non-negative, $-a$ if the number is negative. The symbol $|a|$ is used to represent the absolute value of a. Also called 'magnitude', 'modulus', 'numerical value'.

absorbed overhead. The amount of overhead (usually, production overhead costs) included in product costs by means of absorption rates over a period. In America, called 'applied overhead'.

absorption. 1. Short form of the term 'overhead absorption'.

   2. An arrangement under which the entire business and undertaking of one or more companies are transferred to another existing company and the companies whose assets have been transferred are dissolved.

absorption account. Another term for 'valuation account'.

absorption costing. Treating the total of direct costs and absorbed overhead as the most important measure of the costs of a product. Sometimes called 'full absorption costing' in contrast to marginal costing in which variable overhead costs, but not fixed overhead costs, are considered in the cost of a product. Absorbed overhead may be only production overhead costs or may include non-production overhead costs.

absorption rate. The rate at which the costs of a cost centre or product are increased to represent the portion of overhead (usually, production overhead costs) that should be allocated to the centre or product.

abstract. A summary of information.

a/c. Abbreviation of 'account'.

ACA. 1. Designation of an Associate of the Institute of Chartered Accountants in England and Wales.

   2. Designation of an Associate of the Institute of Chartered Accountants in Ireland.

ACAE. Designation of an associated corporate accounting executive.

ACCA. Designation of an Associate of the Chartered Association of Certified Accountants.

accelerated depreciation. 1. Depreciation of an asset by any method under which the charge for depreciation for a year is greater in any one year than it is in the next succeeding year. The declining balance method is one method of accelerated depreciation.

   2. Depreciation of an asset in such a way that the depreciated value is equal to the estimated residual value after a shorter time than would be usual for that type of asset.

accept. 1. *Verb.* To signify acceptance of a bill of exchange.

   2. *Verb.* To communicate agreement to be bound by a contract proposed by an offeror.

acceptable distribution policy. Payments of dividends by a controlled foreign company, in the manner specified in Part I of Schedule 17 to the Finance Act 1984, which will prevent an apportionment of its chargeable profits being made by the Board of Inland Revenue.

acceptance. 1. Signature of a bill of exchange by its drawee. This signature makes the drawee liable to pay the bill when it is duly presented.

2. A bill of exchange that has been accepted.

acceptance commission. A charge made by a bank for accepting a bill of exchange on behalf of a customer.

acceptance credit. A letter of credit under which bills of exchange drawn by the beneficiary will be accepted by the advising bank or by the issuing bank. See also the entry for 'London acceptance credit'.

accepting house. A merchant bank that specialises in financing the international trade of its customers by accepting bills of exchange drawn in connection with that trade. In Britain, the term is normally applied only to the banks that are members of the Accepting Houses Committee.

acceptor. A drawee of a bill of exchange who has signified, by signing the bill, acceptance of liability to pay the bill when it is duly presented.

accommodation bill. A bill of exchange drawn not to pay a debt owed to the drawer but to provide the drawer with a bill of exchange that can be sold (i.e., discounted) to provide money for (i.e., accommodate) the drawer. The drawee of an accommodation bill accepts it only after making satisfactory arrangements with the drawer for reimbursement of the value of the bill. Also called, colloquially, 'kite' or 'windmill'.

accommodation party. A person who has signed a bill of exchange, either as drawer, acceptor or endorser, without receiving value for doing so. Any person who signs a bill of exchange may be liable to pay it and an accommodation party takes on this liability to show that payment of the bill is guaranteed and thus to make the bill easier to sell (i.e., discount). See Bills of Exchange Act 1882, s. 28.

account. 1. A recorded list of financial transactions, or of events (such as movements of stock) expressed in monetary terms, over a period of time. Usually, an account records only transactions or events of a particular kind, such as transactions between an accounting entity and one other person, or transactions of an accounting entity relating to a particular class of its assets, and the account is given a title referring to the class of transactions recorded.

2. Plural form (accounts). Financial statements—in particular, the annual report and accounts of an accounting entity.

3. Plural form (accounts). Another term for 'accounting records'.

4. A regular customer of a business enterprise; a business relationship between an enterprise and one of its regular customers, e.g., a bank account.

5. Another term for 'charge account'.

6. Another term for 'statement'.

7. On the Stock Exchange, another term for 'dealing period'.

accountability. The state or condition of being accountable.

accountable. *Adjective*. Required to provide a description and analysis of actions, usually so that the action may be evaluated.

accountancy. 1. The profession of accounting.

2. The work of accounting.

accountant. An individual whose work involves the application of accounting in performing some or all of the following: preparing financial statements; conducting financial investigations; preparing, reporting and advising on the purchase and sale of businesses, business combinations, obtaining capital for enterprises, changes in partnerships, fraud and insolvency; preparing tax returns; giving advice on taxation; contesting disputed tax before officials; preparing or reporting on profit forecasts and budgets; planning external and internal audits and supervising audit work; advising on, reorganising, devising, and overseeing the installation and implementation of accounting, bookkeeping and related systems. This description has been adapted from: Department of Employment, *Classification of Occupations and Directory of Occupational Titles* (London: HMSO, 1972).

accountant's lien. The right of an accountant in public practice to retain books and documents of a client on which work has been done until payment for that work is received.

account day. On the Stock Exchange, the day on which a bargain (other than a bargain in gilt-edged securities) made during the preceding dealing period must be settled – i.e., the seller must supply the securities being sold and the buyer must pay for them. It is the sixth business day after the end of the dealing period. Also called 'settlement day'.

account form. A layout for a balance sheet in which items are presented in two columns side by side. In Britain, the practice is to put liabilities and owners' equity in the left column and assets in the right column; in America assets are put in the left column and liabilities and owners' equity in the right column.

accounting. Several definitions of 'accounting' have been published in recent years from which the following have been selected and arranged approximately in order of publication.

'Accounting is the art of recording, classifying, and summarising in a significant manner and in terms of money, transactions and events which are, in part at least, of a financial character, and interpreting the results thereof.' (American Institute of Certified Public Accountants, Committee on Terminology, *Accounting Terminology Bulletin No. 1*, para. 9, August 1953, repeating a definition formulated in 1941.)

'The process of identifying, measuring, and communicating economic information to permit informed judgments and decisions by users of the information.' (American Accounting Association, *A Statement of Basic Accounting Theory* (Evanston, Ill, 1966), p. 1.)

'Accounting is a discipline which provides financial and other information essential to the efficient conduct and evaluation of the activities of any organisaton. . . . It includes the development and analysis of data, the testing of their validity and relevance, and the interpretation and communication of the resulting information to intended users. The data may be expressed in monetary or other quantitative terms, or in symbolic or verbal forms.' (Council of the American Institute of Certified Public Accountants, 'A Description of Public Accounting', 1967.)

'Accounting is a service activity. Its function is to provide quantitative information, primarily financial in nature, about economic entities that is intended to be useful in making economic decisions.' (American Institute of Certified Public Accountants, Accounting Principles Board, *Statement No. 4*, para. 9, October 1970.)

'Accounting is the process of observing, measuring, recording,

4

classifying, and summarising the individual activities of an entity, expressed in monetary terms, and interpreting the resulting information.' (Henry E. Riggs, *Accounting: A Survey* (New York: McGraw-Hill, 1981), p. 7.)

'Briefly, the science of collecting, recording, classifying, summarising and interpreting financial (and associated) data, so that business decisions can be made. A language of business communications.' (D. Pitt Francis, *Accounting Concepts and Methods: Accounting 2* (London: Holt, Rinehart & Winston, 1982), p. 345.)

'The art of collecting, processing, reporting, analysing, interpreting, and projecting financial information.' (D. Dupree and M. Marder, *Principles of Accounting* (Reading, Mass: Addison-Wesley, 1984).)

'Accounting is concerned with the quantification of economic events in money terms in order to collect, record, evaluate and communicate the results of past events and to aid in decision-making.' (R.J. Bull, *Accounting in Business*, 5th edition (London: Butterworths, 1984), p. 4.)

'There is no generally accepted definition of accounting.' (Douglas Garbutt, *Accounting Foundations* (London: Pitman, 1980), p. 6.)

accounting asset. An asset that can be given a value in monetary terms.

accounting bases. Defined in SSAP 2 as the methods by which fundamental accounting concepts are applied to financial transactions and items for the purpose of financial accounts, in particular: (a) for determining the accounting periods in which revenue and costs should be recognised in the profit and loss account, and (b) for determining the amounts at which material items should be stated in the balance sheet.

accounting concept. A term used by some writers on accounting for a simple idea which the writer identifies as underlying the theories and practice of accounting. Different authors identify different ideas for this purpose and give various names to the individual ideas. Some of these concepts are called 'accounting principles' in the Companies Act 1985, Schedule 4, paras 9 to 15; some are called 'fundamental accounting assumptions' in IAS 1; some are called 'fundamental accounting concepts' in SSAP 2.

accounting date. For the purposes of the Corporation Tax Acts, the date to which a company makes up its accounts. Called 'balance sheet date' in other contexts.

accounting entity. Something which is a party to financial transactions, or an activity or scheme for which financial transactions are undertaken, and for which accounting records are kept relating only to its transactions. Some examples of activities which may be accounting entities are: a business enterprise conducted by a sole trader, the administration of a trust fund, the activities of a department of a factory, and the trade of one branch of a chain of retail stores. An activity treated as an accounting entity may be carried on by persons who also have other financial transactions not related to that activity. The idea that those other transactions should not be recorded in the accounts of the accounting entity is known as the 'separate entity concept' or (if the activity is a business enterprise) the 'business entity concept'. The separate entity concept is particularly important in accounting for the business affairs of a sole trader, where it may be necessary to make accounting entries to record money or other assets removed from the business activity and taken for personal use by the proprietor, even though there is no change of ownership of money or assets so taken. Also called 'accounting unit', 'entity'.

accounting equation. The statement that, in relation to an accounting entity:

assets = liabilities + equity

'Liabilities' includes long-term loans and provisions. In some circumstances, equity may be called 'owners' equity', 'capital' or 'shareholders' equity' so that the accounting equation may be stated as:

assets = liabilities + owners' equity
assets = liabilities + capital
assets = liabilities + shareholders' equity.

Some people prefer to subtract 'liabilities' from both sides of the equation so that it reads as:

assets – liabilities = equity

In the past, some people have regarded equity as being a liability and such people would express the accounting equation as:

assets = liabilities.

accounting income. Net profit or loss of an accounting entity for a period, including extraordinary items, as reported in the profit and loss account, before deducting related payments of tax or adding amounts of tax recoverable. See IAS 12.

accounting information system. Abbreviation: AIS. A system for providing information in monetary terms about the effects of transactions and events on an accounting entity.

accounting officer. An individual in a government department who is made personally responsible to Parliament for the regularity of any expenditure from the Supply voted for the department and for rendering an appropriation account.

accounting period. 1. The period of time during which the financial effects have occurred that are reported by financial statements of an accounting entity. A balance sheet reports the financial status of the entity at the end of the accounting period; the profit and loss account (or income and expenditure account) and statement of source and application of funds report changes in financial position from beginning to end of the accounting period.

2. In UK revenue law, a period of time (not exceeding 12 months) for which profits are assessed to corporation tax (Income and Corporation Taxes Act 1970, s. 247).

accounting policies. Defined in SSAP 2 as the specific accounting bases selected by an accounting entity as being, in the opinion of those responsible for the entity, appropriate to its circumstances and best suited to present fairly its results and financial position. SSAP 2 requires accounting policies to be applied consistently and this is also required by the Companies Act 1985, Schedule 4, para. 11. SSAP 2 also requires that the accounting policies followed when dealing with items which are judged material or critical in determining profit and loss and stating the financial position should be disclosed by way of notes to the accounts.

accounting principles. 1. Five principles which, by para. 9 of Schedule 4 to the Companies Act 1985, must be followed in preparing financial statements of a company for the purposes of the Act, unless the directors of the company believe that there are special reasons for departing from them. Four of the principles are the same as the fundamental accounting concepts defined in SSAP 2. The fifth principle is that: 'in determining the aggregate amount of any item the amount of each individual asset or liability that falls to be taken into account shall be determined separately'.

2. Used by some authors as a general term for the concepts, rules, methods and procedures of accounting.

accounting records. Records of financial transactions, or of events (such as uses of stock) expressed in monetary terms, made for the purposes of accounting. Also called 'accounts'.

accounting reference date. The date of the end of an accounting reference period of a company. Successive accounting reference periods must normally end on the same day each year, the date of which may be chosen by the company. If no date is chosen by the company then the accounting reference date is 31 March.

accounting reference period. A period of time ending on an accounting reference date and starting on the day after the preceding accounting reference date. A British registered company must prepare a profit and loss account (or income and expenditure account) for a period (called a 'financial year') starting on the first day of an accounting reference period and ending within seven days of the end of that accounting reference period.

accounting standard. A rule which it is widely accepted should be followed in accounting. In particular a rule propounded in a Statement of Standard Accounting Practice.

Accounting Standards Committee. Abbreviation: ASC. A committee within the Consultative Committee of Accountancy Bodies that prepares Statements of Standard Accounting Practice and Statements of Recommended Practice.

accounting technician. An individual whose work involves accounting but who is not regularly responsible for the performance of the tasks listed in the entry for 'accountant'.

accounting unit. Another term for 'accounting entity'.

account payable. An amount owing to a creditor in respect of delivered goods or completed services.

account receivable. An amount owed by a debtor for delivered goods or completed services. Also called 'receivable'.

account sales. A statement rendered by an agent to whom goods have been sent for sale on consignment, which gives details of goods received, sales, expenses incurred, commission charged, remittances made, and the outstanding balance.

accounts for a financial year. In relation to a British registered company, defined in s. 239 of the Companies Act 1985 as comprising the following documents relating to the financial year:

7

(a) the company's profit and loss account (or income and expenditure account) and balance sheet;

(b) the directors' report;

(c) the auditors' report;

(d) if the company has subsidiaries and is obliged to prepare group accounts, the company's group accounts.

accounts receivable collection period. Term used in America for 'debtor days ratio'.

account stated. A spoken or written admission of indebtedness. The term is usually used to imply that there is a promise to repay the debt, and that the debtor cannot subsequently dispute the debt.

accrual. 1. Recognition of the financial effects of transactions and events as they occur rather than when money is received or paid out.

2. An accrued asset or accrued liability.

accrual accounting. Recognition of revenues and costs in the accounts for the period in which they were earned or incurred rather than the period in which the cash is actually received or disbursed.

accruals basis. A principle, which may be used as a basis for the preparation of financial statements, that revenues and costs should be dealt with in the accounts for the period in which they are earned or incurred, so far as this is consistent with the concept of prudence in accounting. In UK revenue law, called 'earnings basis'.

accruals concept. A fundamental accounting concept that revenues and costs should be dealt with in the accounts for the period in which they are earned or incurred, so far as this is consistent with the concept of prudence in accounting, rather than the period in which the cash is actually received or disbursed. This is one of the fundamental accounting concepts identified in SSAP 2, one of the fundamental accounting assumptions identified in IAS 1 and one of the accounting principles set out in the Companies Act 1985, Schedule 4.

accrued asset. An asset recorded in accounts before it is receivable. Because of the concept of prudence in accounting, few assets are thus recorded.

accrued expense. The amount, as recorded in accounts under the accruals concept, incurred up to a particular time of a liability that builds up over a period, such as a liability for electricity consumed or rent payable in arrears.

accrued income. Another term for 'accrued revenue'.

accrued liability. A liability that is recognised in accounts before it is due for payment, especially an accrued expense.

accrued revenue. Revenue that has been earned but is not yet due for payment. Also called 'accrued income'.

accumulate. *Verb.* To capitalise dividends, rents and other income, e.g., in relation to a fund of money held in trust.

accumulated depreciation. The total depreciation provided on a fixed asset.

accumulated earnings. Term used in America for 'reserves'.

accumulated fund. In the accounts of an unincorporated association that is not for profit, an account recording capital contributed by members to which a surplus of income over expenditure is credited and an excess of expenditure over income is debited. Also called 'capital fund'.

accumulation. Capitalisation of dividends, rents and other income, e.g., in relation to a fund of money held in trust.

accumulation and maintenance trust. A trust for an individual beneficiary who does not have an interest in possession but will have on attaining a certain age, until when income produced by the trust property is to be accumulated in so far as it is not applied for the maintenance, education or benefit of the beneficiary. See Capital Transfer Tax Act 1984, s. 71.

accumulation factor. Another term for 'future amount of 1'.

acid-test ratio. The ratio:

$$\frac{\text{quick assets on a particular day}}{\text{current liabilities on that day}}$$

The acid-test ratio measures the ability of an accounting entity to pay its creditors in the short term. Also called 'quick ratio'.

ACMA. Designation of an Associate of the Institute of Cost and Management Accountants.

acoustic coupler. A device for converting signals representing data produced by a data processing system into sounds suitable for transmission through a telephone system, and for receiving such sounds and converting them into signals suitable for processing by the data processing system.

acquisition. 1. The combining of two business enterprises in such a way that the owners of one of the enterprises give up their interest in exchange for consideration given by the other enterprise. Also called 'take-over'.

2. In SSAP 23, a business combination that is accounted for by acquisition accounting.

3. In IAS 12, 'a business combination that is not a uniting of interests' (para. 3).

acquisition accounting. A method of dealing in the group accounts of a holding company with the fact of a company becoming a subsidiary of that holding company in which the results of the new subsidiary are brought into the accounts only from the date on which it became a subsidiary.

ACT. Abbreviation of 'advance corporation tax'.

activity-on-arrow network. In project network techniques, a network in which the arrows represent the activities. Also called 'arrow diagram'.

activity-on-node network. In project network techniques, a network in which the nodes represent the activities.

activity ratio. Another term for 'production volume ratio'. The ICMA official terminology notes that 'activity ratio' is not recommended as the word 'activity' is capable of difference in interpretation.

act of bankruptcy. An event affecting a debtor which a court in England or Wales will recognise as a ground for making a receiving order (the first stage of making the debtor bankrupt). What constitutes an act of bankruptcy is defined in the Bankruptcy Act 1914, s. 1(1), s. 107(4) and s. 130, the Powers of Criminal Courts Act 1973, s. 39, and the Insolvency Act 1976, s. 11 (which has not yet been brought into force). The 1984 Insolvency Bill proposes the abolition of the requirement that an act of bankruptcy should have occurred before a receiving order may be made.

actuarial method. If an asset is paid for by instalments paid at regular intervals over a period of time then, usually, part of the money so paid is payment of the value of the asset at the beginning of the period (called the 'capital value') and part is a charge for being allowed to spread payment over a period of time (called the 'finance charge' or 'charge for credit'). The 'actuarial method' is a method of dividing each instalment into part capital value and part finance charge assuming:

(a) that the finance charge in an instalment is a certain percentage of the total amount owed immediately before that instalment has been paid; and

(b) that finance charges are regarded as part of the amount outstanding on which later finance charges are levied.

The problem is to find the percentage rate of the finance charge, which is usually done by computer because the solution usually cannot be obtained by an algebraic formula. Compare 'rule of 78'.

actuary. An individual whose work involves the application of mathematical and statistical techniques to the computation of insurance risk, and the preparation of insurance and pensions schemes.

added value. Another term for 'value added'.

added value statement. Another term for 'value added statement'.

addend. A number that is added to another number (called the 'augend').

additional rate. A rate of UK income tax determined by subtracting the basic rate for a year of assessment from the rate of tax which, for that year, is applicable to the second higher rate band (Finance Act 1971, s. 32(1)).

additional voluntary contribution. Abbreviation: AVC. A contribution to a pension scheme over and above the regular contributions, if any, required from a member by the scheme rules, which a member elects to pay in order to secure additional benefits (ED 34, para. 12).

address. 1. *Noun.* In data processing, a character or group of characters that identifies a register or a location in a store, or some other source or destination of data.

2. *Verb.* In data processing, to refer to a register, or a location in a store, by its address (in sense 1), or to an item of stored data by the address (in sense 1) of the location where it is stored.

ademption. Revocation of a gift expressed in a will by the testator selling, destroying or giving away the subject-matter of the gift so as to make the gift impossible. A gift that has been revoked by ademption is said to have been 'adeemed'.

adjudication order. Term used in proceedings under the Bankruptcy Act 1914 for an order of a court in England or Wales making an individual a bankrupt and vesting the individual's property in a trustee in bankruptcy for distribution amongst creditors in accordance with bankruptcy law. The 1984 Insolvency Bill uses the term 'bankruptcy order'.

adjusted trial balance. A trial balance incorporating adjusting entries.

adjusting entry. Another term for 'adjustment'.

adjusting event. A post balance sheet event that provides additional evidence of conditions existing at the balance sheet date.

adjusting journal entry. Abbreviation: AJE. An entry in a journal to record an adjustment which is to be posted to ledger accounts.

adjustment. An entry made in accounts which does not record a transaction but which is made so that the accounts will present a true and fair view of the financial position. It includes entries which correct errors, entries for depreciation, bad debts and accrued expenses. Also called 'adjusting entry'.

ad litem. *Preposition phrase.* Latin for 'for the suit'. Used to describe a personal representative, or the appointment of a personal representative, of a deceased individual for the purpose of bringing or defending legal proceedings relating to the estate of the deceased (apart from proceedings concerning the validity of a will of the deceased or the validity of the appointment of personal representatives of the deceased). Compare *'pendente lite'*.

administration cost. Cost of management, and of secretarial, accounting and administrative services, which cannot be directly related to specific functions of the organisation for which separate costs are stated (for example, production, marketing, or research and development). Costs that are normally not regarded as operating costs, such as interest on loans, taxation of income and capital gains, and losses on sales of fixed assets, are not regarded as administration costs. Also called 'administration overhead'. The term 'administration cost' is used in the ICMA official terminology; in America, the term 'administrative expense' is more common; in the formats for profit and loss accounts specified in Schedule 4 to the Companies Act 1985, the term 'administrative expenses' is used for operating costs other than distribution costs and production costs.

administration cost variance. The difference between the budgeted cost of administration for a budget period and the actual administration cost for that period.

administration order. 1. An order made by a county court in England or Wales for the orderly payment of an individual's debts – usually by weekly instalments – and to preclude any other legal proceedings against the individual for debt where the individual's total indebtedness does not exceed the limit for which the court has jurisdiction (£5,000 as from 1 October 1981).

2. Under a procedure proposed by the 1984 Insolvency Bill, an order of a court directing that the affairs, business and property of a company that is, or will be, unable to pay its debts are to be managed by an administrator appointed by the court.

administration overhead. Another term for 'administration cost'.

administration period. The period commencing with the death of an individual and ending on the completion of the administration of the deceased's estate (Income and Corporation Taxes Act 1970, s. 426(1)).

administrative data processing. Automatic data processing used in accounting or management. Also called 'business data processing'.

administrative expense. 1. Term used in America for 'administration cost'.

2. Plural form (administrative expenses). Term used in the formats for profit and loss accounts in the Companies Act 1985, Schedule 4, for operating costs other than distribution costs and production costs. See also the entry for 'administration cost'.

administrative receiver. An individual who is receiver of an incorporated company's property and undertaking subject to a floating charge, appointed by the chargee to utilise the charged property for the purpose of fulfilling the obligation secured by the charge.

administrator. 1. A personal representative of a deceased individual appointed by the High Court. Compare 'executor'. A female administrator is sometimes called an 'administratrix'.

2. Under a procedure proposed by the 1984 Insolvency Bill, an individual appointed by a court to manage the affairs, business and property of a company that is, or will be, unable to pay its debts.

administratrix. Term sometimes used for a female administrator.

ADP. Abbreviation of 'automatic data processing'.

ad val. Abbreviation of '*ad valorem*'.

ad valorem. Abbreviation: *ad val. Preposition phrase.* According to the value. For example, an *ad valorem* tax is a tax which varies in amount according to the value of the property or transaction being taxed.

advance. 1. *Noun.* A payment, for services being, or to be, supplied, or of a royalty, paid before the due date for payment and, possibly, before the amount payable has been finally ascertained.

2. *Verb.* To pay an amount of money as an advance (in sense 1).

3. *Verb.* In the law of trusts, to pay or use the capital of a trust fund in order to benefit a beneficiary of the trust before the beneficiary becomes absolutely entitled to a share in the trust fund, the amount thus paid or used being regarded, when the beneficiary does become absolutely entitled as a payment already made of the share to which that beneficiary is entitled.

4. *Verb.* In the law of succession, to give property to one's child or spouse with the express or implied intention that after one's death the gift is to be regarded as a payment already made of part of the portion of one's estate to be inherited by that child or spouse.

advance corporation tax. Abbreviation: ACT. A tax paid by a company, which is resident in the UK and subject to corporation tax, whenever it distributes any profits. If the company has paid ACT during a year then the amount paid is deducted from the corporation tax that it has to pay for that year. ACT on a distribution also represents the basic-rate income tax payable by recipients of the distribution and each recipient is credited as having paid basic-rate tax on the distribution. The rate of ACT is set each year in the Finance Act. It is equal to:

$$\frac{\text{basic rate of income tax}}{1 - \text{basic rate of income tax}}$$

Thus, if basic-rate income tax is 30%, the rate of ACT is 3/7.

adverse opinion. An audit report that the financial statements do not present a true and fair view of the financial position, results of operations or changes in financial position of the accounting entity in conformity with accounting standards or statutory requirements.

adverse variance. Abbreviation: A. A variance that results in a reduction of profit. Also called 'unfavourable variance'.

advice note. A document sent separately from a consignment of goods to advise that the goods have been sent, usually stating a description of the goods and the method of transport. Compare 'delivery note'. Also called 'dispatch note'.

advising bank. A bank that advises the beneficiary of a letter of credit that the credit has been issued. A bank located conveniently for the beneficiary is chosen to act as advising bank and acts on the instructions of the issuing bank.

affiliate. In America, another term for 'affiliated enterprise'.

affiliated company. In America, another term for 'affiliated enterprise'.

affiliated enterprise. In relation to one enterprise, an enterprise that directly or indirectly controls, is controlled by, or is under common control with, that enterprise; also, a party with which the enterprise may deal if one party has the ability to exercise a significant influence over the other's operating and financial policies (FAS 65). The terms 'affiliated enterprise', 'affiliate' and 'affiliated company' are used in America with roughly the same meaning as the term 'associated company' in Britain.

after-acquired property. Property acquired by an individual after being adjudged bankrupt.

ageing. American spelling: aging. Short form of 'ageing of accounts receivable'.

ageing of accounts receivable. American spelling: 'aging of accounts receivable'. Term used in America for 'ageing of debtors'. Also called 'ageing' (American spelling: aging).

ageing of debtors. American spelling: aging of debtors. Analysis of debtors by reference to the time for which the debts have been outstanding. In America, the term 'accounts receivable' is used instead of 'debtors'. Also called 'ageing'.

agency. 1. The functions, powers and responsibilities of an agent.

2. The relationship between agent and principal.

3. The business of acting as agent for others.

4. A government department.

agenda. A list of business planned to be transacted by a meeting.

agent. 1. Generally, a person who transacts business on behalf of others.

2. In law, a person who has the power and authority to put another person (who is called a 'principal' of the agent) into binding legal relationships.

aging. American spelling of 'ageing'.

aging of accounts receivable. American spelling of 'ageing of accounts receivable'.

aging of debtors. American spelling of 'ageing of debtors'.

AGM. Abbreviation of 'annual general meeting'.

agreed bid. Another term for 'agreed take-over'.

agreed take-over. Also written: agreed takeover. A business combination in which a take-over bid is made for a company whose directors accept the offer in respect of their own shareholdings and recommend other shareholders to accept the offer. Also called 'agreed bid'.

agreement to sell. A contract of sale of goods under which the property in the goods is to be transferred from the buyer to the seller at a future time or subject to some condition to be fulfilled in the future. An agreement to sell becomes a 'sale' when the time elapses or the conditions are fulfilled subject to which the property in the goods is to be transferred. See Sale of Goods Act 1979, s. 2.

air consignment note. A consignment note used in carriage by air for a shipment that is covered by the Warsaw Convention (convention relating to the unification of certain rules relating to international air carriage, 1929) but not the Hague Protocol, 1955, amending the Warsaw Convention.

air waybill. Abbreviation: AWB. A consignment note used in carriage by air for a shipment that is covered by the Hague Protocol, 1955, amending the Warsaw Convention relating to the unification of certain rules relating to international air carriage, 1929.

AIS. Abbreviation of 'accounting information system'.

AJE. Abbreviation of 'adjusting journal entry'.

algorithm. In mathematics, a routine procedure for calculating the solution to a particular type of problem.

A list. In the winding up of a registered company, a list of contributories who were members of the company at the time the winding up commenced.

allocated stock. Another term for 'reserved stock'.

allocation. 1. Reservation of something for a particular purpose or person. Also the quantity reserved. As in 'allocated stock' (another term for 'reserved stock') and 'allocation problem'.

2. See 'cost allocation'.

3. Defined in FASB Statement of Financial Accounting Concepts 3 as: 'the accounting process of assigning or distributing an amount according to a plan or formula'.

allocation problem. In operational research, a problem concerning the distribution of limited resources among competing alternatives in such a way as to minimise total cost or maximise total income. Also called 'programming problem'.

allonge. A piece of paper attached to a bill of exchange when there is no more room on the bill for the signatures of endorsers.

allotment. Assignment of previously unissued shares to particular holders, giving them an unconditional right to be entered in the register of members in respect of those shares. See the entry for 'allotted share'.

allotment letter. Another term for 'letter of allotment'.

allotted share. A share in a company is allotted when a person acquires the unconditional right to be included in the company's register of members in respect of that share (Companies Act 1985, s. 738(1)). The person who has that right is called the 'allottee' of the share. Also called 'issued share'.

allotted share capital. 1. The allotted shares in a company. Also called 'issued share capital'.

2. The total nominal value of all the shares in a company that have been allotted. Also called 'issued share capital'.

allottee. In relation to a newly issued share in a company, a person who has acquired the unconditional right to be included in the company's register of members in respect of the share.

allowance. A deduction, from the amount of an invoiced charge, granted or accepted by the creditor for damage, delay, shortage, imperfection etc. The term does not include cash discounts and amounts allowed for sales returns.

allowance for doubtful accounts. Term used in America for 'provision for doubtful debts'.

allowance for sales discount. Term used in America for 'provision for discounts allowable'.

allowance for uncollectable accounts. Term used in America for 'provision for doubtful debts'.

alphanumeric. *Adjective.* Involving the use of both digits and letters of the alphabet.

alpha risk. Another term for 'type I risk'.

alternative accounting rules. The rules stated in section C of Part II of Schedule 4 to the Companies Act 1985, which are rules for applying the modified historical cost convention to the preparation of financial statements.

ALU. Abbreviation of 'arithmetic and logic unit'.

amalgamation. 1. Another term for 'uniting of interests'.

2. An arrangement under which the entire business and undertaking of two or more companies are transferred to another company newly formed for the purpose and the old companies are dissolved.

amortisation. 1. In Britain, depreciation of an asset with a definite useful life (for example, a non-renewable lease of land) representing loss of value arising from effluxion of time.

2. In America, step-by-step reduction of an amount over a number of accounting periods, e.g., reduction of a debt by instalments, any form of depreciation. Defined in FASB Statement of Financial Accounting Concepts 3 as: 'an allocation process for accounting for prepayments and deferrals'.

amortise. 1. *Verb.* To calculate an amount of amortisation.

2. *Verb.* To repay a loan gradually or put aside money periodically in order to repay a loan.

amount earned for equity. Another term for 'earnings for equity'.

analog model. American spelling of 'analogue model'.

analogous instrument. A financial document that is not a cheque but to which the provisions of the Bills of Exchange Act 1882 relating to crossed cheques apply and in respect of which a collecting bank has a statutory protection against an action for conversion. The documents that are analogous instruments are listed in s. 4 of the Cheques Act 1957 and SIs 1957 No. 1764, 1972 No. 641, 1972 No. 764, 1972 No. 765.

analogue model. American spelling: analog model. A model in which the variables of a system and the relationships between them are represented by variables and relationships in another system.

analysis of variance. Abbreviation: ANOVA, usually spoken as an acronym. A statistical technique in which the sum of the squares of the deviations of observed values of a dependent variable from their arithmetic mean is divided into component parts associated with various sources of variation for the purpose of testing hypotheses concerning the parameters of a mathematical function being used as a symbolic model of the relationship between the dependent variable and one or more independent variables.

analytical review. Abbreviation: AR. In auditing, comparison of amounts recorded for quantities being measured with the amounts predicted by presumed or possible patterns for those quantities.

ancillary credit business. Defined in the Consumer Credit Act 1974, s. 145(1), as: 'any business so far as it comprises or relates to:

'(a) credit brokerage;

'(b) debt-adjusting;

'(c) debt-counselling;

'(d) debt-collecting; or

'(e) the operation of a credit reference agency'.

ancillary work. Service or any other work related to a machine or process which it is not appropriate to classify as productive work (BS 3138 : 1979).

annual accounts. 1. Financial statements for an accounting period that is a calendar year.

2. Financial statements for a financial year of a company.

3. Financial statements for an accounting entity for which such statements are normally prepared once a year.

annual general meeting. Abbreviation: AGM. A meeting of members of an association held once a year to review the activities of the association, to elect officers and to discuss future policy. Usually an association's rules require the holding of an AGM. In British company law, a meeting of the members of a registered company, described as an annual general meeting in the notice convening it, at which the usual business is the declaration of a dividend, the consideration of the annual accounts, and the reports of the directors and auditors, the election of directors in the place of those retiring and the appointment of, and the fixing of the remuneration of, the auditors. See Companies Act 1985, s. 366.

annualise. *Verb.* To express a quantity that is related to time periods as an amount per year.

annual percentage rate. Abbreviation: APR. The total charge for credit in a consumer credit agreement expressed as an annual rate of compound interest in accordance with regulations made under s. 20 of the Consumer Credit Act 1974. The regulations currently in force are the Consumer Credit (Total Charge for Credit) Regulations 1977 (SI 1977 No. 327). Tables of APRs for various repayment schedules have been published by HMSO with the title *Consumer Credit Tables.*

annual report and accounts. Documents prepared regularly once a year by the managers of an accounting entity to report its activities and financial position. Usually, there are a balance sheet, a profit and loss account (or income and expenditure account), a statement of source and application of funds (unless the turnover or gross income is less than £25,000 – see SSAP 10), an auditor's report and a written report summarising activities and prospects.

annual return. A formal or official report that must be made once a year in response to an authoritative order or legal requirement. In particular, the annual report of details of membership and financial structure that each British registered company is required to send to the Registrar of Companies, who makes it available for public inspection. Until 1 October 1977 a company's annual return had to be accompanied by its annual accounts, but accounts are now submitted separately to the Registrar.

annual value. The rent for an item of real property which might reasonably be expected to be obtained on a letting from year to year if the tenant undertook to pay all usual tenant's rates and taxes, and if the landlord undertook to bear the costs of the repairs and of the insurance, and the other expenses, if any, necessary for maintaining the property in a state to command that rent (Income and Corporation Taxes Act 1970, s. 531).

annuitant. A person to whom an annuity is paid.

annuity. A sum of money paid regularly to a person (called the 'annuitant'), either for a fixed period of time or until a specific individual (usually the annuitant) dies. An annuity payable for a fixed period of time is called an 'annuity certain'; an annuity payable until some individual dies is called a 'life annuity'.

annuity certain. An annuity that is payable for a fixed period of time.

annuity method. A method of calculating depreciation on a fixed asset in which the amount of depreciation provided for a year is the same for each year of the useful life of the asset and the depreciated value at the beginning of a year is calculated as: depreciated value at the beginning of the preceding year plus a fixed percentage of the depreciated value at the beginning of the preceding year minus the annual provision for depreciation.

The amount of the annual provision for depreciation is calculated so that, at the end of the useful life, the depreciated value calculated in this way is equal to the estimated residual value of the asset.

ANOVA. Usually spoken as an acronym. Abbreviation of 'analysis of variance'.

antedate. *Verb.* To give as the date of a document (on the document itself) a date that is earlier than the actual date of writing it. The verb 'backdate' may be used with the same meaning.

anticipatory breach. Repudiation of a contractual obligation before it is due to be performed, e.g., by rendering it impossible to perform.

antilogarithm. If y is the logarithm of x then x is the antilogarithm of y.

APC. Abbreviation of 'Auditing Practices Committee'.

applied overhead. Term used in America for 'absorbed overhead'.

applied research. See the entry for 'research and development expenditure'.

apportionment. 1. In relation to a sum of money payable in respect of a period of time (e.g., an amount of rent payable for a year) payment of part of the sum in respect of part of the period.

2. Calculation of an apportionment (in sense 1).

3. See the entry for 'cost apportionment'.

appraisal. Term used in America for 'valuation'.

appraisal surplus. In America, the amount by which the value of an asset as determined by appraisal exceeds the value previously expressed for the asset in the accounting records.

appropriated stock. Another term for 'reserved stock'.

appropriation account. 1. In the accounts of an incorporated company, a ledger account to which the profit for each financial year is credited (or a loss is debited) and dividends paid to the shareholders are debited. Occasionally transfers may be made from this account to reserve accounts or capital accounts. The balance on this account may also be used to acquire the company's own shares.

2. In the accounts of a partnership, a financial statement showing the net

profit for a period, salaries paid to partners, interest paid to and by partners and the amount of each partner's share of the remaining profits.

3. A financial statement showing the expenditures and receipts of a government department for a financial year.

appropriation budget. A list of permitted or authorised expenditures.

appropriation in aid. In British government finance, money, other than money paid from the Consolidated Fund, received by a government department or agency (e.g., fees received for services) that is regarded as paying some of the costs of the department or agency and so reducing the amount that has to be budgeted as a payment for its costs from the Consolidated Fund rather than as general government revenue that is not specifically associated with that department or agency.

approved pension scheme. Another term for 'approved scheme'.

approved scheme. Defined in the Finance Act 1970, s. 26(1), as a retirement benefit scheme for the time being approved by the Board of Inland Revenue for the purpose of chapter 2 of Part II of the Finance Act 1970. Also called 'approved pension scheme'.

APR. Abbreviation of 'annual percentage rate'.

AR. Abbreviation of 'analytical review'.

argument. In mathematics, an item in the domain of a function.

arising basis. The basis of assessment to UK income tax in which all income arising in a period is taken into account whether the income has been or will be received in the United Kingdom or not.

arithmetic and logic unit. Abbreviation: ALU. In a computer, a part of a processor that performs arithmetic operations, logic operations and related operations.

arithmetic mean. The arithmetic mean of n numbers is the sum of the numbers divided by n. Also called 'average' though not by people who specialise in mathematics or statistics.

arithmetic operation. One of the operations traditionally studied in arithmetic, including addition, multiplication, subtraction and division.

arithmetic progression. A sequence in which each term is the sum of its predecessor and a constant called a 'common difference'. For example:

$$1, 3, 5, 7, \ldots$$

(common difference 2).

arithmetic register. In a computer, a store within a processing unit used for holding temporarily the operands and results of arithmetic operations.

arithmetic weighted average. Another term for 'weighted average'.

arm's-length. *Adjective.* Used to describe a transaction between persons on terms that have not been affected by any connection between the persons.

arrow diagram. Another term for 'activity-on-arrow network'.

articles. Clauses of an agreement, and hence the whole agreement itself. In particular: (a) articles of association, (b) an agreement between partners about the management of their partnership (called a 'partnership agreement' or 'articles of partnership'), (c) an agreement between a professional firm (e.g., of accountants) and a trainee about employment during training.

articles of association. In British company law, the regulations governing a company and by which all its members are bound. Articles cover such matters as rules for meetings of members of the company, powers given by the members to directors, payment of dividends and issue of shares. Often referred to as 'articles'.

articles of partnership. Another term for 'partnership agreement'.

articulation. Interrelationship, e.g., of financial statements.

ASC. Abbreviation of 'Accounting Standards Committee'.

ASCA. Designation of an Associate of the Society of Company and Commercial Accountants.

ASCII. The version of ISO-7 specified by the American National Standards Institute for use in the USA. It is the same as the version used in the UK. The name is derived from the words 'American standard code for information interchange'.

ASIA. Designation of an Associate of the Society of Investment Analysts.

asset. 1. An item of property of an accounting entity that is expected to confer an economic benefit to the entity. In accounting, an item of property can only be an asset if it can be given a value in monetary terms and such an asset is sometimes called an 'accounting asset'.

FASB Statement of Financial Accounting Concepts No. 3 states: 'Assets are probable [footnote omitted] future economic benefits obtained or controlled by a particular entity as a result of past transactions or events' (para. 19). It goes on to identify three essential characteristics of an asset: '(a) it embodies a probable future benefit that involves a capacity, singly or in combination with other assets, to contribute directly or indirectly to future net cash inflows, (b) a particular enterprise can obtain the benefit and control others' access to it, and (c) the transaction or other event giving rise to the enterprise's right to control of the benefit has already occurred' (para. 20).

2. A resource; something which confers an advantage that is not necessarily capable of being objectively valued.

3. Defined in the Capital Gains Tax Act 1979, s. 19(1), as 'all forms of property . . . whether situated in the United Kingdom or not, including:

'(a) options, debts and incorporeal property generally, and

'(b) any currency other than sterling, and

'(c) any form of property created by the person disposing of it, or otherwise coming to be owned without being acquired'.

See also the entry for 'chargeable asset'.

asset account. An account in a nominal ledger dealing with transactions relating to a particular type of asset or one particular asset.

asset cover. The ratio:

$$\frac{\text{net tangible assets before deducting borrowings}}{\text{total borrowings}}$$

Overdrafts are included in 'borrowings'.

asset register. Another term for 'fixed assets register'.

asset stripping. Acquiring an incorporated company in order to sell its fixed assets and usually without intending to continue its business.

assigned stock. Another term for 'reserved stock'.

assignment problem. In operational research, an allocation problem in which exactly one resource unit has to be allocated to each alternative use, and the numbers of alternative uses and resource units are equal.

assisted area. One of the areas of the UK in which special government assistance is available to industry in order to reduce unemployment. The assisted areas are the development areas, the intermediate areas and Northern Ireland.

associated company. For the purposes of SSAP 1, a company is an associated company of another company (or group of companies), which is called an 'investing company' (or 'investing group'), if it is not a subsidiary of the investing company or a member of the investing group, and:

(a) The interest of the investing group or company is effectively that of a partner in a joint venture or consortium and the investing group or company is in a position to exercise a significant influence over the company; or

(b) The interest of the investing group or company is for the long term and is substantial and, having regard to the disposition of other interests in the company, the investing group or company is in a position to exercise a significant influence over the company.

Significant influence over a company essentially involves participation in the financial and operating policy decisions of that company (including dividend policy), but not necessarily control of those policies. Representation on the board of directors is indicative of such participation, but will neither necessarily give conclusive evidence of it, nor be the only method by which the investing company may participate in policy decisions.

The interest of the investing group or company in an associated company is sometimes called a 'trade investment'.

In America, the concept of 'affiliated enterprise' is similar.

associated corporate accounting executive. A student undertaking the professional examination of the Association of International Accountants.

associated operations. For the purposes of capital transfer tax, defined by the Capital Transfer Tax Act 1984, s. 268(1), as: 'any two or more operations of any kind, being:

'(a) operations which affect the same property, or one of which affects some property and the other or others of which affect property which represents, whether directly or indirectly, that property, or income arising from that property, or any property representing accumulations of any such income, or

'(b) any two operations of which one is effected with reference to the other, or with a view to enabling the other to be effected or facilitating its being effected, and any further operation having a like relation to any of those two, and so on,

'whether those operations are effected by the same person or different persons, and whether or not they are simultaneous; and "operation" includes an omission'.

Association of Accounting Technicians. Abbreviation: AAT. An accountancy body for accounting technicians working for accountancy firms in public practice, and working in industry, commerce and the public sector. The council of the Association awards qualifications at two levels: Member, designated MAAT, and Senior Accounting Technician, designated SAT. Membership is attained by passing the Association's examination or obtaining exemption, and gaining three years' accounting experience after registration as a student. A Member may become a Senior Accounting Technician after acquiring a minimum of five years' relevant professional experience at a senior level.

Address: 21 Jockey's Fields, London WC1R 4BN. Telephone: 01-405 4961.

Association of Authorised Public Accountants. A professional association of statutory accountants in the UK. Membership of the Association is restricted to individuals who are qualified for appointment as auditors of companies under British company law. The Association is particularly concerned to represent the interests of accountants who are authorised by the Secretary of State to be appointed as auditors under the Companies Act 1985, s. 389(1)(b) and those who retain an authorisation formerly granted by the Board of Trade or the Secretary of State under the Companies Act 1948, s. 161(1)(b) or the Companies Act 1967, s. 13(1). There are two grades of membership: Associate, designated AAPA, and Fellow, designated FAPA.

Address: 10 Cornfield Road, Eastbourne, East Sussex BN21 4QE. Telephone: Eastbourne 641514.

Association of Corporate Treasurers. A professional association of people whose work is concerned with treasurership in companies. There are two grades of membership: Member, designated MCT, and Fellow, designated FCT. Membership is obtained by examination. A Member must be aged 25 or more and must have been engaged for at least two years in positions of senior responsibility for the corporate treasury function or in teaching treasurership. A Fellow must be aged 30 or more and must have been engaged for at least five years in positions of senior responsibility for the corporate treasury function or in teaching treasurership.

Address: 16 Park Crescent, Regent's Park, London W1N 4AH. Telephone: 01-631 1991.

Association of International Accountants. A world-wide organisation for professional accountants, which promotes international accountancy. Members have senior financial and managerial appointments in commerce and industry, and also work in private practice. Membership is by examination and members must have had an appropriate period of approved practical accountancy experience and must hold an approved accountancy appointment. There are two grades of membership: Associate, designated AAIA, and Fellow, designated FAIA. Members are styled 'international accountant'. A student undertaking the Association's professional examination is styled 'associated corporate accounting executive', designated ACAE.

Address: 2-10 St John's Street, Bedford MK42 0DW. Telephone: Bedford 213577.

at arm's length. *Preposition phrase.* Used to describe a transaction between persons on terms that have not been affected by any connection between the persons.

at call. *Preposition phrase.* Used to describe money lent on condition that it will be repaid immediately when demand for repayment is made – i.e., when repayment is called for – usually with the implication that the borrower is known to be capable of repaying the money at any time.

ATII. Designation of an Associate of the Institute of Taxation.

at par. *Preposition phrase.* In relation to a security, at a price equal to its nominal value.

attachment of earnings. Procedure for obtaining payment from an individual in employment of a judgment debt or an amount payable under a court order in which a county court orders the individual's employer to withhold money from the individual's remuneration and pay it to the court.

attainable standard. A standard that can be attained if a standard unit of work is carried out efficiently, a machine properly operated or material properly used. In setting an attainable standard, allowances are made for normal waste and machine breakdowns so that the standard represents future performance objectives that are reasonably attainable.

attendance bonus. An addition to normal wages which an employer promises to give to employees who achieve a certain standard of timekeeping or lack of absence from work.

attendance time. The total time spent by a worker at a place or places of employment, whether working or available for work, for which payment is made (BS 3138 : 1979).

attest. *Verb.* To make an attestation.

attestation. A description of an occurrence given by an individual who was present at the occurrence and observed it.

attestation clause. A statement in a document in which witnesses describe the execution of the document. In Scotland, called 'testing clause'.

attributable profit. The part of the total profit currently estimated to arise over the duration of a long-term contract (after allowing for likely increases in costs so far as they are not recoverable under the terms of the contract) which fairly reflects the profit attributable to the part of the work performed up to a particular date. There can be no attributable profit until the outcome of the contract can be assessed with reasonable certainty. See SSAP 9.

attributes sampling. In auditing, taking a sample of the records of events or transactions of a particular kind and checking items in the sample for the presence or absence of some attribute (usually, whether the item is erroneous) and recording the number of items that possess the attribute.

audit. 1. *Noun.* For the purposes of British and Irish Auditing Standards and Auditing Guidelines, 'the independent examination of, and expression of opinion on, the financial statements of an enterprise by an appointed auditor in pursuance of that appointment and in compliance with any relevant statutory obligation'. In this definition, 'enterprise' means 'any body corporate or other organisation on the financial statements of which the auditor is reporting'.

2. *Verb.* To carry out an audit (in sense 1).

Audit Commission. Short form of the name 'Audit Commission for Local Authorities in England and Wales'.

Audit Commission for Local Authorities in England and Wales. A corporation established in January 1983 under the Local Government Finance Act 1982 with a primary function of appointing auditors to audit the accounts of local authorities and other bodies concerned with local government in England and Wales. The Commission may have a minimum of 13 and maximum of 17 members who are appointed by the Secretary of State. Its chief officer is called the 'Controller of Audit'. 'Audit Commission' is commonly used as a short form of the name.

audit committee. A committee of directors of a company responsible for facilitating and improving audits of its financial statements and for dealing with matters raised by auditors. An audit committee also usually supervises internal auditing.

audit evidence. Information obtained by an auditor in arriving at the conclusions which form the basis of the auditor's opinion on the financial statements being audited.

audit fee. The fee charged for carrying out an audit.

Auditing Guideline. A statement approved by the councils of the Institute of Chartered Accountants in England and Wales, the Institute of Chartered Accountants of Scotland, the Institute of Chartered Accountants in Ireland and the Chartered Association of Certified Accountants which does not prescribe basic principles and practices, but gives guidance on:

(a) procedures by which Auditing Standards may be applied;

(b) the application of Auditing Standards to specific items appearing in the financial statements of enterprises;

(c) techniques currently being used in auditing;

(d) audit problems relating to particular commercial or legal circumstances or to specific industries.

Auditing Practices Committee. Abbreviation: APC. A committee within the Consultative Committee of Accountancy Bodies that prepares Auditing Standards and Guidelines.

Auditing Standard. A statement approved by the councils of the Institute of Chartered Accountants in England and Wales, the Institute of Chartered Accountants of Scotland, the Institute of Chartered Accountants in Ireland and the Chartered Association of Certified Accountants which prescribes basic principles and practices which members of those institutes are expected to follow in the conduct of an audit.

audit opinion. Another term for 'audit report'.

auditor. For the purposes of British and Irish Auditing Standards and Auditing Guidelines, the individual, or partnership firm, appointed to carry out an audit of the financial statements of an accounting entity. The term is also to be understood to cover employees of such an individual or firm to whom work on the audit has been delegated, and partners of an individual auditor. In practice, the plural form 'auditors' is used to refer to a partnership firm appointed to carry out an audit. 'Auditors' is also used to refer to the staff engaged on an audit.

auditor's opinion. Another term for 'audit report'.

auditor's report. Another term for 'audit report'.

audit report. Any written report by an auditor on a matter on which an opinion has been sought within the terms of the auditor's appointment. In the UK, specifically, the report on a company's financial statements required by s. 236 of the Companies Act 1985. Also called 'audit opinion', 'auditor's opinion', 'auditor's report'.

audit staff. The employees of an individual or of a partnership firm, appointed to carry out an audit, who take a direct part in the audit.

audit trail. A sequence of connected pieces of evidence demonstrating how a figure in financial statements being audited has been derived from original transactions.

augend. A number to which another number (called the 'addend') is added.

authorised auditor. An individual who, though not a chartered accountant or a certified accountant, may, under the Companies Act 1985, s. 389(2), be appointed auditor of a British registered company. Also called 'statutory accountant'.

authorised capital. Another term for 'nominal share capital'.

authorised minimum. The minimum amount of allotted share capital that a public company must have. Under the Companies Act 1985, s. 118(1), the authorised minimum is £50,000 or such other sum as the Secretary of State may otherwise specify by order made by statutory instrument.

authorised share capital. Another term for 'nominal share capital'.

authorised unit trust. A unit trust scheme that has been authorised by order of the Department of Trade and Industry under the Prevention of Fraud (Investments) Act 1958, s. 17, or of the Northern Ireland Department of Commerce under the Prevention of Fraud (Investments) Act (Northern Ireland) 1940, s. 16.

autocorrelation. Dependence of each of a sequence of observed values of a variable on one or more of the preceding observations.

automatic data processing. Abbreviation: ADP. Data processing performed mainly by devices that do not require human intervention while carrying out a job.

automatic resulting trust. A trust that arises as a matter of law where one person transfers property to a second person on trusts which for some reason leave some or all of the beneficial interest undisposed of so that the second person automatically holds the property on a resulting trust for the first person to the extent of the undisposed-of beneficial interest.

available for ordinary. *Adjective phrase.* Used to describe the amount of earnings for equity.

available hour. An hour during which a worker or machine is available for work.

available time. 'The period of time between the placing of a production order and the due date required' (BS 5191 : 1975).

aval. A signature on a bill of exchange put on to indicate that the signatory guarantees payment of the bill.

AVC. Abbreviation of 'additional voluntary contribution'.

AVCO. Usually spoken as an acronym. Abbreviation of 'average cost'.

average cost. Abbreviation: AVCO. A method of determining the purchase price or production cost of some class of stocks and work in progress in which the total cost of the stocks of that class purchased or produced during a period is divided by the number of units purchased or produced and the resulting average cost is multiplied by the number of units in stock at the end of the period.

average deviation. Another term for 'mean deviation'.

average due date. See the entry for 'equation of payments'.

average time of payment. See the entry for 'equation of payments'.

avoidable cost. A cost that is identified with a particular activity and which would not be incurred if that activity were not undertaken.

AWB. Abbreviation of 'air waybill'.

B

BAA. Abbreviation of 'British Accounting Association'.

backdate. 1. *Verb.* To give as the date of a document (on the document itself) a date that is earlier than the actual date of writing it. The verb 'antedate' is used with the same meaning.

2. *Verb.* To declare that a change made at one time in a contract, rule, procedure or law is to be treated as having been made at an earlier time.

back duty. Tax which should have been paid in the past by a person who failed to provide adequate information at the time for a correct assessment to be made of tax payable.

backing store. Another term for 'external store'.

backlog depreciation. In current cost accounting, in relation to a depreciable asset, the effect of changing prices on the accumulated depreciation stated for the asset in historical cost accounts. If accumulated depreciation must be increased to meet the effect of changing prices the amount of the increase is transferred to current cost reserve; if it must be decreased the amount of the decrease is transferred from current cost reserve.

back-to-back credit. An arrangement for financing the purchase of goods which are first supplied to an intermediary who then supplies them to the ultimate purchaser. The ultimate purchaser applies for a letter of credit to be issued in favour of the intermediary; this credit is used by the intermediary as security when applying for the issue of a further credit or credits in favour of the suppliers of the goods.

back-to-back loan. A loan from one person A to another person B in one currency accompanied by a simultaneous loan by B to A in another currency with the loans being approximately equal in value at the time they are made.

backwardation. 1. A fee paid to a stockbroker, by a person for whom the stockbroker has arranged to sell securities, for the privilege of delaying delivery of the securities.

2. A state in which the spot price for something is higher than the forward price for the same thing.

3. The difference between the forward price for something and the spot price for the same thing when the spot price is higher than the forward price.

bad debt. 1. A debt that, it is assumed, will never be paid. Also called 'doubtful debt'.

2. A debt that has not been paid and has been written off.

bailee. The person to whom possession of an item of tangible personal property is given in bailment.

bailment. Giving possession of an item of tangible personal property to a person (called the 'bailee') for a particular purpose on condition that the possession will be given up when the purpose is fulfilled. Bailment occurs, for example, when a thing is given to a person for repair, storage or transportation.

bailor. The person who gives possession of an item of tangible personal property in bailment.

balance. 1. *Noun.* The difference between the total credit entries and the total debit entries made in an account since it was last balanced. When credits are larger than debits there is a 'credit balance'. When debits are larger than credits there is a 'debit balance'.

2. *Verb.* To calculate the difference between the total debit entries made in an account since it was last balanced and the total credit entries made since then, and to make appropriate bookkeeping entries. See the entries for 'balance off' and 'close off'.

balance off. *Verb with particle.* To enter the balance of a ledger account in that account (as a credit if it is a debit balance, or a debit if it is a credit balance) and make the corresponding double entry as the opening balance for the next period in the same account.

balance sheet. A financial statement for an accounting entity which shows its financial position on a particular day (called the 'balance sheet date') by stating the values of its assets and liabilities on that day and, where appropriate, the owners' equity on that day. A balance sheet is a classified summary of the balances on the ledger accounts of the accounting entity after nominal accounts have been closed off. A balance sheet is drawn up in a conventional form. Until recently, the 'account form' was usual, which was in two columns with assets listed in one column and liabilities and owners' equity in the other column: by virtue of the accounting equation, the totals of the two columns would be equal. Nowadays, the 'vertical form' or 'narrative form' is more usual.

balance sheet asset value. In relation to a registered company, the total of the assets of the company minus the total of the liabilities and provisions and any capital the repayment of which, in the event of a winding up, would have priority over the ordinary share capital. By virtue of the accounting equation, the total amount of the balance sheet asset value is equal to the shareholders' equity. Balance sheet asset value is usually expressed as an amount per ordinary share by dividing the total amount by the number of issued ordinary shares.

balance sheet audit. An audit that is restricted to verifying the existence and valuation of assets and liabilities shown in a balance sheet of the entity being audited without examining other financial statements.

balance sheet date. The date at which a balance sheet of an accounting entity describes the financial position of the entity. A balance sheet is often described as the balance sheet 'as at' the balance sheet date.

balance sheet equation. Another term for 'accounting equation'.

balance sheet total. The total value of assets shown in a balance sheet.

balancing adjustment. A balancing allowance or a balancing charge.

balancing allowance. A capital allowance made in certain circumstances where the full amount of the capital expenditure has not been deducted from income or profits by virtue of other capital allowances. See Finance Act 1971, s. 44(2)(b), Capital Allowances Act 1968, ss. 3(1), 58(2), 60(4)(b), and 67(2), Income and Corporation Taxes Act 1970, ss. 379(2) and 386(1), Finance Act 1982, Schedule 12, para. 4.

balancing charge. An extra charge to income tax or corporation tax made when capital allowances exceed the actual amount of capital expenditure.

balancing figure. A figure which will make one quantity equal another.

bank. 1. *Noun.* A person conducting a banking business. A person carries on a banking business if:

(a) The person accepts money from, and collects cheques for, customers and places them to their credit.

(b) The person honours cheques or orders drawn by customers when presented for payment and debits customers accordingly.

(c) The person keeps current accounts in which the credits and debits are entered.

A person carrying on a banking business may not be described to the general public in the UK as a 'bank' unless recognised by the Bank of England under the Banking Act 1979. In much of the legislation relating to banking, the term 'banker' is used instead of 'bank' partly because when the legislation was drafted banks were usually operated by partnerships rather than, as now, incorporated companies.

2. *Verb.* To hand cash or financial documents to a bank (in sense 1) for credit to an account.

bank account. 1. An account recording deposits by the accounting entity of money at a bank, and cheques drawn by the accounting entity on that bank.

2. The relationship between a bank and one of its customers. A bank account may be a 'current account' or a 'deposit account'.

bank agreement. Another term for 'bank reconciliation'.

bank balance. The balance on an account of a customer of a bank, or a total of the balances of all accounts of a customer of a bank.

bank bill. A bill of exchange with a bank as drawee.

bank charge. A charge made by a bank to a customer for the bank's services.

bank confirmation. Term used in America for 'bank report'.

bank draft. Another term for 'banker's draft'.

banker. A person conducting a banking business. The term is commonly thought to imply that the person is an individual rather than an incorporated company for which the term 'bank' would be more appropriate. However, 'banker' is used in many UK statutes including the Bills of Exchange Act 1882, s. 2 of which states that ' "banker" includes a body of persons whether incorporated or not who carry on the business of banking'. A banker may not be described to the general public in the UK as a 'bank' unless recognised by the Bank of England under the Banking Act 1979.

banker's commercial credit. Another term for 'letter of credit'.

banker's discount. Another term for 'simple discount'.

banker's draft. 1. A financial document, drawn by an officer of a bank, by which the bank promises to pay a certain sum of money to a named payee and, usually, on demand. A banker's draft of this type drawn payable to bearer is a banknote. Also called 'bank draft'. In America, called 'cashier's cheque'.

2. A cheque drawn by an officer of a bank on that bank's current account with another bank. Also called 'bank draft'. In America, called 'cashier's cheque'.

banker's order. An order from a customer of a bank to the bank requesting it to make payments of specified amounts at specified times (usually at regular intervals until the order is cancelled) from the customer's account to another bank account.

banker's payment. A banker's draft in favour of another bank used for settlement of business between the banks.

Bank Giro. A system for dealing with bankers' orders, credit transfers and direct debits operated by British banks.

bank mandate. See the entry for 'mandate'.

banknote. A financial document issued by a bank by which the bank promises to pay the bearer of the document, on demand, a specified sum of money. In England and Wales only the Bank of England may issue banknotes.

bank overdraft. Money borrowed from a bank on current account so that interest is charged only on the amount outstanding each day.

bank reconciliation. A statement showing why a balance recorded in a cash book is not the same as the balance recorded on a bank statement. The difference will be made up of unpresented cheques, errors etc. Also called 'bank agreement'.

bank report. A report made by a bank to the auditor of an accounting entity giving details of the entity's dealings with the bank during the period under investigation. In America, called 'bank confirmation'.

bankrupt. 1. *Noun.* An individual against whom a court has made an adjudication of bankruptcy.

2. *Adjective.* In law, having the status of bankruptcy.

3. *Adjective.* Often used imprecisely to mean 'insolvent'.

bankruptcy. Legal status imposed by adjudication of a court on an individual (who is called a 'bankrupt'), in which all property of the bankrupt is transferred to a 'trustee in bankruptcy' to be used to pay the debts of the bankrupt existing at the time of adjudication and under which the creditors at the time of adjudication are not permitted to take proceedings against the bankrupt personally but must deal with the trustee. A bankrupt is usually subject to various disabilities; for example, in England and Wales a bankrupt cannot hold public office or be a director of a company or, without disclosing the bankruptcy, obtain credit of £50.00 or more. The status of bankruptcy continues until 'discharged' and until that time a bankrupt is usually described as an 'undischarged bankrupt'. In most cases in England and Wales discharge occurs automatically on the fifth anniversary of adjudicaton of bankruptcy. The 1984 Insolvency Bill proposes to reduce this period to three years. It is also possible for an adjudication of bankruptcy to be annulled if all the debts existing at the time of adjudication are paid in full.

bankruptcy notice. Under the Bankruptcy Act 1914, a notice sent to a judgment debtor, requiring payment of the debt and warning the debtor that if the payment is not made then proceedings may be commenced to make the debtor bankrupt. A bankruptcy notice must be in the prescribed form stated in the Bankruptcy Act 1914, s. 2. The 1984 Insolvency Bill proposes the abolition of bankruptcy notices.

bankruptcy order. Term used in the 1984 Insolvency Bill for an order of a court adjudging an individual bankrupt.

bankruptcy petition. A petition to a court initiating bankruptcy proceedings and requesting the court to make a receiving order under the Bankruptcy Act 1914 (or a bankruptcy order under the procedure proposed by the 1984 Insolvency Bill).

bank statement. A list of transactions on a customer's bank account provided for the customer by the bank.

bar. Informal. One million pounds sterling. 'Half a bar' is £500,000.

bar diagram. A diagram representing the frequency distribution of a discrete variable. Each value of the variable is represented by a point on a straight line and at each of these points a perpendicular line is drawn with length proportional to the frequency of occurrence of that value.

bare trustee. A trustee who has no active duties to perform and holds the trust property in name only, having undertaken not to do anything with the property except under the direction of some other person.

base rate. 1. A rate of interest that is used as a starting-point for computing the rates to be charged by a bank to a customer for an overdraft or other form of loan.

2. Another term for 'basic rate'.

basic costing method. Another term for 'costing method'.

basic rate. 1. The minimum wage rate for a job excluding any allowances such as overtime premium or bonus. Also called 'base rate', 'basic wage rate'.

2. The minimum wage rate for a job agreed in a national agreement but subject to local increases. Also called 'base rate', 'basic wage rate'.

3. The rate of UK income tax payable on the part of taxable income that does not exceed an amount that is known as the 'basic rate limit'. The basic rate is determined each year by Parliament (Finance Act 1971, s. 32(1)(a)) but the basic rate limit is altered by the Treasury each year in line with inflation in accordance with the Finance Act 1980, s. 24, unless Parliament otherwise determines.

basic research. See the entry for 'research and development expenditure'.

basic standard. A standard established for use over a long period from which a current standard can be developed.

basic wage rate. Another term for 'basic rate'.

basis of apportionment. A rule for allocating indirect costs or overheads to cost centres or products.

basis of assessment. The period during which, and the place at which, financial transactions must occur for them to be taken into account for the purpose of assessing liability to tax for a particular financial year or year of assessment. See the entries for 'arising basis', 'current-year basis', 'preceding-year basis' and 'remittance basis'.

basis period. The period during which financial transactions must occur for them to be taken into account for the purpose of assessing liability to tax for a particular financial year or year of assessment. See the entries for 'current-year basis', 'preceding-year basis'.

For the purposes of claiming capital allowances against UK income tax, the term is defined in detail in the Capital Allowances Act 1968, s. 72.

basis point. One-hundredth of a percentage point.

batch. A definite quantity of some product manufactured or produced under conditions which are presumed uniform, which, for production control purposes, passes as a unit through the same series of operations (see BS 5191 : 1975). Also called 'lot'.

batch cost. The cost of a batch of a number of identical units of output which is considered as a single cost unit.

batch costing. Specific-order costing when used to cost a single batch of a number of identical units of a product. In America, called 'job-lot costing'.

batch processing. 1. In data processing, any way of arranging jobs for execution or data for processing that involves accumulating jobs or data before work starts on them.

2. Executing computer programs in such a way that work on one program is completed before work on the next is started.

baud. In the transmission of data, a unit of signalling speed equal to one signal event or discrete condition per second, e.g., one bit per second in a train of binary signals. The word is taken from the surname of Émile Baudot (1845–1903), a French telegraphic engineer.

BCD notation. Abbreviation of 'binary-coded decimal notation'.

b/d. Abbreviation of 'brought down'.

BDV. Abbreviation of 'Budget Day value'.

B/E. Abbreviation of 'bill of exchange'.

bear. A person who anticipates that the price of something will fall, e.g., by contracting to sell at a fixed price at a future time in the expectation that by then it will be possible to buy in the same market at a lower price.

bearer. 1. The person who is in possession of a financial document payable to bearer. See Bills of Exchange Act 1882, s. 2.

2. The person who is in possession of a bearer security.

bearer bond. A bond that is a bearer security.

bearer debenture. A bearer security issued by a registered company and representing an interest in a marketable loan.

bearer security. A security that can be transferred from one owner to another merely by giving possession of a certificate of ownership. Also, the certificate of ownership of such a security. Compare 'registered security'.

bearer share. 1. A share in a company, ownership of which is evidenced by a bearer security.

2. A bearer security (called a 'share warrant' in Britain) that evidences ownership of a share in a company.

bell-shaped curve. See the entry for 'normal curve'.

below par. *Preposition phrase.* In relation to a security, at a price less than its nominal value.

below the line. *Preposition phrase.* Not taken into account when computing a specified kind of profit; in particular, not taken into account when computing profit on ordinary activities after taxation.

beneficiary. 1. A person to whom a gift is made.

    2. See the entry for 'letter of credit'.

    3. See the entry for 'trust'.

benefit-cost ratio. Another term for 'profitability index'.

bequeath. *Verb.* To give a person an item of property as a legacy in a will.

bequest. Another term for 'legacy'.

bereavement pay. Pay given to an employee who is on leave because a close relative has died.

BES. Abbreviation of 'Business Expansion Scheme'.

beta. In portfolio theory, the percentage change in the risk premium (excess return) of a particular investment that is associated with a 1 per cent change in the risk premium of the market portfolio. The quantity is the regression coefficient in a regression equation with the risk premium of the security as dependent variable and the risk premium of the market portfolio (as measured by, for example, an index of stock exchange prices) as independent variable, and a regression coefficient is traditionally denoted by the Greek letter beta (β). Also called beta coefficient.

beta coefficient. 1. Another term for 'regression coefficient'.

    2. In portfolio theory, another term for 'beta'.

beta risk. Another term for 'type II risk'.

b/f. Abbreviation of 'brought forward'.

bid bond. Another term for 'tender bond'.

bid price. 1. The price at which the manager of a unit trust will buy a unit.

    2. The price at which a jobber will buy a security.

big-ticket lease. A lease of equipment with a high value, say, £5 million or more.

bill. 1. A bill of exchange.

    2. An invoice.

    3. Draft legislation presented to a legislative body for discussion.

    4. A currency note.

    5. A security (usually a bearer security) representing an interest in a marketable loan.

    See also the entries for 'bill of lading', 'bill of materials' and 'bill of sale'.

billion. Abbreviation: bn. Now generally one thousand millions. Formerly, in Britain, one million millions.

bill of exchange. Abbreviation: B/E. Defined in s. 3(1) of the Bills of Exchange Act 1882 as: 'an unconditional order in writing, addressed by one person to another, signed by the person giving it, requiring the person to whom it is addressed to pay on demand or at a fixed or determinable future time a sum certain in money to or to the order of a specified person, or to bearer'.

    The person giving the unconditional order is called the 'drawer' of the bill; the person to whom it is addressed is called the 'drawee' of the bill; and if the bill specifies a person to whom payment is to be made then that person is called the 'payee' of the bill.

    A bill of exchange that is payable on demand, that is, when the bill is presented to the drawee, is called a 'demand bill' or 'sight bill' and may be said to be payable 'at sight'.

    A bill of exchange imposes no liability on its drawee unless the drawee signs the bill. This is traditionally done by writing 'accepted' across the face of the bill and signing it, and the signature is called 'acceptance' of the bill. A drawee of a bill who has accepted it is called the 'acceptor' of the bill.

It is common for bills to be made payable at a fixed time after the date of acceptance, and such bills are called 'time bills' or 'term bills'. The length of time between the date of acceptance and the date on which payment is due is called the 'tenor' of the bill.

A 'cheque' is a bill of exchange drawn on a banker payable on demand.

In international trade, a bill of exchange is usually called a 'draft'.

bill of lading. Abbreviation: B/L. 1. A document signed on behalf of a shipowner stating that certain specified goods have been shipped in a particular ship and setting out the terms of the contract under which the goods have been delivered to and received by the ship.

On arrival at the destination, the goods will be given up to the person who produces the bill of lading. Thus the bill of lading of a shipment of goods confers control over the goods.

2. A document similar to a maritime bill of lading (sense 1) issued by another carrier, e.g., a railway or inland waterway bill of lading.

bill of materials. A list specifying the materials and components required for a particular job and specifying the quantities needed. Also called 'parts list'.

bill of sale. A document by which the owner of goods (called the 'grantor' of the bill) transfers ownership, but not possession, of the goods to another person. A bill of sale may be 'conditional' – i.e., stating that ownership will revert to the grantor on specified conditions (usually, when the grantor repays a loan) – or 'absolute' – i.e., ownership will not revert to the grantor.

bill payable. Abbreviation: B/P. A bill of exchange, payable at some time in the future, considered as a liability of its acceptor.

bill receivable. Abbreviation: B/R. A bill of exchange, payable at some date in the future, considered as an asset of the person entitled to payment of it.

bimodal. *Adjective.* In probability theory and statistics, having two modes.

binary arithmetic operation. An arithmetic operation in which the operands and the result are expressed in the pure binary numeration system.

binary character. A character from a character set that has only two characters, e.g., a binary digit. Also called 'bit'.

binary-coded decimal notation. Abbreviation: BCD notation. A notation system for numbers in which each of the decimal digits is represented by a binary numeral.

binary digit. Either of the digits 0 and 1 when used in the pure binary numeration system. Also called 'bit'.

binary numeral. A representation of a number in the pure binary numeration system.

bin card. A local stock record, normally simplified and kept close to the place where the stock is stored (BS 5191 : 1975).

binomial coefficient. A number denoted by:

$$\binom{n}{p}$$

or by $C_n^{\,p}$ obtained from two non-negative integers n and p by the following formula:

$$\binom{n}{p} = \frac{n!}{p!\,(n-p)!}$$

It is the numerical coefficient of $a^p b^{n-p}$ in the nth power of the binomial $(a + b)$.

binomial distribution. A probability distribution – of a discrete random variable X, that may take as value any integer r, $0 \leqslant r \leqslant n$, where n is a non-negative integer – defined by the formula:

$$P(X = r) = \frac{n!}{r!\,(n-r)!}\ p^r(1-p)^{n-r}$$

where $0 \leqslant p \leqslant 1$.

If p is the probability of something occurring if it has an opportunity to occur then $P(X = r)$ is the probability that it will occur r times if it has n opportunities to occur.

bit. 1. Another term for 'binary character'.

2. Another term for 'binary digit'.

bivariate distribution. A probability distribution that determines the probability that two random variables take any particular pair of values or have values in a particular set of pairs of values.

B/L. Abbreviation of 'bill of lading'.

black economy. Economic activity that is concealed from government agencies, especially taxation authorities, and so is not recorded in official statistics.

black market. Illicit trade in goods or foreign exchange which evades official rationing or prohibition.

B list. In the winding up of a registered company, a list of contributories who were not members of the company on the day the winding up commenced, but were members within the 12 months preceding that day.

blue chip. A listed company which, because of its large size, long history of stability and profitable trading, and good prospects, commands a high level of confidence from investors. Also, an ordinary share in such a company. (Traditionally, the high-value chips in gambling are coloured blue.)

bn. Abbreviation of 'billion'.

Board of Customs and Excise. Collective name for the Commissioners of Customs and Excise.

Board of Inland Revenue. Collective name for the Commissioners of Inland Revenue.

body corporate. Generally, a corporation; however, in the Companies Act 1985, references to a body corporate do not include a corporation sole (s. 740 of the Act).

body of persons. Term used in UK tax legislation to mean 'any body politic, corporate or collegiate, and any company, fraternity, fellowship and society of persons whether corporate or not corporate' (Taxes Management Act 1970, s. 118(1), and Income and Corporation Taxes Act 1970, s. 526(5)).

bona vacantia. Property whose ownership cannot be determined, and which is deemed by law to be property of the Crown. In certain parts of England

and Wales the right to *bona vacantia* has been granted to the Duchies of Cornwall and Lancaster. In Latin, *'bona'* means 'goods' but *'bona vacantia'* may be any form of property, not only goods.

bond. 1. An interest in a marketable loan.

2. A security issued when a marketable loan is raised and evidencing an entitlement to payment of interest and repayment of principal, the amount of principal being the nominal value of the security. Bonds are usually bearer securities and are called 'bearer bonds'.

bond washing. Sale of an interest-bearing security just before an interest payment is due coupled with an agreement to repurchase the security or a similar security just after the interest has been paid in order to avoid paying income tax on the interest payment. Also called 'dividend washing'.

bonus. Part of an employee's remuneration that is related in some way to the value, quantity or quality of work done. In many instances, the value of a bonus is determined by managerial discretion rather than by a term of the employee's contract.

bonus issue. An issue of bonus shares. Also called 'capitalisation issue'.

bonus share. A share in a company that is wholly or partly paid up by capitalisation of realised or unrealised profits or by a transfer from capital redemption reserve to share capital account.

book. A collection of accounting records. In some instances the collection may be actually written in a single bound volume of paper and so will be a 'book' in that sense.

book debt. A debt arising in the course of a business which would, or could, be entered in well-kept books relating to that business. See *Independent Automatic Sales Ltd* v *Knowles & Foster* [1962] 1 WLR 974.

bookkeeper. Also written: book-keeper. An individual whose work is bookkeeping.

bookkeeping. Also written: book-keeping. Recording of financial transactions. Bookkeeping is one aspect of accounting. Transactions may be recorded simply by listing them as they occur or they may be analysed and entered into ledger accounts according to the rules of double-entry bookkeeping. The preparation of financial statements is not usually regarded as a part of bookkeeping.

book of original entry. The journal or one of the books regarded as part of the journal, for example, the cash book, the day books, the returns books. Also called 'book of prime entry'.

book of prime entry. Another term for 'book of original entry'.

book value. The amount at which a thing is valued in accounts. 'Gross book value' is historical cost, or amount substituted for historical cost (e.g., on revaluation); 'net book value' is historical cost less accumulated depreciation. Also called 'carrying amount'.

borrowed capital. Another term for 'debt capital'.

bottom line. Informal. Profit or loss, shown as the final line of a profit and loss account or an account of financial dealings. By extension, the final outcome of an event or enterprise.

bought day book. Another term for 'purchases day book'.

bought ledger. The creditors ledger of a trading enterprise.

bought-out. *Adjective.* Used to describe something used by an organisation which has been purchased from a supplier rather than made within the organisation.

B/P. Abbreviation of 'bill payable'.

B/R. Abbreviation of 'bill receivable'.

branch accounts. 1. Accounting records of transactions between branches of an organisation, treated as separate accounting entities, between branches and the head office of the organisation and between branches and persons outside the organisation.

2. Financial statements for a branch of an organisation treated as a separate accounting entity.

breach of contract. A failure to perform all or part of a contract.

breach of trust. Any act by a trustee, in relation to trust property, in contravention of the duties imposed by the trust or in excess of those duties, or any neglect or omission by a trustee to fulfil the duties imposed by the trust. It is also a breach of trust for one of several trustees to concur or acquiesce in a breach of trust by a co-trustee.

break-even analysis. Also written: breakeven analysis. Computation of costs and revenues for different quantities of a product in order to determine the break-even point.

break-even chart. Also written: breakeven chart. A chart showing the relationship between fixed and variable costs associated with a product and the number of units of the product produced, and the break-even point.

break-even point. Also written: breakeven point. The volume of production at which the income from selling the quantity produced is the same as the costs of producing that quantity so that the producer makes neither a profit nor a loss. Sometimes there may be more than one break-even point for a producer of a product, and the product is then said to have 'multiple break-even points'.

breaking-down time. In production planning, the time required to return a work station to a standard condition after completion of an operation (BS 5191 : 1975).

break-up value. An estimate of the price that could be obtained for the assets of a business enterprise if the enterprise's business activities ceased.

Briggsian logarithm. Another term for 'common logarithm'.

British Accounting Association. Abbreviation: BAA. An association open to any person concerned with or interested in higher education and research in accounting. Membership is open to both individuals and partnership firms. No formal entry qualifications are required and no designating letters are employed.

Address: The Association does not have a permanent headquarters. At the beginning of 1985 the General Secretary and Treasurer was Professor K.T. Maunders, Department of Management Studies, Leeds University, Leeds LS2 9JT. Telephone: Leeds 431751. The Membership Secretary was Mr C. Brown, Department of Economics, University College of North Wales, Bangor, Gwynedd LL57 2DG. Telephone: Bangor 351151.

broker. 1. A person who arranges transactions between other persons and receives a commission for doing so. For example, an insurance broker, a money broker or a stockbroker.

2. A broker (in sense 1) of a particular kind – especially, a stockbroker (securities broker in America).

brokerage. Commission charged by a broker.

brought down. Abbreviation: b/d. *Participle with particle.* Used in bookkeeping to label an entry which repeats the last entry in that account for the preceding period.

brought forward. Abbreviation: b/f. *Participle with particle.* Used to label the first entry in a column on a page when it is the total of the corresponding column on the preceding page.

bubble. Short form of the term 'magnetic bubble memory'.

bubble memory. Short form of the term 'magnetic bubble memory'.

budget. 1. A plan expressed in financial terms; a summary of planned financial expenditures and receipts over a period, prepared before the period begins, or related to an activity, prepared before the activity begins

2. A list of permitted or authorised expenditures. Also called 'appropriation budget'.

3. (Usually capital 'B'.) A plan for the public expenditure of a country and the way it will be financed, such as the one presented by the British Chancellor of the Exchequer to the House of Commons in March or April in each year.

budget account. An arrangement in retail trading under which a customer of a trader is allowed credit in return for making regular (typically monthly) payments to the trader. Usually, the trader will offer to give credit up to a fixed multiple of the regular payment.

budgetary control. Control based on the use of budgets for various activities and comparison of actual performance with budgeted performance. The ICMA official terminology makes it clear that such budgets should relate the responsibilities of individuals to the requirements of a policy and that the purpose of control is to secure by individual action the objective of that policy or to provide a basis for its revision.

budget centre. American spelling: budget center. A part of an organisation for which a separate budget is prepared.

budget cost allowance. The cost expected to be identified with a budget centre in a control period.

Budget Day value. Abbreviation: BDV. For the purposes of UK capital gains tax, the value of an asset on 6 April 1965, which was the day the then Chancellor of the Exchequer presented a Budget proposing the introduction of capital gains tax.

budgeted capacity. The number of standard hours of productive work planned for a budget period, taking into account budgeted sales, supplies, and work-force availability.

budget manual. A set of instructions on the preparation of budgets within an organisation.

budget period. A period for which a budget is prepared and used. It may be divided into 'control periods'.

buffer stock. Stock of work in progress held because of varying production rates, not necessarily planned and usually held on the shop floor (BS 5191 : 1975).

building society. A society established to raise money from its members for lending to members secured by land mortgages. In England and Wales and Scotland, a building society is required to be incorporated by registration under the Building Societies Act 1962.

bull. A person who anticipates that the price of something will rise, e.g., by contracting to purchase in the expectation of being able to resell in the same market at a higher price before payment for the purchase is due.

bulldog bond. An international bond originally issued in Britain for a borrower resident outside Britain.

burden. Term sometimes used in America for 'production overhead cost'.

bus. In electronic data processing, one or more conductors used for transmitting data or power from one or more sources to one or more destinations.

business combination. 1. In SSAP 23, 'A "business combination" arises when one or more companies become subsidiaries of another company' (para. 6).

2. In IAS 12, 'A "business combination" is the result of the acquiring of control of one or more enterprises by another enterprise or the uniting of interests of two or more enterprises' (para. 3). In this context, 'control' means 'ownership, directly, or indirectly through subsidiaries, of more than one-half of the voting power of an enterprise' (para. 3).

business data processing. Another term for 'administrative data processing'.

business day. In England and Wales, any day except:

(a) Saturday, Sunday, Good Friday, Christmas Day.

(b) New Year's Day, Easter Monday, the last Monday in May, the last Monday in August, 26 December and, in any year in which 25 or 26 December is a Sunday, 27 December.

(c) Any day appointed by Royal Proclamation or order of the Treasury.

See Bills of Exchange Act 1882, s. 92, Banking and Financial Dealings Act 1971, and Royal Proclamation of 26 October 1973.

business entity concept. See the entry for 'separate entity concept'.

Business Expansion Scheme. Abbreviation: BES. A scheme providing relief from income tax for money invested between 6 April 1983 and 5 April 1987 by an individual as capital contributed to a company incorporated in the United Kingdom. The scheme applies only to investments in certain kinds of company and the investor must not be connected with the company invested in. The provisions relating to the Business Expansion Scheme are contained in the Finance Act 1981, ss. 52 to 67, Finance Act 1983, s. 26 and Schedule 5, Finance (No. 2) Act 1983, s. 5 and Schedule 1, and Finance Act 1984, s. 37.

business name. The name under which a business or profession is carried on.

business review. In relation to a British registered company, a fair review of the development of the business of the company and its subsidiaries during a financial year and of their position at the end of the year which must be included in the directors' report for the year (Companies Act 1985, s. 235(1)(a)).

business trust. See the entry for 'trust'.

buyer credit. A method of financing exports in which a financing institution (e.g., a bank) in an exporter's country lends money to foreign buyers for purchases from the exporter. Such a deal is usually arranged by the exporter and, in practice, the money is paid direct to the exporter.

buy out. 1. *Verb with particle.* To pay a person or persons to give up entirely an interest in a business enterprise. See also the entry for 'management buy-out'.

2. See the entry for 'bought-out'.

by-product. A product that is recovered incidentally from the manufacture or processing of another product and which is significantly less valuable than that other product. See also the entry for 'joint product'.

byte. In data processing, a string of binary characters (commonly eight) operated on as a unit in a data processing system.

C

CA. Designation of a member of the Institute of Chartered Accountants of Scotland.

calculator. A data processing device that is especially suited to performing arithmetic operations but which has few facilities for storing instructions so that, usually, an instruction for each stage of a calculation must be given to the device by its user when the preceding stage has been completed.

call. 1. *Noun.* A demand made by a company for payment of part or all of the amount still to be paid on partly paid shares in the company.

2. *Noun.* A claim; a demand for the payment of money.

3. *Verb.* To bring a computer program, routine or subroutine into effect.

call-back pay. Another term for 'call-in pay'.

called-up share capital. The total nominal value of the allotted shares in a company less any amount which has not yet been called on partly paid shares. Called-up capital includes calls made, but not yet paid. Compare 'paid-up share capital'.

call-in pay. A guaranteed minimum payment to an employee for being specially called in to work. Also called 'call-back pay'.

call off. *Verb with particle.* Having given a blanket order or bulk order for something, without specific delivery instructions, to request delivery specifying quantity and time.

call up. *Verb with particle.* To make a call for part of the nominal value of partly paid issued shares.

C&F. Abbreviation of 'cost and freight'.

capital. 1. A stock of money or other assets for use in a business enterprise, which will be increased by the profits of that enterprise (to the extent that they are not taken by the owners of the enterprise) and diminished by the losses of the enterprise. Money that is provided as a long-term loan to a business enterprise is sometimes described as 'debt capital' because, like capital, it is a long-term resource of the enterprise.

2. Another term for 'owners' equity'.

See also the entries for 'equity capital' and 'working capital'.

capital account. 1. In a sole trader's accounts an account recording the amount of money set aside by the trader for business purposes and regarded as the capital of the business, plus any accumulated profits that have not been taken by the proprietor for non-business purposes, less realised losses.

2. In the accounts of a partnership, an account recording the amount of

money set aside by the partners for business purposes and regarded as the capital of the partnership plus any accumulated profits that have not been taken by the partners for non-business purposes, less realised losses.

capital allowance. An allowance that, when computing liability to UK income tax or corporation tax, may be deducted from trading profits when there has been capital expenditure.

capital asset. In America, an asset (either tangible or intangible) of an accounting entity, intended for use on a continuing basis in the activities of the entity. In Britain, the term 'fixed asset' is used in this sense.

capital asset pricing model. Abbreviation: CAPM. In portfolio theory, a symbolic model of market prices of investments (especially listed company shares) in which either the expected rate of return on, or expected risk premium of, an investment is expressed as a linear function of the expected risk premium of the market portfolio and in the function the coefficient of the market risk premium is the beta of the investment. For example, if the risk-free rate of return is R, the rate of return on the market portfolio is r_m and the beta of investment i is β_i then the expected rate of return $E(r_i)$ on investment i may be expressed as:

$$E(r_i) = R + \beta_i \, (E(r_m) - R)$$

Also called 'security market line'.

capital budget. Another term for 'capital expenditure budget'.

capital budgeting. The process of choosing, from a number of possible investments, the ones in which to invest.

capital duty. A tax charged when the contributed capital of a limited company is increased. In the UK tax is 1% (rounded up to the nearest £1) of either the value of the assets contributed or the nominal value of shares allotted, whichever is greater.

capital employed. A measurement of the total value of the operating assets of an entity. Different measurements are appropriate for different purposes. In some cases, owners' equity is the appropriate measurement: in an incorporated company, this will be called 'shareholders' capital employed'. In some cases, long-term borrowings may be added to owners' equity, while in others dividends payable by the entity and taxation payable by it may be added.

capital expenditure. Expenditure on fixed assets. This may be expenditure to acquire fixed assets or expenditure to add to fixed assets (provided the addition is intended to benefit future accounting periods) or expenditure which increases the capacity, efficiency, useful life or economy of operation of an existing fixed asset.

capital expenditure budget. A document showing the extent and timing of proposed capital expenditure of an organisation over a future period. It may also show other relevant information such as the revenue that the expenditure is expected to produce, the cost of capital to be used for the expenditure and the net profit that will result. Also called 'capital budget'.

capital fund. Another term for 'accumulated fund'.

capital gain. 1. Profit from the sale of an asset other than a current asset. Also called 'capital profit'.

2. For the purposes of UK capital gains tax, a chargeable gain computed in accordance with the Capital Gains Tax Act 1979 and accruing to a person on the disposal of an asset (Capital Gains Tax Act 1979, s. 1(1)).

capital gains tax. Abbreviation: CGT. A tax levied on capital gains. In the UK, capital gains tax at 30% is charged on chargeable gains accruing to persons resident or ordinarily resident in the United Kingdom, but the capital gains of a company subject to UK corporation tax are subject to corporation tax rather than capital gains tax. The law on capital gains tax in the United Kingdom is contained mainly in the Capital Gains Tax Act 1979.

capital introduced. The contributed capital of an enterprise, especially of a sole trader or a partnership firm.

capitalisation issue. Another term for 'bonus issue'.

capitalise. *Verb.* 1. To compute a single sum that is equivalent to a number of future payments, in particular, by computing the net present value.

2. To decide that a certain sum of money will in future be treated as capital, especially, in a limited company, to decide that some reserves will be treated as share capital.

3. To turn something to one's advantage.

capital issue. An issue of securities made in order to acquire capital for a company.

capital lease. Term used in America for 'finance lease'. A full definition is given in FASB Statement 13, paras 6a and 7.

capital loss. 1. Loss of the contributed capital of an enterprise.

2. Loss on the sale of an asset other than a current asset.

capital maintenance. See the entry for 'concept of capital maintenance'.

capital market line. Abbreviation: CML. In portfolio theory, a graph of alternative combinations of risk and return obtainable by using a fixed amount to invest in the market portfolio and lend at the riskless rate of interest, or by borrowing at the riskless rate of interest so as to invest further in the market portfolio.

capital profit. Another term for 'capital gain'.

capital rationing. Choosing investments in which to invest the funds of an accounting entity when the managers of the entity have determined a maximum limit for the amount of funds that can be invested in a particular period, which limit cannot be exceeded by raising new funds even if those new funds could be invested profitably.

capital receipt. A receipt of money from the sale of an income-producing asset (e.g., a fixed asset rather than a current asset) as opposed to a receipt of income produced by an asset.

capital redemption reserve. An account to which is credited the nominal value of shares that have been redeemed in so far as the redemption was not paid for by the proceeds of a new issue of shares and was not a payment out of capital.

capital reserve. A term used in the past for a reserve of a registered company that may not be distributed to the members of the company otherwise than on a winding up of the company. Compare 'revenue reserve'. The term has been replaced by the term 'undistributable reserves' which has a precise statutory meaning.

capital structure. The proportions of the capital of an accounting entity that are derived from each of its various sources of capital.

capital transfer tax. Abbreviation: CTT. A United Kingdom tax levied on gifts of property made by an individual while alive or on death. The law on capital transfer tax is contained mainly in the Capital Transfer Tax Act 1984, s. 1 of which defines capital transfer tax as a tax 'on the value transferred by a chargeable transfer'.

capital turnover. The ratio:

$$\frac{\text{turnover for a period}}{\text{average capital employed during the period}}$$

CAPM. Abbreviation of 'capital asset pricing model'.

cardinal. Another term for 'cardinal number'.

cardinal number. A number that is used in counting and which indicates how many elements there are in a set of elements, e.g., 1, 2, 3, ... Also called 'cardinal'.

carriage inward. Alternative form: carriage inwards. Expense incurred by an accounting entity in transporting its purchases. The expense is part of the entity's cost of sales. In America, called 'freight in', 'transportation in'.

carriage outward. Alternative form: carriage outwards. Expense incurred by an accounting entity in transporting goods it has sold. Sometimes 'carriage outward' is used for the costs of transporting specific items, especially where those costs are charged to customers, while 'distribution costs' is used for the general cost of distributing all goods to customers. In America, called 'freight out'.

carried down. Abbreviation: c/d. *Participle with particle.* Used in bookkeeping to label an entry which will be repeated as the first entry in that account for the next period.

carried forward. Abbreviation: c/f. *Participle with particle.* Used to label the total of a column of figures on one page which will be entered as the first item in the corresponding column on the next page.

carrier's note. Another term for 'consignment note'.

carry. In performing an addition to, or a multiplication of, a number in a positional representation system, the process of adding the number represented by a carry digit to the number represented by the digit in the appropriate digit place of the number being added to or multiplied.

carry back. *Verb with particle.* To acquire an entitlement to a reduction of tax by virtue of the transactions in one period and use it to reduce the tax payable in respect of an earlier period.

carry digit. In a positional representation system, if the result of adding to, or multiplying, the number represented by a digit is larger than the maximum number that can be represented in its digit place, the carry digit is the digit of that result in the digit place with the next higher weight. A carry digit must be taken to the digit place with the next higher weight for further processing.

carrying amount. The value of a thing as stated in accounts. In relation to a fixed asset, 'carrying amount' may be used to refer to net book value (which may be called 'net carrying amount') or to historical cost or revaluation without deducting provision for depreciation (which may be called 'gross carrying amount'). See also 'book value'.

carrying cost. Another term for 'stockholding cost'.

car tax. A UK tax payable when an enterprise sells a car that it has manufactured in the UK or imported into the UK.

Cartesian product. In relation to n sets, $S_1, \ldots, S_n$, the set of all ordered sets $\{a_1, a_2, \ldots, a_n\}$ in which a_1 is a member of S_1, a_2 is a member of S_2, and so on. The Cartesian product of $S_1, \ldots, S_n$ is denoted by $S_1 \times S_2 \times \ldots \times S_n$. Named after René Descartes (1596-1650), French philosopher and mathematician, who, in his book, *Géométrie* (1647), first used analytical geometry, in which Cartesian products are important.

case-of-need. A person named by the drawer of a bill of exchange as a person who may be asked for further instructions if the bill is dishonoured.

cash. 1. *Noun.* Money in an immediately usable form: coins, banknotes and money deposited in a current account at a bank.

2. *Verb.* To obtain payment in cash of a financial document.

cash account. An account recording receipts of cash and cheques and payments of cash including deposits of money into the accounting entity's bank.

cash at bank. The money of an accounting entity that is deposited with a bank or other deposit-taker from which it may be withdrawn on demand.

cash basis. Another term for 'receipts and payments basis'.

cash before delivery. Abbreviation: CBD. A condition imposed by a business enterprise that items to be supplied by it will not be delivered until payment for them has been received.

cash book. Abbreviation: CB. A section of a ledger containing the cash account and bank account. Sometimes, a note is made in the cash book of discounts received and discounts allowed on individual transactions, and periodically totals of these individual discounts are posted to the discounts allowed and discounts received accounts rather than recording the individual discounts in those accounts. A cash book in which discounts are not recorded may be called a 'two-column cash book' while one in which discounts are recorded is called a 'three-column cash book'.

cash budget. An estimate of monetary receipts and payments of an accounting entity over a future period showing when it will be necessary to borrow money and when there will be surplus money available for investment. Also called 'cash-flow budget'.

cash discount. Part of an invoiced charge that will be cancelled if payment for the invoice is received within a certain time. Usually expressed as a percentage of the total value of the invoice. From the seller's point of view this is called a 'discount allowed'; from the purchaser's point of view it is called a 'discount received'. Nowadays the word 'cash' is inappropriate since business invoices are normally settled by cheque. Also called 'settlement discount'.

cash float. A quantity of notes and coins from which a retailer can give change to customers. In America, called 'change fund'. Also called 'float', 'till float'.

cash flow. 1. A cash inflow or a cash outflow.

2. The pattern and extent of payments and receipts of money by an

accounting entity over a period.

3. The difference between total cash inflows and total cash outflows of an accounting entity over a period. Sometimes called 'net cash flow'.

4. The difference between total cash inflows and total cash outflows for an investment project. Sometimes called 'net cash flow'.

5. In financial analysis, the earnings for equity of a company over a period plus the company's provision for depreciation for that period. Sometimes called 'gross cash flow' when 'net cash flow' means earnings for equity less dividends paid to equity shareholders plus provision for depreciation.

cash-flow budget. Another term for 'cash budget'.

cashier's cheque. American spelling: 'cashier's check'. Term used in America for 'banker's draft'.

cash inflow. An amount of money received.

cash in hand. Cash of an accounting entity in the form of banknotes and coins in the possession of the entity, as opposed to money deposited at a bank or with a licensed deposit-taker or money otherwise invested. In America, called 'cash on hand'.

cash limit. An amount of money that is fixed as the maximum amount that may be spent for a particular purpose over an accounting period whatever changes occur during the period.

cash on delivery. Abbreviation: COD. A method of selling goods in which payment for the goods is made to the person who delivers them and the goods will not be delivered unless payment is received.

cash on hand. Term used in America for 'cash in hand'.

cash outflow. An amount of money paid.

cash with order. Abbreviation: CWO. A condition imposed by a business enterprise that an order for it to supply something must be accompanied by payment for the thing.

cast. *Verb.* To add numbers together.

casualty. An unanticipated substantial reduction in the resources available to an accounting entity, not caused by a financial transaction but by accidents such as fire or flood.

cause of action. A factual situation which entitles one person to obtain a remedy from another person in the courts.

CB. Abbreviation of 'cash book'.

CBD. Abbreviation of 'cash before delivery'.

CCA. Abbreviation of 'current cost accounting'.

CCAB. Abbreviation of 'Consultative Committee of Accountancy Bodies'.

c.c.c. Abbreviation of 'cwmni cyfyngedig cyhoeddus'. Used as the equivalent in Welsh of the abbreviation 'p.l.c.'

c/d. Abbreviation of 'carried down'.

CD. Abbreviation of 'certificate of deposit'.

centered random variable. American spelling of 'centred random variable'.

centered variate. American spelling of 'centred variate'.

central bank. A bank with which the government of a country deposits its money and which is responsible for raising loans for the government and for managing other government financial business. For example, the Bank of England.

central limit theorem. A theorem of probability theory stating that if X_1, ..., X_n are independent random variables that all have the same probability distribution, which has a finite mean μ and a finite variance σ^2, and:

$$s_n = (\sum_{i=1}^{n} X_i - n\mu)/(\sigma\sqrt{n})$$

then the larger n is the closer the distribution of s_n will be to the standardised normal distribution.

central processing unit. Abbreviation: CPU. Another term for 'processing unit'.

central processor. Another term for 'processing unit'.

centred random variable. American spelling: centered random variable. A random variable with a mean of 0. If a random variable X has mean $E(X)$ then the corresponding centred random variable is $X - E(X)$. Also called 'centred variate'.

centred variate. American spelling: centered variate. Another term for 'centred random variable'.

certificate. A document formally attesting a fact. The Council of the Institute of Chartered Accountants in England and Wales has drawn attention to the fact that an accountant may be asked to give a 'certificate' that something has occurred or that a record has been made accurately when the accountant has not been present at the occurrence or at the making of the record. In such circumstances, the accountant should decline to give a 'certificate', but should offer to make a 'report' giving a professional opinion of whether accounting records give a true and fair view. See Council statement 3.915 (S13).

certificate of deposit. Defined in the Finance Act 1968, s. 55, as 'a document relating to money, in any currency, which has been deposited with the issuer or some other person, being a document which recognises an obligation to pay a stated amount to bearer or to order, with or without interest, and being a document by the delivery of which, with or without endorsement, the right to receive that stated amount, with or without interest, is transferable'.

certificate of incorporation. A document given by the Registrar of Companies to certify that a company has been incorporated under the Companies Act 1985 or a former Companies Act. The certificate states the company's name and whether it is a public company. The company is incorporated with the stated name as from the first moment of the date of the certificate.

certificate of insurance. A document certifying that insurance cover of a specified type has been obtained. The certificate is usually given by the person who obtained the insurance rather than by an insurer. The insurer is only bound by the terms of a policy of insurance not by a certificate of insurance.

certificate of misfortune. A certificate granted by a court when discharging a bankrupt stating that the bankruptcy was caused by misfortune without any misconduct on the part of the bankrupt. Possession of such a certificate will free the bankrupt from certain statutory disqualifications from holding public office which normally apply to bankrupts.

certificate of origin. A document used in international trade, stating that goods are the produce of a specified country, and usually countersigned by an official of a chamber of commerce.

certificate of value. A statement in a document certifying that the transaction effected by the document does not form part of a larger transaction, or series of transactions, for which the consideration exceeds a specified amount, so that stamp duty is either not payable or is payable at a reduced rate.

certificate to commence business. A certificate issued by the Registrar of Companies to a company registered as a public company on its original incorporation certifying that the nominal value of the company's allotted share capital is not less than the authorised minimum. A company registered as a public company on its original incorporation must not do business or exercise any borrowing powers until it has a certificate to commence business. In practice, a company is normally initially registered as a private company and then re-registered as a public company so as to avoid the need for a certificate to commence business.

certification of a transfer. A procedure adopted when a transferor of shares in a company is not transferring all of the shares covered by a share certificate. The transferor presents the share certificate and the instrument of transfer to a company official or a Stock Exchange official who certifies on the instrument of transfer that there is prima facie evidence that the transferor owns the shares being transferred. The instrument of transfer is then forwarded to the transferee while the share certificate goes direct to the company or its registrars.

certified accountant. A member of the Chartered Association of Certified Accountants.

certified public accountant. Abbreviaton: CPA. 1. In the USA, an individual given a licence by a state government entitling the individual to describe himself or herself as a certified public accountant after passing a national standardised examination prepared and graded by the American Institute of Certified Public Accountants. In general, only certified public accountants may act as auditors.

2. In Ireland, a member of the Institute of Certified Public Accountants in Ireland.

cestui que trust. A beneficiary of a trust.

ceteris paribus. In economics, assuming that other relevant factors do not change. The phrase is Latin for 'other things being equal'.

c/f. Abbreviation of 'carried forward'.

CFR. Abbreviation of 'cost and freight'.

CGT. Abbreviation of 'capital gains tax'.

chairman's statement. A brief statement by the chairman of the board of directors of a public company published with the company's annual report and accounts, and giving the chairman's views on the current state of the company.

chamber of commerce. An association of business people in a particular geographical area which is formed to promote commerce and industry in

47

the area. Also called 'chamber of commerce and industry'.

change fund. Term used in America for 'cash float'.

changeover time. Also written: change-over time. In production planning, the time required to change a work station from a state of readiness for one operation to a state of readiness for another (BS 5191 : 1975).

channel. In data processing, short form of the term 'input-output channel'.

character. 1. In data processing, a sign, with a conventional shape recognisable by very many people, used to represent, organise or control data.

2. A representation within a data processing system of a character in sense 1.

character set. In data processing, a set of characters available for use in particular circumstances, especially, a set of characters that the input and output units of a data processing system are designed to transmit.

charge. 1. *Noun.* The price at which a person will supply services or goods.

2. *Verb.* To request payment for services or goods.

3. *Verb.* To record in an account of an entity an amount to be paid to the entity for supplying services or goods.

4. *Noun.* An agreement between a person (called the 'chargee') who is owed a financial obligation and the person who owes that obligation that if the obligation is not met when due then the chargee may appropriate certain property (called 'charged' property) of the person who owes the obligation and utilise it to meet the obligation.

5. *Verb.* To make an item of property the subject-matter of a charge (in sense 4).

6. *Noun.* In a profit and loss account, a deduction from revenue.

chargeable asset. An asset upon the disposal of which a chargeable gain or allowable loss may accrue for the purposes of capital gains tax. According to the Capital Gains Tax Act 1979, all assets are chargeable assets apart from:

(a) Savings certificates and non-marketable securities issued under the National Loans Act 1968 or the National Loans Act 1939, or any corresponding enactment forming part of the law of Northern Ireland (s. 71).

(b) A mechanically propelled road vehicle constructed or adapted for the carriage of passengers, except for a vehicle of a type not commonly used as a private vehicle and unsuitable to be so used (s. 130).

(c) The rights of the insurer under any policy of insurance other than one on human life (s. 140).

chargeable gain. For the purposes of UK capital gains tax, the excess of the proceeds of disposing of an asset over the cost of acquiring the asset (including the cost of any improvements made to the asset) computed in accordance with the Capital Gains Tax Act 1979 – called a 'gain' in the Act – unless the gain is expressly exempted from capital gains tax by the Act (Capital Gains Tax Act 1979, s. 28(2)).

chargeable transfer. For the purposes of capital transfer tax, a transfer of value which is made by an individual, but is not an exempt transfer (Capital Transfer Tax Act 1984, s. 2(1)).

charge account. An arrangement for retail credit trading between a retailer and a customer in which the prices of purchases made by the customer are recorded by the retailer and periodically the customer is required to pay the outstanding total. The short form 'account' is also used.

charge by way of legal mortgage. A charge on land in a form defined in the Law of Property Act 1925. Commonly called a 'mortgage'.

charge card. A credit card issued to a cardholder whose dealings with the issuer are on open account.

chargee. In relation to a charge on property, the person entitled to utilise the property when there is default in meeting the obligation which the charge was created to secure.

charge for credit. Another term for 'finance charge'.

charging order. 1. An order of a court, made under the Charging Orders Act 1979, imposing a charge on the property of a person so as to secure the payment of money due, or to become due, from the person under a court order of judgment.

2. An order of a court, made under the Partnership Act 1890, s. 23, imposing a charge on the interest of a partner in the partnership property and profits so as to secure payment of a judgment debt owed by the partner.

3. An order of a court, made under the Solicitors Act 1974, imposing a charge on property recovered or preserved in a suit, matter or proceeding in the court in which a solicitor was employed so as to secure payment of the solicitor's costs.

charitable purposes. See the entry for 'charity'.

charity. A body of persons or a trust established for charitable purposes. The purposes that are recognised in law as being charitable purposes are generally taken to be those stated in a judgment by Lord Macnaghten in *Commissioners for Special Purposes of the Income Tax* v *Pemsel* [1891] AC 531: '"Charity" in its legal sense comprises four principal divisions: trusts for the relief of poverty; trusts for the advancement of education; trusts for the advancement of religion; and trusts for other purposes beneficial to the community, not falling under any of the preceding heads'.

A purpose is charitable only if it benefits the public, except that the relief of poverty is a charitable purpose even if only a restricted group of people are to benefit, such as the employees of a particular company (*Dingle* v *Turner* [1972] AC 601). Nevertheless, a purpose other than the relief of poverty does not have to benefit the whole world in order to be charitable. It is sufficient if it benefits a group of people who are not merely the members of a particular family or the employees of a particular employer.

chartered accountant. A member of the Institute of Chartered Accountants in England and Wales, or of the Institute of Chartered Accountants in Ireland or of the Institute of Chartered Accountants of Scotland.

Chartered Association of Certified Accountants. Professional body of accountants with members in all sectors of the accountancy profession—industry, commerce, the public sector and public practice. There are two grades of membership: Associate, designated ACCA, and, after five years' membership, Fellow, designated FCCA. Members are styled 'certified accountants'.

Address: 29 Lincoln's Inn Fields, London WC2A 3EE. Telephone: 01-

242 6855. Telex: 24381. Also at: 9th Floor, Charlotte House, 78 Queen Street, Glasgow G1 3DN; and 9 Leeson Park, Dublin 6, Republic of Ireland.

chartered company. A company incorporated by a charter granted by the Crown.

chartered corporation. In Britain, a corporation incorporated by royal charter.

Chartered Institute of Public Finance and Accountancy. Abbreviation: CIPFA. Professional institute for individuals who specialise in financial management for public service bodies, e.g., in the health service, the water industry, nationalised industries and other public organisations as well as central and local government. Entry to membership of the Institute is by examination. Membership is designated by the letters IPFA. Members are styled 'chartered public finance accountants'.

Address: 3 Robert Street, London WC2N 6BH. Telephone: 01-930 3456. Telex: 297156.

chartered public finance accountant. A member of the Chartered Institute of Public Finance and Accountancy.

chartist. In investment analysis, a person who uses the pattern of past market prices for an investment (e.g., by looking at a graph of those prices) to predict future prices of the investment.

chart of accounts. A list of the ledger accounts of an accounting entity giving the titles and, possibly, codes of the accounts.

chattel. An item of personal property. The term is often used to refer only to things in possession, sometimes excluding currency.

chattel personal. An item of personal property that is not a chattel real. Also called 'personal chattel'.

chattel real. An interest in land which is not a real-property interest.

check. 1. American spelling of 'cheque'.

2. A token given by a finance house to a consumer and having a nominal value, typically, of one pound, which may be exchanged by the consumer with selected retailers for goods. The consumer makes regular fixed payments to the finance house to repay the nominal value of the checks the consumer has used.

3. A process for determining accuracy.

check card. American spelling of 'cheque card'.

check-off. Withholding, by an employer, from wage payments, of the amount of employees' union subscriptions, which are paid directly to the union by the employer.

check trading. System of retail credit trading involving the use of checks.

cheque. American spelling: check. Defined in the Bills of Exchange Act 1882, s. 73, as 'a bill of exchange drawn on a banker payable on demand'.

cheque card. American spelling: check card. A card issued by a bank to one of its customers, bearing a number unique to the customer. Under certain conditions, which are stated on the back of the cheque card, the bank guarantees to pay any cheque on which the cheque-card number is written.

Chinese Wall. Defined in the Licensed Dealers (Conduct of Business) Rules 1983 (SI 1983 No. 585), r. 2 as: 'an established arrangement whereby information known to persons involved in one part of a business is not available (directly or indirectly) to those involved in another part of the business and it is accepted that in each of the parts of the business so divided decisions will be taken without reference to any interest which any other such part or any person in any other such part of the business may have in the matter'.

A Chinese Wall enables an organisation to deal on behalf of clients in securities in which the organisation itself has interests without raising the suspicion of a conflict of interest.

(The Great Wall of China is a noted work of fortification, dating in its present form from the Ming Dynasty (14th to 17th centuries) and designed to protect China from invasion from the North.)

chip. A thin slice of a crystal of a semiconductor material (usually silicon) with sides of length between about one millimetre and eight millimetres on which a miniature electronic circuit is formed.

chi-squared distribution. The probability distribution of a random variable that is the sum of the squares of a number of independent standardised normal variates. A random variable with a chi-squared distribution takes only non-negative values. The number of standardised normal variates forming a chi-squared distribution is called the number of degrees of freedom of the distribution.

The word 'chi' is the name of the Greek letter χ and the term 'chi-squared distribution' is often written 'χ^2 distribution'.

chi-squared test. A statistical test that depends on the value of a statistic that has a chi-squared distribution. A chi-squared test is used, for example, to test whether the observed frequencies of values correspond to the frequencies that would be expected if the values occurred with a particular probability distribution.

chose in action. Another term for 'thing in action'.

chose in possession. Another term for 'thing in possession'.

CIF. Abbreviation of 'cost, insurance and freight'.

CIPFA. Often spoken as an acronym. Abbreviation of 'Chartered Institute of Public Finance and Accountancy'.

CIR. Abbreviation of 'Commissioners of Inland Revenue' – i.e., the Board of Inland Revenue.

circular chart. Another term for 'pie chart'.

circulating asset. An asset of an accounting entity that is expected to be consumed or sold in the course of the entity's ordinary activities during one operating cycle of the entity and is expected to be replaced by a similar asset. Also called 'floating asset'.

circulating capital. The current assets of an accounting entity.

City Code on Take-overs and Mergers. A document setting out principles and rules of conduct to be observed during take-overs and mergers and which are expected to be observed by 'those who wish to take advantage of the facilities of the securities markets in the United Kingdom' (Introduction to the Code). The Code is issued on the authority of the Council for the Securities Industry on which are represented a number of associations of persons involved in the securities industry, all of which are committed to support the Code. Provisions of the Code are enforced by the Panel on Take-overs and Mergers.

claused bill of lading. A bill of lading that has a clause or notation expressly declaring a defective condition of the goods and/or packaging.

clean bill of lading. A bill of lading that bears no clause or notation expressly declaring a defective condition of the goods and/or packaging.

clean collection. Collection of financial documents not accompanied by commercial documents.

clearing bank. A bank that is represented on the Committee of London Clearing Bankers which runs a national clearing house (the London Bankers' Clearing House) for cheques and credit transfers.

clearing house. An organisation, set up by persons who continually deal with each other, to accumulate and offset financial claims against each other so that they can be settled periodically by single payments.

client account. A bank account in which a professional firm deposits its clients' money. Solicitors and estate agents are required by law to maintain client accounts.

close company. In UK revenue law, an incorporated company that is subject to special rules intended to prevent tax avoidance. In general, a company is a close company if five or fewer persons can determine what dividends the company pays to them. A precise definition is given in the Income and Corporation Taxes Act 1970, ss. 282 and 283.

closed-end fund. In the USA, a corporation similar to a British investment trust.

close off. *Verb with particle.* To enter the balance of a ledger account in that account (as a credit if it is a debit balance, or a debit if it is a credit balance) and make the corresponding double entry in a different ledger account. Totals of credits and debits in the account that has been balanced may be inserted to prove that they are equal after balancing. There will be no opening balance in the balanced account for the next period.

closing balance. An amount recorded as the asset or liability in existence at the end of a period for which an account is kept.

closing entry. An entry in a nominal account in a ledger which closes off the account.

closing rate. In the translation of financial statements from one currency to another, the exchange rate for spot transactions for the exchange of the two currencies on the balance sheet date, which is represented by the arithmetic mean of the buying and selling rates at the close of business on the balance sheet date (SSAP 20, para. 41).

closing rate/net investment method. When consolidating the accounts of an entity with transactions in one currency with the accounts of an entity with transactions in a foreign currency, a method of translating the foreign currency accounts in which the amounts in the balance sheet are translated at the rate of exchange for the balance sheet date and amounts in the profit and loss account are translated at that rate or at an average rate for the accounting period. Compare 'temporal method'.

closing stock. An amount recorded as the value of stock at the end of the period for which an account is kept.

cluster sampling. In statistics, a method of sampling in which the population is divided into groups (called 'clusters') of items that are associated together in some way, a random sample is taken from each cluster and these samples are put together to form a sample from the population.

CML. Abbreviation of 'capital market line'.

CMOS. Usually spoken as an acronym. Abbreviation of 'complementary metal oxide semiconductor'. An electronic component (used in computers as well as in other applications) incorporating a pair of transistors of opposite polarity, the transistors being of the type known as 'MOSFETs' - that is, field-effect transistors (FETs) in which the gate is a layer of metal (or polycrystalline silicon) separated from the semiconductor by a layer of silicon dioxide.

C/N. Abbreviation of 'credit note'.

COBOL. A programming language developed under the auspices of the Conference on Data Systems Languages, first published in 1960, revised 1974, and currently specified in ISO 1989-1978. A further revision was proposed in 1980. The language has been very widely used in administrative data processing. The name is derived from the words 'common business-oriented language'. The Conference on Data Systems Languages, founded 1959, is an association of individuals and institutions, based at Washington DC, USA, who work on designing and developing techniques and languages to assist in data systems analysis, design and implementation.

COD. Abbreviation of 'cash on delivery'.

codicil. A statement made by a testator to add to, alter, explain or confirm a will.

coefficient. A multiplier; especially, a constant that is a multiplier of a variable.

coefficient of correlation. 1. In probability theory, the covariance of two random variables divided by the product of their standard deviations.

2. In statistics, the covariance of a dependent and an independent variable divided by the product of the standard deviations of the variables. Also called 'correlation coefficient', 'product-moment coefficient of correlation', 'Pearson coefficient of correlation'.

coefficient of variation. 1. In probability theory, the standard deviation of a random variable divided by the absolute value of the mean of the random variable.

2. In statistics, the standard deviation of a set of observed values of a quantitative characteristic divided by the absolute value of the arithmetic mean of those values. The coefficient of variation is often expressed as a percentage.

collateral. Term used in America for 'security'.

collateral security. Security for the performance of a financial obligation given by a person other than the person from whom the obligation is due. Also called 'third-party security'.

collecting bank. 1. In Britain, the bank to which a person requiring payment of a cheque or other financial document has entrusted the document so that the bank can carry out the operation of collecting payment. In international banking, according to the Uniform Rules for Collections of the International Chamber of Commerce, such a bank is called the 'remitting bank'.

2. In international banking, according to the Uniform Rules for Collections of the International Chamber of Commerce, any bank, other than the remitting bank, involved in the collection of documents by processing a collection order.

collection. In banking, defined in the Uniform Rules for Collections of the International Chamber of Commerce as: the handling by banks, on instructions received, of financial documents and/or commercial documents in order:

(a) to obtain acceptance and/or, as the case may be, payment, or;

(b) to deliver commercial documents against acceptance and/or, as the case may be, against payment, or;

(c) to deliver documents on other terms and conditions.

The person on whose instructions a collection is carried out is called the 'principal'.

collection order. A written order accompanying documents entrusted to a bank for collection giving instructions on what the principal requires to be done with the documents.

collector of taxes. An individual appointed by the Commissioners of Inland Revenue to demand and collect payment of taxes as notified by Her Majesty's Inspectors of Taxes.

COM. 1. Abbreviation of 'computer output microfiche'.

2. Abbreviation of 'computer output microfilming'.

3. Abbreviation of 'computer output on microfilm'.

combination. A selection made from a set of items is regarded as a combination if the order of items within the selection is immaterial. Compare 'permutation'.

combined transport document. Abbreviation: CTD. A receipt given by a carrier certifying that specified goods have been received by the carrier for carriage to a named destination, the journey to which will involve more than one mode of transport.

comfort letter. A letter, addressed to a bank by the parent company of a company which is seeking to borrow money from the bank, expressing the parent company's awareness of the proposed borrowing and stating that its intention is that the subsidiary company should continue in business but not actually giving any guarantee of the subsidiary's indebtedness. Also called 'letter of comfort'.

Commercial Court. Part of the Queen's Bench Division of the High Court which deals with commercial disputes.

commercial documents. Invoices, shipping documents, documents of title or other similar documents, or any documents, other than financial documents, entrusted to a bank for collection.

commission. 1. *Noun.* Payment made by one person to another who has obtained work, orders or sales for the person paying – especially, a payment that is a fixed percentage of the value of the business transacted. For example:

(a) payment to a sales representative of a percentage of the value of sales made by the representative;

(b) payment to an agent of a percentage of the value of work procured for others.

2. *Noun.* A task entrusted to a person.

3. *Noun.* A body of people given authority to perform a specific task. Especially, a government agency with investigative or administrative duties.

4. *Noun.* A formal document entrusting a task to a person.

5. *Verb.* To entrust a task to a person.

6. *Verb.* To put a piece of machinery into service.

commission account. Part of the nominal ledger recording commissions payable to agents.

commissioner. An individual entrusted with a task, especially by a court, by Parliament or the Crown.

Commissioner for the general purposes of the income tax. Another term for 'General Commissioner'.

Commissioner for the special purposes of the Income Tax Acts. Another term for 'Special Commissioner'.

Commissioner of Customs and Excise. An individual appointed by the Crown, under the Customs and Excise Management Act 1979, s. 6, to be responsible for collecting and managing the revenues of customs and excise, subject to the general control of the Treasury. The Commissioners are collectively known as the Board of Customs and Excise.

Commissioner of Inland Revenue. An individual appointed by the Crown, under the Inland Revenue Regulation Act 1890, s. 1, to be responsible for the collection and management of capital gains tax, capital transfer tax, corporation tax, development land tax, income tax, petroleum revenue tax and stamp duties in the UK. The Commissioners are known collectively as the Board of Inland Revenue.

Commission for Local Authority Accounts in Scotland. A commission whose members are appointed by the Secretary of State and whose main duty is to ensure that the accounts of local authorities in Scotland are audited. The chief officer of the commission is called the Controller of Audit.

commissions received account. Part of the nominal ledger recording commissions receivable.

committee of inspection. A committee of individuals, representing the interests of creditors, who supervise the conduct of a trustee in bankruptcy or of a liquidator in a compulsory winding up or in a creditors' voluntary winding up. The 1984 Insolvency Bill proposes that the term should no longer be used in legislation.

Committee of Public Accounts. A committee of the House of Commons whose main functions are to see that public money is applied for the purposes prescribed by Parliament and to ensure that government departments and agencies carry out their work efficiently, effectively and economically. The committee bases its work on reports made by the Comptroller and Auditor General. By tradition, the chairman of the committee is an Opposition member who has been a Treasury minister. Informally, the name is often altered to 'Public Accounts Committee'.

common cost. The cost of an expenditure incurred for two or more activities, departments or products where the proportion ascribed to each activity is determined, if at all, by an arbitrary decision.

common difference. See the entry for 'arithmetic progression'.

common law. A system of law developed by professional lawyers in court judgments and in textbooks, based on customary rules. In the legal system of England and Wales the term 'common law' is usually used to refer to the system without equity because until 1875 equity was administered by separate courts.

common logarithm. A logarithm to base 10. Also called 'Briggsian logarithm' because an English mathematician, Henry Briggs (1561-1631) promoted the use of logarithms to base 10.

common property. Property owned in common by two or more persons.

common ratio. See the entry for 'geometric progression'.

commorientes. Individuals who died together. The 'law of commorientes' is the rule, contained in the Law of Property Act 1925, s. 184, that where two (or more) persons die in circumstances rendering it uncertain which of them survived the other (or others), deaths are, for all purposes affecting the title to property under a will, presumed to have occurred in order of seniority; accordingly, a younger person would be presumed to have survived an elder. This rule does not apply to a married couple for the purposes of the law relating to intestacy (Administration of Estates Act 1925, s. 46(3)).

Companies Act. 1. A statute regulating the formation, incorporation, management, finance and winding up of registered incorporated companies. In Britain, the Companies Act 1862 was the first statute to be called a Companies Act although there had been earlier legislation on the subject. The 1862 Act and several amending Acts were repealed and replaced by the Companies (Consolidation) Act 1908, in turn replaced by the Companies Act 1929, in turn replaced by the Companies Act 1948. The 1948 Act was amended many times and the British legislation relating to companies was given the collective title 'Companies Acts 1948 to 1983'. These have all now been repealed and have been replaced by the Companies Act 1985 as from 1 July 1985. See the entry for 'former Companies Acts'.

2. Plural form (Companies Acts). In the Companies Act 1985, used to mean the Companies Act 1985, the Companies Consolidation (Consequential Provisions) Act 1985 and the Company Securities (Insider Dealing) Act 1985 (Companies Act 1985, s. 744).

company. 1. An association of persons, especially one formed to carry out a business enterprise or practise a profession. A company may be either unincorporated or incorporated.

An unincorporated company formed to pursue a business or profession for profit is a partnership. The words 'and company' may appear in the name of a partnership firm to refer to the partners whose names are not stated in the firm-name.

In Britain, almost all incorporated companies are registered companies, which, in turn, are almost all limited companies. The word 'company' often means 'limited company' or 'registered company'. Statutory companies and chartered corporations are also types of incorporated company in Britain, but there are very few of them. In the USA, an incorporated company is usually called a 'corporation', but in Canada, other parts of the

Commonwealth and Ireland, an incorporated company is called a 'company'.

2. For the purposes of many statements of standard accounting practice, ' "company" includes any enterprise which comes within the scope of Statements of Standard Accounting Practice' (SSAP 15, para. 24; SSAP 17, para. 15; SSAP 18, para. 11; SSAP 20, para. 34; SSAP 21, para. 13; SSAP 22, para. 27; ED 32, para. 27; ED 36, para. 33). This means any entity for which financial statements are prepared which are intended to give a true and fair view of financial position and profit or loss (Explanatory Foreword to SSAPs, para. 1).

3. In the Companies Act 1985, a company formed and registered under that Act or under the former Companies Acts (except one registered in Ireland) (s. 735(1) of the Act).

4. In the Income and Corporation Taxes Act 1970, unless otherwise stated, any body corporate or unincorporated association, but not a partnership, a local authority or a local authority association (s. 526(5) of the Act).

company law. The law relating to the formation, operation and dissolution of incorporated companies. In the USA (but not Canada), called 'law of corporations'.

company limited by guarantee. In British company law, a company whose members do not contribute capital to the company unless it is necessary to do so when the company is wound up, though even then the amount to be contributed is limited, and in practice is usually nominal. In the past, it was possible for a company limited by guarantee to have a class of members who contributed share capital, but it is no longer possible to form companies like this. Also called 'guarantee company'.

company limited by shares. A limited company in which the limit of a member's liability is the nominal value of the shares allotted to the member.

comparative figure. In relation to an item in a financial statement of an accounting entity for an accounting period, the amount for the same item in the corresponding financial statement for the preceding accounting period. Also called 'corresponding amount'.

compensating balance. Money which a customer of a bank is required to deposit at the bank as a condition for the bank lending money to the customer. The practice of requiring compensating balances is more common in America than Britain.

compensating errors. Two or more errors in accounts whose combined effect, accidentally, does not make the overall balance erroneous. In America, called 'offsetting errors'.

compiler. A computer program used to translate programs that are expressed in a particular high-level language into a particular computer-oriented language. Also called 'compiling program'.

compiling program. Another term for 'compiler'.

completed long-term contract. A long-term contract on which no further work, apart from maintenance work, is expected to take place (SSAP 9, appendix 2).

compliance audit. An examination of the operations of an organisation to check that it is complying with procedures required by law or by contractual agreement.

compliance test. A test that seeks to provide audit evidence that internal control procedures are being applied as prescribed.

component. Another term for 'part'.

composite rate. The rate of withholding tax applied to payments of interest by building societies, banks and other deposit-takers in the UK. It is calculated so as to reflect the average rate of tax payable by customers of deposit-takers.

composition. An agreement between a debtor and a creditor that the creditor will accept as complete settlement something less valuable than was originally claimed from the debtor.

compound discount. A discount calculated by the formula:

$$d = P \{ 1 - (1 + i)^{-t} \}$$

where P is the amount from which the discount d is to be deducted, i is the discount rate per unit of time and t is the number of units of time, and t is a positive integer.

If $0 < t < 1$ then the compound discount on P at discount rate i is:

$$d = Pti$$

If $t > 1$ and t is not an integer, and $[t]$ is the largest integer less than t then the compound discount on P at discount rate i is:

$$d = P \{1 - ([t]i + 1 - ti)(1 + i)^{-[t]} \}$$

Also called 'mathematical discount', 'true discount'.

$P - d$ is called the 'present value' of P.

compound interest. Interest calculated by the formula:

$$P(1 + i)^t - P$$

where P is the principal, i is the rate of interest per unit of time and t is the number of units of time, and t is a positive integer.

If $0 < t \leqslant 1$ then the compound interest on P at an interest rate i is:

$$Pti$$

If $t > 1$ and t is not an integer, and $[t]$ is the largest integer less than t then the compound interest on P at an interest rate i is:

$$P(1 + i)^{[t]} \{ 1 + (t - [t])i \} - P$$

comprehensive income. Term used in FASB Statement of Financial Accounting Concepts 3 to mean the change in the owners' equity (or net assets) of an accounting entity, during a period, from transactions and other events and circumstances but not from contributions of capital by owners or distributions of profits or repayments of capital to them.

compromise. An agreement settling a dispute, without pursuing legal proceedings, in which there is some accommodation by each party to the dispute in favour of the other party or parties.

Comptroller and Auditor General. An officer of the House of Commons appointed by the Crown under s. 6 of the Exchequer and Audit

Departments Act 1866 on an address presented by the House of Commons, who is head of the National Audit Office and who is required to authorise payments out of the Consolidated Fund, to audit all appropriation accounts and to examine the economy, efficiency and effectiveness with which government departments have used resources in discharging their functions.

compulsory liquidation. Another term for 'compulsory winding up'.

compulsory winding up. A winding up of a registered company or any partnership or association with eight or more members or a trustee savings bank ordered by a court under the Companies Act 1985. In the Act, the term 'compulsory winding up' is not used; instead the process is called 'winding up by the court'. Also called 'compulsory liquidation'.

computer. A data processing device capable of performing substantial jobs involving numerous arithmetic operations and logic operations without intervention by a human operator during the performance of a job.

computer language. In relation to a particular computer, the programming language in which instructions presented to the processing unit of the computer must be expressed if the processing unit is to execute them. Also called 'machine language'.

computer network. Two or more interconnected computers. The short form 'network' is often used.

computer-oriented language. A programming language that reflects the structure of a particular computer or class of computers. Also called 'low-level language'.

computer output microfiche. Abbreviation: COM. A microfiche of data received from a computer.

computer output microfilming. Abbreviation: COM. Making microform records of data received from a computer. Also called 'computer output on microfilm'.

computer output on microfilm. Abbreviation: COM. 1. A microfilm of data received from a computer.
2. Another term for 'computer output microfilming'.

computer program. A sequence of instructions to a computer determining how it will carry out a particular data processing job, expressed in a form that can be communicated to the computer so that it can execute the job. The short form 'program' is commonly used.

computer system. One or more computers that use a common main store together with their associated software. Also called 'computing system'.

computing system. Another term for 'computer system'.

concept of capital maintenance. A basis for assessing whether any capital of an accounting entity has been lost. It is usual to draw a distinction between the 'financial' concept of capital maintenance, in which the assessment is based on the amount of net assets shown in a balance sheet, and the 'physical' concept of capital maintenance (also called the 'concept of maintenance of operating capability'), in which the assessment is based on the capacity of the business to supply goods and services. In accounting terms, the operating capability of a business is represented by the net operating assets at current cost.

concept of maintenance of operating capability. A basis for assessing whether any capital of an accounting entity that is a business enterprise has been lost in which profit is determined after allowing for the effects of specific price changes on the funds required to maintain the net operating assets, and thus the operating capability, of the business, after taking account of the way in which these assets are financed. Net operating assets consist of fixed assets, stocks and monetary working capital. The adjustments necessary to show whether the operating capability represented by these assets has been maintained are, respectively, a depreciation adjustment, a cost of sales adjustment, and a monetary working capital adjustment. A gearing adjustment is also necessary to take account of the capital structure of the company.

concert party. Jocular version of the phrase 'persons acting in concert', which is used in the City Code on Take-overs and Mergers to refer to persons who cooperate in buying shares with a view to gaining control of a company. (A 'concert party' was a small group of entertainers giving a theatrical performance consisting of a sequence of short items of a lightly amusing or sentimental character.)

concession note. A document which authorises the further processing of an item of product that does not conform to specification.

condition. In the law of contract, an obligation, which one party has under a contract, that is such an essential feature of the contract that failure to perform it entitles the other party to regard the contract as terminated. Compare 'innominate term', 'warranty'.

conditional bill of sale. A bill of sale of goods under which ownership of the goods will revert to the grantor if specified conditions are fulfilled.

conditional distribution. In probability theory, in relation to a multivariate distribution of n random variables, a probability distribution of k of those variables for fixed values of the other variables.

conditional endorsement. Alternative spelling: conditional indorsement. An endorsement that expresses an intention that the instrument is to be transferred only after fulfilment of a condition.

conditional indorsement. Alternative spelling of 'conditional endorsement'.

conditional probability. In relation to two events A and H for which probabilities are defined, where $P(H) \neq 0$, the conditional probability of A given H, symbolised by $P(A \mid H)$, is:

$$P(A \mid H) = \frac{P(A \text{ and } H)}{P(H)}$$

conditional sale agreement. A contract of sale which is subject to a condition. In the Consumer Credit Act 1974, s. 189(1), defined as 'an agreement for the sale of goods or land under which the purchase price or part of it is payable by instalments, and the property in the goods or land is to remain in the seller (notwithstanding that the buyer is to be in possession of the goods or land) until such conditions as to the payment of instalments or otherwise as may be specified in the agreement are fulfilled'.

confidence coefficient. The probability that a confidence interval includes the value of the population parameter being estimated. Also called 'confidence level'.

confidence interval. A range of numbers, calculated from a sample from a population, which has a specified probability of including the value of a particular population parameter. The specified probability is called the 'confidence coefficient' or 'confidence level'.

A confidence interval is defined by a number or numbers called 'confidence limits'. Usually there are two confidence limits, which may be denoted by T_1 and T_2 with $T_1 < T_2$. If θ is the population parameter and $1 - \alpha$ ($\alpha \neq 1$) is the confidence coefficient and:

$$P(T_1 \leqslant \theta \leqslant T_2) = 1 - \alpha$$

then the interval $[T_1, T_2]$ — i.e., all numbers x such that $T_1 \leqslant x \leqslant T_2$ — is a two-sided $(1 - \alpha)$ confidence interval for θ.

A one-sided confidence interval is defined by one confidence limit T. If:

$$P(T \leqslant \theta) = 1 - \alpha$$

then all the numbers greater than or equal to T form a one-sided $(1 - \alpha)$ confidence interval for θ. Alternatively, if:

$$P(\theta \leqslant T) = 1 - \alpha$$

then all the numbers less than or equal to T form a one-sided $(1 - \alpha)$ confidence interval for θ.

confidence level. Another term for 'confidence coefficient'.

confidence limit. A number calculated, from a sample from a population, as a boundary point of a confidence interval for a population parameter.

confirmation. In Scotland, a decree of a Sheriff Court authorising an executor dative or executor nominate of a deceased individual to deal with the estate of the individual.

confirmed credit. A letter of credit that the advising bank undertakes to honour whether or not it receives funds from the issuing bank.

confirming house. A business enterprise that operates in one country facilitating exports from that country by confirming orders from foreign buyers and undertaking to pay the exporters for those orders. The confirming house collects the money from the foreign buyers and charges them a fee for its services.

consensus ad idem. Latin for 'agreement to the same thing'. An essential feature of an enforceable contract.

conservatism. In accounting, the principle that it is better to understate income, profits and owners' equity than to risk overstating them. One aspect of conservatism is the concept of prudence in accounting; another aspect is the rule that stocks must be valued at the lower of historical cost or net realisable value.

consideration. Something of value given for a promise.

consignee. A person named in a bill of lading or consignment note or similar document relating to the shipment of goods as the person to whom delivery of the goods is to be made on arrival at their destination.

consignment. 1. Goods, sent by one person (called the 'consignor') in one place to a person (called the 'consignee') in another place, that are transported and delivered together and are dealt with in a single set of documents.

2. The act or process of sending goods from one place to another.

3. Arrangement by which the goods of one person (called the 'consignor') are put in the possession of another person (called the 'agent' or 'factor') who offers them for sale and makes all arrangements with buyers. The agent retains an agreed percentage of sales receipts but does not take ownership of the goods so the consignor is left with the risk of them not selling.

consignment accounts. Accounting records of transactions relating to goods consigned to a merchant to sell as agent of the consignor. Such records are kept both by the consignor and the agent.

consignment inward. A batch of goods sent to an agent for sale on consignment – from the point of view of the agent. The form 'consignment inwards' is also used.

consignment note. A document made out by a carrier when goods are received for carriage, identifying the sender, the goods and the destination, and stating the terms of the contract of carriage. Usually, one copy of the note is given to the sender and another copy accompanies the goods. Also called 'carrier's note', 'waybill'.

consignment outward. A batch of goods sent to an agent for sale on consignment – from the point of view of the consignor. The form 'consignment outwards' is also used.

consignor. A person who has sent a consignment of goods.

consistency concept. The fundamental accounting concept that there should be consistency of accounting treatment of like items within each period of account and from one period to the next. This is one of the fundamental accounting concepts identified in SSAP 2, one of the fundamental accounting assumptions identified in IAS 1, and one of the accounting principles set out in the Companies Act 1985, Schedule 4.

console. Another term for 'operator console'.

consolidated accounts. Financial statements in which the financial position of two or more accounting entities is presented as if they were a single entity. The preparation of consolidated accounts involves the elimination of financial transactions between the entities whose results are consolidated. Also called 'consolidated financial statements'.

consolidated balance sheet. A balance sheet which presents the assets and liabilities of two or more accounting entities as though they were a single entity.

consolidated financial statements. Another term for 'consolidated accounts'.

Consolidated Fund. The fund of money held in an account at the Bank of England into which all UK government revenues have to be paid. A withdrawal from the account can be made only if authorised by Parliament – that is, if it is to pay for a Consolidated Fund standing service or a Supply service. The Comptroller and Auditor General is responsible for checking that withdrawals are authorised. If there is a surplus in the fund at the end of a day then that surplus is transferred to the National Loans Fund. If there is a deficit at the end of a day it is made up from the National Loans Fund.

Until the end of the 18th century, government revenues were kept in separate funds according to the source of the revenue but this became too cumbersome and so, in 1787, all funds were 'consolidated'.

Consolidated Fund standing service. A government expenditure that is payable out of the Consolidated Fund by virtue of a statutory provision and which may be incurred in any year while the provision remains in force without specific authorisation for that year by Parliament. The most important Consolidated Fund standing service is payment of interest on money lent to the government.

consolidated income and expenditure account. An income and expenditure account which presents the incomes and expenditures of two or more accounting entities as though they were a single entity. The term is used instead of 'consolidated profit and loss account' for entities which are not business enterprises.

consolidated income statement. Term used in America for 'consolidated income and expenditure account' and for 'consolidated profit and loss account'.

consolidated profit. In relation to a holding company, the profit of the company and its subsidiaries as shown in a consolidated profit and loss account.

consolidated profit and loss account. A profit and loss account which presents the revenues and expenditures of two or more accounting entities as though they were a single entity. Transactions between the entities must be eliminated. Called a 'consolidated income and expenditure account' if the entities are not business enterprises. In America, called 'consolidated income statement'.

consolidated statement of source and application of funds. A statement of source and application of funds which presents the sources and applications of funds of two or more accounting entities as though they were a single entity.

consolidation. 1. Preparation of consolidated accounts.

2. Treatment of the share capital of a company as no longer represented by separate shares.

3. Another term for 'uniting of interests'.

4. Insistence by a creditor who is owed two separate debts by one debtor, secured by two separate charges, that neither charge will come to an end until both debts are paid.

5. Preparation of a consolidation Act.

consolidation accounts. Financial statements for a company in a group of companies in which adjustments (called 'pre-consolidation adjustments') have been made so that there is uniformity of treatment throughout the group of such matters as translation of foreign currencies, format of presentation, and revaluation of fixed assets, and from which consolidated accounts will be prepared.

consolidation Act. An Act of Parliament that repeals previous legislation contained in several statutes and re-enacts the provisions in a single Act.

consortium. 1. A number of companies associated together for a particular purpose, especially where they are the members of another company formed to carry out that purpose.

2. In United Kingdom tax legislation:

(a) for the purposes of the Income and Corporation Taxes Act 1970, s. 256 (group income), 'a company is owned by a consortium if three-quarters or more of the ordinary share capital of the company is beneficially owned between them by companies resident in the United Kingdom of which none beneficially owns less than one-twentieth of that capital, and those companies are called the members of the consortium' (s. 256(6)(c));

(b) for the purposes of the Income and Corporation Taxes Act 1970, ss. 258 to 264 (group relief), 'a company is owned by a consortium if three-quarters or more of the ordinary share capital of the company is beneficially owned between them by companies of which none beneficially owns less than one-twentieth of that capital, and those companies are called the members of the consortium' (s. 258(8)) and in this provision references to a 'company' apply only to bodies corporate resident in the UK (s. 258(7));

(c) for the purposes of the Finance Act 1978, Schedule 9 (profit-sharing schemes), 'a company is a member of a consortium owning another company if it is one of not more than five companies which between them beneficially own not less than three-quarters of the other company's ordinary share capital and each of which beneficially owns not less than one-twentieth of that capital' (para. 17).

constant. In mathematics, in an equation expressing the relationship between a dependent variable and one or more independent variables, a factor or term which has the same value for all values of the independent variable or variables.

If several relationships are being considered which are represented by formulae which are identical except for the value of one constant term or factor then that term or factor may be referred to as a 'parameter'.

constant dollar accounting. Term sometimes used in America for 'constant purchasing power accounting'.

constant purchasing power accounting. Abbreviation: CPP accounting. Method of preparing financial statements so as to account for the effects of changing prices in which the monetary amounts recorded for transactions on the various dates on which they occurred are translated into monetary amounts which, at a specified time, would have the same purchasing power. Purchasing power is measured by a general index of prices such as the General Index of Retail Prices in the UK. In the past called 'current purchasing power accounting'. In America also called 'general price level accounting', 'constant dollar accounting'.

constraint. In operational research, a prior limit on what will be acceptable as a solution to a problem.

constructive trust. A trust automatically imposed by equity in special circumstances in which it is unconscionable for property to be held purely for the benefit of its owner. The term 'constructive trust' is sometimes also used to cover automatic resulting trusts.

consular invoice. In international trade, an invoice that has been certified by a consul appointed by the government of the country where the buyer is domiciled.

Consultative Committee of Accountancy Bodies. Abbreviation: CCAB. An organisation that enables six British and Irish accountancy bodies to consult on matters of common interest. The bodies represented are the Institute of Chartered Accountants in England and Wales, the Institute of Chartered Accountants of Scotland, the Institute of Chartered Accountants in Ireland, the Chartered Association of Certified Accountants, the Institute of Cost and Management Accountants and the Chartered Institute of Public Finance and Accountancy. Three important committees within the organisation are the Accounting Standards Committee, the Auditing Practices Committee, and the Parliamentary and Law Steering Group.

consumables. Materials used by an organisation, but not incorporated into or supplied with its products and not used as a part of the manufacturing process, for example, stationery. Also called 'supplies'.

consumer credit agreement. Defined by the Consumer Credit Act 1974, s. 8, as: an agreement between an individual ('the debtor') and any other person ('the creditor') by which the creditor provides the debtor with credit not exceeding £15,000 (£5,000 before 20 May 1985). 'Credit' includes a cash loan and any other form of financial accommodation. 'Individual' includes a partnership firm or other unincorporated body of persons not consisting entirely of bodies corporate.

consumer credit business. Defined in the Consumer Credit Act 1974, s. 189(1), as: 'any business so far as it comprises or relates to the provision of credit under regulated consumer credit agreements'.

consumer hire agreement. Defined in the Consumer Credit Act 1974, s. 15, as: 'an agreement made by a person with an individual (the "hirer") for the bailment or (in Scotland) the hiring of goods to the hirer, being an agreement which:

'(a) is not a hire-purchase agreement; and

'(b) is capable of subsisting for more than three months; and

'(c) does not require the hirer to make payments exceeding £15,000 [£5,000 before 20 May 1985]'.

consumer hire business. Defined in the Consumer Credit Act 1974, s. 189(1), as: 'any business so far as it comprises or relates to the bailment or (in Scotland) the hiring of goods under regulated consumer hire agreements'.

contango. 1. A fee paid to a stockbroker, by a person who has arranged to buy securities, for the privilege of delaying payment for those securities.

2. A state in which the spot price for something is lower than the forward price for the same thing.

3. The difference between the spot price for something and the forward price for the same thing when the spot price is lower than the forward price.

contemnor. A person who has committed contempt of court.

Contingencies Fund. A fund of money available to the British government for urgent unforeseen expenditure made in anticipation of parliamentary authority. Money paid from the Contingencies Fund is always replaced by a payment from the Consolidated Fund when parliamentary approval has been obtained.

contingency. 1. Something that may happen, but is not certain to happen.

2. In relation to financial statements, a condition which exists at a balance sheet date, of which the outcome will be confirmed on the

occurrence or non-occurrence of one or more uncertain future events. See SSAP 18.

contingency table. When qualitative characteristics of items have been classified according to two or more separate classification schemes, a contingency table states the numbers of items in each class of one scheme that are in each class of the other scheme or schemes.

contingent gain. A gain dependent on a contingency (SSAP 18, para. 14).

contingent interest. An interest, in property, that will come into being if a contingency occurs. Compare 'vested interest'.

contingent liability. A liability dependent on a contingency. Information about contingent liabilities must be given by companies (Companies Act 1985, Schedule 4, para. 50(2)).

contingent loss. A loss dependent on a contingency (SSAP 18, para. 14).

continuous compounding. Calculation of the compound interest on an amount P at an interest rate i per unit of time for t units of time by the formula:

$$Pe^{kt} - P$$

where $k = \ln (1 + i)$.

If t is a positive integer the formula gives the same result as the normal formula for compound interest:

$$P(1 + i)^t - P$$

If t is not an integer the formula for continuous compounding gives an approximation to the correct result.

continuous inventory. Term used in America for 'continuous stock-checking'.

continuous-operation costing. A costing method used when a product results from a sequence of repetitive processes or operations. The costs of the operations or processes for a period are added together and the total is divided by the number of units of the product produced during the period. Also called 'process costing'.

continuous random variable. A random variable, the possible values of which are all the real numbers in a particular range. Compare 'discrete random variable'. Also called 'continuous variate'.

continuous stock-checking. Measurement, each day, of the quantities of a few items of stocks and work in progress held so that over a year all items of stocks and work in progress are measured, and reconciliation of the measured quantities with the quantities recorded by a perpetual inventory system. Also called 'continuous stock-taking', 'cyclic stock check' (the term preferred in BS 5191 : 1975), 'perpetual audit', 'cycle count'. In America, called 'continuous inventory'.

continuous stock-taking. Also written: continuous stocktaking. Another term for 'continuous stock-checking'.

continuous variate. Another term for 'continuous random variable'.

contra accounts. The accounts in the creditors and debtors ledgers of a creditor of an accounting entity who is also a debtor of the entity, particularly where a customer of a trading enterprise is also a supplier to the enterprise.

contract. A promise or set of promises which the law will enforce. In the law of England and Wales, a promise is not enforceable unless either the promise is made in a written statement contained in a deed (in which case there is a 'specialty contract') or something of value (called 'consideration') is given for the promise (in which case there is a 'simple contract'). In practice, almost all contracts are simple contracts and involve two parties, the promise of each being the consideration for the promise of the other.

A simple contract is 'formed' or 'made' when an 'offer' made by one party, which that party has not revoked, is accepted by the other party. The two parties must have agreed to the same thing and must have the legal capacity to make contracts if the contract is to be enforceable. In some circumstances, a contract must be written down or there must be some written evidence that the contract exists for it to be enforceable.

contract cost. The cost of a contract which is considered as a cost unit.

contract costing. Specific-order costing when applied to costing work undertaken to customers' special requirements when each order is of long duration. Compare 'job costing'. Most applications of contract costing are in construction work.

contract for services. Term used in the past for the type of contract which is called a 'contract for the supply of a service' in the Supply of Goods and Services Act 1982.

contract for the supply of a service. Defined in the Supply of Goods and Services Act 1982, s. 12, as 'a contract under which a person ("the supplier") agrees to carry out a service'. A contract of service or apprenticeship is not a contract for the supply of a service (s. 12(2) of the Act). A contract is a contract for the supply of a service whether or not goods are also transferred, or to be transferred or bailed or to be bailed by way of hire under the contract (s. 12(3) of the Act).

contract for the transfer of goods. Defined in the Supply of Goods and Services Act 1982, s. 1(1), as: 'a contract under which one person transfers or agrees to transfer to another the property in goods, other than an excepted contract'. By s. 1(2) of the Act: 'an excepted contract means any of the following:

'(a) a contract of sale of goods;

'(b) a hire-purchase agreement;

'(c) a contract under which the property in goods is (or is to be) transferred in exchange for trading stamps on their redemption;

'(d) a transfer or agreement to transfer which is made by deed and for which there is no consideration other than the presumed consideration imported by the deed;

'(e) a contract intended to operate by way of mortgage, pledge, charge or other security'.

By s. 1(3) of the Act a contract is a contract for the transfer of goods whether or not services are also provided or to be provided under the contract.

contract guarantee. An arrangement under which one party to a contract is promised compensation if the contract is not properly performed by the other party. The major types of contract guarantee are tender bonds, performance guarantees and repayment guarantees.

contract note. A note sent by a broker or dealer advising a client that shares, stock or other securities have been bought or sold for the client.

contract of employment. Another term for 'contract of service'.

contract of sale of goods. Defined in the Sale of Goods Act 1979, s. 2, as: 'a contract by which the seller transfers or agrees to transfer the property in goods to the buyer for a money consideration, called the price'. A contract of sale of goods may be absolute or conditional. If, under a contract of sale of goods, transfer of the property in the goods is to take place at a future time or subject to some condition to be fulfilled in the future, the contract is called an 'agreement to sell'. An agreement to sell becomes a 'sale' when the time elapses or the conditions are fulfilled subject to which the property in the goods is to be transferred, and a contract of sale of goods which transfers the property in the goods from the seller to the buyer at the time the contract is made is also called a 'sale'.

contract of service. A contract under which an individual undertakes personally to perform work as an employee in return for payment. In some instances there is great difficulty in deciding whether an individual undertakes to perform work as an employee under a contract of service or as an independent contractor under a contract for the supply of a service. The distinction is important for UK income tax purposes: earnings from a contract of service are Schedule E income whereas earnings from a contract for the supply of a service are Schedule D income. Also called 'contract of employment', 'service contract'.

contractual pension scheme. According to ED 32, para. 28, a pension scheme 'is "contractual" where the members have rights to benefits, the payment of which may be enforced by legal process or where the arrangements are of long standing and a contractual obligation may in fact have been created by the continued payment of the benefits'.

contra entry. Where a creditor of an accounting entity is also a debtor to that entity, a credit to that debtor's account and a corresponding debit to the creditor's account so as to make the smaller of the balances on the two accounts zero and leave only one amount owing to or owed by the entity.

contributed capital. Money or other assets for use in a business enterprise assigned to the enterprise by its owners or given to the enterprise rather than being earned by the enterprise as retained earnings from its operations or lent to the enterprise. In British companies, share premiums are regarded as undistributable reserves rather than as contributed capital. Also called 'paid-in capital'.

contribution. The difference between the sales value of a product and the total variable costs associated with the product, either 'in total' for a specified quantity of the product or 'per unit' for one unit of the product. Sometimes called 'contribution margin'.

contribution margin. 1. Ratio of the contribution from a certain quantity of a product to the turnover (or net sales) attributable to that quantity of the product. Also called 'contribution margin ratio'.

2. Another term for 'contribution'.

contribution margin ratio. Ratio of the contribution from a certain quantity of a product to the turnover (or net sales) attributable to that quantity of the product. Also called 'contribution margin'.

contribution week. In relation to social security contributions in Britain, a period of seven days beginning at midnight between a Saturday and Sunday.

contributory. In British company law, any person liable to contribute to the assets of a company in the event of its being wound up. If a company is a company limited by shares then the only liability is for a member to pay the amount, if any, unpaid on the shares that member held at the time winding up commenced. See Companies Act 1985, ss. 502 to 507.

control account. An account of totals of amounts that should have been posted from books of prime entry to a particular part of the ledger. The balance on the control account should equal the total of the balances on all the accounts in that part of the ledger. A control account is named after the part of the ledger to which it refers. For example, the debtors control account refers to the debtors ledger and it contains as debit entries the total of credit sales (from the sales day book) and corrections of errors (from the journal); and as credit entries, sales returns (from the sales returns book) cash received (from the cash book), discounts allowed (from the discount column of the cash book), and bad debts written off, contra entries and corrections of errors (from the journal). The balance on the debtors control account should equal the total of the balances on the accounts in the debtors ledger. Also called 'controlling account', 'total account'.

control character. In data processing, a character whose occurrence in a particular context initiates, modifies or stops a control function.

control function. In data processing, an action that affects the recording, processing, transmission or interpretation of data. In America called 'control operation'.

controllable cost. A cost that is attributed to a budget centre or cost centre and can be influenced by the person responsible for that centre. Also called 'managed cost'.

controllable variable. In operational research, a variable, in a system, that is under the control of the managers of the system.

controlled foreign company. Defined by the Finance Act 1984, s. 82, as a company that is:
   (a) resident outside the United Kingdom; and
   (b) controlled by persons resident in the United Kingdom; and
   (c) subject to a lower level of taxation in the territory in which it is resident.

Controller of Audit. 1. The chief officer of the Audit Commission for Local Authorities in England and Wales.
   2. The chief officer of the Commission for Local Authority Accounts in Scotland.

control operation. Term used in America for 'control function'.

control period. A period in respect of which comparisons are made between budgeted and actual results.

control program. A computer program that schedules and supervises the execution of programs in a computer system.

conventional basis. In UK revenue law, a principle for determining the accounting period in which events and transactions should be recorded that is not the earnings basis.

convention of periodicity. Another term for 'periodicity concept'.

conversational mode. A mode of operation of a computer system in which a sequence of alternating entries and responses between a user and the system takes place. Also called 'interactive mode'.

conversion. 1. Actual exchange of an amount of money in one currency for an equivalent amount in another currency. Compare 'translation'.

2. In the law of torts, an act of deliberate dealing with goods or with a negotiable instrument in a manner inconsistent with another person's right whereby that other person is deprived of the use and possession of the goods or negotiable instrument.

3. An exchange of a convertible security for another security.

conversion cost. The cost of converting material input into semi-finished or finished products, i.e., additional direct material cost, direct labour cost, direct expenses and absorbed production overhead.

conversion premium. In relation to a convertible security that is exchangeable for a second security, the difference between the cost of acquiring the second security by using the convertible and the cost of purchasing it directly, usually expressed as a percentage of the cost of purchasing the second security directly.

convertible. *Adjective.* Capable of being converted. When referring to securities, exchangeable for a different security at the option of the holder (for example, securities issued in connection with a marketable loan raised by a company may give holders the option of exchanging them for ordinary shares in the company).

convertible unsecured loan stock. Abbreviation: CULS. Unsecured loan stock of a company which a holder may exchange for another security – usually ordinary shares of the company – on terms fixed on the issue of the loan stock.

COP. Computerisation of PAYE: a scheme of the Inland Revenue to implement computer processing of PAYE throughout the UK by the end of 1987.

core. In a computer, a piece of magnetic material, usually ring-shaped, used as an element of a store. Also called 'magnetic core'.

corporate. 1. *Adjective.* Of, or relating to, a corporation.

2. *Adjective.* Incorporated.

corporate report. The annual report and accounts of an accounting entity, especially one including significantly more information than is required by law.

corporation. An association of persons that is itself regarded, in law, as a separate person which may be put into legal relationships (such as being an owner of property, a party to a contract, or a party to legal proceedings) and which continues in existence until dissolved in accordance with the law.

The persons who are associated together in a corporation are called the 'corporators' or 'members' of the corporation.

An association that is a corporation is said to be 'incorporated'.

The normal method of incorporating an association is by registration with a public official. In Britain, the normal method is by registration as a registered company under the Companies Act 1985. Corporations may also be formed for limited special purposes by registration under the Building

Societies Act 1962, the Charitable Trustees Incorporation Act 1872, or the Industrial and Provident Societies Act 1965. (All the Acts mentioned, except that of 1872, re-enact provisions for registration contained in earlier Acts). A corporation may also be formed by specific legislation or by royal charter.

A reference in the Companies Act 1985 to a 'corporation' does not include a corporation sole.

corporation aggregate. A corporation that may have more than one member at a time.

corporation sole. A corporation that may have only one member at a time.

corporation stock. A stock issued by a British local authority in connection with a marketable loan.

corporation tax. Abbreviation: CT. A United Kingdom tax charged on the income and capital gains of a company resident in the UK. For the purposes of corporation tax, 'company' means any incorporated or unincorporated company apart from a partnership, a local authority or a local authority association.

Corporation Tax Acts. When used in any Act of Parliament or Northern Ireland legislation, defined in the Interpretation Act 1978, Schedule 1, to mean:

(a) Parts X and XI of the Income and Corporation Taxes Act 1970, and

(b) all other provisions of that or any other Act relating to corporation tax or to any other matter dealt with in Part X or Part XI of that Act, and

(c) all the provisions of Part IV of the Finance Act 1965 and of any other enactment which, at 12 March 1970, formed part of or was to be construed with the Corporation Tax Acts.

corporator. One of the persons who are associated together as a corporation. Also called 'member'.

correcting entry. An adjusting entry that corrects an error.

correlation coefficient. Another term for 'coefficient of correlation'.

corresponding amount. Another term for 'comparative figure'.

COSA. Abbreviation of 'cost of sales adjustment'.

cost. 1. *Noun.* In accounting, in relation to a thing, the value of an asset or part of an asset given up, parted with, used or consumed, or a liability or part of a liability incurred, in exchange for the thing – or an aggregate of such values.

2. *Verb.* In relation to a thing, to determine the value of an asset or part of an asset given up, parted with, used or consumed, or a liability or part of a liability incurred, in exchange for the thing – or an aggregate of such values.

3. *Noun.* In economics, opportunity cost.

cost accounting. Defined in the ICMA official terminology as the part of management accounting which is concerned with the establishment of budgets and standard costs and actual costs of operations, processes, departments or products, and the analysis of variances, profitability or the social use of funds.

cost allocation. Attribution of items of cost to cost centres or products without cost apportionment.

cost and freight. Abbreviation: C&F or CFR. Trade terms for the sale of goods that are to be transported to the buyer by sea under which the seller must pay the costs and freight necessary to bring the goods to a destination port nominated by the buyer but the buyer bears the risk of the goods being lost or damaged after they have crossed the ship's rail when being loaded at the start of the sea journey so that the buyer should insure the goods for the sea journey.

cost apportionment. Division of costs between two or more cost centres or products in proportion to the estimated benefit received where direct measurement of the benefit is not possible or not worth while.

cost ascertainment. Collection of costs attributable to cost centres and products of an organisation using the costing methods, principles and techniques adopted by the organisation. Also called 'cost finding'.

cost attribution. The process of deciding which cost centre or product of an organisation should be treated as having incurred a cost that the organisation has incurred. Cost allocation and cost apportionment are two aspects of cost attribution.

cost behaviour. American spelling: cost behavior. The way in which costs per unit of output differ at different output levels.

cost centre. American spelling: cost center. A location, function or item of equipment in respect of which costs may be ascertained and related to cost units for control purposes.

cost control. Influence on costs so that they will not differ from planned amounts.

cost control account. See the entry for 'cost ledger'.

cost convention. The rule that the cost of acquiring or producing an asset is the amount to be recorded as its value in accounts. Also called 'historical cost convention'.

cost finding. Another term for 'cost ascertainment'.

costing method. A method of establishing a product cost when the product is of a particular kind, for example, contract costing, continuous operation costing or service costing. Also called 'basic costing method'.

costing principle. A fundamental assumption about what constitutes the most important indication of the cost of a product, upon which a costing system is based. The two alternative costing principles used are absorption costing and marginal costing.

costing technique. An established system of methods for carrying out the work of cost accounting. The two most important costing techniques are budgetary control and standard costing.

cost, insurance and freight. Abbreviation: CIF. Trade terms for the sale of goods that are to be transported to the buyer by sea under which the seller is responsible for transporting the goods to a destination port nominated by the buyer and must insure the goods against loss during the journey.

cost ledger. A set of accounts used in computing product costs and kept on the double-entry bookkeeping system. Cost accounts are not concerned with personal accounts, capital and reserves, nor with asset accounts other than accounts showing items of stock. However, cost accounts do include accounts for materials, and jobs or products, which do not appear in the normal or 'financial' ledger. For some transactions, only one aspect is a debit or credit to an account in the cost ledger while the other aspect would be an entry in an account that appears only in a financial ledger. For example, a purchase of some raw material is a debit to the account for that material in the cost ledger but is a credit to the supplier's account in the creditors ledger which would not form part of the cost ledger. The cost ledger may be a competely independent system, so that some transactions will be entered in both the financial ledger and the cost ledger, or there may be a system of 'interlocking accounts'. In an independent system, double entries which would be made to accounts not in the cost ledger are instead made to a single account in the cost ledger called the 'cost control account'. In interlocking accounts, the accounts in the financial ledger which also appear in the cost ledger are removed from the financial ledger and replaced by a single account called 'cost ledger control account'. As in the independent system, the cost ledger has a control account for double entries in accounts that are outside the cost ledger, but in interlocking accounts this control account is called 'general ledger control account' or, sometimes, 'cost ledger control account'.

cost ledger control account. See the entry for 'cost ledger'.

cost of capital. The minimum return on investment that is required by persons who invest money in a business enterprise and which is therefore the minimum rate of return that must be provided by any project for which the enterprise uses its capital.

cost of goods manufactured statement. Term used in America for 'manufacturing account'.

cost of goods sold. Another term for 'cost of sales'.

cost of sales. The expenses incurred in producing or acquiring goods that have been sold. Also called 'cost of goods sold'.

cost of sales adjustment. Abbreviation: COSA. In current cost accounting, an adjustment made to the trading profit of an accounting entity for an accounting period, as calculated on the historical cost basis, to allow for the effect of price changes on the value of stock consumed in earning the revenue for the period. In SSAP 16, para. 49, it is defined as the difference between the value to the business and the historical cost of stock consumed during the period.

cost unit. A measured amount of a product used for the expression of the costs of that product, for example, if the product is steel, costs may be expressed per tonne of the product and then the cost unit is one tonne; if the product is bricks, costs may be expressed per thousand bricks and the cost unit is 1,000 bricks.

cost-volume-profit analysis. Analysis of the relationships between actual or potential gross profit from a product and the costs of producing and selling it for different volumes of production and different selling prices.

coupon. A part of a bearer security which the bearer detaches and uses to claim a payment of dividend or interest. Hence, the interest rate (also called 'coupon rate') payable on any marketable loan, whether the securities issued for it are bearer securities or not.

coupon rate. The interest rate payable on a marketable loan. See the entry for 'coupon'.

covariance. 1. In probability theory, in relation to a bivariate distribution of two random variables X and Y, the quantity:

$$E((X - E(X))(Y - E(Y))$$

where E symbolises expectation.

Also called 'product moment'.

2. In statistics, in relation to two sets of observed values, $x_1, \ldots, x_m$ with mean $\bar{x}$ and $y_1, \ldots, y_n$ with mean $\bar{y}$, the quantity:

$$\frac{1}{N} \Sigma(x_i - \bar{x})(y_j - \bar{y})$$

where $N = m + n$.

Also called 'product moment'.

cover note. A memorandum sent by an insurance broker to a client to inform the client that insurance cover requested by the client has been obtained.

CPA. 1. In the USA, abbreviation of 'certified public accountant'.

2. In Ireland, designation of an Associate of the Institute of Certified Public Accountants in Ireland.

CPM. Abbreviation of 'critical path method'.

CPP accounting. Abbreviation of 'constant purchasing power accounting'.

CPU. Abbreviation of 'central processing unit'.

Cr. Abbreviation of 'creditor' used in accounts to mark a credit entry or a column of credit entries.

credit. 1. *Noun.* An entry in an account that represents a decrease in the value of assets or an increase in the amount of liabilities. It is conventional to make credit entries on the right-hand side of a record of an account. Compare 'debit'.

2. *Noun.* An increase in the amount that a customer of a bank has deposited with the bank (which is a liability – see sense 1 – from the point of view of the bank).

3. *Verb.* To make an entry in an account representing a decrease in the value of assets or an increase in the amount of liabilities.

4. *Noun.* An allowance of time for the payment of a debt. In the Consumer Credit Act 1974, ' "credit" includes a cash loan, and any other form of financial accommodation' (s. 9(1) of the Act).

5. *Noun.* Another term for 'letter of credit'.

credit agency. Another term for 'credit-reporting agency'.

credit balance. The amount by which credits exceed debits in an account.

credit-broker. A person carrying on a business of credit brokerage.

credit brokerage. A business concerned with effecting introductions of individuals desiring to obtain credit or goods on hire to persons carrying on consumer credit or consumer hire businesses. A detailed definition is given in the Consumer Credit Act 1974, s. 145(2) to (4), subject to exceptions specified in s. 146. There is also a detailed definition in the Supply of Goods and Services Act 1982, s. 18(1).

credit bureau. Another term for 'credit-reporting agency'.

credit card. A card issued to an individual (called the 'cardholder'), which identifies the cardholder and permits the cardholder to obtain goods or services on credit. Credit cards are either two-party or three-party. A two-party card may be used only to acquire goods or services from the enterprise that issued the card. A three-party card is issued by a specialist enterprise and may be used to obtain goods or services from any supplier authorised by the issuer of the card. The cardholder must pay the card issuer for anything obtained with the card, and dealings between cardholder and issuer may be on open account (in which case the credit card is usually called a 'charge card'), on revolving credit, or (with two-party cards only) on a budget account. A credit card may be a credit-token under the Consumer Credit Act 1974.

credit insurance. Insurance that compensates a seller if a buyer who has been granted credit fails to pay.

credit memorandum. Term used in America for 'credit note'.

credit note. Abbreviation: C/N. A document stating that a credit entry has been made in an account and stating the amount of the entry and the reason for making it. A credit note is sent to a customer to inform the customer that a previously invoiced charge has been cancelled wholly or partly. In America, called 'credit memorandum'.

creditor. 1. In relation to an accounting entity, a person owed money by the accounting entity.

2. Plural form (creditors). The total amount owed by an accounting entity to other persons.

3. See the entry for 'Cr'.

creditor days ratio. The ratio:

$$\frac{\text{trade creditors at the end of a period}}{\text{average daily purchases on credit terms in the period}}$$

or:

$$\frac{\text{average trade creditors during a period}}{\text{average daily purchases on credit terms in the period}}$$

Average daily purchases is calculated by taking the total of purchases during the period and dividing by the number of days in the period. Average trade creditors during the period may be taken as half the sum of trade creditors at the beginning of the period and trade creditors at the end of the period. The ratio measures the average time taken, in days, to pay for purchases bought on credit. In America, known as 'days' purchases in accounts payable ratio'.

creditors ledger. A section of a ledger containing accounts of transactions with trade creditors of the accounting entity. If the accounting entity is a trading enterprise, its creditors will be mainly suppliers of goods for resale by the enterprise, and the creditors ledger may be called the 'purchases ledger' or 'bought ledger'.

creditors' voluntary liquidation. Another term for 'creditors' voluntary winding up'.

creditors' voluntary winding up. A voluntary winding up of a registered company in which no declaration of solvency is made by the directors within the five weeks before the members adopt the resolution to wind up. In a creditors' voluntary winding up the creditors are entitled to appoint the liquidator and to supervise the winding up. Also called 'creditors' voluntary liquidation'.

credit rating. An assessment of how freely credit should be allowed to a person.

credit reference agency. Defined in the Consumer Credit Act 1974, s. 145(8), as: 'a person carrying on a business comprising the furnishing of persons with information relevant to the financial standing of individuals, being information collected by the agency for that purpose'. 'Individual' includes a partnership firm or other unincorporated body of persons not consisting entirely of bodies corporate. See also the entry for 'credit-reporting agency'.

credit-reporting agency. An organisation that supplies information about the financial standing of persons. Also called 'credit agency', 'credit bureau'. See also the entry for 'credit reference agency'.

credit sale. A supply of goods or services by an accounting entity for which payment is not to be received until some time after the time of supply. This term is used in accounting and commerce generally to describe a transaction whatever the legal form of the transaction may be. However, in law, the term 'credit-sale agreement' has a special technical meaning.

credit-sale agreement. Defined in the Consumer Credit Act 1974, s. 189(1), as: 'an agreement for the sale of goods, under which the purchase price or part of it is payable by instalments, but which is not a conditional sale agreement'. 'Goods' has the same meaning as in the Sale of Goods Act 1979.

credit slip. A form completed by, or on behalf of, a customer of a bank when depositing cash and financial documents for credit to the customer's account, listing in detail the items being handed to the bank. Also called 'paying-in slip'.

credit-token. Defined in the Consumer Credit Act 1974, s. 14, as: 'a card, check, voucher, coupon, stamp, form, booklet or other document or thing given to an individual by a person carrying on a consumer credit business, who undertakes:

'(a) that on the production of it (whether or not some other action is also required) he will supply cash, goods and services (or any of them) on credit; or

'(b) that where, on the production of it to a third party (whether or not any other action is also required), the third party supplies cash, goods and services (or any of them), he will pay the third party for them (whether or not deducting any discount or commission), in return for payment to him by the individual'.

'Individual' includes a partnership firm or other unincorporated body of persons not consisting entirely of bodies corporate.

credit-token agreement. Defined in the Consumer Credit Act 1974, s. 14(2) as: 'a regulated agreement for the provision of credit in connection with the use of a credit-token'.

creditworthiness. Extent to which it is prudent to grant credit to a person.

critical event. In an activity-on-arrow network, an event on a critical path.

critical path. In project network techniques, an unbroken sequence of arrows, between two nodes in a network, with least float.

critical path method. Abbreviation: CPM. A project network technique developed, about 1957, by employees of an American chemical producer, E.I. du Pont de Nemours & Co. Two time estimates (called 'normal' and 'crash') are made for each activity. Costs are calculated for performing activities in 'normal' and 'crash' times. If some crash costs are higher than the normal costs, the technique enables an analyst to see how to reduce the overall time of the project in the most economical way.

critical region. In a statistical test, a range of numbers chosen so that if the test statistic has a value within the range then the null hypothesis is to be rejected. The critical region is chosen in such a way that if the null hypothesis is true then the probability of it being rejected is not greater than the probability chosen as the significance level of the test.

The numbers which limit the critical region are called 'critical values'. If a critical region consists of two sets, one the set of numbers less than one critical value and the other the set of numbers greater than a second critical value, then the statistical test is called a 'two-sided test'. If the critical region consists of one set of numbers, either all numbers less than the critical value or all numbers greater than the critical value, then the statistical test is called a 'one-sided test'.

critical value. See the entry for 'critical region'.

cross. *Verb.* To add a crossing to a cheque or other financial document.

crosscast. *Verb.* In Britain, to add figures horizontally across columns. In America, the term 'crossfoot' is used instead of 'crosscast'.

cross-default. Default by a borrower of money from one person which is deemed, by the contract covering the borrowing, to occur when the borrower fails to pay any debt owed to any other person.

crossfoot. *Verb.* To crosscast. More commonly used in America than in Britain.

crossing. Two parallel lines drawn or printed across (from top to bottom of) a cheque, or some other kinds of financial document, as an instruction to the drawee that the money must be paid only to a bank. If the name of a bank is stated between the parallel lines then the crossing is called a 'special crossing'; if not it is called a 'general crossing'.

CT. Abbreviation of 'corporation tax'.

CTD. Abbreviation of 'combined transport document'.

CTT. Abbreviation of 'capital transfer tax'.

CULS. Abbreviation of 'convertible unsecured loan stock'.

cum. *Preposition.* With. Used in describing deals in securities to indicate that a security will be sold with a particular benefit; for example, 'cum dividend' means that the buyer will receive the next dividend payment due on the security; 'cum interest' means that the buyer will receive the next interest payment due on the security.

cum testamento annexo. *Preposition phrase.* Latin for 'with the will attached'. Used to describe letters of administration issued in respect of a deceased individual who left a will, a copy of which accompanies the letters of administration.

cumulative preference share. See the entry for 'preference share'.

cumulative sum chart. Another term for 'cusum chart'.

currency. 1. The coins, banknotes or other objects in general use in a country for settling debts.

2. In Britain, money or monetary units other than sterling.

currency note. A financial document used as currency in a particular place – usually a banknote.

current account. 1. An account with a bank from which deposits are repayable on demand when cheques drawn by the account holder are duly presented.

2. In partnership accounts, an account for a partner recording the partner's drawings and interest charged on them, and the partner's share of the partnership losses (debits), interest on the partner's capital and the partner's share of the partnership profits (credits).

current asset. 1. In British company law, an asset of a company not intended for use on a continuing basis in the company's activities (Companies Act 1985, Schedule 4, para. 77). In this context, any asset that is not a current asset is a fixed asset.

2. In general, an asset of an accounting entity regarded as being capable of providing funds from which liabilities arising from the ordinary activities of the entity can be met. In this context, assets that are not current assets are called 'non-current assets'. The liabilities that are to be met from current assets are usually taken to be the current liabilities – i.e., the liabilities due to be met within one year. Accordingly, an asset of an accounting entity is a current asset if it is expected to be consumed or sold in the course of the ordinary activities of the entity within one year, and so stocks and work in progress are normally current assets. If an accounting entity has an operating cycle that is longer than one year or is indeterminate then, in order that its stocks and work in progress will be counted as current assets, it is necessary to define its current assets as being those expected to be consumed or sold in the course of its ordinary activities within one operating cycle and to define its current liabilities as being those due to be met within one operating cycle. However, because it is often difficult to measure the length of an operating cycle and because the one-year limit is so widely observed in defining current assets and current liabilities, it may be preferable, when an entity has a long or indeterminate operating cycle, not to classify its assets into current and non-current.

According to IAS 13 (in which the one-year limit for the definition of current assets and liabilities is preferred), the following items should normally be included as current assets of an entity:

(a) Cash at bank and in hand.

(b) Marketable securities held as temporary investments.

(c) Trade and other debtors for amounts expected to be paid within one year. (Trade debtors may be included in their entirety in reported current assets, provided that the amount not expected to be paid within one year is disclosed.)

(d) Stocks and work in progress.

(e) Prepayments paid to purchase current assets.

current cost. The current cost of an asset whose value is consumed in the operations of an accounting entity is the amount that it would have cost to acquire the asset at the time when its value was being consumed. Current cost is normally estimated from historical cost by reference to changes in a suitable index of prices from the time of acquisition of the asset to the time of consumption of its value.

Also called 'value to the business'.

current cost accounting. Abbreviation: CCA. Accounting for the effects of changing prices by measuring the value of assets by their current cost and determining profit after providing for the maintenance of the operating capability of the business of the accounting entity. For accounting purposes operating capability is measured by the current cost of the net operating assets of the business.

current cost depreciation. Depreciation calculated on a current cost basis.

current cost operating profit. In relation to an accounting period of an accounting entity, defined in SSAP 16, para. 40, as: 'the surplus arising from the ordinary activities of the business [of the entity] in the period after allowing for the impact of price changes on the funds needed to continue the existing business and maintain its operating capability, whether financed by share capital or borrowing. It is calculated before interest on net borrowing and taxation.'

current cost profit attributable to shareholders. In relation to an accounting period of an accounting entity, defined in SSAP 16, para. 41, as: 'the surplus for the period after allowing for the impact of price changes on the funds needed to maintain their [i.e., the entity's shareholders'] proportion of the operating capability [of the entity]. It is calculated after interest, taxation and extraordinary items.'

current cost reserve. A reserve of profits that have been retained to meet the effects of changing prices.

current liability. In British company law, a financial obligation of a company falling due within one year (Companies Act 1985, Schedule 4, balance sheet formats). The same definition is used generally in accounting. However, if an accounting entity has an operating cycle that is longer than one year or is indeterminate then its current liabilities may be regarded as any liability due to be met within one operating cycle – see the entry for 'current asset'.

Also called 'short-term obligation'.

current purchasing power accounting. Term used in the past for 'constant purchasing power accounting'.

current ratio. The ratio:

$$\frac{\text{current assets at the end of a period}}{\text{current liabilities at the end of the period}}$$

The current ratio is a measure of the liquidity of an enterprise.

current replacement cost. In relation to a fixed asset, the cost at which an identical asset could be purchased or manufactured as computed for the purposes of current cost accounting. Normally, current replacement cost is calculated by applying an index number to the original acquisition cost of the asset but in some circumstances it may be preferable to use an expert opinion of the actual cost of replacement. Current replacement cost is said to be 'gross' if no allowance has been made for depreciation, 'net' if accumulated current cost depreciation has been deducted.

current standard. A standard established for use over a short period of time, related to current conditions.

current-year basis. A basis of assessment to UK tax in which income or gains are charged to tax in the year of assessment or the financial year in which they arise.

custodian trustee. A bare trustee who holds property which is managed by other trustees (called 'managing trustees') who exercise all discretionary powers conferred by the trust.

customs duty. A tax payable on goods exported or imported from a country. Also called 'duty of customs'.

customs entry. A description of imported goods prepared by the importer for customs purposes. Also called 'entry'.

customs invoice. A version of an invoice for goods that is specially prepared for customs authorities.

cusum chart. A graph showing, for each sample in an ordered sequence of samples, the cumulative sum of values of a statistic calculated from that sample and all the preceding samples. Also called 'cumulative sum chart'.

cwmni cyfyngedig cyhoeddus. Abbreviation: c.c.c. The equivalent in Welsh of 'public limited company'.

CWO. Abbreviation of 'cash with order'.

cybernetics. The scientific study of communication and control, concerned especially with comparative studies of control systems.

cycle count. Another term for 'continuous stock-checking'.

cycle stock. In stock control, the portion of stock available or planned to be available for normal demand, excluding excess stock and safety stock (BS 5191 : 1975).

cycle time. In production planning, the time required to complete an operation on one unit of a batch (BS 5191 : 1975). Also called 'floor-to-floor time'.

cyclic stock check. Term used in BS 5191 : 1975 for 'continuous stock-checking'.

D

D/A. A symbol (from 'documents against acceptance') on a documentary bill of exchange payable at a future date indicating that the commercial documents are to be released to the drawee when the bill is accepted. Compare 'D/P'.

DA. Abbreviation of 'development area'.

DAF. Abbreviation of 'delivered at frontier'.

damages. Money ordered by a court to be paid by one person A to another person B as compensation for a loss sustained by B in consequence of an injury committed by A. Damages are described as 'liquidated' if the amount to be paid may be computed by a rule without any need for estimation or opinion, and 'unliquidated' where the opinion of an authority such as a court is required to settle the amount payable.

data. Characters, or records of characters, representing information in a form suitable for data processing. The word is the plural form of the noun 'datum' but the singular form is never used in the sense defined here and so 'data' used in this sense is treated by some as a singular noun.

data bank. A large, comprehensive, central or otherwise significant collection of data; especially when carefully organised and recorded so that information may be derived from it by using electronic data processing. A data bank may be regarded as consisting of a number of 'libraries', where each library consists of a number of files of data. Also called 'database'.

database. Also written: data base. 1. A collection of data stored in a data processing system for use with a number of jobs, especially where organisation of, and access to, the data are controlled by special software (called a 'database management system').

2. Another term for 'data bank'.

database administrator. Also written: data base administrator. Abbreviation: DBA. An individual responsible for designing, maintaining and supervising the operation of a database.

database management system. Also written: data base management system. Abbreviation: DBMS. In data processing, software for organising, and controlling access to, databases.

data bus. In a computer, a bus used to communicate data internally and externally to and from a processing unit, stores and peripheral equipment.

data flowchart. Also written: data flow chart. A diagram of the sequence of jobs, both manual and automatic, performed in processing data for some purpose, specifying the data media used at each stage. Also called 'flowchart', 'system flowchart'.

81

data medium. In data processing, material in or on which data may be represented by altering some physical characteristic of the material. For example, paper and magnetic disks are data media.

data processing. Abbreviation: DP. Systematically operating on data (e.g., by transcription, filing, sorting or computing) in order to rearrange the data, produce new data (e.g., by addition), supply information or revise the data.

data processing system. A collection of units of equipment, methods, procedures and operators organised together for the purpose of carrying out data processing.

datum. See the entry for 'data'.

dawn raid. Purchase on the Stock Exchange of a substantial number of shares in a company in a number of deals carried out rapidly, e.g., at the beginning of a trading day, by offering an attractive purchase price.

day book. See the entries for 'purchases day book' and 'sales day book'.

day rate. Another term for 'time rate'.

days to sell inventory. Term used in America for 'number of days' stock held'.

days' purchases in accounts payable ratio. Term used in America for 'creditor days ratio'.

days' sales in inventory. Term used in America for 'number of days' stock held'.

days' sales in receivables. Term used in America for 'debtor days ratio'.

days' sales outstanding. Term used in America for 'debtor days ratio'.

daywork. 1. Another term for 'timework'.

2. Work that is performed mainly during the hours of daylight.

3. Work, or opportunity for employment, that occurs intermittently; casual work.

DBA. Abbreviation of 'database administrator'.

DBMS. Abbreviation of 'database management system'.

DCF. Abbreviation of 'discounted cash flow'.

DDB. Abbreviation of 'double declining balance'. See the entry for 'double declining balance method'.

DDP. Abbreviation of 'delivered duty paid'.

dealing period. One of the 24 periods into which a calendar year is divided for the purposes of dealing on the Stock Exchange in securities other than gilt-edged securities. Also called 'account'.

death duty. 1. Another term for 'estate duty'.

2. In the Law of Property Act 1925, ' "death duty" means estate duty and every other duty leviable or payable on a death' (s. 205(1)(iv) of the Act).

debenture. 1. In legal usage, a document acknowledging a debt.

2. A written contract by which a company gives a charge on its property as security for payment of a debt, for example, for repayment of a bank overdraft.

3. Debenture stock.

4. In America, another term for 'debenture bond'.

debenture bond. In America, a bond for which the issuer gives no security. Equivalent to 'unsecured loan stock' in Britain.

debenture holder. A person to whom a company is indebted and to whom the company has granted a charge over some or all of its property.

debenture stock. A marketable loan in the form of stock issued by a company which charges its property as security for payment of interest and repayment of principal. Normally a floating charge is given. If there is a significant fixed charge then the stock may be described as a 'mortgage debenture'. Debenture stocks are often called simply 'debentures'.

It is possible to have an 'unsecured debenture' where the issuing company does not charge any property as security for payment of interest and repayment of principal, but in practice such a marketable loan is usually called 'unsecured loan stock'.

debenture stock certificate. A document certifying that a specified person (or the bearer of the certificate) is the owner of a specified quantity of debenture stock.

debit. 1. *Noun.* An entry in an account that represents an increase in the value of assets or a decrease in the amount of liabilities. It is conventional to make debit entries on the left-hand side of an account. Compare 'credit'.

2. *Noun.* A decrease in the amount a customer of a bank has deposited with the bank.

3. *Verb.* To make an entry in an account representing an increase in the value of assets or a decrease in the amount of liabilities.

debit balance. The amount by which debits exceed credits in an account.

debit memorandum. Term used in America for 'debit note'.

debit note. A document stating that a debit entry has been made in an account and stating the amount of the entry and the reason for making it. A debit note is sent by a customer to a supplier to inform the supplier that the amount recorded in the customer's accounts as owing to the supplier has been reduced because of an allowance, return of goods or cancellation. In America, called 'debit memorandum'.

de bonis non. *Preposition phrase.* Used to describe an administrator, or the appointment of an administrator, of a deceased individual appointed when part of the estate of the individual has already been dealt with by another personal representative.

debt-adjusting. Defined in the Consumer Credit Act 1974, s. 145(5), as: 'in relation to debts due under consumer credit agreements or consumer hire agreements:

'(a) negotiating with the creditor or owner, on behalf of the debtor or hirer, terms for the discharge of a debt; or

'(b) taking over, in return for payments by the debtor or hirer, his obligation to discharge a debt; or

'(c) any similar activity concerned with the liquidation of a debt'.

When pursued as a business activity, debt-adjusting is an ancillary credit business.

debt capital. Money which is loaned to a business enterprise for continuing use in financing the activities of the enterprise and on which interest is payable at a rate which does not depend on the amount of profit made by the enterprise. Also called 'borrowed capital', 'loan capital'.

debt-collecting. Taking steps to procure payment of debts. For the purposes of the Consumer Credit Act 1974, defined in s. 145(7) of the Act as: 'the taking of steps to procure payment of debts due under consumer credit agreements or consumer hire agreements'; and it is an ancillary credit business if pursued as a business activity.

debt-counselling. American spelling: debt-counseling. Defined in the Consumer Credit Act 1974, s. 145(6), as: 'the giving of advice to debtors or hirers about the liquidation of debts due under consumer credit agreements or consumer hire agreements'. When pursued as a business activity, debt-counselling is an ancillary credit business. The advice given in debt-counselling is called 'money advice'.

debt-equity ratio. The ratio of total liabilities to shareholders' equity or the ratio of long-term debt to shareholders' equity.

debt factoring. Sale of trade debts to a factor, especially where the fact of the sale is notified to creditors and the factor collects payment of the debts. Compare 'invoice discounting'.

debtor. 1. In relation to an accounting entity, a person who owes money to the entity.

2. Plural form (debtors). The total amount of money owed to an accounting entity.

3. An individual who is the subject of impending bankruptcy proceedings.

4. See the entry for 'Dr'.

debtor-creditor agreement. Defined in the Consumer Credit Act 1974, s. 13, as a regulated consumer credit agreement which is:

(a) a restricted-use credit agreement to finance a transaction between the debtor and a person (the 'supplier') other than the creditor but which is not made by the creditor under pre-existing arrangements, or in contemplation of future arrangements, between the creditor and the supplier; or

(b) a restricted-use credit agreement to refinance any existing indebtedness of the debtor's, whether to the creditor or to another person; or

(c) an unrestricted-use credit agreement which is not made by the creditor under pre-existing arrangements between the creditor and a person (the 'supplier') other than the debtor in the knowledge that the credit is to be used to finance a transaction between the debtor and the supplier.

debtor-creditor-supplier agreement. Defined in the Consumer Credit Act 1974, s. 12, as a regulated consumer credit agreement which is:

(a) a restricted-use credit agreement to finance a transaction between the debtor and the creditor, whether the transaction forms part of that agreement or not; or

(b) a restricted-use credit agreement to finance a transaction between the debtor and a person (the 'supplier') other than the creditor made by the creditor under pre-existing arrangements, or in contemplation of future arrangements, between the creditor and the supplier; or

(c) an unrestricted-use credit agreement which is made by the creditor under pre-existing arrangements between the creditor and a person (the 'supplier') other than the debtor in the knowledge that the credit is to be used to finance a transaction between the debtor and the supplier.

debtor days ratio. The ratio:

$$\frac{\text{trade debtors at the end of a period}}{\text{average daily value of credit sales}}$$

or:

$$\frac{\text{average trade debtors during a period}}{\text{average daily value of credit sales}}$$

Average daily value of credit sales is the total value of credit sales for the period divided by the number of days in the period. Average trade debtors for a period may be calculated as half the sum of trade debtors at the beginning of the period and trade debtors at the end of the period. The ratio measures the average number of days it takes to collect trade debts. In America, known as 'accounts receivable collection period', 'days' sales in receivables', 'days' sales outstanding'.

debtors ledger. A section of a ledger containing accounts of transactions with trade debtors of the accounting entity. If the accounting entity is a trading enterprise the debtors ledger may be called a 'sales ledger' or 'sold ledger'.

debug. *Verb.* To find errors in a computer program and correct them.

decile. A fractile of order p where p is an integral multiple of 0.1.

decimal digit. Any one of the digits 0, 1, 2, 3, 4, 5, 6, 7, 8, 9 when used in a decimal numeration system.

decimal numeral. A representation of a number in the decimal numeration system.

decimal numeration system. A positional representation system in which the ratio of the weight of any digit place to the weight of the digit place with the next lower weight is ten, in which there is a digit place with weight one, and in which the digits used are 0, 1, 2, 3, 4, 5, 6, 7, 8, 9.

decision tree. A diagram of a sequence of decisions, each of which involves choosing between a number of alternatives and depends on the results of the previous decisions.

declaration of solvency. A statutory declaration made by the majority of the directors of a company, at a board meeting, within the five weeks preceding the adoption of a resolution to wind up the company, which is made in order that the winding up may be a members' voluntary winding up.

A declaration must state that the declaring directors have made a full inquiry into the affairs of the company, and have formed the opinion that the company will be able to pay its debts in full within a certain time after the commencement of winding up. The period specified must not exceed 12 months.

A declaration of solvency is of no effect unless it embodies a statement of the company's assets and liabilities as at the latest practicable date before the making of the declaration.

declining balance method. A method of calculating depreciation of a fixed asset in which the amount of depreciation for a year is a fixed fraction (called the 'rate of depreciation') of the preceding year's depreciated value. The rate of depreciation may be any convenient figure or it may be calculated so that the depreciated value of the asset will equal its estimated residual value at the end of its useful life. If s = residual value, t = number of years of useful life, c = historical cost of the asset, then the rate of depreciation given by the following formula will make the depreciated value equal the residual value at the end of the useful life:

$$\text{rate of depreciation} = 1 - (s/c)^{1/t}$$

Also known as 'diminishing balance method', 'diminishing provision method', 'reducing balance method', 'reducing instalment method'. See also the entry for 'double declining balance method'.

deduction at source. An arrangement for the collection of income tax under which a person who pays money to another person is required to withhold some of the payment and pay it instead to a collector of taxes as an advance payment of the other person's tax liability. The amount withheld is called 'withholding tax'.

deed. A document stating a promise of a person which is executed with particular formality to make clear that the person is to be bound by the promise. A deed must be delivered, that is, the promisor must act as though the deed is to be binding, usually by handing it to the person to whom the promise is made. A deed must also bear the seal of the promisor and, unless the promisor is a corporation, must bear the promisor's signature. In practice, a deed made by a corporation usually bears the signature of an officer of the corporation. Thus a deed is said to be 'signed, sealed and delivered'.

In Scotland, seals are used by corporations but not by individuals, and a deed must be signed by at least two individuals who witnessed its execution.

deed of arrangement. A contract made between an insolvent individual and all, or a majority, of the individual's creditors under which an arrangement is made for paying as much of the debts as is possible and the creditors agree to abandon their claims to complete payment. Usually the entire property of the debtor is transferred to a trustee who administers it for the benefit of creditors. The Deeds of Arrangement Act 1914 specifies procedures which must be followed if a deed of arrangement is to be effective.

deed of partnership. A partnership agreement stated in a deed. Also called 'partnership deed'.

deed of postponement. A deed by which a chargee of property agrees that a second chargee of the property will have priority in utilising the property for meeting the secured obligation owed to the second chargee.

deep discount. 1. A large discount, especially on the issue of securities in connection with a marketable loan.

2. The difference between the issue price of a redeemable security and the amount payable on reduction of that security is a deep discount for the purposes of the Finance Act 1984 if it:

(a) represents more than 15% of the amount payable on redemption of that security; or

(b) is 15% or less, but exceeds $\frac{1}{2}y\%$, of the amount so payable (where y is the number of complete years between the date of issue of the security and the redemption date) (Finance Act 1984, s. 36(2)).

defalcation. 1. Misappropriation of property by an individual who was entrusted with the property.

2. Property lost by misappropriation by a person who was entrusted with the property.

default. Failure to fulfil an obligation – for example, (a) failure to pay a debt when due; (b) failure to defend legal proceedings when required by a court.

default notice. A notice that the Consumer Credit Act 1974, s. 87, requires to be served on the creditor under a regulated consumer credit agreement or the hirer under a regulated consumer hire agreement before the agreement can be terminated or other action taken to the detriment of the consumer. The notice must contain the information specified in s. 88 of the Act and in regulations made under s. 88. The Consumer Credit (Enforcement, Default and Termination Notices) Regulations 1983 (SI 1983 No. 1561) have been made to specify the contents of default notices.

default order. In British company law, a court order requiring an officer of a company to make good a default in filing returns or accounts (Companies Act 1985, s. 297(3)(b)).

defended bid. A take-over bid for a company whose directors oppose the bid and recommend shareholders to reject the offer. Also called 'opposed bid'.

deferred asset. An item of deferred expenditure.

deferred charge. An item of deferred expenditure.

deferred credit. An item of deferred revenue.

deferred creditor. A creditor, of an insolvent person, whose debt is a deferred debt.

deferred debit. An item of deferred expenditure.

deferred debt. A debt in a class of debts of an insolvent person which must not be paid by the liquidator or personal representative or trustee in bankruptcy until all other debts of the person have been paid.

deferred expenditure. Expenditure in a period of account which is not treated as an operating cost of that period but is treated as an asset with the intention that it will be an operating cost of a future period. Also called 'deferred revenue expenditure'. An item of deferred expenditure may be called a 'deferred asset', 'deferred charge', 'deferred debit' or 'deferred expense'.

deferred expense. An item of deferred expenditure.

deferred income. Another term for 'deferred revenue'.

deferred liability. 1. Term sometimes used for 'long-term liability'.

2. An item of deferred revenue.

deferred revenue. Revenue received before consideration is given for it. For example, money paid for a subscription to a publication before the publication is published. Also called 'deferred income', 'unearned revenue', 'unrealised revenue'. An item of deferred revenue may be called a 'deferred credit', 'deferred liability', 'payment in advance' or 'prepayment received'.

deferred revenue expenditure. Another term for 'deferred expenditure'.

deferred share. A share in a company bearing the restriction that no dividend can be paid to the shareholder for a financial year unless ordinary shareholders are paid a certain amount of dividend for that year. Companies that have issued deferred shares have often called them 'founders' shares'.

deferred tax. 'Tax attributable to timing differences' (ED 33, para. 17).

deferred taxation. Taxation attributable to timing differences (SSAP 15, para. 22).

deficiency. 1. Amount by which liabilities exceed assets.

2. Amount by which the true quantity of something is less than the amount recorded in accounts.

deficiency account. Part of a statement of affairs showing how assets and liabilities have changed over the past year (up to three years in the case of a company).

deficit. 1. An excess of expenditure over income.

2. The amount by which expenditure exceeds income.

3. A loss of money.

4. An amount of money lost.

5. A reduction of equity not due to an authorised repayment of contributed capital to owners.

6. The amount by which equity has been reduced otherwise than by an authorised repayment of contributed capital to owners.

defined benefit scheme. A pension scheme under which amounts to be paid as retirement benefits are determined by an employee's earnings and/or years of service (ED 32, para. 29).

defined contribution scheme. 'A pension scheme under which amounts to be paid as retirement benefits are determined by the contributions to a fund together with investment earnings thereon' (ED 32, para. 30).

definite integration. Calculation of a change in value of a function between two values of the independent variable, given the derivative of the function.

degree of freedom. Abbreviation: DF or d.f. A dimensionless unit used for a parameter of a probability distribution, as in the chi-squared distribution, F-distribution and t-distribution.

del credere agent. An agent who guarantees debts due to the principal which result from transactions entered into by the agent on behalf of the principal.

delict. In Scotland, a breach of legal duty causing unjustifiable harm for which the courts will provide compensation.

delictual. *Adjective.* Of, or relating to, delict.

delinquent account receivable. In America, a creditor's name for a debt remaining unpaid after the due date. In Britain, called 'overdue account'.

delivered at frontier. Abbreviation: DAF. Trade terms for the sale of goods that are to be transported to the buyer by rail or road under which the seller's obligations are fulfilled when goods have arrived at the frontier of the country named in the contract of sale but before the goods have been cleared for import into that country.

delivered duty paid. Abbreviation: DDP. Trade terms for the sale of goods under which the seller must deliver the goods at the buyer's premises, having paid any import duties, taxes and fees involved in getting the goods to that destination.

delivery note. A document accompanying a consignment of goods stating the description and quantity of goods consigned. It may have to be signed on delivery and returned to the consignor or kept by the carrier as evidence of receipt, or it may be a set of documents, one copy of which is signed and returned. Receipt of a returned delivery note may be the cue for issuing an invoice. A consignment note may serve as a delivery note.

demand bill. A bill of exchange that is payable when it is presented to the drawee. Also called 'demand draft', 'draft at sight', 'sight bill', 'sight draft'.

A drawee is not liable to pay a demand bill unless it has been accepted, which is in practice rare.

demand draft. Another term for 'demand bill'.

demand note. Another term for 'sight note'.

demerger. An arrangement whereby trading activities carried on by a single company or group are divided so as to be carried on by two or more companies not belonging to the same group or by two or more independent groups (Finance Act 1980, s. 117).

demise. 1. *Noun.* A lease of land.

2. *Verb.* To grant a lease of land.

demonstrative legacy. A gift of money that is made by a testator in a will and that is directed by the testator to be paid out of a specific fund.

demurrage. Charges incurred for late collection of goods from a carrier.

denominator. See the entries for 'ratio' and 'rational number'.

departmental accounts. 1. Accounting records of transactions between different departments of an organisation, treated as separate accounting entities, and between departments and persons outside the organisation.

2. Financial statements for a department of an organisation treated as a separate accounting entity.

departmental budget. Another term for 'functional budget'.

dependent relative revocation. A revocation of a will made on condition that some other event occurs (e.g., the making of a replacement will). If the event does not occur, then the revocation is not effective.

dependent variable. One of two or more related variables that is regarded as depending on the others, e.g., because there is a procedure for calculating or estimating its value for any given particular value, or set of values, of the other variable or variables. In particular, where the relationship between variables is represented by a mathematical function, the variable for items in the range of the function. Traditionally, the letter y is used for the dependent variable.

depletion. Depreciation of a mining property, gravel pit or similar property representing loss of value arising from extraction of minerals.

deposit. 1. *Noun.* A sum of money paid by a person (called the 'depositor') to another person on condition that the depositor may call for repayment of an equal sum of money (but not the same notes or coins) either on demand or at a time or in circumstances settled by agreement between the depositor and the person receiving the deposit. A deposit repayable on demand is called a 'demand deposit'. The person receiving the deposit may offer to pay interest on it or may offer to provide banking services. In many instances of making deposits (e.g., in making a deposit in a current account at a bank) the depositor is entitled to call for repayment of any sum of money less than the sum deposited. In other instances (e.g., a deposit in exchange for a certificate of deposit) only the entire amount deposited may be repaid. If banking services are provided then the deposited money may be paid to any person to whom the depositor gives a right to payment (e.g., by issuing a cheque).

For the purposes of licensing deposit-taking businesses, a precise definition of 'deposit' is given in the Banking Act 1979, s. 1(4), (5) and (6).

2. *Verb.* To pay money as a deposit in sense 1.

3. *Noun.* A sum of money paid, as security for the performance of an obligation, on condition that it will be repaid if the obligation is performed. A deposit in this sense is not a deposit for the purposes of the Banking Act 1979 – see s. 1(4)(b) and (6) of the Act.

4. *Noun.* A sum of money paid by a person to reserve for that person goods or services offered for sale and representing part of the purchase price of the goods or services. A deposit in this sense is not a deposit for the purposes of the Banking Act 1979 – see s. 1(4)(b) and (6) of the Act.

deposit account. An account with a bank from which deposits are repayable only to the depositor. Interest is paid on deposits in deposit accounts. Usually, in principle, the depositor must give a period of notice before repayment will be made, but in practice repayment is made immediately on demand with an adjustment of the amount of interest in lieu of the notice period.

deposit-taker. A person carrying on a deposit-taking business.

deposit-taking business. For the purposes of the Banking Act 1979 (which controls deposit-taking businesses in the UK) a business is a deposit-taking business if:

(a) in the course of the business money received by way of deposit is lent to others; or

(b) any other activity of the business is financed, wholly or to any material extent, out of the capital of or the interest on money received by way of deposit.

However, a business is not a deposit-taking business for the purposes of the Act if, in the normal course of the business:

(a) the person carrying it on is not held out as accepting deposits on a day-to-day basis; and

(b) any deposits which are accepted are accepted only on particular occasions, whether or not involving the issue of debentures or other securities.

depreciable amount. In relation to a depreciable asset of an accounting entity, the difference between the historical cost, or other amount substituted for historical cost in the financial statements of the entity, and the estimated residual value of the asset.

depreciable asset. An asset of an accounting entity which:

(a) is expected to be used during more than one accounting period, and

(b) has a limited useful life, and

(c) is held by the entity for use in the production or supply of goods and services, for hire to others, or for administrative purposes.

See IAS 4, which requires that the depreciable amount of a depreciable asset should be allocated on a systematic basis to each accounting period during the useful life of the asset.

In British company law, the Companies Act 1985, Schedule 4, para. 18, requires that the depreciable amount of any fixed asset which has a limited useful economic life should be reduced by provisions for depreciation calculated to write off the depreciable amount systematically over the period of the asset's useful economic life. For the purposes of this Act, therefore, any fixed asset which has a limited useful economic life may be described as a 'depreciable asset'.

depreciate. *Verb.* To make a provision for the depreciation of a fixed asset.

depreciated value. Another term for 'net book value'.

depreciation. 1. 'The measure [in monetary terms] of the wearing out, consumption or other loss of value of a fixed asset whether arising from use, effluxion of time or obsolescence through technological and market changes' (SSAP 12, para. 15). In ED 37, para. 10, it is proposed to amend this definition by changing 'or other loss of value' to 'or other permanent loss of value'. Depreciation representing the loss of value of a mining property, gravel pit or similar property arising from extraction of minerals is often called 'depletion'. Depreciation of assets with a definite useful life (for example, a non-renewable lease of land) representing loss of value arising from effluxion of time is often called 'amortisation'.

2. Term used in IAS 4 for 'depreciation accounting'.

depreciation accounting. Allocation of the depreciable amount of a fixed asset to each accounting period during its useful life and deduction of the amount allocated to each period from the revenue of that period when calculating the profit for the period. Usually, allocation is by a simple computational rule, paying no attention to the actual amount of use, or change in usefulness, of the asset during any period. In IAS 4, called 'depreciation'.

depreciation adjustment. In current cost accounting, an adjustment made to the profit on the ordinary activities of an accounting entity for an accounting period, as calculated on the historical cost basis, to allow for the effect of price changes on the value of fixed assets consumed by the entity during the period. In SSAP 16, para. 49, it is defined as the difference between the proportion of the value to the business of fixed assets consumed during the accounting period and the amount of depreciation charged on the historical cost basis.

depreciation rules. The rules about provision for depreciation in financial statements of registered companies set out in paragraphs 17 to 20 and 22 to 24 of Schedule 4 to the Companies Act 1985 (see para. 29 of the schedule).

deprival value. In relation to an asset of an accounting entity, the loss that the accounting entity would suffer if deprived of the asset.

deputy Special Commissioner. A person appointed by the Lord Chancellor, after consultation with the Lord Advocate, to facilitate the performance of any functions of the Special Commissioners.

derivative. 1. The slope of the best linear approximation at a point on the graph of a function. Also called 'differential coefficient'.

2. In relation to a function, a second function which, for each value of the independent variable, gives the value of the derivative (in sense 1) of the function for that value of the independent variable. The derivative of a function may itself have a derivative, in which case the derivative of the function is called the 'first derivative' of the function and its derivative is called the 'second derivative' of the function, and so on.

despatch note. Alternative spelling of 'dispatch note'.

detail account. Another term for 'subsidiary account'.

devastavit. A violation of the duties of a personal representative, e.g., by misappropriating property.

development. See the entry for 'research and development expenditure'.

development area. Abbreviation: DA. An area of the UK which has been designated by the Secretary of State under the Industrial Development Act 1982, s. 1, and in which industry is given government assistance in order to reduce unemployment. In particular, enterprises may be given regional development grants.

development land tax. Abbreviation: DLT. A tax on a gain which is realised by a person on the disposal of an interest in land in the UK on or after 1 August 1976 and which can be ascribed to a change in the use of the land. The 1985 Finance Bill proposes that the tax shall not be charged in respect of any disposal taking place on or after 19 March 1985.

deviation. In statistics, the difference between an observed value of a quantitative characteristic and some chosen number, which is often the arithmetic mean of the observed values.

devise. 1. *Noun.* A gift of real property made in a will.

2. *Verb.* To make a gift of real property in a will.

devisee. The beneficiary of a devise.

DF. Also written: d.f. Abbreviation of 'degree of freedom' and 'degrees of freedom'.

diagnostic program. A computer program that helps in finding and correcting faults in hardware or errors in computer programs.

dies non. Another term for 'non-business day'.

difference. The result of subtracting one number (called the 'subtrahend') from another number (called the 'minuend').

differential. *Adjective.* Incremental.

differential calculus. A branch of mathematics dealing with differentiation and integration, and the uses of those processes.

differential coefficient. The value of the derivative of a function for a particular value of the independent variable.

differentiation. The process of finding the derivative of a function.

digit. 1. A single character that represents an integer.

2. The integer represented by a digit (in sense 1).

digit place. A position in an ordered set of digits used to represent a number in a positional representation system.

diminishing balance method. Another term for 'declining balance method'.

diminishing provision method. Another term for 'declining balance method'.

direct access. In data processing, access to any location in a store without going through another location. Use of the alternative term 'random access' is deprecated in BS 3527 : Part 12 : 1978.

direct cost. A cost, that has been identified in an organisation which has more than one product, and which can be directly attributed to one of those products – or an aggregate of such costs. It is common to use the term to refer only to production costs. Compare 'indirect cost'. See also the entry for 'direct cost of sales'. A cost will be indirect if it is of anything used for the purpose of more than one product, unless it is possible to measure directly the amount used on each product. For example, it is not possible to measure the portion of the cost of insuring a factory which relates to any particular product of that factory. Sometimes measurement may be theoretically possible, but not worth while in practice, for example, of electricity consumed.

direct cost centre. American spelling: direct cost center. Another term for 'production cost centre'.

direct costing. Term used in America for 'marginal costing'.

direct cost of sales. The sum of direct material costs, direct labour costs, direct expenses and variable production overhead costs for a period for a product or products. Also called 'direct production cost of sales'. The term 'direct cost of sales' is preferred in the ICMA official terminology. Direct cost of sales plus fixed production overhead cost is cost of sales.

direct debit. An amount transferred from a current account of a customer of a bank to a bank account of another person at the request of that other person, the customer in question having given the bank authority to honour such requests. Direct debits will only be made in favour of persons who have been approved by the clearing banks and who have given indemnities against misuse of the system.

direct expense. 1. In Britain, a direct cost which is a cost of something other than materials, supplies and work performed by people (for example, an energy cost), or an aggregate of such costs.

2. In America, another term for 'direct cost'.

direct hour. An hour of work by an employee, renumeration for which is a direct labour cost. 'Direct hour' is the term used in the ICMA official terminology; the term 'direct labour hour' is also common.

direct hours yield. The number of direct hours worked during a period expressed as a percentage of the available hours of direct workers during that period.

direct labor. American spelling of 'direct labour'.

direct labor cost. American spelling of 'direct labour cost'.

direct labor efficiency variance. American spelling of 'direct labour efficiency variance'.

direct labor hour. American spelling of 'direct labour hour'.

direct labor rate variance. American spelling of 'direct labour rate variance'.

direct labor total variance. American spelling of 'direct labour total variance'.

direct labour. American spelling: direct labor. Another term for 'direct labour cost'.

direct labour cost. American spelling: direct labor cost. A cost of work performed by people which is a direct cost, or an aggregate of such costs. Also called 'direct labour', 'direct wages'.

direct labour efficiency variance. American spelling: direct labor efficiency variance. The difference between the standard direct labour cost of the actual quantity of product produced during a budget period and the amount that the direct labour actually used would have cost if it had been paid for at the standard direct labour rate.

direct labour hour. American spelling: direct labor hour. Another term for 'direct hour'.

direct labour rate variance. American spelling: direct labor rate variance. The difference between the standard direct labour rate per hour for a product and the actual direct labour rate per hour paid during a budget period multiplied by the number of hours worked during that period. (Rates may be expressed in terms of any convenient time unit, but the hour is most widely used.)

direct labour total variance. American spelling: direct labor total variance. The difference between the standard direct labour cost of the quantity of a product produced during a budget period and the actual direct labour cost incurred during that period.

direct material. 1. Material entering into and becoming part of a manufactured product, or used in or supplied with a service, expenditure on which is a direct cost.

2. Another term for 'direct material cost'.

direct material cost. A cost of materials or supplies which is a direct cost. Also called 'direct materials cost' (which is the form used in the ICMA official terminology) or 'direct material'.

direct material price variance. The difference between the actual price of the quantities of direct materials used during a budget period and the amount that would have been paid had those quantities been bought at standard prices. Also called 'direct materials price variance'.

direct materials cost. An alternative form of the term 'direct material cost'.

direct materials price variance. Another form of the term 'direct material price variance'.

direct materials total variance. Another form of the term 'direct material total variance'.

direct materials usage variance. Another form of the term 'direct material usage variance'.

direct material total variance. The difference between the standard direct material cost of the quantity of product produced during a budget period and the actual direct material cost of that quantity. Also called 'direct materials total variance'.

direct material usage variance. The difference between the standard direct materials cost of the quantity of product actually produced during a budget period and the cost of the actual quantity used if it had been bought at standard prices. Also called 'direct materials usage variance'.

director. An officer of a registered company who, in collaboration with fellow directors, is responsible for managing the affairs of the company.

Every British public company registered after 1 November 1929 must have at least two directors. Other British companies must have at least one director. In the Companies Acts, provisions relating to directors apply to any person occupying the position of director by whatever name called (Companies Act 1985, s. 741(1)).

director's or higher-paid employment. For the purposes of liability to income tax on certain benefits, under the Finance Act 1976, Part III, employment as a director of a company or employment with emoluments at the rate of £8,500 a year or more (Finance Act 1976, s. 69(1)). An individual who holds office as a director will not be treated as a director for the purposes of Part III of the Finance Act 1976 if two conditions are satisfied (Finance Act 1976, s. 69(5)):

(a) The director has no material interest in the company, that is, if the director and his associates (meaning the directors' relatives, partners, or trustees of a settlement which the director or a relative created) own beneficially or are able to control directly or indirectly no more than 5% of the company's ordinary share capital (Finance Act 1976, s. 72(10)).

(b) Either:

(i) the director is a full-time working director, meaning that substantially the whole of the time of the director is required to be devoted to the service of the company in a managerial capacity (Finance Act 1976, s. 72(9)), or

(ii) the company is non-profit-making (that is, it does not trade or hold investments) or is established for charitable purposes only.

A person holding the office of director who is nevertheless not treated as a director may, however, be treated as a higher-paid employee if emoluments are £8,500 a year or more.

directors' report. In British company law, a report that must be prepared for each financial year of a company and which forms part of the company's accounts for the financial year which have to be presented to its members. If the directors of a company do not prepare for the members a directors' report within certain time-limits then every director of the company is liable to a fine for which there is no limit.

Among many other matters, a directors' report must contain a fair review of the development of the business of the company, and its subsidiaries, during the financial year ending on the balance sheet date and must state the directors' recommendations on how the profits of the year are to be applied. The report must state the principal activities of the company and its subsidiaries during the year and any significant changes that occurred in those activities. It must contain particulars of any important events affecting the company or any of its subsidiaries which have occurred since the end of the financial year and it must indicate likely future developments in the business of the company and its subsidiaries. See Companies Act 1985, s. 235 and Schedule 7.

direct production cost of sales. The sum of the direct material costs, direct labour costs, direct expenses and variable production overhead costs identified with producing the quantity of a product or products sold during a period. Also called 'direct cost of sales', which is the term preferred in the ICMA official terminology. Direct production cost of sales plus fixed production overhead cost is production cost of sales.

direct security. Security for the performance of a financial obligation given by the person from whom the obligation is due.

direct stock. Stock of materials, purchased parts, etc., that are to be incorporated into finished products (BS 5191 : 1975). Also called 'productive stock'.

direct wages. Another term for 'direct labour cost'.

direct worker. An employee whose remuneration is normally a direct labour cost.

disc drive. Alternative spelling of 'disk drive'.

discharge. 1. *Noun.* Release from an obligation, charge or disability.

2. *Verb.* To release from an obligation, charge or disability.

disclaimer of opinion. A statement in an audit report indicating the inability of the auditor to form an opinion on whether the financial statements taken as a whole present a true and fair view.

discontinuance actuarial valuation. Defined in ED 32, para. 31, as a computation by an actuary of the amounts that must be paid to finance a pension scheme on the assumption that at the date of the valuation:

(a) The existing benefits for current and deferred pensions and accrued benefits for current members and their dependants will be paid in due course.

(b) Future pay increases for current members are to be disregarded.

(c) No new members will be admitted to the scheme.

(d) No further payments will be required from the employer or the members.

(e) Future service is not to be included.

discount. 1. *Noun.* A deduction from a standard or nominal price of something that is made to arrive at the price of that thing in a particular transaction. For example:

(a) a cash discount;

(b) a quantity discount;

(c) a trade discount;

(d) a deduction from the nominal value of a security to give the amount payable when the security is issued or when the security is sold;

(e) a deduction from the amount of debt due to be repaid at some time in the future to give the amount that :

(i) the debtor will pay before the due date to discharge the debt; or

(ii) the amount a third party will pay the creditor, before the due date, to take over the creditor's right to receive the money.

2. *Noun.* An addition, which is to be made to the number of units of a foreign currency that will be obtained in a spot purchase for one unit of domestic currency, in order to arrive at the number of units of the foreign currency to be obtained in a forward purchase.

3. *Verb.* To reduce the price of something.

4. *Verb.* To sell to a person the right to receive, at a future date, payment of a debt. In particular, to sell a bill of exchange.

5. *Verb.* To buy the right to receive payment of a debt (e.g., a bill of exchange) for a price that is less than the full amount of the debt.

6. *Verb.* To calculate a present value.

7. *Verb.* To reduce a valuation of something so as to reflect some factor thought to affect the value of the thing.

discount allowed. An amount deducted from a charge invoiced to a customer in consideration of, e.g., prompt payment.

discounted cash flow. Abbreviation: DCF. The present value of a number of cash flows.

discount house. In Britain, an enterprise whose principal business is to buy and sell very liquid securities – in particular, bills of exchange that are due for payment in a short time, Treasury bills, and government stocks and local authority bonds that are due for repayment in a short time (less than 12 months). The term is usually restricted to the companies that are members of the London Discount Market Association.

discount rate. A number (usually expressed as a percentrage) used to determine a discount or a present value. See the entries for 'compound discount', 'present value' and 'simple discount'. In particular, a discount rate (as used for calculating simple discounts) quoted by a bank for discounting bills of exchange.

discount received. An amount deducted from a charge invoiced by a creditor in consideration of, e.g., prompt payment.

disc pack. Alternative spelling of 'disk pack'.

discrete random variable. A random variable that takes only isolated values within its range. Also called 'discrete variate'.

discrete-valued stochastic process. A stochastic process in which all the random variables are discrete random variables.

discrete variate. Another term for 'discrete random variable'.

discretionary trust. A trust in which the trustees may choose whether or not to distribute income to beneficiaries or may choose what proportion of income is to go to each beneficiary or both.

dishonour. American spelling: dishonor. 1. *Verb.* To fail to accept a bill of exchange when it is duly presented for acceptance, or to give a qualified acceptance which is refused by the holder of the bill. A bill dishonoured in this way is said to be 'dishonoured by non-acceptance'.

2. *Verb.* To refuse to pay a bill of exchange, cheque or other financial document when it is duly presented for payment. A bill dishonoured in this way is said to be 'dishonoured by non-payment'.

disk drive. Alternative spelling: disc drive. In data processing, a mechanism for moving a disk pack or a magnetic disk and controlling its movement.

diskette. Another term for 'flexible disk'.

disk pack. Alternative spelling: disc pack. In data processing, a removable assembly of magnetic disks.

dispatch note. Alternative spelling: despatch note. Another term for 'advice note'.

disposals account. An account recording transactions relating to cessation of ownership of fixed assets.

distrain. *Verb.* To seize goods by way of distress.

distress. 1. Seizure and impounding, without court proceedings, of goods of a person who has failed to fulfil an obligation. The goods may be returned to the person if the obligation is fulfilled or they may be sold to pay the obligation.

2. Goods, of a person who has failed to fulfil an obligation, seized and impounded, without court proceedings, and held for return to the person when the obligation is fulfilled or for sale to pay the obligation.

distributable profits. Another term for 'profits available for distribution'.

distribution cost. 1. In the ICMA official terminology, cost identified with warehousing saleable products and with delivering the products to customers. Also called 'distribution overhead'.

2. In America, any cost identified with marketing, selling or distributing the product of an enterprise. Also called 'distribution expense'.

distribution expense. In America, any expense identified with marketing, selling or distributing a product.

distribution-free test. A statistical test in which the distribution function of the test statistic does not depend on the form of distribution function of the population.

distribution function. In probability theory, in relation to the probability distribution of a random variable, a function giving, for every number x, the probability that the random variable is less than or equal to x.

distribution overhead. Another term for 'distribution cost'.

distribution time. In relation to a manufactured object, the period of time between the date it is dispatched from the manufacturer and the delivery date to the customer (BS 5191 : 1975).

diverted hour. An hour of work of a direct worker spent on indirect activities, such as cleaning machines, so that the renumeration for it is an indirect labour cost.

diverted hours ratio. The number of diverted hours during a period expressed as a percentage of the available hours of direct workers during that period.

diverted time. The part of attendance time when a worker is not engaged on productive work or ancillary work (BS 3138 : 1979).

dividend. 1. An amount of a company's profits to be paid to its members. Either the total amount to be paid, expressed as an amount per share, or the amount to be received by a particular member.

2. The amount that is available for distribution to the creditors of an insolvent person. Either the total amount, expressed as a number of pence per pound that is owed, or the amount payable to a particular creditor.

3. A payment of interest on a marketable loan, especially government stock. Either the total amount payable, expressed as a percentage of the nominal value of the stock, or the amount payable to a particular investor.

4. A number that is divided by another number (called the 'divisor').

dividend cover. Another term for 'equity dividend cover'.

dividend equalisation reserve. An amount retained from profits in order to provide for payment of a minimum dividend in future financial years.

dividend mandate. Document by which an owner of registered securities authorises the issuer of the securities to make payments of dividends or interest direct to the owner's bank account.

dividend payout. The dividend paid by a company in respect of a period divided by the earnings for equity for that period. Also called 'dividend payout ratio', 'payout ratio'. The dividend payout is the reciprocal of the dividend cover.

dividend payout ratio. Another term for 'dividend payout'.

dividend per share. The total dividend payable to shareholders of a company in respect of a financial year divided by the number of shares carrying an entitlement to receive the dividend. Sometimes called 'net dividend per share' (see the entry for 'net dividend').

dividend stripping. Taking control of a company with large retained earnings and declaring a large dividend in such a way that tax is avoided.

dividend warrant. Also written: dividend-warrant. A financial document by which a dividend is paid.

dividend washing. Another term for 'bond washing'.

dividend yield. See the entry for 'gross dividend yield'.

divisor. A number by which another number (called the 'dividend') is divided.

DLT. Abbreviation of 'development land tax'.

documentary bill. A bill of exchange accompanied by commercial documents. The commercial documents, such as a bill of lading, give control over the goods being paid for by the bill of exchange and are released to the buyer when the bill is paid or accepted.

documentary collection. Collection of financial documents accompanied by commercial documents or of commercial documents without financial documents.

documentary credit. Another term for 'letter of credit'.

documents against acceptance. See the entry for 'D/A'.

documents against payment. See the entry for 'D/P'.

domain. See the entry for 'function'.

domicile. A concept of private international law by which a person is associated with a legal system of a particular place and that legal system is treated as the person's 'personal law' which will be the law applicable to the personal property of the person and (if the person is an individual) family matters involving the person. The concept of domicile may also be important for taxation purposes. The law of a person's domicile is called the '*lex domicilii*' of the person.

domicile of a bill. An address, usually of a bank, written on a bill of exchange by its acceptor, where the bill may be presented for payment when due.

domicile of choice. A domicile that has been adopted by an individual to replace that individual's previous domicile. In order to adopt a domicile of choice an individual must actually take up residence in the new territory of domicile and must have formed the intention of making his or her sole or principal home there, and of continuing to reside there indefinitely.

domicile of dependency. A domicile that a child is deemed to have because his or her father or mother has changed domicile since the time of the child's birth and before the child has attained the age at which the child has the capacity to decid on a domicile of choice. In English law, the domicile of an unmarried, legitimate child under 16, while living with his or her father follows the domicile of the father. The domicile of an unmarried child under 16 who is illegitimate and who lives with his or her mother, but not his or her father, follows the domicile of the mother.

domicile of origin. The domicile that an individual has at the time of birth, which is the domicile of the individual's mother at that time unless the mother was married (and not separated from) the father at that time, in which case it is the domicile of the father at the time of birth. If nothing is known of the parents of an individual then the domicile of origin of that individual is the place of birth or the place where he or she was found.

donatio mortis causa. A gift made by an individual which will be completely effective (i.e., it cannot be revoked) only when the donor dies but where the donee is provided with physical dominion over the subject-matter of the gift, although it is intended that the gift will be revoked if the donee predeceases the donor. Also called 'gift *mortis causa*', 'gift on account of death'.

dormant company. A registered company is a dormant company during any period during which no transaction which is a significant accounting transaction for that company occurs. Any transaction which is required under the Companies Act 1985, s. 221, to be entered in a company's accounting records is a significant accounting transaction for that company, other than one arising from the taking of shares in the company by a subscriber to the memorandum of the company in pursuance of an undertaking in the memorandum. See Companies Act 1985, s. 252(5). If a dormant company is a private company then its members can resolve not to appoint auditors for the period during which it is dormant.

double brokerage. Brokerage paid by both buyer and seller.

double declining balance method. Abbreviation: DDB method. The declining balance method with the rate of depreciation equal to:

$$2 \ (H - R)/L$$

where H is the historical cost of the asset, R is its estimated residual value and L the number of years in its useful life.

double-entry bookkeeping. A method of making accounting records in which there are several accounts, known collectively as the 'ledger', arranged so that every transaction is recorded both as a credit in one account and a debit in another account.

double taxation relief. Allowance made, when assessing tax on profits or gains, for tax paid on those profits or gains to the authorities in other countries. Also called 'double tax relief' but 'double taxation relief' is the term usually used in UK legislation.

double tax relief. Another term for 'double taxation relief'.

doubtful debt. A debt that, it is assumed, will never be paid. Also called 'bad debt'.

down time. Also written: downtime. Time during which a machine or device or production facility is not in a condition to perform its intended function. This may include time during which work is being done to bring the item back into use ('active maintenance time'). Down time due to failure is considered to commence at the instant the item is determined to have failed and includes any additional time necessary to reach the same stage in the working programme of the item where it was when it failed. See BS 3811 : 1984. Compare 'idle time'.

D/P. A symbol (from 'documents against payment') on a documentary bill of exchange payable at a future date indicating that the commercial documents are to be released to the drawee when the bill is paid. Compare 'D/A'.

DP. Abbreviation of 'data processing'.

Dr. Abbreviation of 'debtor' used in accounts to mark a debit entry or a column of debit entries.

draft. Another term for 'bill of exchange'.

draft at a tenor. Another term for 'time bill'.

draft at sight. Another term for 'demand bill'.

DRAM. Abbreviation of 'dynamic random-access memory'.

drawback. 1. Repayment of customs duty that has been paid on imported goods when those goods are exported again or when they are incorporated in articles that are exported.

2. Repayment of excise duty that has been paid on goods when those goods are exported.

drawee. 1. The person to whom the unconditional written order contained in a bill of exchange or a cheque is addressed.

2. The person to whom documents entrusted to a bank for collection are to be presented.

drawer. The person who gives the unconditional written order contained in a bill of exchange or a cheque.

drawing. 1. Money or trading stock of a sole proprietorship business taken by the proprietor for non-business purposes. Also called 'private drawing'.

2. Money or trading stock of a partnership firm taken by a partner for personal use. Also called 'private drawing'.

drawings account. An account recording drawings.

drop-in. In data processing, an erroneous insertion of a binary character when putting data into, or retrieving data from, a magnetic store.

drop lock. A provision that if a floating rate falls to a particular level then it will be fixed at that level thereafter.

drop-out. In data processing, an omission of a binary character when putting data into, or retrieving data from, a magnetic store.

dump. 1. *Verb.* To record, in one store of a data processing system, the contents of all or part of another store in the system.

2. *Noun.* A record, in one store of a data processing system, of the contents of all or part of another store in the system.

durante absentia. *Participle with noun.* Latin for 'during absence'. Used to describe a personal representative, or the appointment of a personal representative, of a deceased individual to act for another personal representative for a period when the other personal representative is abroad.

durante minore aetate. *Participle with noun phrase.* Latin for 'during minority'. Used to describe a personal representative, or the appointment of a personal representative, of a deceased individual to act on behalf of another personal representative who has not yet attained the age of 18.

duty of customs. Another term for 'customs duty'.

duty of excise. Another term for 'excise duty'.

dyadic operation. An operation with two operands.

dynamic programming. Using mathematical or logical techniques to deal with multistage decision processes – i.e., problems that involve deciding an optimum sequence of decisions where each decision in the sequence depends on the ones before it.

dynamic random-access memory. Abbreviation: DRAM. A random-access memory from which the data stored will be lost in time unless the memory is kept supplied with electricity.

E

e. The irrational number defined by:

$$\Sigma 1/n!$$

where the sum extends over all non-negative integers n.

EAA. Abbreviation of 'European Accounting Association'.

E&OE. Abbreviation of 'errors and omissions excepted'. Put on an invoice or statement of account to indicate that if it contains an error or omission then the person rendering it will refuse to be regarded as precluded from issuing a revised invoice or statement. 'EE' is used with the same meaning.

earmarked stock. Another term for 'reserved stock'.

earned for ordinary. *Verb phrase.* Used to describe the amount of earnings for equity.

earned income. For the purposes of UK income tax, earned income is defined in the Income and Corporation Taxes Act 1970, s. 530. The definition covers all income chargeable under Schedule E and 'any income which is charged under Schedule A, Schedule B or Schedule D and is immediately derived by the individual from the carrying on or exercise by him of his trade, profession or vocation, either as an individual or, in the case of a partnership, as a partner personally acting therein'. In addition, certain other types of income are treated by statute as earned income: Civil List pensions, certain voluntary pensions and social security benefits chargeable under Schedule E (Income and Corporation Taxes Act 1970, s. 530(2)), post-cessation receipts (Income and Corporation Taxes Act 1970, s. 148), annuities paid under an approved retirement annuity scheme (Income and Corporation Taxes Act 1970, s. 226(1)), income from certain patents and know-how (Income and Corporation Taxes Act 1970, ss. 383 and 386(5)), partnership retirement annuities below a certain limit (Finance Act 1974, s. 16(1)), and income from furnished lettings (Finance Act 1984, s. 50(1) and Schedule 11, para. 1(2)(d)).

earned surplus. Term used in the past in America for 'retained earnings'. The Committee on Terminology of the American Institute of Certified Public Accountants recommended that the term was inappropriate and should not be used – see Accounting Terminology Bulletin 1, paras 65-70.

earnings. 1. Money received by an individual from employment.

2. Net profit of an accounting entity measured either with or without deducting payments of corporate income tax, interest on debt capital and preference dividends.

earnings available for ordinary. Another term for 'earnings for equity'.

earnings basis. In UK revenue law, the principle of using accrual accounting in preparing financial statements.

earnings before interest and after tax. Abbreviation: EBIAT. Net profit of an accounting entity over a period after deducting payments of tax but without deducting payments of interest on debt capital.

earnings before interest and tax. Abbreviation: EBIT. Net profit of an accounting entity over a period without deducting payments of interest on debt capital and payments of tax.

earnings for equity. The profit of a limited company for a period (consolidated profit after deducting minority interests if it is a holding company) after tax and after deducting preference dividends, but before taking into account extraordinary items. Earnings for equity normally includes the earnings of associated companies. See SSAP 3, Appendix 1, para. 2. Also called 'amount earned for equity', 'earnings available for ordinary'.

earnings per share. Abbreviation: EPS. In relation to a listed company, defined in SSAP 3 as the earnings of the company for a period – that is, the profit of the company (consolidated profit after deducting minority interests if it is a holding company) after tax and after deducting preference dividends, but before taking into account extraordinary items – divided by the number of issued equity shares on which dividend will be paid for the period. If the figure for earnings per share is negative, that is, if there was a loss before taking account of extraordinary items, then it is called 'loss per share'. Earnings per share is measured in pence per share. See also the entries for 'fully diluted earnings per share', 'net basis of calculating earnings per share' and 'nil distribution basis of calculating earnings per share'.

earnings-related contribution. In British social security law, a Class 1 social security contribution.

earnings retained for use in the business. Term used in America for 'reserves'.

earnings statement. In America, another term for 'income statement'.

EBCDIC. A character set, for use in processing and transmitting data, together with a representation of each character in the character set by a string of eight bits, originally specified by International Business Machines Corporation for use with computers manufactured by it. The term is derived from the words 'extended binary-coded decimal interchange code'.

EBIAT. Abbreviation of 'earnings before interest and after tax'.

EBIT. Abbreviation of 'earnings before interest and tax'.

EBQ. Abbreviation of 'economic batch quantity'.

ECGD. Abbreviation of 'Export Credits Guarantee Department'.

economic batch quantity. Abbreviation: EBQ. The quantity of a manufactured item made in batches that should be produced in one batch in order to meet a particular regular demand with minimum production and stockholding costs. Also called 'economic lot size'.

economic lot size. Abbreviation: ELS. Another term for 'economic batch quantity'.

economic manufacturing quantity. Abbreviation: EMQ. The economic order quantity of an item that is to be manufactured within the organisation rather than purchased.

economic order quantity. Abbreviation: EOQ. In stock control, the quantity of an item, which is normally kept in store, that should be ordered so as to minimise the total cost of ordering, purchasing and storing. If there is a constant usage rate, and if the item must never be out of stock, and if delivery of fresh stock can be arranged to coincide with the exhaustion of the existing stock, then the economic order quantity is given by the 'square-root formula':

$$Q = \sqrt{(2sr/k)}$$

where Q = economic order quantity, s = quantity used per year, r = ordering cost per order to be placed, k = stockholding costs per unit per year.

economic purchase quantity. Abbreviation: EPQ. The economic order quantity of an item that is to be purchased rather than manufactured within the organisation.

ECU. Also written: ecu. Usually spoken as an acronym. Abbreviation of 'European currency unit'. Coincidentally, *ecu* was the name of various gold and silver coins used in France from the 14th to the 19th centuries.

ED. Abbreviation of 'exposure draft'. In this dictionary, used only for exposure drafts issued by the Accounting Standards Committee.

EDP. Abbreviation of 'electronic data processing'.

EE. Abbreviation of 'errors excepted'. Put on an invoice or statement of account with the same meaning as 'E&OE'.

efficiency ratio. The ratio:

$$\frac{\text{actual standard hours of production in a budget period}}{\text{actual number of direct labour hours during the period}}$$

The ratio measures the efficiency of direct labour and is usually expressed as a percentage.

efficient portfolio. A portfolio of investments chosen from a particular collection of possible investments in such a way that no other portfolio chosen from those investments will offer a higher expected rate of return for the same risk or the same or a higher expected rate of return with less risk.

EFTPOS. Abbreviation of 'electronic funds transfer at point of sale'.

EGM. Abbreviation of 'extraordinary general meeting'.

eight-bit. *Adjective.* Used to describe a computer or processor that is designed to deal principally with words that are eight bits long and so, for example, has data buses with eight parallel conductors and has arithmetic registers that store eight bits.

eighty-twenty. Also written: 80/20. *Adjective.* Used to describe a situation in which 20% of the items under consideration have 80% of the total of some quantitative attribute. See also the entry for 'ABC analysis'.

elasticity. In relation to a function, for a particular value x of the independent variable (for which the value of the function is y), the quantity:

$$\frac{x \; \mathrm{d}y/\mathrm{d}x}{y}$$

where $\mathrm{d}y/\mathrm{d}x$ is the value of the derivative of the function at x.

electronic data processing. Abbreviation: EDP. Automatic data processing carried out by electronic devices.

electronic funds transfer at point of sale. Abbreviation: EFTPOS. A system for making payments for retail purchases in which banks transfer money from purchasers' bank accounts to retailers' bank accounts following instructions recorded at the retailers' premises and transmitted electronically to the banks.

electronic mail. Transfer of written messages between people by electronic means.

element. In relation to a set, a thing that, according to the rules defining the set, is included in the set. Also called 'member'.

elements of cost. The elements into which product costs are traditionally analysed, namely, expenses, labour costs and material costs.

eligible bank. One of the banks on a list published by the Bank of England, being a bank whose acceptances the Bank of England is willing to purchase. Discount houses need to be able to sell acceptances to the Bank of England on occasion and will therefore pay slightly more (i.e., buy at a lower rate of discount) for the acceptances of eligible banks.

eligible bank bill. A bill of exchange accepted by an eligible bank – i.e., an acceptance of an eligible bank.

ELS. Abbreviation of 'economic lot size'.

embezzle. *Verb.* To take for one's own use property that has been entrusted to one's care.

emblements. Crops and vegetable produce of land taken within a year of sowing. Unlike trees, emblements are not considered to form part of the land on which they are produced and are treated as goods rather than as real property.

emoluments. The total payment in money, or in goods or services that have a monetary value, for services or work done. By the Income and Corporation Taxes Act 1970, s. 183(1), tax is chargeable 'on the full amount of the emoluments' of an office or employment, 'and the expression "emoluments" shall include all salaries, fees, wages, perquisites and profits whatsoever'.

employees' share scheme. A scheme for encouraging or making it easier for the employees of a company to own shares in the company. In the Companies Act 1985, s. 743, the term is defined as: 'a scheme for encouraging or facilitating the holding of shares or debentures in a company by or for the benefit of:

'(a) the bona fide employees or former employees of the company, the company's subsidiary or holding company or a subsidiary of the company's holding company, or

'(b) the wives, husbands, widows, widowers or children or stepchildren under the age of 18 of such employees or former employees'.

employment. In revenue law, a contract of employment (*Fall* v *Hitchen* [1973] 1 WLR 286); the job someone is employed to perform.

employment cost. A cost identified with employing people, including costs of salaries, social security contributions, pension contributions, protective clothing or subsidised meals, or an aggregate of such costs.

employment report. Part of an annual report and accounts of an accounting entity giving information about its employees, including numbers employed, their distribution between various locations, hours worked, employment costs and training costs.

EMQ. Abbreviation of 'economic manufacturing quantity'.

EMV. Abbreviation of 'expected monetary value'.

encryption. Creation of an abnormal representation of data, for the purposes of recording or transmitting the data, in order to restrict the number of people to whom a record or transmission will be intelligible.

encumbrance. Alternative spelling: incumbrance. A charge on property, especially on land, to secure the due performance of an obligation.

endorse. Alternative spelling: indorse. *Verb.* To make an endorsement on a negotiable instrument.

endorsee. Alternative spelling: indorsee. A person who is designated in an endorsement of a negotiable instrument as the person to whom the endorser is transferring the instrument.

endorsement. Alternative spelling: indorsement. 1. A statement written on (traditionally on the back of) a negotiable instrument (such as a bill of exchange or a cheque or a negotiable bill of lading) by a holder of the instrument which will transfer ownership of the instrument to another person when the holder delivers the instrument to that other person (or an agent of that other person). The person who makes an endorsement is called the 'endorser'. An endorsement consists of the endorser's signature with other words as necessary. An endorsement may name the person to whom the instrument is to be transferred, in which case the endorsement is called a 'special endorsement' and the named person is called the 'endorsee'. An endorsement which does not name an endorsee is called an 'endorsement in blank'; it consists of the endorser's signature only and it makes the negotiable instrument payable to the bearer.

2. An alteration to a policy of insurance written on a piece of paper attached to the policy document.

endorsement in blank. Alternative spelling: indorsement in blank. An endorsement in which no endorsee is specified.

endorser. Alternative spelling: indorser. A person who makes an endorsement.

energy cost. A cost of electricity, gas or other sources of energy – such as coal and petroleum products – used, or an aggregate of such costs.

engagement letter. Another term for 'letter of engagement'.

enterprise zone. An area designated by the Secretary of State for the Environment under the Local Government, Planning and Land Act 1980. In an enterprise zone, non-domestic buildings are generally free from local authority rates and there are special planning procedures to encourage the establishment of businesses.

entity. Short form of 'accounting entity'.

entry. 1. A record, made in an account, of a transaction or event.

2. A record, made in a register, or other file of data, of a description of an

occurrence, transaction or proceeding, or of data relating to a particular person or thing.

3. The act of making an entry (in sense 1 or 2).

4. A description of imported goods prepared by the importer for customs purposes. Also called 'customs entry'.

5. In this dictionary, a word, phrase, prefix or abbreviation, printed in bold type, and an accompanying description of its meaning.

EOQ. Abbreviation of 'economic order quantity'.

EPQ. Abbreviation of 'economic purchase quantity'.

EPS. Abbreviation of 'earnings per share'.

equal-instalment depreciation. American spelling: equal-installment depreciation. Another term for 'straight-line depreciation'.

equated time of payment. See the entry for 'equation of payments'.

equation of payments. Calculation of a date on which, if the total amount of several payments due at different dates is paid, no interest will be charged – the interest payable on the overdue ones being cancelled by the discount claimed on those paid early. The date calculated is called the 'average due date', 'equated time of payment' or 'average time of payment'.

equitable apportionment. Apportionment of payments in accordance with rules developed by courts applying the principles of equity.

equitable mortgage. 1. A contract, by which one person agrees to create a legal mortgage over property when required to do so by another person, that a court will enforce by ordering the first person to create the legal mortgage.

2. A mortgage of an equitable interest in property.

equity. 1. The residue left after subtracting the value of the liabilities of an accounting entity from the value of its assets, where an obligation to return contributed capital and an obligation to distribute the residue itself to particular persons are not counted as liabilities. If there are persons who may be regarded as owners of the entity, to whom the entity's equity would be paid if the entity were wound up, then the equity is called 'owners' equity' (or 'owner's equity' if there is only one owner). In some entities there are classes of owners with different entitlements on winding up: often the claims of owners whose entitlement is subject to a maximum limit are treated as liabilities and deducted from the value of assets so that equity represents the value of the entity to those of its owners who have an unlimited entitlement to be paid from the assets of the entity on winding up – see the entry for 'shareholders' equity'. See also the entry for 'net assets'.

2. A system of law originating in the English Chancery courts which provides rules for deciding disputes involving personal rights and duties.

3. The value of the equity of redemption – that is, the value of an asset after all charges on the asset to secure fulfilment of obligations have been discharged.

equity capital. Capital contributed to a business enterprise in return for a right to participate in distributions of profits (either while the enterprise is a going concern or on its winding up) not limited to any specified amount. In particular, capital contributed for equity shares.

equity dividend cover. The earnings of a company for a period – that is, the profit of the period (consolidated profit after deducting minority interests if it is a holding company) after tax and after deducting preference dividends, but before taking into account extraordinary items – divided by the dividend payable on equity shares in respect of the period. Often simply called 'dividend cover', which is the term used in the ICMA official terminology.

quity method. A method of recording investment in an associated company in which the balance sheet shows:

(a) the cost of the investment; and

(b) the share of the post-acquisition retained profits and reserves of the company attributable to the investing company or group; less

(c) any amounts written off in respect of (a) and (b);

and in which the profit and loss account shows separately the share of the profit before tax, taxation and extraordinary items of the company attributable to the investing company or group. See SSAP 14, para. 14, and Companies Act 1985, Schedule 4, para. 65.

equity of redemption. The right of a person who has mortgaged or otherwise charged property as security for the fulfilment of an obligation to recover the property by fulfilling the obligation at any time. Usually, a contract of mortgage or charge gives the mortgagee or chargee the right to sell the property after default in fulfilling the secured obligation, and exercise of an agreed right of sale brings to an end the equity of redemption, although the mortgagee or chargee is not permitted to retain any profit from the sale.

equity share. A share in a company carrying rights to participate in distributions of profits (either while the company is a going concern or on its winding up) not limited to any specified amount. The ordinary shares of a company are usually equity shares.

equity share capital. The part of the share capital of a company represented by equity shares.

equity shareholder. In relation to a company, a shareholder whose shares are equity shares.

equivalent unit. A cost unit multiplied by a fraction representing the portion of an element of product cost identified with work in progress. For example, if 1,000 units of work in progress have reached a stage with which 50% of the direct labour cost element of product cost can be identified, then they may be treated as:

1,000 × 50% = 500 equivalent units.

Equivalent units are added to completed units when valuing stocks of finished and partly finished goods.

erroneous. *Adjective.* Containing an error.

error. 1. A discrepancy between a recorded statement, value or condition, or a value shown by measuring instruments or obtained by calculation, and the true or theoretically correct statement, value or condition. The term is usually used when it is not intended to imply that there has been deliberate falsification by the person making the record, measurement or calculation.

2. A discrepancy between an actual value or condition and a specified or theoretically correct value or condition.

3. The amount of an error (in sense 1 or 2).

error of the first kind. See the entry for 'statistical test'.

error of the second kind. See the entry for 'statistical test'.

errors and omissions excepted. See the entry for 'E&OE'.

errors excepted. See the entry for 'EE'.

escape clause. Another term for 'exemption clause'.

estate. 1. In land law, the rights that a property owner has over a piece of real property. Nowadays, the term is used only in the phrase 'legal estate', all other forms of ownership of real property being known as 'interests'.

2. The total assets of a person (especially of a deceased individual at the time of death).

3. For the purposes of capital transfer tax, a person's estate is defined in the Capital Transfer Tax Act 1984, s. 5, as 'the aggregate of all the property to which he is beneficially entitled, except that the estate of a person immediately before his death does not include excluded property'. In determining the value of a person's estate at any time for the purposes of capital transfer tax the person's liabilities at that time shall be taken into account, except as otherwise provided by the Capital Transfer Tax Act 1984 (s. 5(3) of the Act). The liabilities to be taken into account in determining the value of a transferor's estate immediately after a transfer of value include the transferor's liability for capital transfer tax on the value tansferred but not the transferor's liability (if any) for any other tax or duty resulting from the transfer (s. 5(4) of the Act).

estate duty. A tax formerly charged in the UK on the value of the estate of a deceased individual. It has been replaced by capital transfer tax and has not been payable in respect of any death occurring after 13 March 1975. Also called 'death duty'.

estate owner. The owner of a legal estate in land (Law of Property Act 1925, s. 205(1)(v)).

estimator. In statistics, a statistic used to estimate a population parameter.

estoppel. Insistence by a court that a party to legal proceedings who has in the past misrepresented a state of affairs cannot benefit from the true position but must accept the consequences of the misrepresentation.

Euro-. *Prefix.* Of, or relating to, the lending of an amount of the currency of one country in a place outside that country. For example, 'Eurodollar', a US dollar lent outside of the USA and its possessions. Most trading in loans of currencies outside their country of origin occurs in European financial centres.

Eurobond. A bearer bond issued in connection with a marketable loan which has a nominal value expressed in the domestic currency of one country but is originally issued outside that country.

European Accounting Association. Abbreviation: EAA. An association of accounting scholars and researchers which organises a major accounting congress every year.

Address: 40 rue Washington, B-1050 Brussels, Belgium. Telephone: Brussels 6480385.

European currency unit. Abbreviation: ECU or ecu. Unit of account used in the European Community and defined as the sum of certain amounts of the national currencies of the members of the community. The precise amounts of each of the currencies in the definition are altered from time to time.

evolving budget. Another term for 'rolling budget'.

EWMA. Abbreviation of 'exponentially weighted moving average'.

ex. 1. *Preposition.* Without. Used in describing deals in securities to indicate that a security will be sold without a particular benefit, e.g., 'ex dividend' means that the buyer will not receive the next dividend payment due on the security.

2. *Preposition.* From. Used to indicate that a buyer of goods must collect them from a specified place, e.g., 'ex factory'.

3. *Preposition.* From. Used to indicate a source of supply, e.g., 'ex stock'.

except-for opinion. In America, an audit report stating that a particular matter has not been properly reflected in the financial statements, but that otherwise the statements are fair. Also called 'with-the-exception-of opinion'.

exceptional item. An item, in the accounting records of an entity, that derives from an event or transaction within the ordinary activities of the entity but which, because of its size or incidence, should be disclosed separately in the entity's financial statements if those statements are to give a true and fair view. See ED 36, para. 28.

except opinion. In Britain, a statement in an audit report that a particular matter has not been properly reflected in the financial statements, but that the matter is not fundamental for the purposes of giving a true and fair view of the financial position being reported on.

excess. 1. Amount by which one number, quantity or value is greater than another.

2. Amount by which assets are greater than liabilities.

3. Amount by which expenditure is greater than income in an income and expenditure account.

4. Amount by which the correct value of something exceeds the value recorded in accounts.

excess return. Another term for 'risk premium'.

excess stock. In stock control, the portion of stock on hand which is over and above the maximum stock level (BS 5191 : 1975).

exchange. 1. *Noun.* In accounting theory, reciprocal transfers of resources or obligations between one accounting entity and one or more other persons in which the entity either sacrifices resources or incurs obligations in order to obtain other resources or satisfy other obligations. The resources involved may or may not be monetary.

2. *Noun.* In law, reciprocal transfers of property between two persons in which either both persons are transferring only money or neither person is transferring only money. If what is transferred by one person is partly money and partly some other property then the exchange is called a 'part-exchange' and the money is called 'payment for equality'.

3. *Verb.* To participate in a reciprocal transfer of property.

4. *Noun.* An organisation which provides facilities for dealers in a particular type of property, providing, for example, premises in which they can trade, standard forms of contract and terms of business, and supervision to protect the reputation of the dealers generally.

exchange cheque. American spelling: exchange check. A cheque given in exchange for cash.

exchange control. Restriction or regulation by a government of a country of the making of payments to non-residents by residents of the country.

exchange gain. An increase in the value of a transaction that is carried out in one currency as recorded in accounts expressed in another currency caused by a change in the exchange rate used for translation or a difference between the exchange rate used for conversion and that used for translation.

exchange loss. A decrease in the value of a transaction that is carried out in one currency as recorded in accounts expressed in another currency caused by a change in the exchange rate used for translation or a difference between the exchange rate used for conversion and that used for translation.

exchange rate. The number of units of one currency which may be bought or sold for one unit (or, in many cases, 100 units) of another currency.

exchange risk. The risk that exchange rates will vary and that accordingly a future payment in foreign currency will be more expensive, or a future receipt of foreign currency less valuable, than expected. Also called 'foreign exchange risk'.

excise duty. A tax charged in the UK on the manufacture or production of certain goods in the UK, on excise licences and on betting and gaming. Also called 'duty of excise'.

excise licence. A licence issued under a scheme for taxation in which it is declared unlawful to carry on some activity without purchasing a licence from the taxation authorities. In the UK, excise licences are required:

(a) to use a mechanically propelled vehicle;

(b) to manufacture or produce beer, spirits, tobacco, mechanical lighters and matches; and

(c) to carry on a limited number of trades or businesses.

In practice, only vehicle licence duty raises significant amounts of taxation. The object of imposing the other duties is to ensure that an authoritative register is kept of manufacturers and distributors in particular trades.

excise licence duty. The fee paid for an excise licence.

excluded property. Property that may be transferred by an individual without incurring liability to capital transfer tax. The main categories of excluded property are as follows:

(a) Property situated outside the United Kingdom if the person beneficially entitled to it is an individual domiciled outside the United Kingdom (Capital Transfer Tax Act 1984, s. 6(1)).

(b) Government stock beneficially owned by a person who is neither domiciled nor ordinarily resident in the United Kingdom if the securities have been exempted from taxation (Capital Transfer Tax Act 1984, s. 6(2)).

(c) National Savings securities and trustee savings bank deposits if beneficially owned by a person domiciled in the Channel Islands or the Isle of Man (Capital Transfer Tax Act 1984, s. 6(3)).

(d) Property of members of visiting armed forces (Capital Transfer Tax Act 1984, s. 155(1)).

(e) Reversionary interests in settled property, subject to certain conditions (Capital Transfer Tax Act 1984, s. 48).

exclusion clause. Another term for 'exemption clause'.

execution. 1. The performance of all formalities necessary to make a document legally effective. This may involve signing, sealing, signing in the presence of witnesses, registration with a public official, etc.

2. Complete performance of all aspects of a contract by all parties to the contract.

3. Enforcement of the judgment or order of a court by a public officer – usually by seizing the goods of the person against whom the judgment or order was made.

4. The carrying out, by a computer, of an instruction, or of the instructions of a computer program.

execution creditor. A person for whose benefit a writ of execution has been issued – i.e., the person who is to benefit from the court judgment or order which the writ seeks to enforce.

execution debtor. A person ordered to pay money by a court judgment or order in respect of which a writ of execution has been issued.

executive program. Another term for 'supervisory program'.

executor. Abbreviation: exor. A personal representative of a deceased individual appointed in the will of the deceased. A female executor is sometimes called an 'executrix'.

executor according to the tenor. A person who is clearly intended by a testator to be an executor of the testator, but is not expressly appointed as such in the will.

executor dative. In Scotland, a person appointed by a Sheriff Court to administer the estate of a deceased individual when there is no executor nominate. An executor dative is equivalent to an administrator in England and Wales and in America.

executor de son tort. A person who, in relation to the estate of a deceased individual, acts as a personal representative though not appointed as such. Also called 'executor in his own wrong' or 'executor in her own wrong'.

executor in his own wrong. Or: executor in her own wrong. Another term for 'executor de son tort'.

executor nominate. In Scotland, a person appointed in the will of a deceased individual to administer that individual's estate after death. An executor nominate is equivalent to an executor in England and Wales and in America.

executorship. The office and duties of a personal representative.

executor's year. A period of one year after the death of an individual during which no legal proceedings may be taken to force the personal representatives of the deceased to distribute the estate – see Administration of Estates Act 1925, s. 44.

executory. 1. *Adjective.* Of a contract, not completely performed by all the parties.

2. *Adjective.* Of consideration for a promise, not yet given, in whole or in part.

executrix. Term sometimes used for a female executor.

exempt approved scheme. An approved scheme, for providing pensions, that is exempted from income tax and capital gains tax under the Finance Act 1970, s. 21.

exemption clause. A term of a contract excluding or limiting a liability that a party would have if the term were not part of the contract. Also called 'escape clause', 'exclusion clause'.

exempt supply. A supply of goods or services of a description specified in Schedule 6 to the Value Added Tax Act 1983 (see s. 17 of the Act). No value added tax is chargeable on an exempt supply.

exempt transfer. A transfer of value by an individual which is defined by the capital transfer tax legislation to be an exempt transfer and is therefore not subject to capital transfer tax. By the Capital Transfer Tax Act 1984, s. 1(2): 'A transfer of value made by an individual and exempt only to a limited extent:

'(a) is, if all the value transferred by it is within the limit, an exempt transfer, and

'(b) is, if that value is partly within and partly outside the limit, a chargeable transfer of so much of that value as is outside the limit as well as an exempt transfer of so much of that value as is within the limit'.

The main categories of exempt transfer are:

(a) the annual exemption (Capital Transfer Tax Act 1984, s. 19)

(b) the exemption for small gifts (Capital Transfer Tax Act 1984, s. 20)

(c) normal expenditure out of income (Capital Transfer Tax Act 1984, s. 21)

(d) gifts in consideration of marriage (Capital Transfer Tax Act 1984, s. 22)

(e) mutual transfers (Capital Transfer Tax Act 1984, ss. 148 and 149)

(f) any transfer to the spouse of the transferor (Capital Transfer Tax Act 1984, s. 18)

(g) gifts to charities (Capital Transfer Tax Act 1984, s. 23)

(h) gifts to political parties (Capital Transfer Tax Act 1984, s. 24)

(i) gifts for national purposes (Capital Transfer Tax Act 1984, s. 25)

(j) gifts for the public benefit (Capital Transfer Tax Act 1984, s. 26).

exercise price. The price to be paid if an option is exercised. Also called 'striking price'.

ex gratia. Preposition phrase. From generosity; without legal compulsion; without admitting legal liability.

exor. Abbreviation of 'executor'.

ex parte. Preposition phrase. Latin for 'on behalf of'. Used to describe:

(a) an application made to a court by one party to legal proceedings without giving the other party a chance to appear;

(b) an application made to a court during legal proceedings by a person who has an interest in the matter but is not a party to the proceedings, e.g., a person who has an interest in insolvency proceedings.

expectation. In probability theory, a number that represents the average value of a random variable.

For a discrete random variable X taking values x_i with probabilities p_i the expectation $E(X)$ is defined as:

$$E(X) = \Sigma p_i x_i$$

For a continuous random variable X with probability density function $f(x)$ the expectation $E(X)$ is defined as:

$$E(X) = \int x f(x)\, dx$$

Also called 'mean'. The symbol μ is often used for expectation.

expected exit value. Another term for 'net realisable value'.

expected monetary value. Abbreviation: EMV. In relation to an action, the weighted average of the possible payoffs of the action where the weighting factors are the probabilities of the payoffs. If the payoffs of an action are $v_1, v_2, \ldots, v_n$ with probabilities $p_1, p_2, \ldots, p_n$ then the expected monetary value of the action is:

$$\Sigma p_i v_i$$

Also called 'expected payoff', 'expected value'.

expected payoff. Another term for 'expected monetary value'.

expected standard. In relation to a future budget period, a standard expected to be attained during that period.

expected value. Another term for 'expected monetary value'.

expenditure. A giving up of money or other assets, or an incurrence of a liability, in exchange for a benefit received or to be received.

expense. 1. *Noun.* An amount of money or other assets given up, used or consumed, or a liability incurred, in the course of the ordinary activities of an enterprise.

FASB Statement of Financial Accounting Concepts No. 3 states: 'Expenses are outflows or other using up of assets or incurrences of liabilities (or a combination of both) during a period from delivering or producing goods [footnote omitted], rendering services, or carrying out other activities that constitute the entity's ongoing major or central operations' (para. 65).

2. *Noun.* In Britain, a cost of something other than materials, supplies or work performed by people – or an aggregate of such costs. An expense may be a 'direct expense' or an 'indirect expense' depending on whether it is a direct cost or an indirect cost.

3. *Noun.* A small payment of money for something incidental to performing a job.

4. *Verb.* To treat an expenditure as an expense or loss of the current period of account; to write down or write off.

expert system. A data processing system that can solve complex problems within a particular area of expertise, using the knowledge that a human expert in that area would use, imitating the problem-solving techniques of such an expert and providing an explanation of its suggested solution.

expired cost. An expenditure from which no further benefit is expected.

expiry date. The date on which something expires, e.g., the latest date on which an option may be exercised.

exponent. In mathematics, a particular value of x for which the value of a^x is to be calculated. Also called 'index', 'power'.

exponential distribution. The probability distribution of a continuous random variable, which takes only non-negative values, with the distribution function:

$$P(X \leqslant x) = 1 - e^{-\lambda x}$$

where λ is a positive number. The distribution is useful for describing a variable that occurs only with non-negative values, most of which are small and very few of which are very large.

exponential function. A function defined for all numbers x by the equation:

$$y = a^x$$

where a is a positive number called the 'base' of the function. If no value is specified for the base then it is presumed to be e where:

$e = \Sigma 1/n!$ where the sum extends over all non-negative integers n

The value of the exponential function to base e may be represented by the symbol:

exp x

The exponential function to base e is defined as:

exp $x = \Sigma x^n/n!$ where the sum extends over all non-negative integers n

If n is a positive integer then x^n is defined to be the product of n factors each equal to x and x^0 is defined to be equal to 1. The value of the exponential function to any base a other than e is defined to be:

$$a^x = \exp (x \ln a)$$

where ln a is the natural logarithm of a.

exponentially weighted moving average. Abbreviation: EWMA. See the entry for 'exponential smoothing'.

exponential smoothing. A method of smoothing a time series. If the ith observed value is y_i then the corresponding trend value T_i calculated by exponential smoothing is:

$$T_i = (1 - \alpha)T_{i-1} + y_i$$

where $T_1 = y_1$ and α is a chosen number between 0 and 1 called a 'smoothing constant'. T_i is sometimes called an 'exponentially weighted moving average'.

Export Credits Guarantee Department. Abbreviation: ECGD. A British government department that provides credit insurance for British exporters.

exposure draft. Abbreviation: ED. A document issued when preparing, e.g., a Statement of Standard Accounting Practice, setting out a draft on which comments are invited from interested persons.

express trust. A trust created by the express statement of a settlor, whether the settlor actually used the word 'trust' or expressed the intention in some other way. Compare 'implied trust'.

EXQ. Abbreviation of 'ex quay'.

ex quay. Abbreviation: EXQ. Trade terms for the sale of goods that are to be transported to the buyer by sea under which the seller must make the goods available to the buyer on the quay at the destination port named in the contract of sale. The seller has to bear the full cost and risk involved in transporting goods to that destination.

EXS. Abbreviation of 'ex ship'.

ex ship. Abbreviation: EXS. Trade terms for the sale of goods that are to be transported to the buyer by sea under which the seller must make the goods available to the buyer on board a ship at a destination port named in the contract of sale. The seller has to bear the full cost and risk involved in transporting the goods to that destination.

extend. *Verb.* To multiply a unit price or cost by a number of units to arrive at a total price or cost.

extended trial balance. A trial balance to which additional columns, headed 'trading account', 'profit and loss account' and 'balance sheet', are added and each figure in the trial balance is repeated in the appropriate column. Used for illustration and teaching purposes.

external audit. An audit of an accounting entity carried out by an auditor who is not employed by that entity or by its managers and is, as far as possible, independent of the persons who manage the entity.

externally funded scheme. A pension scheme where the benefits are provided from a fund held externally to the employing company (ED 32, para. 32).

external reconstruction. See the entry for 'reconstruction'.

external store. In a computer, a store that is accessible only through input-output channels. Also called 'backing store'.

extraordinary general meeting. Abbreviation: EGM. A general meeting that is not an annual general meeting. The word 'extraordinary' is used because an annual general meeting used to be called an 'ordinary general meeting'.

extraordinary item. An amount which is, or should be, reported specially in a financial statement because it derives from an event or transaction outside the ordinary activities of the entity being reported on, is material and is not expected to recur frequently or regularly. A prior-year item should not be regarded as an extraordinary item merely because it relates to a prior year. (This definition is given in SSAP 6, para. 11.) In IAS 8 called 'unusual item'.

extraordinary resolution. In British company law, a resolution of the members of a company that is valid only if approved by three-quarters or more of the votes cast on it at a meeting of the members of which notice was given specifying that the resolution was to be proposed as an extraordinary resolution. No minimum period of notice is required for an extraordinary resolution. Compare 'ordinary resolution', 'special resolution'.

extrapolation. Where values of a dependent variable are known for values of the independent variable between certain limits, estimation of the value of the dependent variable for a value of the independent variable outside those limits. Compare 'interpolation'.

EXW. Abbreviation of 'ex works'.

ex works. Abbreviation: EXW. Trade terms for the sale of goods by a manufacturer under which the only responsibility of the seller is to make the goods available at the works or factory of the seller. The buyer bears the full cost and risk involved in bringing the goods from the factory to the desired destination.

F

F. Abbreviation of 'favourable variance'.

FA. Abbreviation of 'Finance Act'.

FAAI. Designation of a Fellow of the Institute of Administrative Accountants.

face value. A nominal value stated on a security or other document.

factor. 1. *Noun.* An agent who is provided by the principal with possession of goods of the principal for sale, where the goods may be sold in the name of the agent.

2. *Noun.* An enterprise which purchases (i.e., acquires the right to receive payment of) trade debts owed to other enterprises. Usually, the fact that a debt has been purchased by a factor is notified to the debtor so that there is a legal assignment of the debt.

3. *Verb.* To sell debts to a factor (see sense 2).

4. *Noun.* A part of a mathematical expression that is to be multiplied by another part of the expression.

factorial. The factorial of a non-negative integer n is denoted by $n!$ and is defined as follows:

$$0! = 1$$

$$n! = n(n - 1)! \qquad (n \neq 0)$$

Thus the factorial of a positive integer is the product of the integer and all the positive integers less than itself.

factory burden. Term sometimes used in America for 'production overhead cost'.

factory cost. Another term for 'production cost of sales'.

factory expense. Term used in America for a cost identified with manufacturing other than direct material costs and direct labour costs, or an aggregate of such costs. Also called 'manufacturing expense'.

factory order. Another term for 'production order'.

factory overhead. See the entry for 'production overhead cost'.

factory overhead cost. See the entry for 'production overhead cost'.

FAD. Used as a symbol for the trade terms 'FOB airport'.

FAIA. Designation of a Fellow of the Association of International Accountants.

fair value. 1. In International Accounting Standards, the amount for which an asset could be exchanged between a knowledgeable, willing buyer and a knowledgeable, willing seller in an arm's-length transaction (IAS 16, para. 6; IAS 17, para. 2; IAS 18, para. 4; IAS 22, para. 3).

2. In SSAP 21, the price at which an asset could be exchanged in an arm's-length transaction less, where applicable, any grants receivable towards the purchase or use of the asset (SSAP 21, para. 25).

3. In SSAP 22, the amount for which an asset (or liability) could be exchanged in an arm's-length transaction (SSAP 22, para. 25).

false accounting. An offence in the criminal law of England and Wales defined in s. 17 of the Theft Act 1968 as occurring when: 'a person dishonestly, with a view to gain for himself or another or with intent to cause loss to another:

(a) destroys, defaces, conceals or falsifies any account or any record or document made or required for any accounting purpose; or

(b) in furnishing information for any purpose produces or makes use of any account, or any such record or document as aforesaid, which to his knowledge is or may be misleading, false or deceptive in a material particular'.

For the purposes of this definition, it is provided in s. 17(2) that 'a person who makes or concurs in making in an account or other document an entry which is or may be misleading, false or deceptive in a material particular, or who omits or concurs in omitting a material particular from an account or other document, is to be treated as falsifying the account or document'.

fan club. Informal. A number of investors in securities who buy and sell securities in imitation of one particular investor whom they admire.

FAPA. Designation of a Fellow of the Association of Authorised Public Accountants.

FAS. 1. Abbreviation of 'Statement of Financial Accounting Standards' issued by the Financial Accounting Standards Board.

2. Abbreviation of 'free alongside ship'.

FASB. Abbreviation of 'Financial Accounting Standards Board'.

fate. In banking, whether or not a financial document presented for acceptance or payment has been accepted or paid.

favourable variance. American spelling: favorable variance. Abbreviation: F. A variance that results in increased profit.

FCA. 1. Designation of a Fellow of the Institute of Chartered Accountants in England and Wales.

2. Designation of a Fellow of the Institute of Chartered Accountants in Ireland.

FCCA. Designation of a Fellow of the Chartered Association of Certified Accountants.

FCMA. Designation of a Fellow of the Institute of Cost and Management Accountants.

FCPA. Designation of a Fellow of the Institute of Certified Public Accountants in Ireland.

FCT. Designation of a Fellow of the Association of Corporate Treasurers.

***F*-distribution.** The probability distribution of a random variable

$$F = \frac{X_1^2/v_1}{X_2^2/v_2},$$

where X_1^2/v_1 and X_2^2/v_2 are independent random variables, X_1^2 is a chi-squared distribution with v_1 degrees of freedom and X_2^2 is a chi-squared distribution with ν_2 degrees of freedom. The F-distribution is said to have ν_1, ν_2 degrees of freedom. The letter F is used in honour of an English statistician, Sir Ronald Aylmer Fisher (1890–1962).

fee. 1. A sum of money payable in return for the provision of a service.

2. A right to hold land granted to an individual without a provision that it will come to an end on the death of the individual (but see the entry for 'fee tail') or at a definite date in the future. Because a fee normally continues after the death of the individual to whom it is granted, it may be inherited from that individual and is accordingly described as a 'heritable' interest.

3. In Scotland, the interest that a person (called the 'fiar') has in the capital of an asset that is subject to a liferent.

feedback. Part of the output of a system that is used to evaluate the performance of the system.

fee simple absolute. The right to possess land granted without any provisions under which the right could come to an end. If a fee simple absolute is 'in possession' (meaning that the owner of the fee simple absolute has the immediate right to possession of the land) then it is a legal estate, which is commonly called a 'freehold'. If, however, the right to possession will arise only in the future, e.g., on the happening of a particular event, then the fee simple absolute is only an equitable interest.

The adjective 'absolute' distinguishes a fee simple absolute from a fee simple that will come to an end when a specified event occurs, known as a 'determinable fee simple', and from a fee simple which exists only as long as some condition is fulfilled, known as a 'conditional fee simple'. The adjective 'simple' distinguishes a fee simple from a right to possession of land which endures only so long as the individual to whom it was originally granted or a lineal descendant of that individual is alive, called a 'fee tail'.

fee simple absolute in possession. An interest in land that is a fee simple absolute that gives its owner entitlement to possession of the land now, subject to any right of possession that the owner may have granted to a leaseholder.

fee tail. A right to hold land granted to an individual with a provision that it will continue only while the individual to whom it was granted or any lineal descendant of that individual is alive. A fee tail is described as an 'entailed' interest. Usually, any holder of an entailed interest is entitled to 'bar the entail', i.e., to declare that the provision requiring lineal descendants to be alive no longer applies – the fee tail is thereby converted into a fee simple.

fellow. An individual in a senior class of membership of a professional institute. In some institutes a member who has practised the profession for a minimum number of years is qualified to become a fellow; in others an examination has to be taken or a thesis submitted.

fellow subsidiary. In relation to a corporation A which is a subsidiary of a corporation B, a corporation that is also a subsidiary of B but is not a subsidiary or a holding company of A (Companies Act 1985, Schedule 4, para. 80).

fiar. In Scotland, in relation to a capital asset that is subject to a liferent, the person who is entitled to receive the asset on the death of the liferenter.

FICM. Designation of a Fellow of the Institute of Credit Management.

fictitious asset. An item recorded as an asset in a balance sheet, but which could not be sold for value, for example, preliminary expenses (which must not now be shown as an asset in a balance sheet of a British registered company), and many prepaid expenses such as insurance premiums.

fiduciary. 1. *Adjective.* Involving or depending on confidence or trust.

2. *Noun.* A person in whom confidence or trust has been placed.

FIFO. Usually spoken as an acronym. Abbreviation of 'first in, first out'.

51 per cent subsidiary. See the entry for 'subsidiary'.

FII. Abbreviation of 'franked investment income'.

file. In data processing, a collection of similar groups of data, each of which is called a 'record'. Usually a file contains data giving information of a particular kind for each of a number of transactions, persons or things and the group of data relating to each transaction, person or thing is regarded as a single record within the file.

file maintenance. Adding data to, changing data in, and deleting data from, files so as to record new information or to correct information already stored.

file processing. Data processing concerned with creating, merging, sorting, updating and extracting information from files.

final accounts. Financial statements for an accounting period, consisting of a balance sheet and profit and loss account (or income and expenditure account) with perhaps a statement of source and application of funds. Usually produced annually and called 'annual accounts'.

final adjustments. Adjusting entries made so that final accounts may be drawn up.

final dividend. A payment of dividend by a company to its members which completes the payment of dividend for a financial year in which an interim dividend has been paid.

final pay scheme. A pension scheme in which a member's benefit is calculated by reference to the member's pensionable pay for a period ending at or not long before retirement (ED 32, para. 33). A final pay scheme is a type of defined benefit scheme.

final settlement. A composition, especially for a particular debt.

finance. 1. *Noun.* Plural form (finances). Monetary resources.

2. *Noun.* Activity, or study, of dealing with money, investing money and persuading investors to invest in particular projects.

3. *Noun.* Money provided for a particular purpose.

4. *Verb.* To provide money for a particular purpose.

Finance Act. Abbreviation: FA. The usual short title (apart from the year of enactment) of annual UK Acts of Parliament which impose income tax and corporation tax and amend the law relating to taxation.

finance bill. 1. Another term for 'accommodation bill'.

2. (Usually written with capital F and B.) A bill that is a draft of a Finance Act.

finance charge. A charge made for being allowed to delay paying for an asset for a period of time. Also called 'charge for credit'.

finance company. Another term for 'finance house'.

finance house. An enterprise which finances credit purchases of consumer durables and industrial and commercial equipment, often by purchasing the goods itself and hiring them on hire-purchase terms to the ultimate buyer. Also called 'finance company'.

finance lease. A lease that transfers substantially all the risks and rewards of ownership of the thing leased to the lessee (SSAP 21, para. 15). In America, called 'capital lease' (FASB Statement 13, paras 6a and 7).

financial accounting. Recording of the financial transactions of an accounting entity, in monetary terms, and analysis of them to show the effect of transactions over periods of time and at the ends of periods.

Financial Accounting Standards Board. Abbreviation: FASB. An independent body established by a number of associations of accountants and related professions in the USA to investigate principles and standards of financial accounting. The Board's Statements of Financial Accounting Standards are regarded as establishing generally accepted accounting principles. Also of great importance are its Statements of Financial Accounting Concepts.

financial document. A document used for obtaining payment of money, for example, a cheque, or a bill of exchange.

financial gearing. Another term for 'gearing'.

financial leverage. Term used in America for 'gearing'.

financial management. Management of the acquisition of money for use by an accounting entity.

financial position. The total assets and total liabilities of an accounting entity and their relationship to its contributed capital, if any. The financial position of an entity is shown by its balance sheet.

financial statement. A statement, in monetary terms, of the results of an accounting entity's transactions over a period, giving totals for classes of transaction rather than details of individual transactions and presented in a commonly used form. The forms of financial statement commonly prepared are the balance sheet, profit and loss account (or income and expenditure account), and statement of source and application of funds. Each of these statements may be accompanied by notes giving supplementary information. Each of the statements may be prepared both under the historical cost convention and under the current cost convention (or some other convention for accounting for the effects of changing prices). It is usual to prepare financial statements regularly once a year for an accounting entity, reporting the financial position on the same date each year, and such statements are called 'annual accounts'. The annual accounts of a British registered company must be accompanied by a directors' report which may accordingly be regarded as part of the company's financial statements.

In SSAPs, the term 'financial statements' is defined as: 'balance sheets, profit and loss accounts, statements of source and application of funds, notes and other statements, which collectively are intended to give a true and fair view of financial position and profit or loss' (SSAP 14, para. 10, SSAP 15, para. 23, SSAP 17, para. 14, ED 32, para. 26, ED 33, para. 19).

In Auditing Standards and Guidelines the term 'financial statements' is defined as: 'balance sheets and profit and loss accounts (or other forms of income statement) together with such additional statements and notes as are identified as being within the scope of the audit opinion' (Explanatory Foreword to Auditing Standards and Guidelines).

financial year. 1. In British company law, the period of time between one balance sheet date and the next (whether or not it is twelve months). (Companies Act 1985, ss. 227 and 742(1)(c)).

2. For the purposes of UK corporation tax, the period of time from 1 April of one year to 31 March of the next year, identified by the year in which it finishes. For example, the 'financial year 1985' means the period ending 31 March 1985. (Income and Corporation Taxes Act 1970, s. 527(1).)

3. In UK government finance, the period from 1 April one year to 31 March of the next year.

fine bill. A bill of exchange that can be discounted at the finest (meaning smallest) rate because of the reputation of the acceptor.

fine rate. 1. The smallest rate of interest – charged by banks to their most valued customers.

2. The smallest rate of discount – applied when buying and selling bills of exchange of the highest quality.

finished goods. Products of a manufacturer on which no further work has to be done and which are ready for supply to customers.

finished goods stock. Stock of a manufacturing organisation's products available for supply to purchasers, excluding items that have been invoiced to purchasers. See BS 5191 : 1975. Also called 'finished products stock' or, where the product is normally purchased as a part for incorporation in some other product, 'finished parts stock'.

finished parts stock. Another term for 'finished goods stock'.

finished products stock. Another term for 'finished goods stock'.

firm. 1. Collective noun for persons who have entered into partnership with one another (Partnership Act 1890, s. 4).

2. Any business enterprise – whether organised as a corporation, a partnership or a sole proprietorship – considered as a unit of economic activity.

firm-name. The name under which the business or profession of a partnership is carried on (Partnership Act 1890, s. 4).

first in, first out. Abbreviation: FIFO. A method of determining the purchase price or production cost of stocks and work in progress on the basis that the quantities in hand represent the latest purchases or production.

first-year allowance. Abbreviation: FYA. A capital allowance given where:

(a) a person carrying on a trade incurs capital expenditure on the provision of machinery or plant for the purposes of the trade, and

(b) in consequence of incurring the expenditure, the machinery or plant belongs to the person at some time during the chargeable period related to the incurring of the expenditure.

If the allowance is being claimed against corporation tax then 'the chargeable period related to the incurring of the expenditure' means the accounting period (for the purposes of corporation tax) in which the expenditure is incurred. If the allowance is being claimed against income tax then the phrase means the year of assessment in the basis period for which the expenditure is incurred.

The rules relating to first-year allowances are stated mainly in Part III of the Finance Act 1971.

fiscal year. 1. In Britain, another term for 'year of assessment'.

2. In America, an accounting period of one year, which, in practice, may be:

    (a) 12 consecutive calendar months; or

    (b) 52 consecutive weeks plus one day (two days in leap years); or

    (c) 52 weeks and, occasionally, 53 weeks.

Fisher's ideal index. An index number that is computed as the geometric mean of a Laspeyres index and a Paasche index. Named after an American economist, Irving Fisher (1867-1947).

fixed asset. In British company law, an asset of a company intended for use on a continuing basis in the company's activities (Companies Act 1985, Schedule 4, para. 7). This definition would probably be acceptable for most purposes. The major types of fixed asset are:

    (a) intangible assets – development costs; concessions, patents, licences, trade marks and similar rights and assets; goodwill; payments on account for intangible assets;

    (b) tangible assets – land and buildings; plant and machinery; fixtures, fittings, tools and equipment; assets in course of construction and payments on account for tangible assets;

    (c) investments – shares in and loans to other companies.

In America, the term 'fixed asset' is restricted to tangible assets and the term 'capital asset' is used in the same sense as 'fixed asset' is used in Britain.

fixed assets register. A file of information on fixed assets, stating, for example, description, original cost, estimated residual value, useful life, method of depreciation, and present net book value. Also called 'asset register'.

fixed asset statement. A statement showing the value of fixed assets held by an accounting entity at the beginning of an accounting period, acquisitions and disposals during the period, depreciation, and the value at the end of the period.

fixed assets turnover ratio. The ratio:

$$\frac{\text{turnover for a period}}{\text{average net book value of fixed assets during the period}}$$

fixed budget. A budget which does not include a procedure for altering the budgeted figures in accordance with changes in the level of activity of the budget centre. Compare 'flexible budget'. Also called 'rigid budget', 'static budget'.

fixed capital. The fixed assets of an accounting entity.

fixed charge. 1. A charge given as security for the fulfilment of a financial obligation which is a charge on a specific and identifiable item of property giving the chargee the right to utilise that particular item of property if the obligation is not fulfilled. Compare 'floating charge'. Also called 'specific charge'.

2. A recurring liability (e.g., to pay rent or interest on a long-term loan) of an enterprise which is the same amount whatever the level of activity of the enterprise within a very wide range. Often taken to include fixed overhead costs.

fixed cost. Another term for 'fixed overhead cost'.

fixed expense. Another term for 'fixed overhead cost'.

fixed overhead cost. A cost, or an aggregate of costs, such as of rent, interest on a loan, or management salaries, which would be the same whatever the level of activity, within a relatively wide range of levels of activity.

A cost is a fixed overhead cost even if it is not completely unvarying, provided the level of activity is not one of the causes of variation. 'Fixed overhead cost' is the term used in the ICMA official terminology; it is also known as 'fixed cost', 'fixed expense', 'policy cost'. See also the entry for 'period cost'.

fixed production overhead. Another term for 'fixed production overhead cost'.

fixed production overhead cost. Fixed overhead cost of an organisation attributable to its production function. Also called 'fixed production overhead'.

fixed-sum credit. Defined in the Consumer Credit Act 1974, s. 10, as any facility, other than running-account credit, under a personal credit agreement whereby the debtor is enabled to receive credit (whether in one amount or by instalments).

fixing. A meeting of dealers to establish buying and selling prices.

flexed allowance. The difference between the values of a budgeted cost, revenue or profit in a flexible budget for a particular level of activity and for a planned or standard level of activity. Also called 'flexed budget allowance'.

flexed budget. The figures for costs, revenues and profits in a flexible budget after it has been adjusted for a particular level of activity.

flexed budget allowance. Another term for 'flexed allowance'.

flexible budget. A budget in which there is a procedure for altering the budgeted figures in accordance with changes in the level of activity of the budget centre. Compare 'fixed budget'.

flexible disc. Alternative spelling of 'flexible disk'.

flexible disk. Alternative spelling: flexible disc. A flexible magnetic disk enclosed in a protective container. Also called 'diskette'. Use of the alternative term 'floppy disk' is deprecated in BS 3527 : Part 12 : 1978.

float. 1. *Noun.* A quantity of notes and coins from which a retailer can give change to customers. In America, called 'change fund'. Also called 'cash float', 'till float'.

2. *Noun.* A quantity of cash provided to the person in charge of petty cash under the imprest system.

3. *Noun.* In project network techniques, the time available for an activity or path minus the estimated or actual time required for completing it.

4. *Verb.* To arrange the flotation of securities.

floating asset. Another term for 'circulating asset'.

floating charge. A charge given as security for the fulfilment of a financial obligation in which the property charged is defined by naming a type of property and if the financial obligation is not fulfilled the chargee has the right to utilise whatever property of that type happens to be owned by the giver of the charge at the time when the charge is enforced. Compare 'fixed charge'.

Floating charges were invented in order to charge current assets, which were sometimes called 'floating assets'. Nowadays the most commonly encountered form of floating charge is a charge given by a registered company over its whole property and undertaking. In Britain, legal formalities make it practically impossible for an individual or a partnership to give a floating charge, unless engaged in agriculture.

floating-point representation. A representation of a number by two numbers called the 'fixed-point part' F and the 'exponent' E where there is understood to be a number B, called the 'floating-point base' or 'floating-point radix', such that the number represented is equal to:

$$F \times B^E$$

For example, if the floating-point base is 10 then 123 may be represented as:

1.23   2

because:

$$123 = 1.23 \times 10^2$$

floating rate. A rate of interest payable by a borrower which may be altered from time to time in accordance with a procedure settled at the time the loan was made.

floating-rate certificate of deposit. Abbreviation: FRCD. A certificate of deposit with a floating rate of interest.

float time. In production planning and control, the time available for an activity in addition to its duration (BS 5191 : 1975). Compare 'float'.

floor-to-floor time. Another term for 'cycle time'.

floppy. Short form of the term 'floppy disk'.

floppy disc. Alternative spelling of 'floppy disk'.

floppy disk. Alternative spelling: floppy disc. An alternative term for 'flexible disk', use of which is deprecated in BS 3527 : Part 12 : 1978. Also shortened to 'floppy'.

flotation. The process of arranging for shares in a company, or other securities, to be held by and traded among investors generally.

FOB. Abbreviation of 'free on board'.

FOB airport. Trade terms for the sale of goods that are to be transported by air under which the seller must arrange for transportation by air at the buyer's risk and expense to a destination airport nominated by the buyer (unless the buyer arranges the air transport) and the seller must deliver the goods to the air carrier at the airport of departure. 'FAD' is used as a symbol for these trade terms.

f.o.c. Abbreviation of 'free of charge'.

folio. In accounting, two facing pages of an open book. In account books, both pages of a folio are given the same number.

FOR. Abbreviation of 'free on rail'.

foreclosure. Legal proceedings taken by a mortgagee to foreclose (meaning, bring to an end) the mortgagor's equity of redemption. If foreclosure is ordered then the mortgagee becomes absolute owner of the mortgaged property. However, in practice, the court almost always orders sale of the property so that any profit can be returned to the mortgagor.

foreign bill. A bill of exchange that is not an inland bill (Bills of Exchange Act 1882, s. 4(1)).

foreign emoluments. For the purposes of UK income tax, emoluments of a person not domiciled in the United Kingdom from an office or employment under or with any person, body of persons or partnership resident outside, and not resident in, the United Kingdom (Income and Corporation Taxes Act 1970, s. 181(1)).

foreign exchange. 1. Currencies of foreign countries.

2. Methods of exchanging one currency for another.

foreign exchange risk. Another term for 'exchange risk'.

formation expenses. Another term for 'preliminary expenses'.

former Companies Acts. Term used in the Companies Act 1985 to mean the Joint Stock Companies Act 1856, the Joint Stock Companies Act 1857, the Joint Stock Banking Companies Act 1857, the statute 21 & 22 Vict c. 91, the Companies Act 1862, the Companies (Consolidation) Act 1908, the Companies Act 1929 and the Companies Acts 1948 to 1983 (Companies Act 1985, s. 735).

forward cover. An amount of foreign currency bought for delivery at a fixed time in the future to cover a known future obligation.

forward price. A price for delivery at some specified future time.

forward rate. An exchange rate for delivery of foreign currency at some specified future time.

FOT. Abbreviation of 'free on truck'.

founders' shares. Name often given by companies to deferred shares, with the implication that they are issued to the founders of the business of the company. It used to be common for founders' shares to be entitled to a large proportion (e.g., one-third or one-quarter) of all profits left after a dividend of a certain amount had been paid on ordinary shares.

fractile. In relation to the probability distribution of a random variable X and in relation to a number p (called the 'order' of the fractile) in the range $0 < p \leqslant 1$, the number x_p for which:

$$P(X \leqslant x_p) = p$$

Also called 'quantile'.

franchise. A right, granted to one person (called the 'franchisee') in a geographical area, to conduct a certain line of business in a particular manner, using, for example, a certain business name or trade mark, trading in certain products, or using certain procedures, equipment or processes, use of which is controlled by the person (called the 'franchisor') who grants the franchise.

franchisee. A person granted a franchise.

franchisor. A person who grants a franchise.

frank. *Verb.* To make free from liability to further charges, such as taxes or postage charges.

franked investment income. Abbreviation: FII. Defined in the Finance Act 1972, s. 88(1), as: 'income of a company resident in the United Kingdom which consists of a distribution in respect of which the company is entitled to a tax credit (and which accordingly represents income equal to the aggregate of the amount or value of the distribution and the amount of that credit)'.

If a company that has received franked investment income then distributes the money as a dividend, the company does not itself pay advance corporation tax on it (as the tax has already been paid).

franked payment. 'The sum of the amount or value of a qualifying distribution and such proportion thereof as corresponds to the rate of advance corporation tax in force for the financial year in which the distribution is made' (Finance Act 1972, s. 84(3)).

franked SORP. A Statement of Recommended Practice, on a matter affecting enterprises in a particular industry, prepared under the supervision of the Accounting Standards Committee.

fraud. Deception, either by stating what is false or by suppressing what is true, in order to induce a person to give up something of value.

fraudulent conveyance. A disposition of property made with intent to defraud creditors. By the Law of Property Act 1925, s. 172, a court may declare such a disposition void at the instance of any person prejudiced by it. The 1984 Insolvency Bill proposes the repeal of s. 172 and proposes a more general provision for avoiding transactions defrauding creditors.

fraudulent preference. Treatment of a creditor of a person more favourably than other creditors with the intention of preferring that creditor to other creditors. The treatment in question may be actual payment of a debt or giving security for payment of the debt. The word 'fraudulent' is inappropriate because no fraud, in the usual legal sense of that word, need be committed. In the 1984 Insolvency Bill the term 'preference' is used instead and the Bill proposes the repeal of all enactments containing the term 'fraudulent preference'.

fraudulent trading. In British company law, carrying on the business of a company with intent to defraud creditors of the company or creditors of any other person or for any fraudulent purpose (Companies Act 1985, s. 458).

FRCD. Abbreviation of 'floating-rate certificate of deposit'.

free alongside ship. Abbreviation: FAS. Trade terms for the sale of goods that are to be carried by sea transport under which the seller's obligations are fulfilled when the goods have been placed on the quay alongside a ship named by the buyer, or in a lighter if the ship is lying offshore.

free balance. Another term for 'order cover'.

free capital. The monetary working capital of a bank.

freehold. Commonly used term for the legal estate in land known as 'fee simple absolute in possession'.

freeholder. The owner of a fee simple absolute in possession.

free-issue system. System for making materials, consumables etc., available in which stock is held in store and is issued for use on demand without a stores requisition. See BS 5191 : 1975.

freely negotiable credit. A negotiation credit that authorises the beneficiary to choose any bank to negotiate bills drawn under the credit.

free on board. Abbreviation: FOB. Trade terms for the sale of goods that are to be transported to the buyer by sea under which the seller must place the goods on board a ship nominated by the buyer at a port of shipment nominated by the buyer.

free on rail. Abbreviation: FOR. Trade terms for the sale of goods under which the seller must deliver the goods to a railway operator for transport to a destination nominated by the buyer. If the volume of the goods is sufficient to fill a wagon or to obtain quantity rates for wagon loading, the seller must order the wagon from the railway and load it. Also called 'free on truck'.

free on truck. Abbreviation: FOT. Another term for 'free on rail'.

freight. Consideration charged for carrying goods.

freight in. Also written: freight-in. Term used in America for 'carriage inward'.

freight out. Also written: freight-out. Term used in America for 'carriage outward'.

frustration. In relation to a contract, prevention of complete performance due to a change of circumstances, beyond the control of any party to the contract, rendering performance impossible, illegal or futile.

FSCA. Designation of a Fellow of the Society of Company and Commercial Accountants.

FSIA. Designation of a Fellow of the Society of Investment Analysts.

_F_-test. A statistical test that depends on the value of a statistic that has an F-distribution. An F-test is used, for example, to test whether two normal distributions have the same variance.

FTII. Designation of a Fellow of the Institute of Taxation.

full absorption costing. Another term for 'absorption costing'.

full accounts. In relation to a British registered company, the accounts for a financial year of the company (as defined in s. 239 of the Companies Act 1985, see the entry for 'accounts for a financial year') or, if the company is a small company or a medium-sized company, the modified accounts it is permitted to deliver to the Registrar of Companies.

full capacity. Production volume, expressed in standard hours, that could be achieved if sales orders, supplies and work-force were available for all of an organisation's production facilities.

full consolidation. A method of preparing consolidated accounts for a holding company and a subsidiary that is not a wholly owned subsidiary in which all the results of the subsidiary are included in the consolidated accounts which include a statement of minority interests. Compare 'proportional consolidation'.

fully diluted earnings per share. Earnings per share of a listed company for a period calculated by dividing earnings by the number of equity shares that have been issued or which the company is contractually obliged to issue, whether or not dividend for the period is payable on them.

fully paid share. A share in a company is a fully paid share if the value of the capital contributed to the company for the share (ignoring any share premium) is equal to the nominal value of the share.

fully secret trust. Another term for 'secret trust'.

function. In mathematics, a relationship, between the items in two sets, in which each item in one set (which set is called the 'domain' of the function) is associated with exactly one item in the second set (which set is called the 'range' of the function). (Domain and range may be the same set.)

A function may be defined symbolically in which case the symbol used as variable for the items in the domain is called the 'independent variable' and the symbol used for items in the range is called the 'dependent variable'. Traditionally, x is used as the independent variable and y is used as the dependent variable. The terms 'independent variable' and 'dependent variable' are also applied to the items in, respectively, the domain and range of a function. If the domain of a function is the Cartesian product of n sets then n variables may be used to define the function, which may be described as a 'function of n independent variables'.

The domain and the range of a function are sets of numbers and it may be the case that the number y in the range associated with a particular number x in the domain may be computed by applying a sequence of mathematical operations to x. This then may be expressed as an equation stating that y is equal to the result of performing a stated sequence of operations on x. Such an equation (for example, $y = 2x + 3$) is called an 'explicit equation' of a function. An 'implicit equation' states the equality of the results of performing two sequences of operations on both x and y (for example, $5xy - 3 = 6x/y$).

An item in the domain of a function is called an 'argument' of the function, and the item in the range associated with it is called the 'value' of the function for that argument.

functional budget. A budget for a particular function within an organisation, for example, marketing, personnel or purchasing. Also called 'departmental budget'.

functional currency. In FAS 52, in relation to an accounting entity, the currency of the primary economic environment in which the entity operates. In SSAP 20, this is called 'local currency'.

function costing. Costing a service centre.

fund. 1. *Noun.* A stock or sum of money, especially one set aside for a particular purpose.

2. *Verb.* To provide money for a particular purpose.

3. *Noun.* Plural form (funds). Financial resources; finances.

4. *Noun.* Plural form (funds). Another term for 'working capital'.

5. *Noun.* Plural form written with capital F (Funds). British government stocks. (Originally, before the creation of the Consolidated Fund, the taxes or funds charged with repayment of loans; then the loans themselves.)

6. *Verb.* To provide for a financial obligation by borrowing money for a fixed period, especially for a long period.

7. *Verb.* To provide for a future financial obligation by setting aside money and lending it to earn interest; to create a sinking fund.

fundamental accounting assumptions. Assumptions that the International Accounting Standards Committee recognise as underlying the preparation of financial statements and which it is not necessary to disclose although there must be disclosure and an explanation if financial statements are not based on the assumptions. The fundamental accounting assumptions as stated in IAS 1 are:

(a) Going concern. The enterprise is normally viewed as a going concern, that is, as continuing in operation for the foreseeable future. It is assumed that the enterprise has neither the intention nor the necessity of liquidation or of curtailing materially the scale of its operations.

(b) Consistency. It is assumed that accounting policies are consistent from one period to another.

(c) Accrual. Revenues and costs are accrued, that is, recognised as they are earned or incurred (and not as money is received or paid) and recorded in the financial statements of the periods to which they relate.

SSAP 2 defines four 'fundamental accounting concepts' which are the three fundamental accounting assumptions plus the concept of 'prudence' in accounting which IAS 1 regards as a consideration which should govern the selection and application of appropriate accounting policies rather than a fundamental accounting assumption. See also the entry for 'accounting principles'.

fundamental accounting concepts. Defined in SSAP 2 as the broad basic assumptions which underlie periodic financial accounts of business enterprises. SSAP 2 identifies four concepts as being generally accepted at present. They are the 'accruals' concept, the 'consistency' concept, the 'going-concern' concept and the concept of 'prudence' in accounting.

Many writers on accounting have sought to identify simple ideas which may be regarded as underlying the subject, and have called such ideas 'concepts', 'conventions', 'principles' or 'rules'. See the entries for 'accounting principles', 'fundamental accounting assumptions'.

fundamental analysis. In investment analysis, assessment of whether to buy or sell shares in a company based on consideration of the financial position and prospects of the company; consideration of whether to buy or sell other types of investment based on assessment of their intrinsic value. Compare 'technical analysis'.

fundamental error. An error in a financial statement which is so significant that the statement cannot be said to present a true and fair view.

funds-flow statement. A statement of the way in which the net current assets of an accounting entity have changed over a period of time.

funds statement. Another term for 'statement of source and application of funds'.

fungible. *Adjective.* Consisting of indistinguishable or interchangeable items.

fusion. Another term for 'uniting of interests'.

future amount. Another term for 'terminal value'.

future amount of 1. The factor $(1 + i)^t$ used to find a terminal value when t is a positive integer. Also called 'accumulation factor'.

FYA. Abbreviation of 'first-year allowance'.

G

GAAP. Abbreviation of 'generally accepted accounting principles'.

GAAS. Abbreviation of 'generally accepted auditing standards'.

gain. For the purposes of UK capital gains tax, the excess of the proceeds of disposing of an asset over the cost of acquiring the asset (including the cost of any improvement made to the asset) computed in accordance with the Capital Gains Tax Act 1979.

game theory. Mathematical analysis of situations in which there are conflicts of interest between two or more persons. The situations that can be analysed are the ones that have very simple structures involving rules that assign to each possible action of the conflicting persons a known outcome to which each person involved can assign a value (called a 'payoff') and the analysis is concerned with choosing the action each person should take in order to maximise the payoff of that person. The simplicity of this structure is reminiscent of the rules of a game. Also called 'theory of games'.

Garner v ***Murray.*** A case in partnership law decided in the High Court and reported at [1904] 1 Ch 57, in which it was held that if a partnership loses capital and one partner is unable to contribute to making up the loss, because of insolvency, then the amounts to be contributed by the other partners are not increased.

garnishee. A person against whom a garnishee order is made.

garnishee order. An order made in garnishee proceedings.

garnishee proceedings. Legal proceedings for the attachment of a debt for the execution of a court order or judgment. The proceedings are taken against a person (called the 'garnishee') who owes money to the judgment debtor. A 'garnishee order' is made requiring the garnishee to pay the money to the judgment creditor instead of the judgment debtor.

gearing. Financing the operations of an incorporated company with money on which only a fixed rate of interest or dividend is payable in the belief that income from the operations thus financed will be greater than the fixed interest or dividends payable, the difference being for the benefit of the holders of equity shares of the company. Also called 'financial gearing'. In America, called 'financial leverage', 'leverage', 'trading on the equity'.

gearing adjustment. In the current cost accounts of an entity for an accounting period, the proportion of the depreciation adjustment, cost of sales adjustment and monetary working capital adjustment associated with items financed by net borrowing. SSAP 16, para. 50, requires it to be calculated by multiplying the sum of the depreciation, cost of sales and monetary working capital adjustments by the gearing proportion.

132

gearing proportion. In current cost accounting, in relation to an accounting period of an accounting entity, the ratio:

$$\frac{\text{average net borrowing of the entity during the period}}{\text{average net assets of the entity during the period}}$$

gearing ratio. A ratio that measures the extent of the gearing of a company. Several ratios are used for this purpose, for example, the ratio of prior-charge capital to equity capital, the ratio of prior-charge capital to the sum of prior-charge capital plus equity capital plus reserves, or the ratio of prior-charge capital to capital employed.

general acceptance. An acceptance of a bill of exchange that assents without qualification to the order of the drawer (Bills of Exchange Act 1882, s. 19(2)).

General Commissioner. An individual who is appointed to hear appeals by taxpayers against assessments. A General Commissioner is appointed to a 'division' which covers a particular geographical area. General Commissioners for divisions in England and Wales are appointed by the Lord Chancellor. General Commissioners for divisions in Scotland are appointed by the Secretary of State. General Commissioners receive only travelling allowances and subsistence allowances and are otherwise unpaid. Also called 'Commissioner for the general purposes of the income tax'.

general crossing. A crossing on a cheque or other financial document which does not specify the bank to which the money must be paid.

general gift. A gift in a will of an amount of property of a particular description – in practice, almost always money. Compare 'specific gift'.

general ledger. The section of the ledger containing the accounts that are not in the cash book, the creditors ledger and the debtors ledger. Also called 'impersonal ledger', 'nominal ledger'. If the accounting entity is a sole trader's business or the business of a partnership, the general ledger may be called the 'private ledger' because it contains accounts of transactions with a proprietor or partners, which may be kept confidential. Alternatively, the proprietorship accounts may be referred to as the 'private ledger' and the term 'general ledger' may be used for all the other accounts apart from the cash book and creditors and debtors ledgers.

generally accepted accounting principles. Abbreviation: GAAP. In America, the conventions, rules and procedures of accounting that an auditor believes should have been followed in preparing the accounts of an entity in order for those accounts to present fairly the financial position of the entity. The Council of the American Institute of Certified Public Accountants adopted, in October 1964, a resolution to the effect that accounting principles accepted in Opinions of the Accounting Principles Board must be regarded by members of the Institute as generally accepted accounting principles. Any other principle that has substantial authoritative support is also regarded as a generally accepted accounting principle.

generally accepted auditing standards. Abbreviation: GAAS. Principles that must be followed by members of the American Institute of Certified Public Accountants when conducting external audits and which have been expressed, briefly and not in detail, by the Institute. The brief statements of principle are interpreted by Statements on Auditing Standards issued by the Institute.

general meeting. A meeting that all members, or all members of a particular class, of an association may attend.

general partner. See the entry for 'limited partnership'.

general partnership. A partnership that is not a limited partnership – i.e., a partnership in which every partner has unlimited liability for the debts of the partnership.

general power. A power of appointment that the donee may exercise without restriction (and which may therefore be exercised in favour of the donee).

general price level accounting. Term used in America for 'constant purchasing power accounting'.

general rate. A rate made and levied for the whole of its rating area, at a uniform amount per pound of the rateable value of each hereditament in the area, by a district council, a London borough council, the Common Council of the City of London or the Council of the Isles of Scilly.

geometric mean. The geometric mean of n numbers (which must all be non-negative) is the (non-negative) nth root of the product of the numbers. If G is the geometric mean of the two numbers a and b then a, G, b is a geometric progression.

geometric progression. A sequence in which each term is the product of its predecessor and a constant called the 'common ratio'. For example:

1, 2, 4, 8, 16, . . .

(common ratio 2).

gift *mortis causa*. Another term for '*donatio mortis causa*'.

gift on account of death. Another term for '*donatio mortis causa*'.

gilt-edged securities. British government stocks, and marketable loans raised for public corporations, repayment of which is guaranteed by the Treasury. (The name suggests the high quality of the securities as investments in the sense that there is negligible risk of default. In the past the best quality notepaper was made with a very narrow margin of gold leaf at each edge). For the purposes of the Capital Gains Tax Act 1979, 'gilt-edged securities' means the securities specified in Part II of Schedule 2 to the Act and securities specified by order made by the Treasury by statutory instrument. For Stock Exchange purposes, 'gilt-edged securities' are the securities listed in rule 97(1) of the Rules and Regulations of the Stock Exchange. Also called 'gilts'.

gilts. Another term for 'gilt-edged securities'.

going-concern concept. Assumption made when valuing the assets and liabilities of an accounting entity that the entity will continue to carry on its activities for the foreseeable future. This assumption is one of the fundamental accounting concepts identified in SSAP 2, one of the fundamental accounting assumptions identified in IAS 1, and one of the accounting principles set out in the Companies Act 1985, Schedule 4.

golden handcuffs. Informal. An arrangement by which the buyer of a business which has been bought from partners or a sole proprietor whose expertise is essential to the success of the business will pay the purchase price only in instalments over a period of years and payment will be made only if the previous proprietors continue to work in the business.

golden handshake. Informal. A present given by an employer to an employee at the end of that employee's period of employment.

golden parachute. Informal. A provision in a director's fixed-term contract of service that a large payment must be made to the director if the contract is brought to an end prematurely.

golden share. A share in a company carrying the right that its holder must give permission for any changes to specified provisions of the memorandum and/or articles of association of the company. A typical provision which cannot be altered without the permission of the holder of a golden share is a provision setting a maximum limit on any one person's shareholding in the company.

goods. For the purposes of the Sale of Goods Act 1979, ' "goods" includes all personal chattels other than things in action and money, and in Scotland all corporeal movables except money; and in particular "goods" includes emblements, industrial growing crops, and things attached to or forming part of the land which are agreed to be severed before sale or under the contract of sale' (s. 61 of the Act). The definition is acceptable for most purposes though in some other statutes 'goods' is given a special meaning.

goods in process. Term used in America for 'work in progress'.

goods received note. Abbreviation: GRN. A document prepared when goods are delivered to an organisation, giving a description of the goods and quantity delivered. Used within the organisation for the purposes of stock control, checking suppliers' invoices and so on. A supplier's delivery note may serve as a goods received note.

goodwill. 1. In accounting, the difference between the value of a business as a whole and the aggregate of the fair values of its separable net assets (SSAP 22, para. 21).

2. In law, the probability that customers of a business enterprise will continue to deal with it despite any change of ownership, arising from the reputation of the name of the business or of its trade mark or of the premises where it is conducted or of the person who has been carrying on the business.

go public. *Verb with adjective.* To become listed on a stock exchange for the first time.

government stock. A security in the form of stock issued in connection with a marketable loan raised to finance British government expenditure.

grant in aid. In UK government finance, a grant of money made during a financial year without a condition that any part of the money not spent during that year must be surrendered to the Consolidated Fund.

grant of representation. Grant of probate or of letters of administration.

greenmail. Threat, by a person who owns shares in a company, to make a take-over bid, which would be opposed by the management of the company, with an indication that the bid will not be made if the threatener's shares are purchased from the threatener at a sufficiently high price.

GRN. Abbreviation of 'goods received note'.

gross. 1. *Adjective.* Before any deductions have been made.

2. *Verb.* To gain as an amount before any deductions have been made.

3. *Noun.* Twelve dozen.

gross book value. The historical cost of an asset of an accounting entity, or the amount substituted for historical cost in the financial statements of the entity (e.g., on revaluation), without deducting any provision for depreciation. Also called 'gross carrying amount'.

gross carrying amount. The historical cost of an asset of an accounting entity, or other amount substituted for historical cost in the financial statements of the entity, without deducting any provision for depreciation.

gross cash flow. See the entry for 'cash flow'.

gross current replacement cost. Current replacement cost from which no allowance for depreciation has been deducted.

gross dividend. The dividend paid by a company to its shareholders plus the value of the tax credit received by the shareholders, which is the same as the amount of advance corporation tax paid on the dividend. Compare 'net dividend'.

gross dividend per share. An amount calculated by adding the total dividend paid by a company to its shareholders in respect of a financial year to the value of the tax credit received by the shareholders and dividing the sum by the number of shares carrying an entitlement to receive the dividend.

gross dividend yield. The gross dividend payable per share in a listed company expressed as a percentage of the market price per share. Before the introduction of the imputation system of corporation tax, this percentage was usually described as 'dividend yield', but that might now be a misleading term since 'dividend' normally means 'net dividend'.

gross income. In the accounts of an accounting entity that is not a trading enterprise, the total revenue for a period without deducting any costs of obtaining the revenue.

gross investment in a lease. The total of the minimum lease payments and any unguaranteed residual value accruing to the lessor (SSAP 21, para. 21).

gross loss. The difference between cost of sales and turnover (or net sales) when cost of sales is the greater item. See also the entry for 'gross profit'.

gross margin. 1. Term used in America for 'gross profit'. ('Gross margin' was said to be preferable to 'gross profit' in American Institute of Certified Public Accountants, Accounting Terminology Bulletin 2, para. 10.)

2. The ratio of gross profit for a period to turnover for the period. Also called 'gross margin ratio', 'gross profit percentage'.

gross margin ratio. The ratio of gross profit for a period to turnover for that period. Also called 'gross margin', 'gross profit percentage'.

gross profit. Turnover, or net sales, over a period minus cost of sales. Gross profit measures the profit from selling things without taking into account the expenses of selling or the expense of financing and administering the enterprise. The gross profit from a business enterprise's normal activities over a period is sometimes called its 'trading profit'. Gross profit is often expressed as a percentage of sales revenue or net sales. The term is not defined in any statute or SSAP. Also called 'gross margin'. If cost of sales is greater than turnover the difference is called 'gross loss'.

gross profit percentage. Gross profit for a period expressed as a percentage of turnover (or net sales) for the period. 'Gross profit percentage' is the term used in the ICMA official terminology; also called 'gross margin', 'gross margin ratio'.

gross residual value. Value of an asset at the end of its useful life before deducting the expenses of realising that value.

gross sales. Term used in America for 'turnover'.

gross turnover. Turnover including the value added tax or other sales taxes charged on the sales and, possibly, including trade discounts. It is not usual to include either of these items in accounts as part of the value of sales.

gross up. *Verb with particle.* To calculate, from the net amount left after making a deduction (e.g., of tax), the gross amount from which the deduction was made.

gross working capital. The total value of current assets.

group. 1. A holding company and its subsidiaries.
2. A parent company and its subsidiaries.

group accounts. A set of financial statements for a group of companies. The Companies Act 1985, s. 229, requires a holding company to prepare group accounts and requires these to be consolidated accounts unless the holding company's directors are of the opinion that it will be easier for the members of the company to appreciate the accounts if they are presented in some other way. Also called 'group financial statements'.

group company. In relation to a company for which accounts are being prepared and which is a member of a group of companies, another company in that group (Companies Act 1985, Schedule 4, para. 81).

group financial statements. Another term for 'group accounts'.

group income. For the purposes of UK corporation tax, a dividend of a corporation resident in the UK received by another corporation resident in the UK (or by another person on behalf of or in trust for it) to which s. 256(1) of the Income and Corporation Taxes Act 1970 applies by virtue of an election jointly made by the paying and receiving corporations. If a dividend is group income then the corporation paying it does not have to pay advance corporation tax on it and the dividend is not franked investment income of the corporation receiving it. In order to be eligible to treat a dividend as group income, the corporation paying it must be:
    (a) a 51 per cent subsidiary of the corporation receiving it; or
    (b) a 51 per cent subsidiary of a company (as defined for the purposes of corporation tax) resident in the UK of which the corporation receiving the dividend is also a 51 per cent subsidiary; or
    (c) a trading company or a holding company owned by a consortium the members of which include the corporation receiving the dividend.
    In this context, 'trading company' means a company whose business consists wholly or mainly of the carrying on of a trade or trades, where 'trade' includes vocation and includes also an office or employment or the occupation of woodlands. The definitions of 'consortium' and 'holding company' are given in the entries for those terms in this dictionary.

group relief. An entitlement, to relief from UK corporation tax, which is transferred from one corporation resident in the UK (called a 'surrendering company') to another (called the 'claimant company'). Group relief can operate between two corporations if:

(a) one is the 75 per cent subsidiary of the other or both are 75 per cent subsidiaries of a third corporation resident in the UK; or

(b) one of the corporations is a member of a consortium and the other is a trading company which is owned by the consortium and which is not a 75 per cent subsidiary of any company; or

(c) one is a member of a consortium and the other is a trading company which is a 90 per cent subsidiary of a holding company owned by the consortium and which is not a 75 per cent subsidiary of a company other than the holding company; or

(d) one is a member of a consortium and the other is a holding company which is owned by the consortium and which is not a 75 per cent subsidiary of any company.

In this context, 'trading company' means a corporation resident in the UK whose business consists wholly or mainly of the carrying on of a trade or trades, and 'trade' includes vocation and includes also an office or employment or the occupation of woodlands. See also the entries for 'consortium' and 'holding company'. See Income and Corporation Taxes Act 1970, s. 258.

growth rate. If a dependent variable y is a function of an independent variable x then its growth rate at any particular value of x is:

$$\frac{\mathrm{d}y/\mathrm{d}x}{y}$$

where $\mathrm{d}y/\mathrm{d}x$ is the differential coefficient.

guarantee. Common American spelling: guaranty. 1. In law, a promise by one person (called the 'guarantor') to make good any failure by a second person (called the 'principal debtor') to meet financial obligations owed to a third person (called the 'principal creditor'). In the law of England and Wales, such a promise cannot be enforced by legal proceedings unless there is a written memorandum of it signed by the guarantor or an authorised agent of the guarantor (Statute of Frauds 1677, s. 4).

2. A promise that any defects discovered in goods sold will be repaired or any defective work carried out will be corrected.

guarantee company. Another term for 'company limited by guarantee'.

guarantor. A person who gives a guarantee.

guaranty. Common American spelling of 'guarantee'.

H

hacker. An individual who, as a pastime, makes unauthorised use of computers that may be accessed by the public telephone system.

half-secret trust. A gift of property in the will of the donor with a statement in the will that the recipient of the gift is to hold it in trust but without naming, in the will, a beneficiary of the trust.

hard disc. Alternative spelling of 'hard disk'.

hard disk. Alternative spelling: hard disc. In data processing, a magnetic disk that is not flexible.

hardware. Physical apparatus used for some purpose (especially, for data processing) as opposed to procedures, rules, computer programs and associated documentation concerned with the use of the apparatus.

harmonic mean. The harmonic mean of n numbers (which must all be non-zero) is the reciprocal of the arithmetic mean of the reciprocals of the numbers. If H is the harmonic mean of two numbers a and b then a, H, b is a harmonic progression.

harmonic progression. A sequence of numbers whose reciprocals form an arithmetic progression. For example:

$$1, 1/3, 1/5, 1/7 \ldots$$

the reciprocals of which form the arithmetic progression:

$$1, 3, 5, 7 \ldots$$

head lease. A lease that is not a sublease.

hedge. *Verb.* To protect oneself against financial loss, especially loss that would occur if prices or exchange rates were to vary.

hereditament. In local government finance, a unit of property subject to a rate and shown as a separate item in the local valuation list – that is, the list of rateable values for the area.

hidden reserves. Reserves of an accounting entity that are not apparent from its published balance sheet because of the way in which assets and liabilities are stated, usually because there is insufficient analysis of total figures for items in the balance sheet. Also called 'secret reserves' although that term is sometimes used only where assets have been deliberately understated or liabilities overstated.

high-level language. A programming language that does not reflect the structure of a particular computer or class of computers and is intended instead to reflect the requirements of programmers.

high street bank. A bank with branches in the shopping areas of many towns.

hire. 1. *Noun.* An arrangement between two persons, called the 'owner' and the 'hirer', by which the hirer is granted the right to exclusive possession and use of specified goods which are the property of the owner. The owner retains a good title to the thing hired, and the right to use and possession of the thing reverts to the owner when the period of hire ends. Payment to be made by the hirer as consideration for the right to use the goods is called the 'rent' or 'rental' or 'hire charge'. Compare 'lease'. In Scotland the term 'letter' is used rather than 'owner'.

    2. *Verb.* To be the hirer of a thing.

    3. *Verb.* To employ someone.

hire charge. The charge made for the hire of goods.

hire-purchase. An arrangement under which goods are hired and the hirer has the option to purchase the goods, usually for a nominal sum, after a specified amount has been paid in hire charges.

hire-purchase agreement. For the purposes of UK law, defined by the Consumer Credit Act 1974, s. 189(1) as: 'an agreement, other than a conditional sale agreement, under which:

    '(a) goods are bailed or (in Scotland) hired in return for periodical payments by the person to whom they are bailed or hired; and

    '(b) the property in the goods will pass to that person if the terms of the agreement are complied with and one or more of the following occurs:

        '(i) the exercise of an option to purchase by that person;

        '(ii) the doing of any other specified act by any party to the agreement;

        '(iii) the happening of any other specified event'.

hirer. The person to whom goods are hired in hiring or hire-purchase.

histogram. A diagram that represents the frequency of occurrence of values within adjacent classes of values of a random variable. Classes are represented by adjacent intervals on a straight line. Each of these intervals is used as the base of a rectangle and the area of the rectangle is proportional to the frequency of occurrence of values within the class represented by the interval.

historic. *Adjective.* Famous in history. Often wrongly used when the word 'historical' would be more appropriate.

historical cost. The cost of acquiring or producing an asset – sometimes, after deducting a provision for depreciation.

historical cost accounting. The preparation of financial statements on the basis that assets are valued at historical cost, and that depreciation is concerned with allocating the historical cost of each asset over the period of its useful life.

historical cost accounting rules. The rules set out in section B of Part II of Schedule 4 to the Companies Act 1985, which are rules for determining the amounts at which assets are to be shown in financial statements.

historical cost accounts. Financial statements in which the assets are valued at their historical costs, and depreciation is concerned with allocating the historical cost of each asset over the period of its useful life.

historical cost convention. The rule that the cost of acquiring or producing an asset is the amount to be shown as the value of that asset in accounts.

holder. The person who is in possession of a negotiable instrument and who, if the instrument has been made payable to a named payee or endorsee, is that named payee or endorsee.

holder in due course. Defined in the Bills of Exchange Act 1882, s. 29(1), as: 'a holder who has taken a bill, complete and regular on the face of it, under the following conditions; namely:

'(a) that he became the holder of it before it was overdue, and without notice that it had been previously dishonoured, if such was the fact;

'(b) that he took the bill in good faith and for value, and that at the time the bill was negotiated to him he had no notice of any defect in the title of the person who negotiated it'.

holding company. 1. In British company law, in relation to a corporation S, a corporation H that:

(a) is a member of S and:

(i) holds more than half of the equity share capital of S; or

(ii) controls the composition of the board of directors of S; or

(b) is a holding company of a company that is a holding company of S.

S is called a 'subsidiary' of its holding company. In determining whether a corporation is a holding company of another, membership and shareholdings in the name of a nominee or subsidiary of a corporation are to be regarded as the membership and shareholdings of the corporation itself. However, if one corporation holds another's equity shares only as a trustee or as security for a loan given in the ordinary course of business then they will not count in determining whether or not it has a majority equity shareholding. Corporation H is deemed to control the composition of the board of directors of corporation S if all or a majority of the directors of S may only be appointed by, or with the approval of, H, including cases in which H itself or a subsidiary of H is a director of S and in which a director of H is ex officio a director of S. A corporation sole is never to be regarded as a subsidiary or as a holding company. See Companies Act 1985, s. 736.

2. For the purposes of group relief in UK corporation tax, a company the business of which consists wholly or mainly in the holding of shares or securities of companies which are its 90 per cent subsidiaries, and which are trading companies, where 'trading company' means a company whose business consists wholly or mainly of the carrying on of a trade or trades (Income and Corporation Taxes Act 1970, s. 258(5)). 'Company' means a body corporate resident in the UK (s. 258(7) of the Act).

3. In America, a corporation which has other corporations as subsidiaries and which has no substantial business activities other than managing those subsidiaries.

holding gain. An increase, over a period, in the price for which an asset could be sold due to an increase in prices generally.

holding loss. A decrease, over a period, in the price for which an asset could be sold due to a decrease in prices generally.

holograph will. A will in the testator's own handwriting.

homoscedastic. *Adjective.* Of a dependent variable, having the same variance for all values of the independent variable.

hotchpot. In the law of succession, a reckoning of the estate of a deceased individual including amounts advanced by the individual before death.

human asset accounting. Another term for 'human resource accounting'.

human resource accounting. Measurement, in monetary terms, of the value to an accounting entity of its employees. Also called 'human asset accounting'.

hyperinflation. Inflation at a very high rate. Sometimes the term is used to refer only to inflation at an extreme rate, e.g., over one million per cent a year as in Hungary in 1945/46. Sometimes the term is used to mean inflation at a rate higher than would be tolerated in North America or Western Europe, e.g., one hundred per cent a year or more.

hypothecation. Creation of a charge on goods, which is not a legal mortgage of the goods, without giving the chargee possession of the goods.

I

IA. 1. Abbreviation of 'initial allowance'.

2. Abbreviation of 'intermediate area'.

IAS. Abbreviation of 'International Accounting Standard'.

IASC. Abbreviation of 'International Accounting Standards Committee'.

ICAEW. Abbreviation of 'Institute of Chartered Accountants in England and Wales'.

ICAI. Abbreviation of 'Institute of Chartered Accountants in Ireland'.

ICAS. Abbreviation of 'Institute of Chartered Accountants of Scotland'.

ICM. Abbreviation of 'Institute of Credit Management'.

ICMA. Abbreviation of 'Institute of Cost and Management Accountants'.

iconic model. A model that looks like the system it represents.

ICTA 1970. Abbreviation of 'Income and Corporation Taxes Act 1970'.

ideal standard. A standard that can be obtained under the most favourable conditions. In setting an ideal standard, no provision is made for, e.g., shrinkage, spoilage or machine breakdowns.

idle capacity ratio. The ratio:

$$\frac{\text{practical capacity less budgeted capacity}}{\text{practical capacity}}$$

This is usually expressed as a percentage.

idle time. Time for which a machine or device or production facility is available for production, but is not used because, for example, there is a shortage of materials.

IFAC. Abbreviation of 'International Federation of Accountants'.

immaterial. *Adjective*. Not material.

immovable. A thing which is the subject of property interests and which is land or anything (such as a building) regarded as part of land.

impact day. The first day on which the size and terms of an issue of securities may be announced in the UK if the issue is subject to control under the Control of Borrowing Order 1958 (SI 1958 No. 1208).

impersonal account. A ledger account that is not a personal account. Impersonal accounts are usually classified as real accounts or nominal accounts.

impersonal ledger. Another term for 'nominal ledger'.

implied trust. A trust that arises in law though never expressly created by a settlor. Compare 'express trust'. Implied trusts are usually classified into presumed resulting trusts, automatic resulting trusts and constructive trusts. Sometimes the term 'implied trust' is used to cover only presumed resulting trusts or only presumed and automatic resulting trusts but not constructive trusts.

impressed stamp. A mark made on a document by pressing it between two dies, in particular, as evidence that a tax has been paid.

imprest system. A system for supplying and controlling petty cash, in which the person responsible for petty cash is given an initial stock of cash (called a 'float') sufficient for a period of time: for each disbursement a petty cash voucher must be written out; at the end of the period a fresh amount of cash is supplied equal in value to the vouchers for the period, so that the stock of petty cash should be restored to its initial level. The same principle may be used for controlling stocks of supplies and materials. Originally an 'imprest' was a government official's stock of cash for spending on official business.

imputation system. A system for taxing the profits of companies in which profits are taxed at the same rate whether or not they are distributed to members, tax is payable when a distribution is made and the recipient of the distribution is credited with having paid income tax on the payment. In the United Kingdom, corporation tax has been on an imputation system since 1973, and in the Republic of Ireland the imputation system has been applied to corporation tax since 1976.

in arrears. *Preposition phrase.* Late. Rent for a period of use of land or goods is payable 'in arrears' if it is payable at the end of the period – in contrast to rent payable 'in advance', which is payable at the beginning of the period. A person liable to make regular payments is 'in arrears' if any payment is overdue.

inchoate. *Adjective.* Of a document, incomplete, requiring further words to be effective.

income. An amount of money, or other valuable benefits, received or expected to be received by an accounting entity, either from its usual activities or from other sources, apart from contributions of capital to the entity, loans made to the entity, and capital receipts. In America, it is usual to use the term 'income' for a net amount after deduction of some or all of the expenses of obtaining the income, but this restriction is not so commonly observed in Britain. The distinction between capital receipts and income is of great importance in taxation since the two kinds of receipts are subject to different tax rules. For a business entity the main mark of distinction is that a capital receipt is a receipt of money for the sale of a fixed asset rather than a current asset. In other contexts, an analogy is sometimes drawn with a tree and its fruit: capital is represented by the tree and income by the fruit so that sale of an income-producing asset involves a capital receipt whereas the produce of an asset is income.

Income and Corporation Taxes Act 1970. Abbreviation: ICTA 1970. A UK statute that consolidated the law relating to income tax and corporation tax but which has since been heavily amended.

income and expenditure account. The equivalent in an accounting entity that is not a business enterprise of a profit and loss account. An income and expenditure account shows how the excess of expenditure over income or surplus of income over expenditure is computed starting with income. In the Companies Act 1985, unless the contrary intention appears, any reference to a profit and loss account shall be taken in the case of a company not trading for profit as referring to its income and expenditure account (s. 742(1)(d) of the Act). Also called 'revenue account'. In America, called 'income statement'.

income statement. A term used in America for 'profit and loss account' and for 'income and expenditure account'.

income tax. A tax on the income received by a person. In the UK, only individuals are liable to pay income tax; an incorporated company or unincorporated association is liable to pay a separate tax on its income called corporation tax.

UK income tax is charged by Parliament each year, for one year at a time, by passing a Finance Act. The rules about how income is to be calculated for the purposes of taxing it and the law on the administration of income tax are contained in the Income and Corporation Taxes Act 1970 and the Taxes Management Act 1970 as amended.

UK income tax is based on an individual's statutory income for each year of assessment. Any individual liable to income tax must inform the Board of Inland Revenue of that fact; inspectors appointed by the Board may require an individual to complete a tax return. An individual's personal reliefs are deducted from the individual's statutory income. Income tax is charged on the remainder which is divided into bands or 'slices' that are taxed at progressively increasing rates.

Income Tax Acts. When used in any Act of Parliament or Northern Ireland legislation, defined in the Interpretation Act 1978, Schedule 1, to mean 'all enactments relating to income tax, including any provisions of the Corporation Tax Acts which relate to income tax'.

income tax month. In the UK, a period beginning on the sixth day of any calendar month and ending on the fifth day of the following month.

in common. *Preposition phrase.* Used to describe ownership or holding of land by two or more persons concurrently where there is agreement between the co-owners about the proportion of the property that each owns and where the share that each owns may be disposed of separately and, in particular, if a co-owner is an individual, will form part of the estate of the co-owner after death because the interest in the property does not end with death as in joint ownership.

incomplete records. Accounting records for an entity without a complete double-entry ledger. It may be that all the transactions of the entity have been recorded, but only in books of prime entry, or that some transactions were never recorded at all or that some records have been lost. In practice, a ledger is not maintained for many accounting entities with only a small number of transactions, but it is easy to prepare final accounts periodically if all transactions have in fact been recorded. If some records are missing, it may be possible to compute missing amounts as balancing figures.

incorporate. 1. *Verb.* To provide an association with the legal status of a corporation.

2. *Verb.* To make one object or substance a part of another – e.g., as part of a mixture, or as one of a number of components or as a material that is changed in form.

incorporated accounting technician. A Licentiate of the Institute of Administrative Accountants.

incorporated administrative accountant. An Associate or Fellow of the Institute of Administrative Accountants.

incorporated company and commercial accountant. A member of the Society of Company and Commercial Accountants working otherwise than in public practice.

Incoterms. A set of rules for the interpretation of the trade terms that are commonly used in international trade. The rules are drawn up by, and published by, the International Chamber of Commerce and are almost always adopted in international trade.

incremental. *Adjective.* Relating to the difference between two alternative courses of action. For example, 'incremental cost' is the difference between the costs of two alternative courses of action. The adjective 'differential' has the same meaning.

incumbrance. Alternative spelling of 'encumbrance'.

indemnifier. A person who gives an indemnity.

indemnify. *Verb.* To give an indemnity.

indemnity. A promise to a person of reimbursement for losses incurred in defined circumstances, in particular, a promise to pay for goods or services supplied to, or to repay loans made to, a specified third party.

independent. *Adjective.* In probability theory, one random variable is said to be independent of a second random variable if the distribution function of the first random variable is the same for all possible values of the second random variable. If two random variables are independent then their probability distributions are also said to be independent.

independent variable. A variable that is one of two or more related variables and is not the dependent variable.

index. 1. *Noun.* Another term for 'exponent'.

2. *Noun.* Another term for 'index number'.

3. *Verb.* To arrange for a monetary amount to be altered from time to time as an index number (usually a cost-of-living index) alters. The verb 'index-link' has the same meaning.

indexation. The practice, or an instance, of indexing.

indexation allowance. A sum that may be deducted from the amount of a capital gain to reflect the changing value of money. The rules for calculating the allowance are contained mainly in the Finance Act 1982, ss. 86 and 87.

index-link. *Verb.* To arrange for a monetary amount to be altered from time to time as an index number (usually a cost-of-living index) alters. The verb 'index' has the same meaning.

index number. A number calculated so as to provide a comparison between one quantity and a standard or base quantity, often as one of several comparisons of quantities with the same base quantity. The simplest form of index number is the quantity to be compared expressed as a percentage of the base quantity and is called a 'relative'. More complicated forms of index numbers are used to compare weighted averages – see the entries for 'Fisher's ideal index', 'Laspeyres index', 'Paasche index'. Also called 'index'.

indirect cost. A cost, that has been identified in an organisation which has more than one product, but which cannot be directly attributed to one of those products – or an aggregate of such costs. It is common to use the term to refer only to production costs. Compare 'direct cost'. See also the entry for 'production overhead cost'. In America, also called 'indirect expense'.

indirect cost centre. American spelling: indirect cost center. Another term for 'service cost centre'.

indirect expense. 1. In Britain, an indirect cost which is a cost of something other than materials, supplies or work performed by people – or an aggregate of such costs. For example, a cost of insurance.

2. In America, another term for 'indirect cost'.

indirect labor. American spelling of 'indirect labour'.

indirect labor cost. American spelling of 'indirect labour cost'.

indirect labour. American spelling: indirect labor. Another term for 'indirect labour cost'.

indirect labour cost. American spelling: indirect labor cost. A cost of work performed by people which is an indirect cost – or an aggregate of such costs. Also called 'indirect labour', 'indirect wages'.

indirect material. 1. Material, expenditure on which is an indirect cost.

2. Another term for 'indirect material cost'.

indirect material cost. A cost of materials or supplies used which is an indirect cost – or an aggregate of such costs. An alternative form is 'indirect materials cost' (which is the form used in the ICMA official terminology). Also called 'indirect material'.

indirect materials cost. An alternative form of the term 'indirect material cost'.

indirect stock. Stock of materials that are not incorporated into finished products (e.g., stationery, tools, cleansing materials). Stock of materials that are incorporated into the finished product but in indefinite quantities (e.g., paint) is sometimes regarded as indirect stock. See BS 5191 : 1975. Also called 'non-productive stock'. See also the entry for 'consumables'.

indirect wages. Another term for 'indirect labour cost'.

individual accounts. Financial statements of a company that are not group accounts.

indorse. *Verb.* Alternative spelling of 'endorse'.

indorsee. Alternative spelling of 'endorsee'.

indorsement. Alternative spelling of 'endorsement'.

indorsement in blank. Alternative spelling of 'endorsement in blank'.

indorser. Alternative spelling of 'endorser'.

infix notation. A notation for dyadic operations in which the symbol for the operation is written between the operands. For example, the addition of the numbers 5 and 3 is written 5 + 3.

inflation. A continuing increase in the general level of prices in an economy.

inflation accounting. Preparation of financial statements for an accounting entity which reflect the effects of changing prices on the financial position of the entity.

information retrieval. 1. Recovery of information on a subject from stored data.

2. Methods and procedures for recovering information from stored data.

147

information technology. Abbreviation: IT. Technology relating to the transmission and storage of information.

information theory. The mathematical theory of the transmission of information.

inheritance according to the stocks. Another term for 'inheritance *per stirpes*'.

inheritance *per stirpes*. A system of inheritance by descendants of an individual in which the amount to be inherited is divided equally among the individuals in the first generation of descendants but if a member of that first generation has already died then that member's share is divided equally between that member's children, and so on. Also called 'inheritance according to the stocks'.

initial allowance. Abbreviation: IA. A capital allowance in respect of:

(a) Capital expenditure on the construction of a building or structure which is to be an industrial building or structure occupied for the purposes of a trade carried on by the person incurring the expenditure or, under certain conditions, a lessee.

(b) Qualifying expenditure on the construction of works in connection with the working of a mine, oil well or other source of mineral deposits of a wasting nature.

(c) Capital expenditure on dredging for certain purposes.

(d) Capital expenditure on the construction of farmhouses, farm or forestry buildings, cottages, fences or other works incurred for the purposes of husbandry or forestry on agricultural or forestry land.

See Capital Allowances Act 1968, ss. 1, 56, 67 and 68.

injunction. An order of a court by which a person is required to refrain from doing a particular act or thing (called a 'restrictive injunction') or is required to do a particular act or thing (called a 'mandatory injunction').

inland bill. A bill of exchange that is both drawn and payable within the area consisting of the United Kingdom of Great Britain and Northern Ireland, the Isle of Man, and the Channel Islands, or is drawn within that area upon some person resident in that area (Bills of Exchange Act 1882, s. 4).

innominate term. In the law of contract, an obligation, which one party has under a contract, that, if it is not performed, may be treated as either a conditon or a warranty depending on the circumstances or effect of the failure to perform the obligation. The other party may treat the obligation as a condition (i.e., may treat the contract as terminated) only if the party who has failed to perform the obligation has thereby renounced all obligations under the contract or rendered them impossible to perform or if the consequences of the failure are so serious as to deprive the innocent party of substantially the whole benefit of the contract. Also called 'intermediate term'.

input device. Another term for 'input unit'.

input-output. Abbreviation: I/O. *Adjective.* In data processing, concerned with, consisting of, or relating to, both entry of data into, and delivery of data from, a data processing system or a part of a data processing system.

input-output channel. Part of a computer that handles the transfer of data between the processing unit and peripheral equipment. Also called 'channel'.

input process. In data processing, a process that consists of the reception of data into a data processing system or a part of a data processing system.

input tax. The value added tax on the supply to a taxable person of any goods or services, and the value added tax paid or payable by that person on the importation of any goods, provided those goods or services are used or are to be used for the purposes of a business carried on or to be carried on by that person. If goods or services supplied to a taxable person, or goods imported by that person, are used or are to be used partly for the purposes of a business carried on or to be carried on by that person and partly for other purposes, tax on supplies and importations is apportioned so that only so much as is referable to the business purposes is counted as input tax of the person (Value Added Tax Act 1983, s. 14).

input unit. In a data processing system, a device by which data can be entered into the system. Also called 'input device'.

insider deal. A transaction in securities of a company, carried out by someone (an 'insider') who has acquired information about the company, by virtue of being connected with the company (e.g., by being an auditor, a director or a senior employee), which information is not generally available and will affect the price of the securities when it is generally known.

insider dealing. Buying or selling company securities so as to take advantage of information acquired about the company by an insider (see the entry for 'insider deal'). In certain circumstances, insider dealing is a criminal offence under the Company Securities (Insider Dealing) Act 1985.

insolvency. Inability of a person to pay debts as they fall due. This is sometimes called 'practical insolvency' when the term 'absolute insolvency' is used to mean that the liabilities of a person are greater than the assets of the person.

insolvency practitioner. An individual who administers the estates of insolvent persons or who acts as an administrative receiver of a company. The 1984 Insolvency Bill proposes that it should be an offence for an individual to act as an insolvency practitioner in Great Britain unless authorised to do so by the Secretary of State.

Insolvency Practitioners Association. A professional association whose members work in insolvency administration as liquidators, receivers and trustees.

Membership of the association is by examination, and candidates must be continuously engaged full time in insolvency work.

Membership of the association is designated by the letters MIPA.

Address: 29 Lincoln's Inn Fields, London WC2A 3EE. Telephone: 01-405 3911.

insolvent. *Adjective.* Unable to pay debts as they fall due. See the entry for 'insolvency'.

inspector of taxes. An individual appointed by the Board of Inland Revenue to supervise the assessment (but not collection) of income tax and corporation tax.

Institute of Accounting Technicians in Ireland. Professional institute for accounting technicians. Membership, designated MIATI, is by examination; candidates for membership are required to have completed three years of relevant practical experience.

Address: Chartered Accountants House, 87/89 Pembroke Road, Dublin 4, Republic of Ireland. Telephone: Dublin 680400. Telex: 30567. Also at: 11 Donegall Square South, Belfast BT1 5JE. Telephone: Belfast 221600.

Institute of Administrative Accountants. A professional institute for people working in commerce, industry and the public sector as employees dealing with accounting-based office administration and management. The basic qualification for membership is the passing of a four-part examination. There are two grades of membership: Associates, designated AAAI, and Fellows, designated FAAI. Associates and Fellows are styled 'incorporated administrative accountants'. Associates must have a minimum of three years' business experience in an accounting environment; Fellows must have five years' accounting experience in a senior capacity. There is also a grade of Licentiate, designated LAAI, styled 'incorporated accounting technician', for which the basic qualification is the passing of parts 1 and 2 of the examination and a minimum of two years' appropriate business experience.

Address: Burford House, 44 London Road, Sevenoaks, Kent TN13 1AS. Telephone: Sevenoaks 458080.

Institute of Certified Public Accountants in Ireland. A professional institute of accountants working in private practice as well as in industry, commerce and government. Members are styled 'certified public accountant'. There are two grades of membership: Associate, designated CPA, and Fellow, designated FCPA. Membership may be achieved only by examination and the acquisition of relevant practical experience.

Address: 22 Upper Fitzwilliam Street, Dublin 2, Republic of Ireland. Telephone: Dublin 767353.

Institute of Chartered Accountants in England and Wales. Abbreviation: ICAEW. Professional institute for accountants with members engaged in a wide range of activities in private practice, industry, commerce and government service.

Members of the Institute are styled 'chartered accountants'. There are two grades of membership: Associate, designated ACA, and Fellow, designated FCA. In order to qualify for membership a student must have two A levels or a university degree and must enter a training contract with a practising firm authorised to train students. A student must pass the professional examinations of the Institute before admission to membership. Newly admitted members are Associates, but after five years of membership, and meeting the Institute's continuing professional education requirements a member can become a Fellow.

Address: PO Box 433, Chartered Accountants' Hall, Moorgate Place, London EC2P 2BJ. Telephone: 01-628 7060. Telex: 884443. There is also an office at: Gloucester House, 399 Silbury Boulevard, Witan Gate East, Central Milton Keynes MK9 2HL. Telephone: Milton Keynes 668833. Telex: 827502.

Institute of Chartered Accountants in Ireland. Abbreviation: ICAI. A professional institute for accountants engaged in public practice and employed in industry and commerce. There are two grades of membership: Associate, designated ACA, and Fellow, designated FCA. A candidate for membership is required to have completed a specified period of training under a formal training contract and to have passed an examination. A member is admitted as an Associate and, at a later date, awarded fellowship on the basis of experience.

Address: Chartered Accountants House, 87/89 Pembroke Road, Dublin 4, Republic of Ireland. Telephone: Dublin 680400. Telex: 30567. Also at: 11 Donegall Square South, Belfast BT1 5JE.

Institute of Chartered Accountants of Scotland. Abbreviation: ICAS. Professional institute for accountants, whose members work in industry and commerce, in private practice, in local and central government and in education.

Members of the Institute are styled 'chartered accountants'. There is only one grade of membership, designated CA. To qualify for admission to membership an applicant must have passed the Institute's final examination and have completed a training contract with members of the Institute engaged in public practice in the UK.

Address: 27 Queen Street, Edinburgh EH2 1LA. Telephone: 031-225 5673. Telex: 727530.

Institute of Cost and Management Accountants. Abbreviation: ICMA. Professional institute for cost and management accountants. Membership can be gained only by examination and practical experience. There are two grades of member: Associate, designated ACMA, and Fellow, designated FCMA. An Associate must have completed the Institute's examinations and have had not less than three years' practical experience of management accountancy and related work. A Fellow must have had not less than three years' practical experience at more senior level than that required for associateship.

Address: 63 Portland Place, London W1N 4AB. Telephone: 01-637 2311. Telex: 25816.

Institute of Credit Management. Abbreviation: ICM. A professional body for individuals working in credit management. There are two professional grades of membership: Associate, designated MICM or, when obtained by examination, MICM (Grad), and Fellow, designated FICM. Entry to the Associate grade is open to those who satisfy the council of the Institute either by examination or by thesis or by direct entry in exceptional cases. A Fellow must be at least 30 years old and must have been an Associate for not less then seven years, must have been in an executive position and had the direction and control of credit staff for not less than seven years, and must satisfy the council of the Institute of his or her appropriate experience and standing. There are also Affiliates of the Institute who have experience in credit management but are not professionally qualified.

Address: Easton House, Easton on the Hill, Stamford, Lincolnshire PE9 3NH. Telephone: Stamford 56777.

Institute of Taxation. A professional institute for people whose work involves dealing with taxation. Most members of the Institute are partners or employees of accountancy practices. Others are solicitors or their employees, or barristers, bank employees, mainly in taxation departments, staff in the Inland Revenue, and employees in insurance, industry and commerce in general.

The two grades of membership are: Associate, designated ATII, and Fellow, designated FTII.

To become an Associate it is necessary to pass the intermediate stage (unless exempted) and the final stage of the Institute's associateship examination.

To become a Fellow it is necessary to submit an acceptable thesis on a topic concerning UK taxation, which has been approved in advance by the Institute's Education Committee and to satisfy the Council of specialised practical experience in taxation during a minimum period of three years immediately preceding the date of the application. Candidates for fellowship who are not already members of the Institute are required to demonstrate practical experience of a reasonably broad nature as well as that directly related to the topic of the thesis.

Address: 3 Grosvenor Crescent, London SW1X 7EL. Telephone: 01-235 8847.

instrument. A written document, especially a formal document intended to effect a legal or financial transaction.

insurance company. For the purposes of the Insurance Companies Act 1982, a person or body of persons (whether incorporated or not) carrying on insurance business (s. 96(1) of the Act).

intangible. Short form of the term 'intangible asset'.

intangible asset. An asset that is intangible property. The short form 'intangible' is also used.

intangible property. Property in a thing in action. The benefit conferred by such property is the right to be paid money or to receive some other benefit enforceable by legal action rather than the right to possession of a physical, tangible object.

integer. A whole number. One of the numbers used for counting: $1, 2, 3, \ldots$, or 0, or one of the corresponding negative numbers: $-1, -2, -3, \ldots$.

integer programming. Mathematical programming in which the decision variables have only integer values so that a solution to the programming problem must be a set of integers.

integrated accounts. A set of accounting records which provides financial and cost accounts using a common input of data for all accounting purposes.

integration. The process of finding a function from its derivative.

interactive mode. Another term for 'conversational mode'.

intercompany. *Adjective.* Relating to transactions between companies in a group.

interest. 1. An entitlement to use, possess or derive some benefit from an item of property. Interests are usually classified as 'legal' and 'equitable'. An equitable interest in an item of property automatically comes to an end if the item is sold to a person who does not have notice that the equitable interest exists, whereas a legal interest does not come to an end in such circumstances.

2. Payment made for borrowing another person's money or for delaying payment to another person of an obligation owed to that person. The amount of interest to be paid is calculated with reference to the amount of money borrowed or owed, called the 'principal', the time for which it is

borrowed or owed and a number called the 'rate of interest'. Two methods of calculating interest are in common use. One produces an amount called 'simple interest', the other an amount called 'compound interest'. In law, if interest is payable it is presumed to be simple interest unless there is a specific agreement or established custom that compound interest is payable (*Fergusson* v *Fyffe* (1841) 8 Cl & F 121). It is an established custom that banks charge compound interest (*Commissioners of Inland Revenue* v *Holder* [1931] 2 KB 81). If P is the principal, t the number of units of time for which interest is being charged and i the rate of interest per unit of time, then the formula for calculating simple interest is:

Pti

and the formula for calculating compound interest (provided t is a positive integer) is:

$P(1 + i)^t - P$

If compound interest is to be charged for a period less than one unit of time then it is calculated using the formula for simple interest. If compound interest is to be charged for a whole number of time units plus a fraction of a time unit then the compound interest for the whole number of time units is calculated, added to the principal and simple interest is charged on the sum for the fraction of a time unit.

interest cover. The ratio of earnings before interest and tax of an accounting entity for an accounting period to the interest payable by the entity for the period. Also called 'times interest covered'.

interest in possession. For the purposes of capital transfer tax, the interest of a person in settled property is an interest in possession if the person has the immediate entitlement (subject to any prior claim by the trustees for expenses or other outgoings properly payable out of income) to any income produced by that property as the income arises. A discretion or power, in whatever form, which can be exercised after income arises so as to withhold it from a beneficiary prevents that beneficiary having an interest in possession. See Inland Revenue press notice dated 12 February 1976 and *Pearson* v *Commissioners of Inland Revenue* [1981] AC 753.

interest number. In calculating simple interest, the product of principal and number of days for which interest is to be charged. The amount of interest may be calculated from the interest number by multiplying it by the rate of interest per day.

interest rate implicit in a lease. The discount rate that at the inception of a lease, when applied to the amounts which the lessor expects to receive and retain, produces an amount (the present value) equal to the fair value of the leased asset. The 'inception of the lease' is the date the asset is brought into use or the date from which rentals first accrue, whichever is earlier. The 'amounts which the lessor expects to receive and retain' comprise (a) the minimum lease payments to the lessor, plus (b) any unguaranteed residual value, less (c) any part of (a) and (b) for which the lessor will be accountable to the lessee. If the interest rate implicit in a lease is not determinable in this way, it should be estimated by reference to the rate which a lessee would be expected to pay on a similar lease. See SSAP 21, para. 24.

interest receivable account. An account recording interest received and accrued.

interest yield. In relation to a security on which a fixed rate of interest is paid each year, the amount of interest payable for a year on the security, expressed as a percentage of the purchase price of the security.

interim accounts. In relation to an accounting entity for which financial statements are normally prepared showing the financial position on the same date in each year, financial statements showing the position on another date prepared in addition to the regular annual statements.

interim dividend. A dividend paid by a company to its members during a financial year and regarded as a part-payment of the dividend for that year.

interim injunction. Another term for 'interlocutory injunction'.

interim receiver. Under a procedure proposed in the 1984 Insolvency Bill, an individual appointed, by a court to which a bankruptcy petition has been presented, to take possession of the debtor's property pending the court's decision whether to grant or dismiss the petition.

interleave. *Verb.* To arrange parts of one sequence of things or events (such as the instructions in a computer program) so that they alternate with parts of one or more other sequences of the same nature while retaining the identity of each sequence.

interlocking accounts. A system of accounts providing both financial and cost information in which the cost accounts are distinct from the financial accounts, the two sets of accounts being kept continuously in agreement by the use of control accounts or made readily reconcilable by other means.

interlocutory injunction. An injunction granted while legal proceedings are in progress and having effect only until final judgment is given in the case. Also called 'interim injunction'.

intermediate area. Abbreviation: IA. An area of the UK designated by the Secretary of State under the Industrial Development Act 1982, s. 1, in which some government assistance is given to industry in order to reduce unemployment but regional development grants are not available.

intermediate stock. A manufacturing organisation's completed parts, subassemblies and assemblies held available in stores and regarded as part of its work in progress (BS 5191 : 1975).

intermediate term. Another term for 'innominate term'.

internal audit. The function, carried out within an organisation, of examining, evaluating and reporting on accounting and other controls on the operations of the organisation.

internal control system. Defined in the explanatory foreword to the British and Irish Auditing Standards and Auditing Guidelines as 'the whole system of controls, financial and otherwise, established by the management in order to carry on the business of the enterprise in an orderly and efficient manner, ensure adherence to management policies, safeguard the assets and secure as far as possible the completeness and accuracy of the records'. In this definition, 'enterprise' means any body corporate or other organisation on the financial statements of which an auditor is reporting.

internally financed scheme. A pension scheme in which the benefits are provided directly by the employer (ED 32, para. 34).

internal rate of return. Abbreviation: IRR. The discount rate at which the net present value of something is zero.

internal reconstruction. Term sometimes used for 'reduction of capital'.

internal store. In a computer, a store that is accessible to the computer without using input-output channels.

international accountant. A member of the Association of International Accountants.

International Accounting Standard. Abbreviation: IAS. A statement of an accounting standard relating to some matter issued by the International Accounting Standards Committee.

International Accounting Standards Committee. Abbreviation: IASC. A committee formed by accountancy bodies in 45 countries with the objectives of:

(a) formulating and publishing, in the public interest, accounting standards to be observed in the presentation of financial statements, and promoting the world-wide acceptance and observance of those standards; and

(b) working generally for the improvement and harmonisation of regulations, accounting standards and procedures relating to the presentation of financial statements.

international bond. A bearer bond issued in connection with a marketable loan which was, or is to be, raised from lenders most of whom are not resident in the same country as the borrower.

International Federation of Accountants. Abbreviation: IFAC. A federation of 80 accountancy bodies from 59 countries.

interpolation. Where values of a dependent variable are known for values of the independent variable between certain limits, estimation of the value of the dependent variable for a value of the independent variable within those limits. Compare 'extrapolation'.

interquartile range. The difference between the first and third quartiles.

inter vivos. Preposition phrase. Between living people. Used to describe a gift made by an individual which becomes effective as a gift (i.e., it cannot be revoked by the donor) during the donor's lifetime, as opposed to a gift which only becomes effective on the death of the donor and can be revoked at any time before death.

intestacy. Death of an individual without leaving an effective will. See also the entry for 'partial intestacy'.

intestate. A deceased individual who left no effective will.

intragroup. *Adjective.* Within a group; between companies that are members of a group.

intra vires. Preposition phrase. Within the powers; within the authority or legal capacity of an agent, incorporated company, public official, etc.

in trust. *Preposition phrase.* Used to indicate that property is held by a trustee subject to an enforceable obligation to deal with it for the benefit of particular persons or charitable objects.

inventory. 1. A quantity of something that is kept or stored for use as the need arises; e.g., materials, supplies, work in progress or finished goods. Also called 'stock'.

2. A detailed list of goods or articles in a particular place, such as a list of

tangible assets or a list of tangible assets other than fixed assets. A list of the assets of a deceased individual.

3. In BS 5191 : 1975, given as another term for 'stock' in the sense of 'stocks and work in progress'.

4. In America, another term for 'stock-taking'.

5. Plural form (inventories). Term used in America and in IAS 2 for 'stocks and work in progress'.

inventory control. Term used in America for 'stock control'.

inventory turnover. Term used in America for 'stock turnover'.

invest. *Verb.* To buy something (called an 'investment') because one expects to receive money in the future:

(a) through using the thing as a fixed asset in a business enterprise;

(b) because the thing carries an entitlement to receive payments, e.g., of interest, dividends or royalties;

(c) by reselling the thing if a favourable opportunity for resale should occur (buying something for resale in the normal course of a business of trading in things of that type on the assumption that it will be resold within the operating cycle of the business is not regarded as investing).

investee. In relation to an accounting entity, a company whose shares have been bought by the accounting entity as an investment.

investing company. The company in relation to which a company is an associated company.

investing group. The group in relation to which a company is an associated company.

investment. 1. An act, or the activity of, investing.

2. A thing purchased in investing.

3. An amount spent on investing.

investment bank. Term used in America for 'issuing house'.

investment company. 1. In British company law, a public company that has given notice to the Registrar of Companies that it intends to operate as an investment company and has since complied with the requirements of the Companies Act 1985, s. 266, which are that:

(a) the business of the company consists of investing its funds mainly in securities, with the aim of spreading risk and giving members of the company the benefit of the result of the management of its funds;

(b) none of the company's holdings in companies (apart from other investment companies) represents more than 15% by value of the company's total investments;

(c) distribution of the company's capital profits is prohibited by its memorandum or articles of association;

(d) the company does not retain more than 15% of its income from securities.

These are virtually the same as the conditions under which a company will be recognised as an investment trust by the Board of Inland Revenue in order to be exempt from capital gains tax. An investment company must state on all its business letters and order forms that it is an investment company (Companies Act 1985, s. 351(1)).

2. In UK revenue law, the term 'investment company' is given a statutory definition for certain purposes in the Income and Corporation

Taxes Act 1970, s. 304(5), the Finance Act 1972, s. 101(5), and the Finance Act 1980, s. 37(12).

investment exchange. Defined in the Company Securities (Insider Dealing) Act 1985, s. 13(2), as: 'an organisation maintaining a system whereby an offer to deal in securities made by a subscriber to the organisation is communicated, without his identity being revealed, to other subscribers to the organisation, and whereby any acceptance of that offer by any of those other subscribers is recorded and confirmed'.

investment income. Another term for 'unearned income'.

investment property. Defined in SSAP 19 as an interest in land and/or buildings:

(a) in respect of which construction work and development have been completed; and

(b) which is held for its investment potential, any rental income being negotiated at arm's length.

According to para. 8 of SSAP 19 the following are exceptions from the definition:

(a) A property which is owned and occupied by an accounting entity for its own purposes is not an investment property.

(b) A property let to and occupied by another company in the same group of companies as the accounting entity is not an investment property for the purposes of its own accounts or group accounts.

investment revaluation reserve. A reserve to which changes in the open market value of investment properties are debited or credited.

investment trust. In Britain, a registered company (in practice, always a listed company) whose primary business is investment in a wide range of marketable securities. No 'trust' in the legal sense is involved nowadays: the term appears to have survived from the first half of the 19th century when it was usual for the property of any company to be held by trustees. In practice, an investment trust has to be approved by the Board of Inland Revenue under the Income and Corporation Taxes Act 1970, s. 359, because an approved investment trust is exempt from capital gains tax (Finance Act 1980, s. 81). One of the conditions for approval is that ordinary shares of the company must be listed on the Stock Exchange. In the USA, a corporation similar to a British investment trust is called a 'closed-end fund'.

investment value. The price at which it is estimated a convertible security would sell if it were not convertible.

investor. A person who invests.

invitation to treat. An invitation (to a particular person or to the world at large) to offer to make a contract.

invoice. A document sent by a seller to a purchaser stating the charges that the seller will make for supplying the goods or services described in the document. From the seller's point of view, this is a 'sales invoice'; from the purchaser's point of view it is a 'purchase invoice'.

invoice discounting. Sale by an enterprise of debts owed to the enterprise (i.e., transfer of the right to receive payment of the debts) but without informing the debtors of the sale. The enterprise collects payment of the debts on behalf of the purchaser. Compare 'debt factoring'.

157

invoice register. A list of purchase invoices recording such information as date of receipt of the invoice, name of supplier, and invoice value.

invoice value. The total charge stated on an invoice.

I/O. Abbreviation of 'input-output'.

IPFA. Designation of membership of the Chartered Institute of Public Finance and Accountancy.

IRC. Abbreviation of 'Inland Revenue Commissioners' – i.e., the Board of Inland Revenue.

IRR. Abbreviation of 'internal rate of return'.

irrational number. A number that cannot be expressed in the form M/N where M and N are integers.

irrecoverable ACT. Defined in SSAP 8, para. 21, as advance corporation tax, paid or payable by a company on outgoing dividends paid and proposed, other than recoverable ACT.

irrevocable credit. A letter of credit that can be withdrawn or amended only by agreement between applicant and beneficiary.

ISO-7. A character set, for use in processing and transmitting data, together with a representation of each character in the character set by a string of seven bits, specified in ISO 646–1973. Of all the possible strings of seven bits that could be used to represent characters, seven are left free by ISO 646 for allocation by national standardisation bodies, in particular to represent accented letters, though if no allocation is made it is assumed that these seven strings represent the graphic characters allocated to them in the International Reference Version of ISO-7. For the UK the British Standards Institution has allocated the seven free strings in the same way as in the International Reference Version and the resultant coded character set is called 'ISO-7-UK' or 'United Kingdom 7-bit data code', which is specified in BS 4730 : 1974. For the USA the American National Standards Institute has made the same allocations and the resultant coded character set is called 'ASCII'.

ISO-7-UK. The United Kingdom 7-bit data code: the version of ISO-7 specified in BS 4730 : 1974 for use in the UK. It is the same as ASCII.

issue. 1. *Verb.* In relation to company shares, to go through the process by which members of a company take its shares in exchange for contributions of capital. The process ends with allotment, which is when individual shares are definitely assigned to particular holders.

2. *Noun.* A number of shares in a company that are simultaneously made available for allotment, on identical terms, and which are dealt with together by the company.

3. *Verb.* In relation to securities, to go through the process which results in persons becoming the first holders of the securities.

4. *Noun.* A number of securities that are simultaneously made available for persons to become first holders of them, on identical terms, and which are dealt with together by the issuer.

5. *Verb.* In relation to financial documents, to deliver for the first time a bill of exchange or a promissory note, which is complete in form, to a person who takes it as a holder (Bills of Exchange Act 1882, s. 2).

issued share. Another term for 'allotted share'.

issued share capital. Another term for 'allotted share capital'.

issue note. A document which records the issue of products or raw materials from stores and which is used for the purposes of stock control.

issuing house. In Britain, an enterprise that specialises in obtaining capital for its clients and advises them on when to issue shares and other securities and at what price. In America, called 'investment bank'.

IT. Abbreviation of 'information technology'.

J

JDS. Abbreviation of 'Joint Disciplinary Scheme'.

job. 1. *Noun.* The collection of tasks, duties and assignments that an employee is employed to perform. Also called 'position', 'post'.

    2. *Noun.* A piece of work. A single item or unit of work, complete in itself, performed by a person or by a machine (in particular, by a computer, see BS 3527 : Part 10 : 1979). In work study, called 'task' (see BS 3138 : 1979).

    3. *Verb.* To do small pieces of work for a variety of customers.

    4. *Verb.* To buy and sell securities as a jobber.

jobber. 1. A wholesaler.

    2. A business enterprise that buys and sells securities (especially on the Stock Exchange) taking ownership of them (unlike a stockbroker, who arranges purchases and sales of securities as an agent without taking ownership). Also called 'stockjobber'.

job card. Another term for 'operation card'.

job cost. The cost of a single piece of work carried out to a customer's specific orders, which is considered as a single cost unit.

job costing. Specific-order costing when applied to costing work undertaken to customers' special requirements when each order is of comparatively short duration. Compare 'contract costing'. Also called 'job-order costing'.

job-lot costing. Term used in America for 'batch costing'.

job-order costing. Another term for 'job costing'.

job-related accommodation. For the purposes of UK income tax, living accommodation provided for an individual by reason of that individual's employment, or for his spouse by reason of hers in any of the following cases:

    (a) where it is necessary for the proper performance of the duties of the employment that the employee should reside in that accommodation;

    (b) where the accommodation is provided for the better performance of the duties of the employment, and it is one of the kinds of employment in the case of which it is customary for employers to provide living accommodation for employees;

    (c) where, there being a special threat to the employee's security, special security arrangements are enforced and the employee resides in the accommodation as part of those arrangements.

    Living accommodation is also job-related for a person if, under a contract entered into at arm's length and requiring him or his spouse to carry on a particular trade, profession or vocation, he or his spouse is bound:

(a) to carry on that trade, profession or vocation on premises or other land provided by another person (whether under a tenancy or otherwise); and

(b) to live either on those premises or on other premises provided by that other person.

These definitions are contained in the Finance Act 1974, Schedule 1, para. 4A, which also imposes various conditions.

job sheet. Another term for 'operation card'.

job ticket. Another term for 'operation card'.

joint. *Adjective.* Used to describe ownership of property, liability, tenancy of land, etc., by two or more persons who must all act together in relation to the property, liability, land, etc., which is not divided into separate pieces for each of the persons. Each person is deemed to have the whole of the property, liability, land, etc., which is said to be in 'undivided shares'. If the persons are individuals and one dies then that individual's interest in the property, liability, land, etc., comes to an end and the property, etc., goes to the survivors. Compare 'in common'.

joint adventure. A cooperative enterprise of two or more persons which is confined to a particular project, speculation or voyage and for which no firm-name is used.

joint and several liability. Liability of two or more persons that is both a joint liability of the persons and their several liability.

joint audit. An audit for which two or more firms of accountants are responsible and on which they prepare jointly an audit report.

joint cost. A cost identified with producing joint products before their separation point.

Joint Disciplinary Scheme. Abbreviation: JDS. A scheme established in 1979 by the Institute of Chartered Accountants in England and Wales, the Institute of Chartered Accountants of Scotland and the Chartered Association of Certified Accountants, for investigating and regulating the professional and business conduct, efficiency and competence of members of those accountancy bodies in circumstances which give rise to, or include questions of, public concern. Administration of the scheme is the responsibility of an executive committee of eight individuals and a chairman. Each of the three participating bodies appoints two of its own members to the committee; the other two members (who are non-accountants) and the chairman are appointed by agreement between the participating bodies. When any of the participating bodies considers that a matter has arisen that gives rise to public concern and should be the subject of an inquiry under the scheme it reports the matter to the executive committee which then appoints a committee of inquiry to prepare a report. If a committee of inquiry makes an adverse finding against a firm of accountants then it may decide on the sanction to be imposed and its finding will be published. If a committee finds against an individual accountant then the matter is referred to the participating body to which the accountant belongs and this body decides on the sanction to be imposed.

joint estate. Partnership property of a partnership firm against which bankruptcy proceedings are being taken.

joint product. One of two or more products of manufacturing or processing in which, initially, a single stream of materials and components is operated on until a 'separation point' after which different products are operated on separately. Products are called 'joint products' if they are of approximately equal significance; if one joint product is relatively less significant than the others it may be called a 'by-product'. In America, a separation point is called a 'splitoff point'.

joint-stock bank. In the first half of the 19th century, a bank that was a joint-stock company rather than a partnership. Nowadays, one of the large banks that have numerous branches and conduct a substantial proportion of their business with customers on current account.

joint-stock company. A company that trades for the benefit of all its members and divides its profits among members according to the size of their contributions to its stock (i.e., contributed capital). In general, members do not take part in the day-to-day running of the company's business. Joint-stock companies may be distinguished from associations of traders who each trade for their own account and from partnerships in which each partner takes an active part in running the business. A joint-stock company is normally incorporated and its members' interests are normally represented by shares or stock. See also Companies Act 1985, s. 683.

joint venture. A business association between two or more persons for a special purpose which is of less importance than the ordinary activities of the persons which they continue to pursue independently.

joint will. A single will stating gifts of property of two or more individuals to be made after death.

journal. A record of transactions, giving, for each transaction, a note of which ledger accounts are to be debited and credited. In principle, every transaction is entered in the journal when it occurs and postings are later made to the ledger in accordance with the notes in the journal. In practice, the most important parts of the journal have become separate books – the cash book, the purchases day book, the purchases returns book, the sales day book and the sales returns book. It is not necessary to post both a debit and a credit for each entry in the day books and returns books; a periodic total of either debits or credits, depending on the book, is sufficient (see the entries in this dictionary for the individual books), and the nature of the posting to be made is obvious from the book in which the entry is made so that no annotation is necessary. The cash book is treated as both a part of the journal and a part of the ledger so that no posting of entries is required. Journal entries, especially adjusting entries, with annotations may still be made from transactions that are not recorded in the day books, returns books or cash book. Journal entries are also used in teaching bookkeeping. The journal and the separate books into which it has been divided are known as 'books of original entry' or 'books of prime entry'.

journalise. *Verb.* To make an entry for a financial transaction in a journal.

judgment creditor. A person who has been declared by a court judgment to be owed a sum of money by another person.

judgment debt. A sum of money which a court has ordered to be paid. The person who must pay it is called a 'judgment debtor' and the person to whom the money is due is called a 'judgment creditor'.

judgment debtor. A person who has been declared by a court judgment to owe a certain sum of money to another person.

junior. *Adjective.* In relation to securities, having a lower priority as a claim for payment than one or more other claims.

K

key factor. Another term for 'limiting factor'.

kite. Colloquial. Another term for 'accommodation bill'.

kiting. Term used in America for a form of window-dressing in which an accounting entity that has two current accounts at banks draws a cheque on one account payable to itself and pays it in for credit to the second bank account on the last day of an accounting period. The amount of the cheque appears as a credit in the second bank account but is not debited within that period to the account on which it is drawn, thus temporarily overstating the amount of money that the entity has.

know-how. Knowledge of the techniques and practical details that enable a process or operation to be carried out efficiently. A statutory definition for taxation purposes is given in the Income and Corporation Taxes Act 1970, s. 386(7).

L

LAAI. Designation of a Licentiate of the Institute of Administrative Accountants.

labor cost. American spelling of 'labour cost'.

labor turnover. American spelling of 'labour turnover'.

labour cost. American spelling: labor cost. A cost of work performed by people, or an aggregate of such costs. A labour cost may be either a 'direct labour cost' or an 'indirect labour cost' depending on whether it is a direct cost or an indirect cost.

labour turnover. American spelling: labor turnover. The rate at which employees leave an employer. Commonly measured by the ratio:

$$\frac{\text{number of employees leaving during a year}}{\text{average number of employees during that year}}$$

LAN. Abbreviation of 'local area network'.

land. In law, the term 'land' includes any ground, soil or earth, such as meadows, pastures, woods, moors, waters, marshes and heath; houses and other buildings upon land; the air space above land, and all mines and minerals beneath it. Rivers, lakes, ponds, and so on, are land because they are regarded as earth covered by water. The term 'land' also includes anything fixed to land, as well as growing trees and crops, except emblements. For the purpose of ownership, land may be divided horizontally, vertically or otherwise and either below or above the ground. So different persons may own different storeys of the same building.

land mortgage. Any charge on land created as security for the fulfilment of an obligation.

language. Short form of the term 'programming language'.

lapping. In America, fraudulently withholding money received from a customer, and making up for it by stealing money from a subsequent customer, and so on.

lapse. In relation to a gift expressed in a will, revocation of the gift, as a matter of law, because the beneficiary predeceased the testator (or, if the beneficiary was a corporation, the beneficiary was dissolved before the testator died). If the intended beneficiary was a child or remoter descendant of the testator, then there will not be a lapse of the gift if issue of the intended beneficiary were living at the time of the testator's death (Wills Act 1837, s. 33). A gift saved by the section goes, *per stirpes*, to the issue of the intended beneficiary. This provision applies in England and Wales.

Laspeyres index. An index number that is used to describe items in a time series of weighted averages of observations, the same things being observed on each occasion and the same weights used on each occasion. For example, if the observations are the prices $p_{1t}, p_{2t}, \ldots, p_{nt}$ of n goods on occasion t and the comparisons are with occasion 0 when $q_{10}, q_{20}, \ldots, q_{n0}$ were the quantities of goods bought, then the Laspeyres price index for occasion t is:

$$\frac{100 \sum\limits_{i=1}^{n} p_{it} q_{i0}}{\sum\limits_{i=1}^{n} p_{i0} q_{i0}}$$

A Laspeyres price index measures the change in the price of a standard 'basket' of items (cf. Paasche index). Named after its inventor, a German statesman and economist, Étienne Laspeyres (1834–1913).

last-bag system. Another term for 'two-bin system'.

last in, first out. Abbreviation: LIFO. A method of determining the purchase price or production cost of stocks and work in progress on the basis that the quantities in hand represent the earliest purchases or production.

law of corporations. Term used in the USA (but not Canada) for 'company law'.

law of succession. The law relating to the distribution of the property of individuals after death.

lay-off pay. A payment given to employees who are not required to attend for work because there is no work for them to do.

L/C. Abbreviation of 'letter of credit'.

LCM. Abbreviation of 'lower of cost or market'.

lead time. A period of time between recognition that a thing must be purchased or manufactured and the time when the thing has been delivered and is ready for use.

lease. 1. *Noun.* A contract between two persons, called 'lessor' and 'lessee', by which the lessee is granted the right to exclusive possession and use of a tangible thing which is the lessor's property and this right is granted for a definite period of time (called the 'term'). The lessor retains a good title to the thing leased, and the right to use and possession of the thing reverts to the lessor at the end of the term. The payment to be made by the lessee as consideration for the right to use the property is called 'rent' or 'rental'. The lessee has the right to exclusive possession for the term of the lease but may, in principle, grant that right to another person under a further lease (called a 'sublease') though this is forbidden by the provisions of many leases.

It is common for a lease to be renewed at the end of its term for a further term of the same or a different duration. A lease may contain a provision by which it will be renewed automatically at the end of each term for a further term of the same length unless either party gives notice to the contrary –

such a lease is called a 'periodic lease'.

A lease may be initially for a fairly long term (called the 'primary term') after which it automatically becomes a periodic lease for fairly short terms.

'Demise' and 'tenancy agreement' are alternative terms for a lease of land. 'Contract of hire' and 'rental agreement' are alternative terms for a lease other than land. See also 'finance lease' and 'operating lease'.

2. *Verb*. (a) (Used actively.) To be a party to a lease (in sense 1) of something. The lessor is said to lease the thing 'to' the lessee; the lessee is said to lease 'from' the lessor.

(b) (Used passively.) To be the subject-matter of a lease (in sense 1).

lease back. *Verb with particle*. To become lessee of some property immediately after one has sold it.

leasehold. Commonly used term for the legal estate in land known as a 'term of years absolute'.

leaseholder. The owner of a term of years absolute.

least-squares method. Another term for 'method of least-squares'.

ledger. 1. A collection of accounting records in which all of an accounting entity's financial transactions are entered. It is divided into 'ledger accounts' each of which records transactions of a particular type, for example, transactions with a particular debtor of the accounting entity or transactions relating to a particular type of fixed asset. Every transaction of the accounting entity must in principle appear as a credit entry in one ledger account and as a debit entry in another account. An accounting system may also have other accounting records called 'books of prime entry', from which the records in the ledger are prepared. The final accounts of the accounting entity may be prepared from the records in the ledger alone. Transactions are not necessarily entered individually in the ledger but may be aggregated in some convenient way, for example, each individual retail sale for cash is not recorded, only the total sales for a day. Also called 'financial ledger' when it is necessary to distinguish it from other types of ledger.

2. A collection of accounting records made up by double-entry bookkeeping concerning transactions and events other than those recorded in a financial ledger, for example, a stock ledger recording values of stocks and work in progress, or a cost ledger used for recording production costs.

ledger account. An account within a ledger recording the accounting entity's transactions of a particular type, for example, its transactions with a particular debtor or class of debtors, or its transactions relating to a particular class of fixed assets.

ledgerless bookkeeping. A system of bookkeeping in which files of documents, such as invoices, serve as accounts.

legacy. A gift of personal property in a will. Also called 'bequest'.

legal estate. An estate, interest or charge authorised to subsist or to be created as a legal estate by the Law of Property Act 1925. The three most important types of legal estate are:

(a) an estate in fee simple absolute in possession;

(b) a term of years absolute;

(c) a charge by way of legal mortgage.

The legal estates are defined in the Law of Property Act 1925, s. 1. A legal estate in land confers a right over the land to the estate owner which must be recognised by every other person, whether given notice of the existence of the legal estate or not.

legal mortgage. A form of charge given as security for the performance of some obligation in which ownership but not possession of the charged property is transferred to the chargee (who is called the 'mortgagee') on condition that it will revert to the person giving the mortgage (who is called the 'mortgagor') when the obligation is fulfilled. In the law of England and Wales, it is not possible to create a legal mortgage over land but land can be charged in a very similar way using a 'charge by way of legal mortgage'. Also called 'mortgage'.

legal tender. Means of payment which cannot in law be regarded as unacceptable by a creditor when tendered (i.e., offered) in payment of a debt.

legatee. The beneficiary of a legacy.

length of order book. The time that it will take an enterprise that produces goods or provides services to fulfil orders that have been received from customers but have not yet been completed, calculated by dividing the sales value of the orders by the sales value of what can be produced by the enterprise per unit of time.

lessee. In relation to a lease of a thing, the person to whom the lease grants possession and use of the thing.

lessor. In relation to a lease of a thing, the person who has property in the thing and grants possession and use of it to another person.

letter of allotment. A letter sent by a company to a person to whom the company has allotted newly issued shares, informing the allottee of the number of shares allotted, the amounts to be paid for them and the procedure to be followed if the letter is renounceable or provisional. If the letter of allotment is renounceable then the allottee can, within a certain period (usually six weeks), sell the allotment to another person who will be substituted as the allottee. A provisional letter of allotment is sent in connection with a rights issue – it contains an offer by the company to allot new shares to the addressee of the letter and the allotment will not take place if the addressee does not accept the offer and does not renounce it in favour of someone else. Also called 'allotment letter'.

letter of comfort. Another term for 'comfort letter'.

letter of credit. Abbreviation: L/C. An arrangement between a bank (called the 'issuing bank') and a person (called the 'applicant for the credit' – usually a customer of the issuing bank) under which debts of the applicant incurred with a named third party (called the 'beneficiary of the credit') are assured of payment.

Letters of credit are of two main types. In one type the issuing bank undertakes that when the beneficiary presents stipulated documents (typically, documents evidencing shipment of specified goods to the applicant for the credit), the bank will make payment to, or to the order of, the beneficiary or will pay, accept or negotiate bills of exchange drawn by the beneficiary, provided that the terms and conditions of the letter of credit are complied with. In the second type, the issuing bank authorises another bank (called the 'advising bank') to make payments, or deal with bills of exchange, against stipulated documents, and makes arrangements to reimburse the advising bank. Also called 'documentary credit' because it involves the presentation of documents, 'credit', 'bankers' commercial credit'.

letter of engagement. A letter from an accountant in private practice to a client defining the work which the accountant is to carry out for the client.

letter of insurance. A document sent by a seller of goods to the buyer stating that insurance cover for the transportation of the goods has been obtained.

letter of regret. A letter sent, when there has been an invitation to the public to subscribe for new securities, by the issuer of the securities to persons whose offers have been refused because there were offers to take more securities than were being issued.

letter of representation. A signed written statement made by persons responsible for the operations of an accounting entity to the auditor of that entity providing information for the purposes of an audit, especially on matters that cannot be directly verified by the auditor.

letters of administration. A document issued by the Family Division of the High Court appointing a person as administrator of a deceased individual. If the individual left a will then a copy of the will is attached to the letters of administration and the document is described as 'letters of administration with the will attached' (or 'letters of administration *cum testamento annexo*').

leverage. Term used in America for 'gearing'.

lex domicilii. The law of the domicile of a person.

lex fori. The law of the forum. The legal system under which a court is constituted and which will be applied to all questions to be decided by the court except where, by applying the rules of *lex fori*, it concludes that a different legal system (e.g., *lex domicilii* or *lex situs*) must be applied.

lex situs. The law of the place where a thing is situated. Courts in England and Wales apply *lex situs* in deciding questions concerning immovable property.

liability. A claim against an accounting entity which, it is expected, will be settled by the entity parting with assets or in some other way losing an economic benefit.

Traditionally, the claims of the owners of an accounting entity to be repaid contributed capital and to have reserves distributed to them on the winding up of the entity were regarded as liabilities of the entity at all times and were so described in balance sheets. Nowadays, however, they would not be regarded as liabilities until the claims became enforceable, which would happen, for example, when a limited company resolved to pay shareholders a dividend out of profits or went through the correct procedure for authorising a repayment of capital.

'Liability' and the plural form 'liabilities' are also used for the value of a claim, or an aggregate of the values of claims, against an accounting entity. The estimated value of a liability which is either likely to be incurred, or certain to be incurred although of an uncertain amount or at an uncertain time, is usually called a 'provision' and is included in liabilities.

FASB Statements of Financial Accounting Concepts No. 3 states:

'Liabilities are probable [footnote omitted] future sacrifices of economic benefits arising from present obligations [footnote omitted] of a particular entity to transfer assets or provide services to other entities in the future as a result of past transactions or events' (para. 28). It goes on to identify three essential characteristics of a liability:

'(a) it embodies a present duty or responsibility to one or more other entities that entails settlement by probable future transfer or use of assets at a specified or determinable date, on occurrence of a specified event, or on demand, (b) the duty or responsibility obligates a particular enterprise, leaving it little or no discretion to avoid the future sacrifice, and (c) the transaction or other event obligating the enterprise has already happened' (para. 29).

LIBOR. Abbreviation of 'London inter-bank offered rate'.

library program. A computer program taken from a program library.

licensed deposit-taker. A licensed institution.

licensed institution. An enterprise that is licensed by the Bank of England, under the Banking Act 1979, to operate a deposit-taking business in the UK but which has not been granted recognition as a bank. A licensed institution must not suggest to the general public that it is a bank but should describe itself as a 'licensed deposit-taker'.

lien. Where goods are in the possession of a person who is providing services to the owner of the goods, a right of the provider of the services to retain possession of the goods until paid for the services. For example, a carrier normally has a right to retain possession of goods until charges for carrying them have been paid. A banker's lien applies to financial documents in the possession of a bank.

life annuity. An annuity that is payable until a specified individual (usually the annuitant) dies.

life interest. An interest that a person (called the 'life tenant') has in property and which will end on the death of a particular individual. Usually, it is the life tenant who is the individual whose death brings a life interest to an end. If a life interest is to end on the death of someone other than the life tenant then the interest is said to be 'pur autre vie'.

liferent. In Scotland, a right of an individual (called a 'liferenter') to receive, during that individual's own lifetime, the income from a capital asset but not to receive any of the capital, which will, on the liferenter's death, be paid to another person (called the 'fiar').

liferenter. In Scotland, a person entitled to the income but not the capital of property that is subject to a liferent.

life tenant. A person who has a life interest in property.

LIFO. Usually spoken as an acronym. Abbreviation of 'last in, first out'.

limitation. 1. In property law, definition of the extreme period for which an estate or interest is to subsist.

2. In legal procedure, definition of the maximum period (called the 'limitation period') within which legal action must be commenced after the cause of action has arisen.

limitation period. The maximum period within which a legal action must be commenced after the cause of action has arisen.

Limited. Abbreviation: Ltd. Used as an element of the name of an incorporated company to show that the liability of the members of the company to contribute capital to the company is limited to an amount fixed by agreement between the company and each member.

limited company. A company whose members are required to contribute capital to the company, but only up to a known limited amount agreed between member and company. No further contribution can be required, even if the company is unable to pay its debts, unless fraud can be proved. The most important type of limited company in Britain is the registered company limited by shares. Also called 'limited-liability company'.

limited liability. A liability of a member of a company to contribute capital to the company that is limited to a known amount agreed between the member and the company.

limited-liability company. Another term for 'limited company'.

limited partner. See the entry for 'limited partnership'.

limited partnership. A partnership in which one or more (but not all) of the partners is liable to contribute only a fixed amount of capital (the amount is agreed between the partners) and is not required to contribute any further to the payment of the partnership's debts. A partner whose liability to contribute capital is limited in this way is called a 'limited partner' while a partner whose liability is not limited is called a 'general partner'. A limited partner is not permitted to participate in the management of partnership affairs. In Britain, limited partnerships are governed by the Limited Partnership Act 1907.

limiting factor. A class of materials, labour, finance or production facilities of which, at some level of activity, no further supplies are available so that the level of activity cannot be increased. Also called 'key factor'.

linear function. A mathematical function of n independent variables x_1, ..., x_n, in which the dependent variable y may be calculated by the formula:

$$y = b_0 + b_1 x_1 + b_2 x_2 + \ldots + b_n x_n$$

where $b_0, b_1, \ldots, b_n$ are constants.

linear programming. Abbreviation: LP. Mathematical programming when the objective function is a linear function and all the constraints are linear functions. Any linear programming problem may be expressed in the form:

$$\text{maximise} \sum_{j=1}^{n} c_j x_j$$

$$\text{subject to} \sum_{j=1}^{n} a_{ij} x_j \leqslant b_i \quad \text{for } i = 1, 2, \ldots, m$$

$$\text{and} \qquad x_j \geqslant 0 \qquad \text{for } j = 1, 2, \ldots, n$$

where m and n are positive integers, $x_1, \ldots, x_n$ are the decision variables,

$$\sum_{j=1}^{n} c_j x_j$$

is the objective function, and the inequalities are the constraints.

liquid. *Adjective.* Capable of being exchanged for cash.

liquidate damages. Term used in Scotland for 'liquidated damages'.

liquidated damages. Damages that can be quantified by using a rule without any need for estimation or opinion. In Scotland, called 'liquidate damages'.

liquidation. 1. Termination of indebtedness or liability.

2. Another term for 'winding up'.

3. The state of being wound up.

liquidator. An individual appointed to manage the winding up of a company.

listed. 1. *Adjective.* In relation to a security, included in a list, maintained by the authorities of a stock exchange, of securities in which dealers on the exchange deal. Also called 'officially listed', 'quoted'.

2. *Adjective.* Used to describe a company that has issued securities that are listed (in sense 1). Also called 'officially listed', 'quoted'.

listing. In relation to a security, inclusion in a list maintained by the authorities of a stock exchange of securities in which dealers on the exchange deal. Also called 'official listing', 'quotation'.

listing particulars. A statement which must be published when application is made for listing of securities on a stock exchange. The particulars are intended to enable investors and their investment advisers to make an informed assessment of the assets and liabilities, financial position, profits and losses, and prospects of the issuer and of the rights attaching to the securities. The matters which must be included in listing particulars in the UK are specified in the Stock Exchange (Listing) Regulations 1984 (SI 1984 No. 716) reproducing an EEC Council Directive.

loan capital. Another term for 'debt capital'.

loan creditor. In relation to a company, defined by the Income and Corporation Taxes Act 1970, s. 303(7), as: 'a creditor in respect of any debt incurred by the company:

'(a) for any money borrowed or capital assets acquired by the company, or

'(b) for any right to receive income created in favour of the company, or

'(c) for consideration the value of which to the company was (at the time that the debt was incurred) substantially less than the amount of the debt (including any premium thereon),

'or in respect of any redeemable loan capital issued by the company:

'provided that a person carrying on a business of banking shall not be deemed to be a loan creditor in respect of any loan capital or debt issued or incurred by the company for money lent by him to the company in the ordinary course of that business.'

A person who is not the creditor in respect of any debt or loan capital to which subsection (7) applies but nevertheless has a beneficial interest therein is treated as a loan creditor in respect of that debt or loan capital.

Loan Guarantee Scheme. A scheme under which the Department of Trade and Industry provides a guarantee as security for a medium-term loan by a bank or other financial institution to a small business. The scheme is operated under s. 8 of the Industrial Development Act 1982. The Department charges an annual fee of 5% of the amount of the loan outstanding as consideration for giving a guarantee under the scheme. Only 70% of the amount of any loan will be guaranteed.

loan stock. Stock representing interests in a marketable loan.

local area network. Abbreviation: LAN. A system of connections between a number of computers enabling data to be transmitted from one computer to another at high speed, operating within a small geographical area, such as a single building.

local authority. 1. In the Local Government Act 1972, 'a county council, the Greater London Council, a district council, a London borough council or a parish or community council' (s. 270(1) of the Act). The 1984 Local Government Bill proposes the repeal of the words 'the Greater London Council' in this definition.

2. In the Local Government (Scotland) Act 1973, 'a regional, islands or district council' or any combination of those councils (s. 235(1) and (2) of the Act).

3. Defined for the purposes of the Tax Acts and the enactments relating to capital gains tax by s. 52(2) of the Finance Act 1974 as follows: ' "Local authority" means:

'(a) any authority having power to make or determine a rate;

'(b) any authority having power to issue a precept, requisition or other demand for the payment of money to be raised out of a rate;

'and in this subsection "rate" means a rate the proceeds of which are applicable for public local purposes and which is leviable by reference to the value of land or other property.'

local authority association. For the purposes of exemption from taxation in the United Kingdom, 'any incorporated or unincorporated association of which all the constituent members are local authorities, groups of local authorities or local authority associations and which has for its object or primary object the protection and furtherance of the interests in general of local authorities or any description of local authorities; and for this purpose, if a member of an association is a representative of or appointed by any authority, group of authorities or association, that authority, group or association (and not he) is to be treated as a constituent member of the association' (Income and Corporation Taxes Act 1970, s. 353(4)).

local currency. The currency of the primary economic environment in which a company operates and generates net cash flows (SSAP 20, para. 39). In FAS 52, called 'functional currency'. In FAS 52, 'local currency' means currency of a particular country being referred to.

local loan. A loan by the Public Works Loan Board to a local authority.

location. In data processing, a part of a store that can be explicitly and uniquely identified by an address. Also called 'storage location'.

locus sigilli. See the entry for 'LS'.

lodgement. American spelling: lodgment. Delivery of money, cheques and other financial documents to a bank for credit to an account.

log-normal distribution. A probability distribution that is the distribution of a continuous random variable X that can take any value greater than a where a is a positive number, and which has the property that the probability distribution of the random variable ln $(X - a)$ is a normal distribution.

logarithm. If $x = a^y$, where a is a positive number other than 1, then y is the logarithm of x to base a, denoted by $\log_a x$.

logic operation. An operation of a type studied in symbolic logic, of which the operations involving the logical connectives 'and', 'or' and 'not' are fundamental.

London acceptance credit. An arrangement for the finance of exports made between an exporter and a London merchant bank. When the exporter sells goods, the exporter draws a bill of exchange on the buyer, payable at some time in the future so as to give the buyer a period of credit. The accepted bill of exchange is then pledged to the merchant bank which, in return, accepts an accommodation bill drawn by the exporter. Because of the reputation of the merchant bank in London, its acceptance can be discounted there readily to provide immediate cash for the exporter whereas the foreign buyer's acceptance may have little or no value in the discount market.

London inter-bank offered rate. Abbreviation: LIBOR. The rate of interest at which banks in London offer to lend each other money in a particular currency for a particular period.

long lease. In Schedule 4 to the Companies Act 1985, in relation to a financial year of a company, a lease with 50 years or more to go from the end of that financial year to the end of the term for which the lease was granted.

long-term contract. A contract entered into for manufacture or building of a single substantial object or the provision of a service where the time taken to manufacture, build or provide is such that a substantial proportion of all the contract work will extend for a period exceeding one year (SSAP 9, para. 22).

long-term debt. A debt or the aggregate of debts due to be paid more than one year hence.

long-term liability. A financial obligation of an accounting entity not due to be met within the next year or the next operating cycle. Also called 'long-term obligation', 'deferred liability'.

long-term obligation. Another term for 'long-term liability'.

Lorenz curve. A graph showing the distribution of a quantitative attribute among the population of individuals to which it is attributed. The graph plots proportion of the total quantity of the attribute against proportion of population to which that proportion of the attribute is attributed. Named after Max Otto Lorenz, a statistician from the USA born 1876.

loss per share. Term used for the earnings per share of a company for a period during which it made a loss before taking account of extraordinary items.

loss relief. Relief from payment of tax on an amount of income – received from carrying on a trade, profession or vocation in one year of assessment or financial year – that is equal to the amount of a loss made from carrying on the trade, profession or vocation in another year.

lot. Another term for 'batch'.

lower of cost or market. Abbreviation: LCM. The lesser of:

(a) purchase price or production cost of a current asset;

(b) cost of replacing the asset by purchase or manufacture.

Used as the basis of a rule for valuing current assets. SSAP 9, IAS 2 and the Companies Act 1985, Schedule 4, paras 22 and 23, now require current assets to be valued at the lesser of:

(a) purchase price or production cost;

(b) net realisable value.

However, there may be circumstances in which replacement cost is a better measure of value than net realisable value.

low-level language. Another term for 'computer-oriented language'.

LP. Abbreviation of 'linear programming'.

LS. Abbreviation of '*locus sigilli*' (a Latin phrase meaning 'the place of the seal') used:

(a) on a copy of a document to indicate that a seal was attached to the original;

(b) on a form to show where a seal should be affixed when the form is completed.

Ltd. Abbreviation of 'Limited'.

Łukasiewicz notation. Another term for 'prefix notation'.

M

m. Abbreviation of 'million'.

MAAT. Designation of a Member of the Association of Accounting Technicians.

machine language. Another term for 'computer language'.

magnetic bubble memory. Abbreviation: MBM. A computer store utilising an established pattern of positions in a magnetic thin film. At each position a magnetic bubble (a small cylindrical magnetic domain magnetised perpendicular to the film surface) may be created and the whole pattern of positions is propagated along known pathways at a definite rate by a rotating magnetic field. As the pattern of positions moves past a fixed point data may be recorded by creating a pattern of magnetic bubbles or an existing pattern of bubbles may be detected in order to read stored data. Also called 'bubble', 'bubble memory'.

magnetic card. In data processing, a card with a magnetisable surface on which data can be stored by magnetic recording.

magnetic core. Another term for 'core'.

magnetic disc. Alternative spelling of 'magnetic disk'.

magnetic disk. Alternative spelling: magnetic disc. In data processing, a thin flat disk of material with a magnetisable surface layer used for storing data by magnetic recording.

magnetic drum. In data processing, a cylinder with a surface layer of magnetisable material on which data may be stored by magnetic recording.

magnetic recording. In data processing, a method of recording data in which small areas of a piece of magnetic material are selectively magnetised.

magnetic store. In data processing, a store in which data are stored by using magnetic recording.

magnetic thin-film store. In data processing, a magnetic store in which the data medium is a layer of magnetisable material only one molecule thick deposited on some other material (usually glass). Also called 'thin-film store'.

magnitude. Another term for 'absolute value'.

mainframe. Also written: main frame. 1. In the past, another term for 'processing unit'.

2. A large, powerful, expensive general-purpose computer capable of executing instructions very rapidly and usually physically bulky.

main memory. Another term for 'main store'.

main store. In a computer, a program-addressable store from which

176

instructions and other data can be loaded directly into processor registers for subsequent execution or processing. Also called 'main memory'.

mainstream corporation tax. Abbreviation: MCT. The amount of UK corporation tax due on a company's profits earned in an accounting period less the advance corporation tax that may be offset against this liability.

maintenance of operating capability. See the entry for 'concept of maintenance of operating capability'.

make a market. *Verb with noun phrase.* To provide investors with opportunities both to buy and to sell a particular investment (e.g., a particular security) by, for example, being ready to act as a broker or as a dealer in the investment.

make-or-buy decision. The decision whether to manufacture all or part of a product or purchase it from another enterprise.

maker. The person who, in a promissory note, gives the unconditional promise to pay money.

managed cost. Another term for 'controllable cost'.

management accountant. 1. An individual performing a job which mainly consists of management accounting.

2. A member of the Institute of Cost and Management Accountants.

management accounting. Defined in the ICMA official terminology as the provision of information required by management for such purposes as: (a) formulation of policies, (b) planning and controlling the activities of the enterprise, (c) decision-taking on alternative courses of action, (d) disclosure to persons external to the entity (shareholders and others), (e) disclosure to employees, (f) safeguarding assets. The ICMA regards management accounting as including long-term planning, budgeting, profit planning, financial accounting, cost accounting, financial control, treasurership and internal audit.

management accounting guidelines. 'Statements of good management accounting practice which are advisory not mandatory issued by companies and professional accountancy bodies and in particular by the Institute of Cost and Management Accountants' (ICMA official terminology).

management buy-out. An arrangement, made on the initiative of the managers of one or all of the businesses of a company, under which the company is paid money to give up its ownership of the business that those managers manage. Usually, the managers, and possibly other employees, become the new owners of the business.

management information system. Abbreviation: MIS. A system for providing managers with information relating to their management tasks.

management ratio. A ratio used in ratio analysis of an accounting entity by, or on behalf of, the managers of the entity.

managing trustee. A trustee who exercises discretionary and management powers over property held by a custodian trustee.

mandate. A document given by a customer of a bank to the bank requesting the bank to open an account in the customer's name and to honour cheques and other orders for payment drawn on that account, and stating the names of persons whose signatures may be accepted by the bank for operations on the account. A mandate will also contain specimen signatures of the persons named.

mandatory injunction. An injunction by which a person is required to do a particular act or thing.

manufacturing account. A financial statement analysing the cost of goods manufactured over a period. It usually gives direct expenses, direct labour cost, direct material cost and production overhead cost to arrive at production cost of sales which will form all or part of cost of sales in the trading and profit and loss account. (Production cost of sales will be only part of cost of sales if the enterprise also purchased goods for resale.) This information may be included in the trading and profit and loss account, which may then be called a 'manufacturing, trading and profit and loss account'. In America, called 'cost of goods manufactured statement', 'manufacturing statement'.

manufacturing cost. Another term for 'production cost of sales'. Commonly used in America.

manufacturing cost of goods produced. Another term for 'production cost of sales'.

manufacturing expense. In America, another term for 'factory expense'.

manufacturing lead time. The period of time between the placing of a production order and its completion.

manufacturing order. Another term for 'production order'.

manufacturing overhead. See the entry for 'production overhead cost'.

manufacturing profit. In relation to goods that have been manufactured by an accounting entity, the excess of the cost of buying those goods from another supplier over the entity's production cost of sales. Also called 'profit on manufacture'.

manufacturing statement. Term used in America for 'manufacturing account'.

manufacturing time. In relation to a manufactured object, the period of time between the start and finish dates of manufacture (BS 5191 : 1975).

manufacturing, trading and profit and loss account. A trading and profit and loss account which includes an analysis of the cost of goods manufactured.

marginal. *Adjective.* Relating to the change in a dependent variable associated with an increase of one unit in the independent variable. For example, the 'marginal cost' of a product is the change in costs associated with increasing the level of production by one unit.

marginal cost. An additional cost incurred in producing one more unit of a product. The total of all such costs associated with the product.

marginal costing. Treating the total variable costs of a product as the most important measure of the cost of the product. (The variable costs of one unit of a product are the 'marginal' cost of the product.) Known in America as 'direct costing'.

margin of safety. The excess of normal or actual production quantity over the production quantity at the break-even point, measured either in units of product or in sales value.

margin-of-safety ratio. The ratio:

$$\frac{\text{actual quantity of product minus quantity at the break-even point}}{\text{actual quantity of product}}$$

Normally expressed as a percentage.

marketable loan. A loan that is arranged so that a lender's right to payment of interest and repayment of principal may conveniently be sold in whole or part. In some marketable loans a lender is supplied with a document (called a 'bill', 'bond', 'certificate' or 'note') having a nominal value equal to the amount of principal repayable in respect of the document, and the lender's rights may be transferred by delivery of the document (i.e., it is a bearer security). Usually, only a few nominal values of securities are available. In other marketable loans, the loan is treated as stock and transfers are made by alteration of entries in a register kept by or on behalf of the borrower although bearer stock certificates are also sometimes made available. It is often convenient to refer to all forms of interest in marketable loans as 'bonds'.

marketable security. A security that can be readily sold. A security is judged to be marketable if there is at least one reputable dealer willing to give quotations for it at all times.

marketing cost. A cost identified with acquiring and maintaining markets for an enterprise's products and ensuring that the enterprise's output reaches those markets, or with collecting payments from customers. Or, an aggregate of such costs. Also called 'selling overhead'.

marketing cost variance. The difference between the budgeted marketing cost for a budget period and the actual marketing cost for that period.

marketing research. Term used in America for 'market research'.

market overt. A place in England where goods are traded and where a buyer of goods, who buys them in good faith without notice of any defect or want of title on the part of the seller, acquires a good title to the goods despite any other person's claim to them. A public and legally constituted market or fair – i.e., one held in accordance with a grant by the Crown of the privilege of holding a market or fair, or one held under statutory authority – is market overt for goods sold according to the usage of the market. The part of any shop within the City of London to which the public is admitted without special invitation is market overt between sunrise and sunset on all days except Sundays and holidays for the sale by the shopkeeper of such goods as the shopkeeper professes to trade in.

market price. The price at which a thing is sold when it is put up for sale in the way that is usual for things of its type.

market portfolio. In portfolio theory, a portfolio containing all available investments (or all investments of the type being considered—usually listed company shares) in amounts proportional to the total market values of the amounts of those investments held by investors.

market research. Systematic and objective research for, and analysis of, information concerning the actual or potential markets for products. In America, usually called 'marketing research'.

market risk premium. Another term for 'risk premium'.

market value. 1. The price which, it is estimated, an item of property would fetch if it were put up for sale in the way that is usual for property of its type. The term 'open-market value' is sometimes used to emphasise that the price is not affected by connections between buyer and seller or artificial restriction of the number of buyers given an opportunity to buy the property.

2. Defined in the Capital Gains Tax Act 1979, s. 150, as follows:

'(1) In this Act "market value" in relation to any assets means the price which those assets might reasonably be expected to fetch on a sale in the open market.

'(2) In estimating the market value of any assets no reduction shall be made in the estimate on account of the estimate being made on the assumption that the whole of the assets is to be placed on the market at one and the same time.'

There are special rules for determining the market value of listed shares or securities, and units of unit trusts.

Markov chain. See the entry for 'Markov process'.

Markov process. A stochastic process, representing the state of a system at various times, that has the property that, for any one of those times t, the state of the system at any future time is not influenced at all by the sequence of states the system went through in getting to its state at time t. In other words, if the present state of a system in a Markov process is known then its past has no influence on its future.

If the process is defined only for discrete (isolated) times and the random variables representing states of the system are discrete random variables then the process is called a 'Markov chain'. The conditional probability that the system in a Markov chain will be in a state E_k at time t_{n+1} given that it is in state E_j at time t_n is called a 'transition probability' and is denoted by $p_{jk}(n)$. If a Markov chain has the property that, for each pair (j, k), $p_{jk}(n)$ is the same for all n then the chain is said to have 'stationary' transition probabilities. The Markov processes that are most easily studied and applied are chains with stationary transition probabilities.

Named after a Russian mathematician, Andreĭ Andreevich Markov (1856–1922), who laid the foundations for the study of stochastic processes of this type.

Markowitz model. A model that analyses the problem of choosing a portfolio of investments in terms of the expectation and variance of returns on investments and which was developed by an American economist, Harry Max Markowitz (born 1927) and published in full in his book, *Portfolio Selection: Efficient Diversification of Investments* (Cowles Foundation Monograph 16) (New York: Wiley, 1959; 2nd revised printing, New Haven, Conn: Yale University Press, 1970). Markowitz introduced the ideas of efficient portfolios, the market portfolio and the capital market line.

martingale. A discrete stochastic process $\{X(t)\}$ with the property that for the random variable $X(t_{n+1})$ representing the state of the system at time t_{n+1}, the expectation of the conditional distribution of $X(t_{n+1})$ for given values of all the distributions relating to preceding times is equal to the value $x(t_n)$ of the distribution $X(t_n)$ for the immediately preceding time. Mathematicians took the term 'martingale' from gamblers who apply it to a betting system applicable to games that are discrete stochastic processes. The system is attractive at first sight but in fact use of it by a gambler has no effect on the amount won or lost. Accordingly, in French, the system was called '*martingale*', a word used to describe people from the Provençal town of Martigues, whose inhabitants had a reputation for naïvety.

master budget. The budget which is prepared from, and consolidates, budgets for the separate functions of an organisation to give a single budget for the whole organisation.

matching. Recognising revenues and costs in the accounts for the period in which they are earned or incurred rather than when cash is actually received or disbursed, in accordance with the accruals concept. The 'matching convention' is the rule that matching must be carried out.

material. *Adjective*. Of a transaction or event affecting an accounting entity, so large in size or effect that consideration must be given to whether it is correctly treated in accounting records and financial statements of the entity. FASB Statement of Financial Accounting Concepts No. 2 suggests that whether or not an item is material depends on whether omitting it or misstating it in accounts would affect any decisions taken by experienced people on the basis of those accounts.

material cost. A cost of materials or supplies used, or an aggregate of such costs. A material cost may be either a 'direct material cost' or an 'indirect material cost' depending on whether it is a direct cost or an indirect cost. An alternative form of the term is 'materials cost'.

materiality. The degree to which something is material.

materials cost. An alternative form of 'material cost'.

materials requisition. A document used within an organisation to require the issue from stores of specified materials. The approval of a particular person may be necessary before the materials requisition becomes effective. Also called 'stores requisition'.

materials returned note. A document used within an organisation to record the return of unused material to store.

materials transfer note. A document used within an organisation to record the transfer of material from one store to another, from one cost centre to another, or from one use to another.

maternity pay. In the employment legislation of England and Wales, and Scotland, pay to which a woman who is absent from work because of pregnancy is entitled under Part III of the Employment Protection (Consolidation) Act 1978. Payment is made by the woman's employer who is reimbursed via the Maternity Pay Fund.

Maternity Pay Fund. A fund under the control and management of the Secretary of State, consisting of a proportion of secondary Class 1 social security contributions, from which employers are reimbursed for payments of maternity pay. Any temporary deficit in the Fund is overcome by a loan from the National Loans Fund.

mathematical discount. Another term for 'compound discount'.

mathematical programming. Using mathematical techniques to find optimum programmes of action where there are several related activities and there are limitations (called 'constraints') on what actions may be undertaken. The activities to be programmed are represented by variables with values representing different possible states of the activities. These variables are called 'decision variables'. The overall effect of each possible combination of states of the activities is expressed as a function (called the 'objective function') of the values of the decision variables. The constraints are limits on the values that the decision variables can take. The problem is to find a programme – i.e., a set of values of the decision variables, within the constraints – that will give an optimum value to the objective function.

The simplest form of mathematical programming is when the objective function is a linear function and all the constraints are linear functions of decision variables so that it is a problem of linear programming, for which straightforward techniques of solution have been developed.

matrix. A rectangular array of numbers or symbols in which individual items are arranged in 'rows' (i.e., written or printed so that they are read from left to right), with each row having the same number of items, and the rows are placed one under another so that the items fall into 'columns'. For example, in the matrix:

$$\begin{pmatrix} 1 & 2 & 3 \\ 4 & 5 & 6 \\ 7 & 8 & 9 \\ 10 & 11 & 12 \end{pmatrix}$$

(1 2 3) is the first row and:

$$\begin{pmatrix} 1 \\ 4 \\ 7 \\ 10 \end{pmatrix}$$

is the first column. If the numbers of rows and columns are the same the matrix is called a 'square matrix'.

mature. *Verb.* To become due for payment.

maturity. 1. The time at which a financial obliation is due to be fulfilled – for example, the time at which a debt is due to be paid.

2. The time at which a bill of exchange (other than one payable at sight) is due to be paid.

maturity yield. The internal rate of return of purchasing a redeemable security and holding it until it is redeemed, taking account of both receipts of income and repayment of capital. Calculation of the maturity yield is only feasible if the income from the security is a fixed rate of interest. In America, called 'yield to maturity'.

maximin criterion. A criterion used when making decisions that the decision taken should maximise the minimum payoff that can be achieved.

maximum. 1. Generally, a largest value.

2. In mathematics, in relation to a function, a value of the independent variable for which the dependent variable has a larger value than for any other nearby value of the independent variable.

maximum stock level. In stock control, the planned highest level of stock, above which stock is considered to be in excess. See BS 5191 : 1975.

MBM. Abbreviation of 'magnetic bubble memory'.

MCT. 1. Abbreviation of 'mainstream corporation tax'.

2. Designation of a Member of the Association of Corporate Treasurers.

mean. 1. In probability theory, another term for 'expectation'.

2. In statistics, a statistic giving a central or typical value of a set of numbers, usually the arithmetic mean. See also the entries for 'geometric mean' and 'harmonic mean'.

mean absolute deviation. Another term for 'mean deviation'.

mean deviation. In statistics, the arithmetic mean of the absolute values of the deviations of observed values of a quantitative characteristic from some chosen number (which is usually the arithmetic mean of the observations). Also called 'average deviation', 'mean absolute deviation'.

median. 1. In probability theory, the fractile of order 0.5 of a probability distribution.

2. In statistics, the middle value of a number of different observed values arranged in order of greatness. If there are an even number of observed values then their median is the arithmetic mean of the two middle values.

If the number of observed values is n and the integers 1 to n are assigned to the observed values in such a way that for any integer k which is greater than 1 and less than or equal to n, the value to which k is assigned is greater than the value to which $k - 1$ is assigned and n is odd, then the median is the value to which $\frac{1}{2}(n + 1)$ is assigned. If n is even, the median is the arithmetic mean of the values to which $\frac{1}{2}n$ and $\frac{1}{2}(n + 1)$ have been assigned.

medium-sized company. In order to file modified accounts with the Registrar of Companies for a particular financial year, a private company is a medium-sized company if, in respect of that year and the preceding financial year (or that year alone if it is the company's first financial year), it satisfies any two or more of the following conditions (Companies Act 1985, ss. 248(2) and (5) and 249):

(a) its turnover does not exceed £5.75 million (or a proportionate amount if the financial year is not 12 months);

(b) its balance sheet total does not exceed £2.8 million;

(c) its weekly average number of employees during the financial year does not exceed 250.

member. 1. In relation to an association, one of the persons associated together in the association. In an incorporated association a member may also be called a 'corporator'. In a company limited by shares, a member is almost invariably a shareholder.

2. In relation to a pension scheme, an individual for whom the scheme provides, or is to provide, a pension.

3. In relation to a set, a thing that, according to the rules defining the set, is included in the set. Also called 'element'.

members' voluntary liquidation. Another term for 'members' voluntary winding up'.

members' voluntary winding up. A voluntary winding up of a registered company in which, within the five weeks preceding adoption of the resolution to wind up, a majority of the directors of the company make, at a board meeting, a statutory declaration of the company's solvency. The declaration may be made on the same day as the members' meeting provided it is made before the meeting. If the company has only two directors then both must make the declaration; and if it has only one director then that one director must make the declaration. The declaration must state that the declaring directors have made a full inquiry into the affairs of the company, and have formed the opinon that the company will be able to pay its debts in full within a certain time after the commencement of winding up, which time must not exceed 12 months. See Companies Act 1985, s. 577. Also called 'members' voluntary liquidation'.

memorandum. Short form of 'memorandum of association'.

memorandum of association. In British company law, a document which must be presented to the Registrar of Companies on the registration of any company stating important facts about the company, including its name, whether it is a public company, whether it is a limited company, and the objects for which the company is established. The matters which must be stated in the memorandum of association are specified in the Companies Act 1985, but there is no prohibition on providing additional information. The members of a company may alter the terms of its memorandum by following special procedures specified in the Companies Act 1985. Often referred to as a 'memorandum'.

memory. Term used in computing for 'store' though use of the term is deprecated in BS 3527 : Part 12 : 1978.

menu. In data processing, a list of items or services available from a data processing system, displayed to a user of a system together with instructions for obtaining each item or service.

mercantile agent. A person who carries on a commercial or trading business in the customary course of which the person has authority either to sell goods, or to consign goods for the purpose of sale, or to buy goods, or to raise money on the security of goods, as an agent for other persons (Factors Act 1889, s. 1(1); Sale of Goods Act 1979, s. 26).

merchandise advance. A loan by a bank to pay most of the cost of goods bought for resale, especially where the goods are imported. Usually, a bank takes control of the goods as security for repayment of its loan, e.g., by having the goods warehoused in its name or by taking possession of the bill of lading for the goods. Called a 'produce advance' or 'produce loan' when the goods are agricultural or horticultural produce.

merchantable quality. In relation to goods sold in the course of a business, defined by the Sale of Goods Act 1979, s. 14(6), as the quality of being 'as fit for the purpose or purposes for which goods of that kind are commonly bought as it is reasonable to expect having regard to any description applied to them, the price (if relevant) and all the other relevant circumstances'.

merger. 1. Another term for 'uniting of interests'.

2. In SSAP 23, a business combination that is accounted for by merger accounting.

3. Cessation of a limited form of property in a thing on acquisition of a form of property in the thing that includes the limited form. For example, cessation of a leasehold interest in land on acquisition of the freehold of the land.

merger accounting. A method of dealing in the group accounts of a holding company with the fact of a company becoming a subsidiary of that holding company in which the financial statements of the new subsidiary and the rest of the group are consolidated and presented as if the new company had always been a member of the group.

method of least squares. A method of estimating one or more parameters of a mathematical function being used as a symbolic model of the relationship between a dependent variable and one or more independent variables, in which the parameters are chosen so as to minimise the quantity:

$$\Sigma(y_i - \hat{y}_i)^2$$

where y_i is the observed value of the dependent variable for a particular set of values of the independent variables and $\hat{y}_i$ is the value that the model predicts will be taken by the dependent variable for that set of values of the independent variables, and the sum extends over all observed values. Also called 'least-squares method'.

MIATI. Designation of a Member of the Institute of Accounting Technicians in Ireland.

MICM. Designation of an Associate of the Institute of Credit Management.

MICM (Grad). Designation of an Associate of the Institute of Credit Management who has qualified by examination.

micro. Another term for 'microcomputer'.

microcomputer. A computer small enough to be placed for use on an office desk, or smaller, and having a single chip as processor. Also called 'micro'.

microprocessor. A computer processor on a single chip.

milliard. One thousand millions. In English used mainly by foreign-exchange dealers who often use the colloquial abbreviated form 'yard'. One thousand millions is now commonly called 'billion' in English.

minimax criterion. A criterion used when making decisions that the decision taken should minimise the maximum loss that can occur.

minimum. 1. Generally, a smallest value.

2. In mathematics, in relation to a function, a value of the independent variable for which the dependent variable has a smaller value than for any other nearby value of the independent variable.

minimum lease payments. Defined in SSAP 21, para. 20, as the minimum payments over the remaining part of the lease term (excluding charges for services and taxes to be paid by the lessor) and:

(a) from the point of view of the lessee, any residual amounts guaranteed by the lessee or by a related party; or,

(b) from the point of view of the lessor, any residual amounts guaranteed by the lessee or by an independent third party.

minimum lending rate. Abbreviation: MLR. The rate of interest charged by the Bank of England on short-term loans to discount houses if financial documents, bearing the very lowest risk of default, are pledged as security. In August 1981 the Bank decided that, normally, it would make no public announcement of minimum lending rate. However, in exceptional circumstances, e.g., the decline in value of the pound in terms of the US dollar in January 1985, a minimum lending rate is announced.

minimum stock level. In stock control, the planned lowest level of stock. If stock falls below this level then replenishment orders are given special attention. See BS 5191 : 1975.

minority interests. The interests, in an incorporated company that is a subsidiary of another corporation, of the members other than the companies in the group to which the subsidiary belongs and nominees of those companies. Also called 'outside shareholders' interests'.

minority shareholders. The shareholders, in an incorporated company that is a subsidiary of another corporation, other than the companies in the group to which the subsidiary belongs and nominees of those companies. Also called 'outside shareholders'.

minuend. A number from which another number (called the 'subtrahend') is subtracted.

MIPA. Designation of a Member of the Insolvency Practitioners Association.

MIRAS. Abbreviation of 'mortgage interest relief at source'.

MIS. Abbreviation of 'management information system'.

misfeasance. Improper performance of an action that is in itself lawful.

misfeasance proceedings. Court action during the winding up of a company to recover property of the company that has been misapplied by persons who formed or managed the company. The proceedings are now taken under s. 631 of the Companies Act 1985, though the 1984 Insolvency Bill proposes to replace this section with a new provision.

misrepresentation. In relation to a contract, a false statement of fact, stated, before the contract was made, by one of the parties to the other, whose belief in the truth of the statement was an inducement to enter into the contract.

mixed cost. Another term for 'semi-variable cost'.

MLR. Abbreviation of 'minimum lending rate'.

MM. Abbreviation of 'Modigliani-Miller'.

mode. 1. In probability theory, a value of a random variable for which the probability (if it is a discrete random variable) or the probability density function (if it is a continuous random variable) is a maximum.

2. In statistics, a value of a variable for which the frequency of occurrence is a maximum.

modem. In data processing, a device for converting signals representing data produced by a data processing system into a modulated electromagnetic wave that can be transmitted through a telephone system, and for converting such a modulated wave received by the device into signals suitable for processing by the data processing system. (The word was formed by blending the words 'modulator' and 'demodulator'.)

modified accounts. Annual accounts of a British registered company from which some details have been omitted before delivery of the accounts to the Registrar of Companies. A private company may file modified accounts if it is a small company or a medium-sized company.

modified historical cost convention. A conventional basis for the preparation of financial statements in which, for some assets, the amount stated as the value of the asset is not the historical cost but is either current cost or an amount determined by valuation.

Modigliani-Miller. Abbreviation: MM. *Adjective.* Of, or relating to, discoveries in economic theory made by two US economists, Franco Modigliani (born Italy 1918, naturalised US citizen 1946) and Merton

Howard Miller (born 1923). In particular, three propositions (or, often, just the first of them) expressed in an article, 'The cost of capital, corporation finance and the theory of investment', *American Economic Review*, vol. 48 (1958), pp. 261–97. The propositions concern a company financed entirely by equity shares and marketable loans that are traded in a market in which company shares are in classes with all shares in the same class k having the same expected rate of return r_k. The propositions are:

(a)   If the market is in equilibrium the market value of all the securities of the company does not depend on the ratio of the market value of the marketable loans D to the market value of the equity shares S. (In this context 'market value' means market price per security multiplied by number of securities issued.)

(b)   The expected rate of return on a share of the company is:

$$r_k + (r_k - R)D/S$$

where R is the risk-free rate of return.

(c)   If the company is acting in the best interest of its shareholders at the time of the decision it will exploit an investment opportunity if, and only if, the expected rate of return on it is greater than or equal to r_k.

modulus. Another term for 'absolute value'.

monadic operation. An operation with one operand. Also called 'unary operation'.

monetary asset. Money or a claim to receive a sum of money the amount of which is fixed or determinable without reference to future prices of specific goods or services.

monetary item. A monetary asset or a monetary liability.

monetary liability. An obligation to pay a sum of money the amount of which is fixed or determinable without reference to future prices of specific goods or services.

monetary measurement convention. The principle that only transactions, facts and events that may be measured in monetary terms are recorded in accounts.

monetary working capital. In relation to an accounting entity, defined in SSAP 16, para. 44, as follows: '"Monetary working capital" is the aggregate of:

'(a)   trade debtors, prepayments and trade bills receivable, plus

'(b)   stocks not subject to a cost of sales adjustment, less

'(c)   trade creditors, accruals and trade bills payable,

'in so far as they arise from the day-to-day operating activities of the business [of the accounting entity] as distinct from transactions of a capital nature.

'Bank balances and overdrafts may fluctuate with the volume of stock or the items in (a), (b) and (c) above. That part of bank balances or overdrafts arising from such fluctuations should be included in monetary working capital, together with any cash floats required to support day-to-day operations of the business, if to do so has a material effect on the current cost operating profit.

'In the case of banks and other financial businesses this definition is extended to cover other assets and other liabilities in so far as they also arise from the day-to-day operating activities of the business as distinct from transactions of a capital nature.'

monetary working capital adjustment. Abbreviation: MWCA. In current cost accounting, an adjustment made to the profit on the ordinary activities of an accounting entity for an accounting period, as calculated on the historical cost basis, to allow for the effect of price changes on the amount of finance needed for monetary working capital. In SSAP 16, para. 11, it is said that this adjustment should represent the amount of additional (or reduced) finance needed for monetary working capital as a result of changes in the input prices of goods and services used and financed by the entity.

money. The means used for discharging debts, making payments and measuring value.

money advice. Advice to individuals in financial difficulty about dealing with their debts. Giving such advice in relation to consumer credit agreements or consumer hire agreements may be debt-counselling under the Consumer Credit Act 1974.

monitor. 1. *Noun.* A device for observing continuously the activity or output of a system so as to indicate deviations from a planned or normal state.

2. *Verb.* To observe or measure continuously the activity or output of a system in order to discover variations from a planned or normal state.

3. *Noun.* In data processing, another term for 'monitor program'.

monitoring program. Another term for 'monitor program'.

monitor program. A computer program that observes, regulates, controls or verifies the operations of a data processing system. Also called 'monitor', 'monitoring program'.

Monte Carlo method. A technique for simulating a long sequence of states of a system that has uncontrollable variables which occur with known probability distributions. For each simulated state, the value of an uncontrollable variable comes from a part of its probability distribution chosen by using a table of random numbers. The use of random numbers to determine states of the system is reminiscent of games on which people gamble at casinos, of which the most famous is at Monte Carlo in Monaco.

monthly statement. A statement of account sent monthly.

moratorium. An agreement between the creditors of a person who is in financial difficulty that they will not press for payment of their debts for a period in the hope that the fortunes of the debtor will improve during that period.

mortgage. 1. *Noun.* A term used imprecisely for various types of charge, namely, a charge by way of legal mortgage, an equitable mortgage, a legal mortgage, or a fixed charge.

2. *Verb.* To create a mortgage (in sense 1) over one's property.

mortgagee. A chargee of property whose charge is a charge by way of legal mortgage, an equitable mortgage (in which case the mortgagee may be described as an 'equitable mortgagee'), a legal mortgage (in which case the mortgagee may be described as a 'legal mortgagee') or a fixed charge.

mortgage interest relief at source. Abbreviation: MIRAS. A system under which an individual – who pays interest on money lent by a UK building society, or other UK financial institution participating in the scheme, for purchasing, improving or developing land owned by the individual in the UK or the Republic of Ireland used as the only or main residence of the individual or of a dependent relative or former or separated spouse of the individual – may withhold basic-rate income tax from the payment. For this purpose, 'land' includes a large caravan that is subject to a general rate and a houseboat designed or adapted for use as a place of permanent habitation. The financial institutions participating in the scheme are listed in para. 14 of Schedule 7 to the Finance Act 1982. The scheme does not apply to a loan exceeding £30,000.

mortgagor. A person whose property has been charged by a charge by way of legal mortgage, an equitable mortgage, a legal mortgage, or a fixed charge.

movable. A thing which is the subject of property interests and which is not an immovable.

moving average. In relation to an ordered set of numbers (especially, a time series) { $x_1, \ldots, x_n$ }, one of the weighted averages u_t of k successive elements (where k is an integer, $1 < k < n$ and k is usually odd):

$$u_t = \sum_{j=1}^{k} w_j x_{t+j} \quad (t = 1, 2, \ldots, n - k + 1)$$

where $w_1, \ldots, w_k$ are the weights and:

$$\sum_{i=1}^{k} w_i = 1$$

The number k is called the 'order' of the moving average. If each weight is $1/k$ the moving average is said to be 'simple'. For example, in relation to the ordered set {2, 6, 1, 5, 3, 7 }, the simple moving averages of order 3 are:

$(2 + 6 + 1)/3, \qquad (6 + 1 + 5)/3, \qquad (1 + 5 + 3)/3, \qquad$ etc.

i.e., 3, 4, 3, etc.

multimodal. *Adjective.* In probability theory and statistics, having more than one mode.

multiple break-even points. Also written: multiple breakeven points. Two or more different volumes of production which are all break-even points for a producer of a product.

multiple regression analysis. Regression analysis where there are two or more independent variables.

multiplicand. A number that is multiplied by another number (called the 'multiplier').

multiplier. A number by which another number (called the 'multiplicand') is multiplied.

multiprocessor. A computer that has two or more processing units that have access to a common main store.

multiprogramming. 1. A mode of operation of a computer providing for interleaved execution of two or more computer programs by a single processor.

2. Concurrent execution of two or more computer programs by a computer.

multi-stage consolidation. Preparation of consolidated accounts involving one or more subconsolidations.

multitasking. A mode of operation of a computer that provides for the concurrent performance or interleaved execution of two or more tasks.

multi-user. *Adjective.* Used to describe a computer that is capable of being used simultaneously by several users with separate user terminals.

multivariate distribution. In probability theory, a probability distribution that determines the probability that the ordered set made up of the values of a number n of random variables is the same as a particular ordered set or is in a particular collection of such ordered sets.

mutual fund. In the USA, a corporation that is engaged in investing in securities or other investments and which issues redeemable securities. An American mutual fund offers the same service to investors as a British unit trust. Also called 'open-end fund'.

MWCA. Abbreviation of 'monetary working capital adjustment'.

N

narration. A statement written in an account to explain an entry in the account.

narrative form. Another term for 'report form'.

National Audit Office. The establishment, constituted by the Comptroller and Auditor General and staff, which audits appropriation accounts and examines the economy, efficiency and effectiveness with which government departments have used resources in discharging their functions.

National Insurance Fund. A fund under the control and management of the Secretary of State that is made up of social security contributions (apart from small amounts paid to the Maternity Pay Fund and Redundancy Fund) and a grant from the Consolidated Fund, and from which benefits payable under the Social Security Act 1975 are paid.

national insurance number. A number allocated to an individual by the Secretary of State for Social Services and used to identify the individual for the purposes of the social security scheme.

National Loans Fund. Abbreviation: NLF. A fund of the Treasury held in an account at the Bank of England from which loans are made to nationalised industries, local authorities and similar bodies. At the end of each working day, if there is a surplus in the Consolidated Fund then that surplus is transferred to the National Loans Fund; if there is a deficit in the Consolidated Fund then it is made up by a transfer from the National Loans Fund. Money for the National Loans Fund is obtained primarily by the issue of government stocks.

natural business year. In America, a fiscal year of an accounting entity which ends during a season when the business of the entity is less active than usual and it is therefore more convenient to conduct stock-taking and prepare financial statements.

natural logarithm. A logarithm to base e, where:

$$e = \Sigma \ 1/n!$$

where the sum extends over all non-negative integers n.

The natural logarithm of x may be denoted by ln x.

NBV. Abbreviation of 'net book value'.

negative interest. A charge made by a bank for taking a deposit of money from a customer for a period.

negative pledge. Where a charge has been created on property, an undertaking that no other charge with a higher priority will be created over the same property.

negotiable. *Adjective.* Of property, capable of being transferred from one person to another in such a way that the transferee may ignore all prior claims to it.

negotiable instrument. A financial document that is negotiable.

negotiate. 1. *Verb.* Generally, to discuss with a person with whom one has a difference or dispute possible terms for the settlement of the difference or dispute.

2. *Verb.* In property law, to transfer property in such a way that the transferee can ignore all previous claims to it. Property which is capable of being transferred in such a way is said to be 'negotiable'.

3. *Verb.* In banking, to buy or sell a time bill before it has been accepted.

negotiation credit. A letter of credit under which the beneficiary's bills of exchange will be negotiated by a bank named in the letter of credit – that is, the bills will be purchased by the bank before they have been accepted.

net. 1. *Adjective.* After specified deductions have been made.

2. *Adjective.* Not subject to any further deductions.

3. *Adjective.* To be sold at not less than a certain price.

4. *Verb.* To gain as an amount left after certain deductions have been made.

5. *Verb.* To compute the amount left after certain deductions have been made.

net assets. The total assets of an accounting entity less its total liabilities. In this context, 'liabilities' includes long-term loans and provisions. This definition is the same as that given for the purposes of the Companies Act 1985 in s. 264(2) of the Act. If liabilities exceed assets then the difference is called 'net liabilities' and the entity is absolutely insolvent. See also the entry for 'equity'.

net assets statement. In relation to a pension scheme, a summary of the assets of the scheme at the disposal of the trustees, after deducting ascertained liabilities (i.e., disregarding future liabilities to pay pensions and related outgoings), presented as part of the scheme's accounts (ED 34, para. 21).

net basis of calculating earnings per share. A method of calculating earnings per share of a company subject to UK corporation tax in which the charge for taxation used in determining earnings includes:

(a) any irrecoverable ACT; and

(b) any tax due outside the UK on the payment or proposed payment of dividends where the dividend payment is taxable in the UK and the UK tax authorities refuse to allow the payment of non-UK tax to be deducted from the amount of UK tax due (such tax is called 'unrelieved overseas tax').

Compare 'nil distribution basis of calculating earnings per share'.

net book value. Abbreviation: NBV. The historical cost of a fixed asset less the accumulated depreciation for that asset. Also called 'depreciated value', 'net carrying amount', 'written-down value'.

net borrowing. In current cost accounting, defined in SSAP 16, para. 45, as 'the excess of:

'(a) the aggregate of all liabilities and provisions fixed in monetary terms (including convertible debentures and deferred tax but excluding proposed dividends) other than those included within monetary working capital and other than those which are, in substance, equity capital; over

'(b) the aggregate of all current assets other than those subject to a cost of sales adjustment and those included within monetary working capital'.

net carrying amount. Another term for 'net book value'.

net cash. A condition declared by a seller of goods or services that no credit will be allowed to a purchaser and no discounts will be deducted from the advertised prices.

net cash flow. See the entry for 'cash flow'.

net cash investment in a lease. Defined in SSAP 21, para. 23, as the amount of funds invested in a lease by a lessor, comprising the cost of the leased asset plus or minus the following related payments or receipts:

(a) government or other grants receivable towards the purchase or use of the asset;

(b) rentals received;

(c) taxation payments and receipts, including the effect of capital allowances;

(d) residual values, if any, at the end of the lease term;

(e) interest payments (where applicable);

(f) interest received on cash surplus;

(g) profit taken out of the lease.

net current assets. The value of an accounting entity's current assets minus the value of its current liabilities at a particular time. This is usually regarded as the 'working capital' of the entity. Net current assets may be called 'net working capital' if the total value of current assets is called 'gross working capital'.

net current cost. Current cost less accumulated current cost depreciation.

net current liabilities. The value of an accounting entity's current liabilities minus the value of its current assets at a particular time when current liabilities is the greater amount.

net current replacement cost. Current replacement cost from which accumulated current cost depreciation has been deducted.

net dividend. The dividend actually paid by a company to its shareholders, excluding the value of the tax credit received by the shareholders. Compare 'gross dividend'. The term 'dividend' used alone always means 'net dividend'.

net dividend per share. Another term for 'dividend per share'.

net income. Term usually used in America instead of 'net profit'.

net investment in a lease. Defined in SSAP 21, para. 22, as the gross investment in a lease less gross earnings allocated to future periods.

net liabilities. Total liabilities of an accounting entity less total assets of the entity when liabilities exceed assets. 'Liabilities' includes long-term loans and provisions.

net liquid funds. Cash at bank and in hand and cash equivalents (e.g., investments held as current assets) less bank overdrafts and other borrowings repayable within one year (SSAP 10, para. 8).

net loss. 1. The amount by which the total expenses associated with a sale exceed the proceeds of the sale.

2. The financial loss made by an accounting entity over a period measured after allowing for all expenses incurred during the period including taxation and interest on long-term loans.

net monetary items. The difference between the total value of monetary assets and the total value of monetary liabilities of an accounting entity.

net operating assets. The fixed assets (including trade investments), stocks and monetary working capital dealt with in a historical cost balance sheet of an accounting entity (SSAP 16, para. 38).

net present value. Abbreviation: NPV. The total of the present values of sums receivable in connection with something minus the total of the present values of sums payable in respect of that thing.

net profit. 1. The amount by which the proceeds of a sale exceed the total expenses associated with the sale.

2. The financial gain made by an accounting entity over a period measured after allowing for all expenses incurred during the period including taxation and interest on long-term loans. The term is now not often used in this sense in Britain because the Companies Act 1985, Schedule 4, now requires that in a profit and loss account this item must be called 'profit for the financial year'. In America the term 'net income' is more commonly used than 'net profit' in this sense. In the past 'net profit' sometimes referred to profit measured without deducting either taxation or interest on long-term loans or both.

net purchases. Purchases less purchases returns.

net quick assets. The total quick assets of an accounting entity less its total current liabilities.

net realisable value. The sales value (allowing for trade discounts, but ignoring settlement discounts) of stocks and work in progress (after completion if they are not finished goods or goods bought for resale) less the costs of completing, marketing, selling and distributing them (see SSAP 9, para. 21). Also called 'expected exit value'.

net residual value. The value of an asset at the end of its useful life less expenses of realising that value.

net sales. The amount receivable by an accounting entity in respect of sales made over a period in the course of its ordinary activities (not counting trade discounts, value added tax and other taxes based on sales) after deducting sales returns, allowances, and, usually, cash discounts and quantity discounts. In America, the amount reported as 'sales' in a financial statement is net sales for the period. In Britain, an entity normally reports its turnover, which is the figure for gross sales before deducting allowances, sales returns, cash discounts and quantity discounts. However, it may be that, in practice, the amount reported as turnover by many entities in Britain is net sales.

net turnover. Defined in the EEC Council Directive on Listing Particulars, which is incorporated in the Stock Exchange (Listing) Regulations 1984 (SI 1984 No. 716), as 'the amounts derived from the sale of products and provision of services falling within [an] undertaking's ordinary activities, after deduction of sales rebates and of value added tax and other taxes directly linked to the turnover'. This is the same as 'turnover' as defined in the Companies Act 1985, Schedule 4, para. 95.

network. 1. In project network techniques, a diagram that represents interrelated activities and/or events and shows their interrelationships and dependencies. A network consists of lines, called 'arrows', that join points called 'nodes'. Also called 'project network'.

2. Short form of the term 'computer network'.

network analysis. Another term for 'project network analysis'.

net working capital. The amount by which the current assets of an accounting entity exceed its current liabilities. Also called 'net current assets', 'working capital'.

net worth. Another term for 'owners' equity'.

next in, first out. Abbreviation: NIFO. A method of valuing a class of stocks and work in progress in which the articles consumed or sold during a period are valued at their replacement cost at the end of the period.

NIFO. Usually spoken as an acronym. Abbreviation of 'next in, first out'.

nil distribution basis of calculating earnings per share. A method of calculating earnings per share of a company subject to UK corporation tax in which the charge for taxation used in determining earnings generally excludes:

(a) any irrecoverable ACT; and

(b) any unrelieved overseas tax arising from the payment or proposed payment of dividends, except in so far as such taxation arises in respect of preference dividends.

Compare 'net basis of calculating earnings per share'.

90 per cent subsidiary. See the entry for 'subsidiary'.

NLF. Abbreviation of 'National Loans Fund'.

N/N. Abbreviation of 'not to be noted', written on a bill of exchange to indicate to the bank collecting payment that the expense of noting is not to be incurred if the bill is dishonoured.

nominal account. A ledger account, the balance on which will be transferred to the profit and loss account (or income and expenditure account). Also called 'temporary account'.

nominal capital. Another term for 'nominal share capital'.

nominal ledger. The part of the ledger remaining when the cash book, creditors ledger and debtors ledger are treated as separate sections. The nominal ledger may include control accounts for the other parts of the ledger. Also called 'general ledger', 'impersonal ledger', 'private ledger'.

nominal share capital. The share capital of a registered company as stated in its memorandum of association. It indicates the maximum number of shares which the company may issue. The nominal share capital of a company may be increased by the members by a simple procedure. Also called 'authorised share capital', 'authorised capital', 'nominal capital'. The terms 'authorised share capital' and 'nominal share capital' are both used in companies legislation. In the Companies Acts, nominal share capital is often called simply 'share capital'.

nominal value. A monetary amount assigned to something (such as a security) for purposes of description or identification or to serve as the basis for a calculation.

nominee. A person who is named as the owner of an item of property (e.g., in a register of owners of registered securities) but who has undertaken to exercise all rights of ownership only as instructed by, and for the benefit of, another person.

non-adjusting event. A post balance sheet event that concerns conditions which did not exist at the balance sheet date.

non-business day. A day that is not a business day. Also called '*dies non*'.

non-cumulative preference share. See the entry for 'preference share'.

non-current asset. An asset that is not a current asset.

non-current liability. A liability that is not a current liability.

non-linear programming. Mathematical programming in which either the objective function or the constraints, or both, are not linear functions.

non-monetary asset. An asset that is not a monetary asset.

non-monetary liability. A liability that is not a monetary liability.

non-operating. *Adjective.* In America, not related to ordinary activities. For example, non-operating revenue is revenue of an accounting entity which is not derived from the entity's ordinary activities.

non-production overhead cost. An operating cost of an enterprise which is not attributable to the production of its products. Marketing cost and administration cost are usually classified as non-production overhead costs.

non-productive stock. Another term for 'indirect stock'.

non-profit. *Adjective.* Term used in America for 'non-profit-making'.

non-profit-making. *Adjective.* Operating under rules which require all income to be applied to future activities of the same type (usually charitable) and forbidding distribution of profits to, for example, suppliers of capital. (The term is not to be taken literally: a non-profit-making organisation may make profits for its own purposes but not in order to enrich others.) In America, the adjectives 'non-profit' and, more recently, 'not-for-profit' are used instead of 'non-profit-making'.

non-purchased goodwill. Goodwill other than purchased goodwill.

non-qualifying distribution. A distribution that is not a qualifying distribution (Finance Act 1972, s. 88(6)).

non-voting share. A share in a company which confers no right to vote at general meetings of members of the company apart from a right to vote at meetings of the class of non-voting shareholders in certain circumstances.

normal curve. The graph of the probability density function of a normal distribution. Often alleged to be shaped like a bell and called a 'bell-shaped curve', but the shape depends on the standard deviation of the distribution and on the scales to which the curve is drawn.

normal distribution. The probability distribution of a continuous random variable that has the probability density function:

$$f(x) = \frac{1}{\sigma\sqrt{(2\pi)}} \exp(-\tfrac{1}{2}(x - \mu)^2/\sigma^2)$$

where σ (which is the standard deviation of the distribution) and μ (which is the expectation of the distribution) are constants.

normalised form. A floating-point representation of a number, to a particular floating-point base, in which the fixed-point part lies within a prescribed range chosen so that every number will have one and only one floating-point representation with that floating-point base. For example, if the floating-point base is 10 it is usual to require the fixed-point part F to be in the range $1 \leqslant F < 10$ so that 10 is 1 1 and not 10 0. Also called 'standard form'.

normal loss. General term for normal shrinkage, normal spoilage and normal waste.

normal shrinkage. Cost of material, work in progress or finished goods lost through shrinkage that cannot be avoided, or not without incurring unacceptable costs, and which is regarded as part of the product cost.

normal spoilage. Amount of spoilage that cannot be avoided, or at least not without incurring unacceptable costs, and which is regarded as part of the product cost.

normal variate. A random variable with a normal distribution.

normal waste. Amount of waste that cannot be avoided, or at least not without incurring unacceptable costs, and which is regarded as part of the product cost.

notary public. An individual who is appointed to draw up and certify documents in order to guarantee their authenticity. Appointments of notaries public were originally made by the Church. In England they are still made by the Court of Faculties of the Archbishop of Canterbury. In Wales, however, appointments are made by the Clerk of the Crown in Chancery.

note. 1. *Noun.* Supplementary information about an item in a financial statement.

2. *Noun.* A banknote.

3. *Noun.* A promissory note.

4. *Verb.* To write on a bill of exchange, or on a slip of paper attached to a bill, a memorandum that it has been presented, for acceptance or payment, by a notary public and has been dishonoured. The memorandum is called a 'noting' and is written by the notary.

note payable. A promissory note, payable at some date in the future, considered as a liability of its maker.

note receivable. A promissory note, payable at some date in the future, considered as an asset of the person entitled to payment of it.

not-for-profit. *Adjective.* Term used in America for 'non-profit-making'.

not negotiable. *Adjective phrase.* Words which, when written on a cheque, dividend warrant or analogous instrument, which has been crossed, mean that a person who takes the document does not have and shall not be capable of giving a better title to the document than that which the person from whom he took it had (Bills of Exchange Act 1882, ss. 81, 95; Cheques Act 1957, s. 5).

novation. An arrangement by which a contract between two persons A and B is rescinded and replaced by a similar contract between A and a third person C.

NPV. Abbreviation of 'net present value'.

number of days' stock held. The ratio:

$$\frac{\text{value of stock of goods for sale held at the end of a period}}{\text{average daily cost of sales in the period}}$$

In America, called 'days to sell inventory' or 'days' sales in inventory'.

numeral. A representation of a number by characters.

numerator. See the entries for 'ratio' and 'rational number'.

numeric. *Adjective.* Involving the use of numerals.

numerical value. Another term for 'absolute value'.

nuncupative will. A will that is not written. In the law of England and Wales, a nuncupative will has no effect unless it was made by a member of Her Majesty's Armed Forces on actual military service or by a sailor or mariner at sea.

nursed account. A supplier whose invoices are always paid immediately by an enterprise that does not bother to pay other suppliers' invoices. The supplier with the nursed account can be relied on to provide a good trade reference when the enterprise seeks to deal with a new supplier.

O

objective function. In a mathematical-programming problem, a function that relates each set of values of the decision variables (representing a combination of states of the activities to be programmed) to the value of some measure of the overall effect of the combination of states represented by that set of decision-variable values.

objects clause. The clause of a memorandum of association of a company that specifies the objects for which the company is established.

occupational pension scheme. A scheme for the provision of pensions to employees.

off-balance-sheet financing. Use by an accounting entity of a source of finance creating a liability not reported in a balance sheet of the entity; in particular, using a finance lease not reported in the balance sheet.

offer. A proposal made by one person (called the 'offeror') to another person (called the 'offeree') of the terms of a contract and an indication that acceptance of the proposal by the offeree will make a contract between the offeree and the offeror. The offeror may specify the way in which acceptance must be communicated or may limit the time in which acceptance must be made.

offeree. 1. A person to whom an offer is made.

2. An offeree company.

offeree company. The company whose shares are the subject-matter of a take-over bid. Also called 'offeree'.

offeror. A person who makes an offer.

offer price. 1. The price at which the manager of a unit trust will sell a unit.

2. The price at which a jobber will sell a security.

office. 1. A collection of duties and responsibilities carried out by an appointed person (called the 'holder' of the office) – especially where several persons may be appointed holder in succession with no change in the nature of the duties and responsibilities, and the holder is not under a contract of employment or the duties are of a public nature.

2. A place where business (especially clerical and administrative rather than retailing and manufacturing) is carried out.

3. The room that a particular person or group of people use to perform non-manual work.

4. An insurance company.

official listing. Another term for 'listing'.

officially listed. *Adjective phrase.* Another term for 'listed'.

official receiver. An individual appointed by the Department of Trade and Industry and assigned to a county court or to the High Court to investigate the causes of insolvencies that are dealt with by the court. An official receiver becomes receiver of the property of an individual against whom a receiving order is made and commonly acts as a trustee in bankruptcy and as liquidator of companies in compulsory winding up.

off-line. Also written: offline. *Adjective.* Not under the control of a computer.

offset account. Another term for 'valuation account'.

offshore. *Adjective.* In relation to a company or other scheme in which investments are made, not resident in the country where the persons making the investments are resident.

offshore fund. For UK taxation purposes, a company or other scheme that is not resident in the UK, but in which persons resident in the UK have made investments. A precise definition is given in the Finance Act 1984, s. 94.

oncost. Term sometimes used in Britain for 'production overhead cost'.

on demand. *Preposition phrase.* Whenever a demand is made – used to describe an obligation (e.g., of a deposit-taker to return a customer's deposit) that must be fulfilled as soon as a demand is made for it to be fulfilled.

on-demand guarantee. A contract guarantee under which the compensation must be paid on a demand being made by the buyer without further proof that the seller has defaulted.

one-sided confidence interval. See the entry for 'confidence interval'.

one-sided test. See the entry for 'critical region'.

on-line. Also written: online. *Adjective.* Under the control of a computer.

open account. System of trading in which the seller renders an invoice for goods or services provided and the buyer pays on receipt of the invoice or after an agreed period of credit.

open cheque. American spelling: open check. A cheque that is not crossed.

open-end fund. Another term for 'mutual fund'.

opening balance. An amount recorded as an asset or liability in existence at the beginning of a period for which an account is kept.

opening stock. An amount recorded as the value of stock in existence at the beginning of a period for which an account is kept.

open-market value. See the entry for 'market value'.

operable time. Another term for 'up time'.

operand. An element of an ordered set of elements that is an argument of an operation.

operating capability. The amounts of goods and services that a business is able to supply with its existing resources in a specified period. These resources are represented in accounting terms by the net operating assets at current cost. See SSAP 16, para. 39.

operating-capability maintenance. See the entry for 'concept of maintenance of operating capability'.

operating cycle. For a business enterprise, the time between purchasing materials and receiving money from the sale of the products made from those materials or between purchasing goods for resale and receiving money from reselling them.

operating lease. 'A lease other than a finance lease' (SSAP 21, para. 17).

operating profit. The profit for an accounting period of an accounting entity derived from its ordinary activities and measured without deducting interest payable on long-term loans, preference dividends or corporation tax (or any other form of income tax).

operating system. A computer program or collection of computer programs for controlling the execution by a computer of any other computer program.

operating time. Time during which a machine or device or production facility actually performs its intended function.

operation. 1. In mathematics, in relation to a set S, a function assigning a value in S to each ordered set of n elements of S, where n is a positive integer. If n equals 1, the operation is called a 'monadic operation' or 'unary operation'; if n equals 2, the operation is called a 'dyadic operation'. Each element in an ordered set of elements that is an argument of an operation is called an 'operand' and the value associated by an operation with any particular set of operands is called the 'result' of the operation.

2. In data processing, in relation to a function that is an operation in sense 1, the action of obtaining, from particular operands, the result the function assigns to those operands.

operational audit. A review of activities, methods and procedures of an organisation to determine whether they are being carried out effectively and efficiently.

operational research. Abbreviation: OR. Activity, process, or study of applying scientific (especially mathematical) methods to the solution of problems involving the operations of a system. The usual aim of operational research is to provide those in control of the system with an optimum plan for the operation of the system. In America, called 'operations research'.

operation card. A document which records the times spent by individual workers on a particular job, or the materials used on a particular job or both. It may also give instructions on how to do the job. Also called 'job card', 'job sheet', 'job ticket', 'work ticket'.

operations research. Abbreviation: OR. Term used in America for 'operational research'.

operation time. In production planning, the period of time that is required to carry out an operation on a complete batch exclusive of set-up time and breaking-down time (BS 5191 : 1975).

operator. 1. An individual who operates a machine.

2. In data processing, a symbol showing that an operation is to be performed.

operator console. Part of a computer containing devices by which an operator of the computer can communicate with it. Also called 'console'.

opportunity cost. In relation to a course of action, the value of an alternative course of action that could have been pursued, but which was forgone in favour of the course being costed.

opposed bid. Another term for 'defended bid'.

optimise. *Verb.* To find the most favourable possible state of a system.

optimum. The most favourable possible state of a system.

option. An arrangement by which one person (called an 'option holder') is entitled, at some time in the future, to buy something from, or to sell something to, a second person (called the 'writer of the option') at a price (called the 'exercise price' or 'striking price') fixed at the time of making the arrangement, or may choose not to buy or sell the thing. An option to buy is called a 'call option'. An option to sell is called a 'put option'.

OR. 1. Abbreviation of 'operational research'.
 2. Abbreviation of 'operations research'.

order cheque. American spelling: order check. A cheque drawn payable to a named payee or to the order of that payee (indicated by the words 'or order'), meaning that the payee may direct that the cheque be paid to another person, by endorsing it.

order cover. In stock control, 'the sum of stock physically on hand and on order, less any reserved stock' (BS 5191 : 1975). Also called 'free balance'.

ordered pair. An ordered set containing only two elements.

ordered set. In mathematics, a set, with elements stated in a particular order, which is considered to be different from a set containing the same elements stated in a different order.

order point. See the entry for 'reorder-level system'.

order processing time. The period of time between the recognition that a thing must be purchased or manufactured and the placing of the necessary order or requisition.

ordinal. Another term for 'ordinal number'.

ordinal number. A number designating the position of an item in an ordered sequence, e.g., first, second, third, ... Also called 'ordinal'.

ordinary activity. In relation to an accounting entity, an activity that is usually undertaken by the entity or a related activity engaged in by the entity in furtherance of, incidental to, or arising from, activities usually undertaken by it. See ED 36, para. 31.

ordinary resolution. 1. In British company law, a resolution that is valid if approved by a simple majority of votes cast on it and without any minimum period of notice to members that the resolution is to be proposed. Compare 'extraordinary resolution', 'special resolution'.
 2. In the bankruptcy law of England and Wales, under the Bankruptcy Act 1914, a resolution of creditors which is valid if approved by a majority in value of the creditors present and voting in person or by proxy at a meeting of creditors.

ordinary share. A share in a company carrying the ordinary benefits usually associated with membership of a company. The most important of these benefits are the right to a share of the company's profits, rather than a payment of a fixed amount out of profits (compare 'preference share'), and the right to a vote at all meetings of members of the company (though there have been 'non-voting ordinary shares' which do not carry a right to vote).
 In practice, the term 'equity share' means the same as 'ordinary share'.

ordinary share capital. Share capital contributed for ordinary shares.

ordinary shareholder. A shareholder whose shares are ordinary shares. See also the entry for 'equity shareholder'.

ordinary shareholders' equity. The equity of an incorporated company that would be distributed to ordinary shareholders if the company were wound up. It is calculated as the value of the assets of the company minus the value of the liabilities of the company (including long-term loans) and minus the amount of any capital that, in winding up, would have to be repaid to preference shareholders or any other class of member having priority over the ordinary shareholders. In practice, most companies only have one class of shareholder – ordinary shareholders – so that ordinary shareholders' equity is usually called 'shareholders' equity'. Even if a company does have preference shareholders it is commonly assumed that they do not count as 'shareholders' for the purpose of calculating equity so that in this case also the term 'shareholders' equity' is used to mean 'ordinary shareholders' equity'. Also called 'ordinary shareholders' funds'.

ordinary shareholders' funds. Another term for 'ordinary shareholders' equity'.

organisation costs. Term used in America for 'preliminary expenses'.

organisation expenses. Term used in America for 'preliminary expenses'.

originating timing difference. A timing difference that arises in an accounting period when the treatment of a transaction or event in financial statements differs from the treatment accorded to the same transaction or event for taxation purposes (SSAP 15, para. 20).

OTC. Abbreviation of 'over-the-counter'.

out-of-date cheque. American spelling: out-of-date check. Another term for 'stale cheque'.

out-of-pocket expense. A minor expense paid for by an individual, on incurring the expense, by cash, cheque or charge card.

output device. Another term for 'output unit'.

output process. In data processing, a process that consists of delivering data from a data processing system or a part of a data processing system.

output tax. Value added tax on supplies made by a taxable person.

output unit. In a data processing system, a device by which data can be received from the system. Also called 'output device'.

outside shareholders. Another term for 'minority shareholders'.

outside shareholders' interests. Another term for 'minority interests'.

outstanding cheque. American spelling: outstanding check. From the point of view of an accounting entity, a cheque that has been drawn on its bank account but has not yet been presented for payment.

over-absorbed overhead. Absorbed overhead (usually, absorbed production overhead costs) for a period less actual overhead for the period when absorbed overhead is the greater amount. In America, called 'over-applied overhead'.

over-applied overhead. Term used in America for 'over-absorbed overhead'.

overcapitalised. *Adjective.* Having more contributed capital and/or reserves than is necessary for the scale of operations being conducted.

overcast. *Verb.* To record an erroneous total that is larger than the true total.

overdraft. See the entry for 'bank overdraft'.

overdue account. An account receivable not paid at the end of the agreed period of credit. In America, called 'delinquent account receivable'.

overhead. 1. In an enterprise which manufactures goods or provides services, any cost other than a direct cost identified with producing a product. In a trading enterprise, any cost other than cost of goods sold. Or, an aggregate of such costs.

2. Overhead cost; production overhead cost.

overhead absorption. Allocation of overhead (usually, production overhead costs) to products or cost centres.

overhead cost. The sum of indirect expenses, indirect labour cost and indirect material cost. This is the definition given in the ICMA official terminology and it refers only to production costs. However, to avoid confusion with the term 'overhead', which usually refers to selling and administration costs as well as indirect production costs, it may be better to use the term 'production overhead cost'.

overhead efficiency variance. Where standard variable overhead cost is measured in terms of something other than units of production, the difference between the standard overhead cost of the actual quantity of the product produced during a budget period and the standard overhead cost that would be allocated to that production for the actual number of units of measurement taken. For example, if the standard variable overhead cost is measured in terms of direct labour hours, then the overhead efficiency variance is the difference between the standard overhead cost of the actual quantity of product produced in the budget period and the standard overhead cost that would be allocated to the actual number of direct labour hours used during the period.

overhead expenditure variance. The difference between the standard overhead cost for the budgeted or standard quantity to be produced during a budget period and the actual overhead expenditure incurred during that period.

overhead total variance. The difference between the standard overhead cost for the actual quantity produced during a budget period and the actual overhead cost incurred during that period.

overhead volume variance. Where standard variable overhead cost is measured in terms of something other than units of production, the difference between the standard overhead cost that would be allocated to the actual number of units of measurement taken and the overhead cost given by the flexed budget for that number of units of measurement.

oversea company. A company incorporated in a place outside England, Wales and Scotland which has a place of business in England, Wales or Scotland (Companies Act 1985, s. 744).

oversubscribed. *Adjective.* Used to describe an issue of securities when there has been an invitation to the public generally to subscribe for the securities and the number of securities which the public offer to take is greater than the number being issued.

over-the-counter. Abbreviation: OTC. *Adjective.* Used to describe a purchase of securities from, or sale of securities to, a dealer otherwise than on a stock exchange.

overtrading. Expansion of the production and sales of a business without adequate financial support.

owners' equity. The equity of an accounting entity that has owners. It is equal to the capital contributed to the accounting entity by the owners of the entity (or their predecessors) plus the reserves of the entity or minus the deficit of the entity. In principle, this is the amount of money which should be distributed to the owners if the entity were dissolved. If there is only one owner, as with a sole trader, the term is spelled 'owner's equity'. Also called 'capital', 'net worth', 'owners' interest', 'ownership interest'.

ownership interest. Another term for 'owners' equity'.

owners' interest. Another term for 'owners' equity'.

P

p.a. Abbreviation of 'per annum'.

Paasche index. An index number that is used to describe items in a time series of weighted averages of observations, the same things being observed on each occasion but different weights being used on each occasion. For example, if the observations are the prices $p_{1t}, p_{2t}, \ldots, p_{nt}$ of n goods on occasion t, on which $q_{1t}, q_{2t}, \ldots, q_{nt}$ were the quantities of goods bought, and the comparison is with occasion 0, then the Paasche price index for occasion t is:

$$\frac{100 \sum_{i=1}^{n} p_{it} q_{it}}{\sum_{i=1}^{n} p_{i0} q_{it}}$$

A Paasche index measures the change in the price of quantities of items actually bought (cf. Laspeyres index). Named after a German economist, Hermann Paasche (1851-1925).

Pacioli, Luca. An Italian mathematician who is sometimes described as 'the father of accounting' because he wrote the first printed treatise on double-entry bookkeeping. Pacioli was born in Sansepolcro (formerly Borgo San Sepolcro), Tuscany, circa 1445 and died in the same town in 1517. He was a Franciscan friar who spent most of his life teaching mathematics at various universities in Italy including those at Perugia, Naples, Rome, Milan and Pisa. He published several works on mathematics and on chess and translated Euclid into Latin. Pacioli was a friend of Leonardo da Vinci, who illustrated one of Pacioli's books on mathematics. His important work for the history of accounting was *Summa de arithmetica, geometria, proportioni et proportionalita*, which was published in Venice in 1494. Written in Italian, it contains a general treatise on theoretical and practical arithmetic, elements of algebra, a table of moneys, weights and measures, a summary of Euclid and the treatise on double-entry bookkeeping which is called *De Computis et scripturis*. Double-entry bookkeeping was for some time known as the 'method of Venice', reflecting the widespread dissemination and popularity of Pacioli's work.

packet. In the transmission of data, a string of binary digits, primarily conveying data but also including control characters, which is routed and transmitted as a unit and in which the data and the control characters are arranged in a standard format.

packet switching. The process of routing and transferring data by means of addressed packets so that a channel is occupied only during transmission of a packet, after which the channel is available for the transfer of other packets.

packing note. A document sent to a customer advising of the contents of a package.

paid. *Participle.* When added to a financial document or invoice: payment has been made of the amount due.

paid-in capital. Another term for 'contributed capital'.

paid-up share capital. The nominal value of all allotted shares in a company less any amounts not yet called on partly paid shares and any amounts called but not yet paid on partly paid shares.

P and L. Abbreviation of 'Parliamentary and Law Steering Group'.

P and L account. Abbreviation of 'profit and loss account'.

paper. Informal. Securities traded on a stock exchange; financial documents that are traded and held as investments.

para. Abbreviation of 'paragraph'.

parametric test. A statistical test in which the distribution function of the test statistic depends on the form of distribution function of the population.

parent company. A company that controls, directly or indirectly, one or more other companies by ownership of voting rights. In IAS 2, defined as a company that has one or more subsidiaries, where a 'subsidiary' is a company controlled by a parent company and 'control' of a company means ownership, directly, or indirectly through subsidiaries, of more than one-half of the voting power of the company. In British company law the term 'holding company' has a precise statutory meaning similar to that of 'parent company'.

parenthesis-free notation. Another term for 'prefix notation'.

Pareto analysis. Another term for 'ABC analysis'.

pari passu. At the same rate; equally.

Parliamentary and Law Steering Group. Abbreviation: P and L. A committee within the Consultative Committee of Accountancy Bodies that coordinates the views and representations of accountancy bodies on governmental and legislative proposals affecting the accountancy profession.

parol. A spoken, not written, statement.

part. Something which, with other things, will make up something, but which is itself regarded as an indivisible unit for the purposes of planning and control. Also called 'component'.

partial derivative. A derivative of a function of two or more variables calculated on the assumption that all but one of the variables are constant.

partial differential coefficient. In relation to a function of two or more variables, the differential coefficient for a particular set of values of the independent variables calculated on the assumption that all but one of the variables are constants.

partial differentiation. The process of finding a partial derivative.

partial intestacy. Death of an individual without leaving a will to deal with part of his or her estate.

participating preference share. A preference share, that carries the additional right to an extra dividend from profits whenever ordinary shareholders are paid a dividend exceeding a certain amount.

participator. For the purposes of determining whether a company is a close company, a 'participator' is 'a person having a share or interest in the capital or income of the company, and . . . includes:

'(a) any person who possesses, or is entitled to acquire, share capital or voting rights in the company;

'(b) any loan creditor of the company;

'(c) any person who possesses, or is entitled to acquire, a right to receive or participate in distributions of the company . . . or any amounts payable by the company (in cash or in kind) to loan creditors by way of premium on redemption; and

'(d) any person who is entitled to ensure that income or assets (whether present or future) of the company will be applied directly or indirectly for his benefit'.

See Income and Corporation Taxes Act 1970, s. 303.

partly paid share. A share in a company is a partly paid share if the value of the capital contributed to the company for the share (ignoring any share premium) is less than the nominal value of the share.

partner. A person who carries on a business or profession in partnership with others.

partnership. Defined in the Partnership Act 1890, s. 1(1), as: 'the relation which subsists between persons carrying on a business in common with a view of profit'. By s. 45 of the Act: 'the expression "business" includes every trade, occupation, or profession'. By s. 1(2) of the Act, the relation between members of any incorporated company is not a partnership within the meaning of the Act.

partnership agreement. An agreement between partners about the operation of their partnership, covering such matters as capital, profit-sharing ratios, and what is to happen to the partnership if any partner dies or becomes bankrupt. Also called 'articles of partnership'. A partnership agreement is usually in a deed and so may be called a 'deed of partnership' or 'partnership deed'.

partnership deed. Another term for 'deed of partnership'.

partnership property. In relation to a partnership, property that must be dealt with exclusively for the purposes of the partnership and in accordance with the partnership agreement, and which, on dissolution of the partnership, must be used to pay the debts and liabilities of the partnership with any surplus being distributed among the partners. The Partnership Act 1890, s. 20, states that 'All property and rights and interests in property originally brought into the partnership stock or acquired, whether by purchase or otherwise, on account of the firm or for the purposes and in the course of the partnership business, are . . . partnership property'.

parts list. Another term for 'bill of materials'.

par value. The nominal value of a security.

Pascal. A programming language that is specified in BS 6192 : 1982, which has been endorsed by ISO 7185-1983. The language was designed by Niklaus E. Wirth (born 1934), a professor at the Institut für Informatik of the Eidgenössische Technische Hochschule, Zürich, Switzerland, originally for teaching programming though subsequently it has been adopted in everyday use. The language is named after Blaise Pascal (1623–62), a French mathematician usually regarded as the first person to design and manufacture a calculating machine.

pass. 1. *Verb.* Where one is expected to pay interest or dividends at regular times, intentionally to miss making a payment at one of those times.

2. *Verb.* In relation to a resolution of a meeting, to adopt.

passbook. A small account book given to a customer of a deposit-taker in which the deposit-taker records for the customer all transactions between them.

password. A string of characters that a user of a data processing system must enter into the system in order to use the system or a particular file or program.

pawn. 1. *Noun.* An article subject to a pledge.

2. *Verb.* To pledge something.

pay plan. Another term for 'payment system'.

payback. Another term for 'payback period'.

payback method. A technique of appraising investments by calculating their payback periods.

payback period. The length of time necessary for the returns (usually measured after tax has been paid) on an investment to equal the initial sum invested. Also called 'payback', 'payoff period', 'payout time'.

payee. The person named in a financial document as being entitled to payment of money. Usually a named payee is entitled to order payments to be made to some other person. Some financial documents do not name a payee, but are payable to bearer.

paying bank. A bank paying a financial document of which it is drawee.

paying-in slip. Another term for 'credit slip'.

payment credit. A letter of credit under which the beneficiary is to receive immediate payment on presentation of the stipulated documents.

payment in advance. Another term for 'prepayment'.

payment on account. A payment of part of a debt, leaving the remainder to be paid at some later date.

payment system. The principles, rules and procedures by which the rates of pay of employees of an employer are determined. Also called 'pay plan'.

payoff. Also written: pay-off. The value of a possible result or outcome of a decision.

payoff period. Also written: pay-off period. Another term for 'payback period'.

payout ratio. Another term for 'dividend payout'.

payout time. Another term for 'payback period'.

payroll. A record of the payments to be made to each employee of an employer, showing gross pay, deductions and net pay.

PCB. Abbreviation of 'petty cash book'.

PDB. Abbreviation of 'purchases day book'.

Pearson coefficient of correlation. Another term for 'coefficient of correlation', using the name of an English scientist, Karl Pearson (1857-1936), who, in 1896, was the first to use the coefficient of correlation.

pecuniary. *Adjective.* Consisting of money.

pendente lite. *Participle with noun.* Pending suit. Used to describe a personal representative, or the appointment of a personal representative, of a deceased individual for the purpose of administering the estate of the deceased until settlement of legal proceedings concerning the validity of a will or the validity of a previous grant of representation. Compare '*ad litem*'.

pension. A regular payment to an individual who has retired from a particular job or from working generally.

pension fund. The fund of money from which pensions will be paid under a pension scheme.

pension scheme. An arrangement for providing a defined class of individuals (called 'members') with pensions. A pension scheme may also provide other benefits to members and may provide benefits to dependants of deceased members.

per annum. Abbreviation: p.a. *Preposition phrase.* Yearly.

P/E ratio. Also written: P-E ratio. Abbreviation of 'price/earnings ratio'.

per cent. *Preposition phrase.* In America, written: percent (*adverb*). Of each hundred. Used following a number to indicate that it should be divided by 100 to arrive at the actual quantity being stated.

percentage. The numerator of a rational number whose denominator is 100.

percentage error. If a is an approximation to a quantity then the percentage error of the approximation is the absolute error of the approximation expressed as a percentage of a.

percentage point. 1. In discussing the size of one thing as a percentage of the size of a second thing, 1% of the size of the second thing. In discussing a rate of change of something, a rate of change of that thing of 1%.

2. Another term for 'percentile'.

percentage profit on turnover. Defined in the ICMA official terminology as the profit before interest and tax for a period expressed as a percentage of the turnover for that period. See also the entry for 'profit-to-turnover ratio'.

percentile. A fractile, the order of which is expressed as a percentage. Also called 'percentage point'.

per diem. *Preposition phrase.* For each day.

performance guarantee. An arrangement under which a guarantor promises to pay compensation to a buyer if a sales contract is not properly performed.

performance measure. The measure that is used to evaluate alternative plans, or possible states of a system, in an operational research problem.

period cost. A cost, such as of rent or insurance, arising from being in business during a period of time, as opposed to a cost identified with producing a product. Though considered from a different viewpoint, period costs are probably the same as 'fixed overhead costs'.

periodic inventory. Term used in America for 'periodic stock-taking'.

periodicity concept. An assumption made in accounting that it is possible to identify the effects of the transactions and events affecting an accounting entity with particular periods of time for which financial statements may be prepared. Also called 'convention of periodicity', 'time-period concept', 'time-period principle'.

periodic review system. Another term for 'reorder-interval system'.

periodic stock check. Term used in BS 5191 : 1975 for 'periodic stock-taking'.

periodic stock-taking. Also written: periodic stocktaking. Measurement of quantities of stocks and work in progress held at the end of an accounting period by counting or otherwise measuring all items on a single day (or over a period during which no movements of stocks are permitted). In BS 5191 : 1975, called 'periodic stock check'. In America called 'periodic inventory'.

period of account. For the purposes of corporation tax, the period for which a company's accounts are prepared, which is the period between one accounting date and the next, which is the period between one balance sheet date and the next.

peripheral. In data processing, short form of the term 'peripheral equipment'.

peripheral equipment. In a data processing system, any hardware distinct from the processing unit. Also called 'peripheral'.

permissible capital payment. An amount which a private company may pay, but which is not covered by available profits or the proceeds of a new issue of shares, when redeeming or repurchasing its own shares under chapter VII of Part V of the Companies Act 1985.

permutation. A selection made from a set of items is regarded as a permutation if the order of items within the selection is material. Compare 'combination'.

perpetual audit. Another term for 'continuous stock-checking'.

perpetual inventory. A method of recording the quantities, and sometimes values, of stocks by recording each receipt and issue of stock as it occurs.

perpetuity. 1. An annuity payable for ever.

2. A disposition of property to a person in such a way that it is possible that the person may not acquire a vested interest in the property until after a time-limit set by law. In English law, the time-limit is normally the expiration of a life or lives in being at the time of creation of the disposition plus 21 years.

person. A participant in legal or financial transactions, whether an individual human being, a partnership firm, an unincorporated association, or an incorporated company. In any Act of Parliament passed after the year 1889 and subordinate legislation made after 1 January 1979, 'person' includes a body of persons corporate or unincorporate (Interpretation Act 1978, Schedule 1).

personal account. An account recording the accounting entity's transactions with one person as either debtor or creditor.

personal chattel. Another term for 'chattel personal'.

personal computer. Abbreviation: PC. A general-purpose computer designed to be used by one individual, and sold at a price which makes it economic to purchase the device for such limited use.

personal credit agreement. Defined by the Consumer Credit Act 1974, s. 8, as: 'an agreement between an individual ("the debtor") and any other person ("the creditor") by which the creditor provides the debtor with credit of any amount'. 'Credit' includes a cash loan and any other form of financial accommodation. 'Individual' includes a partnership firm or other unincorporated body of persons not consisting entirely of bodies corporate. If the amount of credit provided under a personal credit agreement does not exceed £15,000 (£5,000 before 20 May 1985) the agreement is a consumer credit agreement.

personal property. Any property that is not real property. Also called 'personalty'.

personal relief. 1. A deduction, which an individual may claim from the amount of income subject to UK income tax, specified in the Income and Corporation Taxes Act 1970, s. 8. The amount to be claimed depends on the taxpayer's marital status and age.

2. Any of the reliefs from income tax specified in the Income and Corporation Taxes Act 1970, ss. 8 to 21.

personal representative. Abbreviation: PR. A person who administers the estate of a deceased individual. In England and Wales, a personal representative may be either:

(a) a person appointed in the deceased's will – called an 'executor' of the deceased; or

(b) a person appointed by the High Court – called an 'administrator' of the deceased.

See also the entry for 'executor de son tort'.

personalty. Another term for 'personal property'.

per stirpes. See the entry for 'inheritance *per stirpes*'.

PERT. Acronym from 'programme evaluation and review technique'. A project network technique developed by the US Navy Special Projects Office and an American firm of management consultants, Booz, Allen & Hamilton. The technique is used to deal with uncertainty in estimating the durations of activities in a project by making three estimates of each duration: a most optimistic estimate, a most likely estimate and a most pessimistic estimate. A certain type of probability distribution is assumed for estimates of activity durations and a critical path is found for an activity-on-arrow network.

petroleum revenue tax. Abbreviation: PRT. A tax, governed by the Oil Taxation Act 1975, on profits made from extracting oil from wells in any part of the United Kingdom or its territorial waters or the United Kingdom sector of the Continental Shelf.

petty cash. Small amounts of cash used for minor everyday payments.

petty cash book. Abbreviation: PCB. A book recording minor payments and receipts of cash.

phasing. Division of a budget period into control periods.

physical inventory. Finding the quantity of stocks and work in progress held by actually counting or otherwise measuring them.

'Physical inventory' is the term used for this activity in the ICMA official terminology. Compare 'physical stock check'.

physical stock check. A check on stock by direct measurement or scrutiny together with subsequent comparison with, and reconciliation to, stock records (BS 5191 : 1975). In the ICMA official terminology the activity of directly measuring stock is referred to as 'physical inventory' without reference to checking stock records.

pictogram. A diagram in which numbers of things are represented by pictures of the things which are either repeated or changed in size in proportion to the number to be represented.

piece rate. A rate of payment for an individual's work per unit of product worked on by the individual.

pie chart. A diagram showing the relative sizes of the components of some quantity by means of a circle divided into sectors with areas proportional to the sizes of the components. Also called 'circular chart'.

PINCCA. Abbreviation of *'Price Index Numbers for Current Cost Accounting'*.

pixel. A small element into which a pictorial image is divided for handling by a data-processing system.

PL. Abbreviation of 'private ledger'.

placement. Term used in America for 'placing'.

placing. A method of issuing or selling a block of securities in which the whole block is taken by a small number of persons, some or all of whom may be securities dealers who will resell to their clients. In America called 'placement'.

plc. Abbreviation of 'public limited company'.

pledge. 1. A form of charge on goods in which possession or control of the goods is given to the chargee (who is called the 'pledgee') on condition that the goods will be returned when the secured obligation is fulfilled. A pledgee has an implied right to sell the goods if the secured obligation is not fulfilled.

2. A promise to make a gift to a charity.

pledgee. A person to whom goods are given in pledge.

pledgor. A person who gives goods in pledge.

PNA. Abbreviation of 'project network analysis'.

PNT. Abbreviation of 'project network technique'.

Poisson distribution. A probability distribution – of a discrete random variable X, that may take as value any non-negative integer – defined by the formula:

$$P(X = r) = e^{-m}m^r/r!$$

where m is a positive number. If an event is unlikely to occur but there are many opportunities for it to occur and m is the most likely number of occurrences then $P(X = r)$ is the probability that it will occur r times.

policy cost. Another term for 'fixed overhead cost'.

Polish notation. Another term for 'prefix notation'.

population. In statistics, the totality of items under consideration.

population parameter. In statistics, in relation to some quantitative or qualitative characteristic of the items in a population, represented by a random variable, a number used to describe the probability distribution of the random variable.

port. The point on a data processing device at which a connection may be made to some other device for the purpose of transferring data between them.

portfolio. A collection of investments.

portfolio theory. A theory about how investments should be chosen to make up a portfolio.

position. The collection of tasks, duties and assignments that an employee is employed to perform. Also called 'job', 'post'.

positional representation system. A notation for the representation of numbers in which a number is represented by an ordered set of digits, the integer represented by each digit is multiplied by a factor (called a 'weight') that depends on the position of the digit in the set, and the sum of the products so obtained is the number represented. A position in an ordered set of digits used to represent a number in a positional representation system is called a 'digit place'.

positive integer. One of the numbers used for counting: 1, 2, 3, ...

post. 1. *Verb.* To make an entry in one accounting record based on one or more entries in another record; in particular to make an entry in a ledger account based on one or more entries in a journal.

2. *Noun.* The collection of tasks, duties and assignments that an employee is employed to perform. Also called 'job', 'position'.

post balance sheet event. An event affecting the financial state of an accounting entity that occurs between a balance sheet date and the date when that balance sheet is approved by the directors or other senior officers of the entity for publication. In America, called 'subsequent event'.

post-cessation receipts. Sums arising from the carrying on of a trade, profession or vocation received after the trade, profession or vocation has been permanently discontinued. Also called 'receipts after discontinuance'.

post-date. *Verb.* To give as the date of a document (on the document itself) a date that is later than the actual date of writing it.

postfix notation. A notation for dyadic operations in which the symbol for an operation is preceded by its operands. For example, the addition of the numbers 5 and 3 and multiplication of the sum by 2 is written 5 3 + 2 ×. Also called 'reverse Polish notation', 'suffix notation'.

post-retirement award. An increase, whether contractual or discretionary, in a pension being paid (ED 32, para. 36).

power. 1. In law, in relation to a transaction or legal relationship, the quality of a person that the person may enter into the transaction or relationship without thereby making it void.

2. In mathematics, a value of a^x for a particular number a.

3. In mathematics, another term for 'exponent'.

4. In statistics, in relation to a statistical test, the probability of not accepting the null hypothesis when the null hypothesis is not true.

power of appointment. A right to create or dispose of beneficial interests in property which the person with the power does not own absolutely. A person with a power of appointment is called the 'donee' of the power.

PR. Abbreviation of 'personal representative'.

practical capacity. Full capacity less an allowance for known unavoidable volume losses.

practical insolvency. Inability to pay debts as they fall due. Used when a distinction is made between absolute insolvency and practical insolvency. See the entry for 'insolvency'.

practice. Another term for 'private practice'.

PRB. Abbreviation of 'purchases returns book'.

preceding-year basis. A basis of assessment to UK tax in which income or gains are charged to tax in the year of assessment or financial year after the one in which they arise.

precept. A demand, made by a body that carries out public functions in a local area, requiring the local authorities in the area to pay a specified amount for those functions out of money raised by a general rate.

pre-consolidation adjustments. See the entry for 'consolidation accounts'.

pre-emption. 1. Acquisition by existing members of a company of newly issued shares in the company before outsiders have a chance to acquire them.

2. Acquisition by members of a company of shares which a fellow member wishes to sell before outsiders have a chance to acquire them.

preference. See the entry for 'fraudulent preference'.

preference dividend. A fixed amount payable each year to the holders of preference shares.

preference share. A share in a company carrying a right to be paid a fixed amount (called a 'preference dividend') each year out of the company's profits, other members of the company being left to share whatever profits are left after payment of the preference dividends. The size of a preference dividend is usually expressed as a percentage of the nominal value of a share.

Preference shares are said to be 'cumulative' if a preference dividend that is not paid in one year, because of lack of profits, has to be paid in the next year in which sufficient profits are made. With 'non-cumulative preference shares', if the profits of a particular year are not sufficient to pay the preference dividend for that year, then it is lost. Preference shares are assumed to be cumulative unless otherwise stated. Preference shares usually do not carry a right to vote at meetings of members of the company. Compare 'ordinary share'.

preference share capital. Share capital contributed for preference shares.

preference shareholder. A shareholder whose shares are preference shares.

preferential creditor. A creditor of an insolvent person whose debt is a preferential debt.

preferential debt. A debt that must be paid in preference to other debts if the debtor is formally recognised as being insolvent. The circumstances in which debts must be recognised as preferential are:

(a) When an individual is adjudged bankrupt.

(b) When the estate of a deceased individual, who was not adjudged bankrupt while alive, is found to be insolvent.

(c) When a receiver is appointed of all, or substantially all, of the property of a company under a floating charge.

(d) When a company passes a resolution to wind up.

(e) When a winding-up order is made against a company or a provisional liquidator is appointed.

The preferential debts are principally rates and taxes and remuneration due to employees. The costs and expenses of administering the property of the insolvent person must be paid before the preferential debts. There are some debts which have an even higher priority than preferential debts and these are called 'pre-preferential debts'.

prefix notation. A notation for dyadic operations in which the symbol for an operation is writen before its operands. For example, the addition of the numbers 5 and 3 and multiplication of the sum by 2 is written × + 5 3 2. Also called 'Łukasiewicz notation', 'parenthesis-free notation', 'Polish notation'. The notation was invented by Jan Łukasiewicz (1878-1956), a Polish logician, while he was professor of philosophy at Warsaw University (1920-1939) and leader of a group of logicians called the 'Polish school'.

preliminary expenses. Legal costs and fees paid in connection with the incorporation of a new company. Also called 'formation expenses' or, tautologously, 'preliminary and formation expenses'. In America, called 'organisation costs' or 'organisation expenses'.

premium on redemption. Another term for 'redemption premium'.

prepaid asset. Another term for 'prepayment paid'.

prepaid expense. Another term for 'prepayment paid'.

preparation time. 'The period of time between the placing of a production order and the commencement of manufacture' (BS 5191 : 1975).

prepayment. Payment made for something before the thing is received. From the point of view of the payer, a prepayment is deferred expenditure and is called a 'prepayment paid'; from the point of view of the recipient of the payment, it is deferred revenue and is called a 'prepayment received'. In the Companies Act 1985, Schedule 4, balance sheet formats, 'prepayment' is used to mean 'prepayment paid'. Also called 'payment in advance'.

prepayment paid. Payment made for something before the thing is received – from the point of view of the payer. In the balance sheet formats in the Companies Act 1985, Schedule 4, called 'prepayment'. Also called 'prepaid asset', 'prepaid expense'.

prepayment received. Payment made for something before the thing is received – from the point of view of the recipient of the payment.

pre-preferential debt. A debt of an insolvent person which must be paid in priority to any other claim against the person. For example, if a bankrupt was an officer of a friendly society and had money of the society's by virtue of his or her office then that must be repaid in preference to any other debt or claim (Friendly Societies Act 1974, s. 59).

presenting bank. In relation to the collection of documents, the collecting bank which presented the documents to the person named by the principal in the collection order. The person to whom the documents are to be presented is called the 'drawee'.

present value. Abbreviation: PV. The value now of a sum of money to be paid or received in the future. The present value of an amount P is calculated as the amount which, if invested now to earn compound interest would have a terminal value equal to P at the time when P is to be paid or received. The rate of interest used in this calculation is called the 'discount rate'. The present value, at a discount rate i per time period, of an amount P to be paid or received at the end of t time periods, is, if t is a positive integer:

$$\frac{P}{(1 + i)^t}$$

If $0 < t < 1$ then the present value is:

$P(1 - ti)$

If $t > 1$ and t is not an integer, and $[t]$ is the largest integer less than t then the present value is:

$$\frac{P([t]i + 1 - ti)}{(1 + i)^{[t]}}$$

Also called 'present worth'.

present value of 1. The factor $1/(1 + i)^t$ used to calculate a present value when t is a positive integer.

present worth. Another term for 'present value'.

presumed resulting trust. A trust that arises as a matter of law where one person transfers property to a second person gratuitously in such a way that the second person is presumed to hold the property on trust for the first person unless the second person can prove that the transfer was in fact a gift.

pre-trading expenditure. Expenditure incurred by a person for the purposes of carrying on a trade before commencing to carry on that trade.

price/earnings ratio. Abbreviation: P/E ratio. Also written: price-earnings ratio; abbreviation: P-E ratio. The market price of an equity share in a listed company divided by the company's earnings per share.

Price Index Numbers for Current Cost Accounting. Abbreviation: PINCCA. A publication compiled by the Business Statistics Office and published by HMSO giving price indices for use in calculating the current replacement cost of assets in the UK. A summary volume (*Business Monitor MO 18*) was published in 1983 giving data for the years 1974 to 1982 and this is updated by monthly supplements (*Business Monitor MM 17*). Fourteen issues of an earlier series with the same title, compiled by the Government Statistical Service, were published by HMSO from 1976 to 1981.

primary auditor. The auditor of a holding company of a group of companies for which group accounts have to be prepared.

prime cost. The total of direct material costs, direct labour costs and direct expenses for a period for a product or products. Prime cost plus variable production overhead cost is direct production cost of sales.

principal. 1. The person on whose behalf an agent transacts business.

2. The person on whose instructions a bank carries out a collection.

3. An amount of money on which interest is payable.

principal beneficiary. See the entry for 'protective trust'.

principal budget factor. A limiting factor which is used as the starting-point in preparing a budget.

prior-charge capital. Debt capital and preference share capital. Interest and dividends on prior-charge capital must be paid before dividends can be paid on ordinary shares and, on winding up, the nominal value of prior-charge capital must be repaid before any distribution is made to the holders of ordinary shares.

priority. Order in which claims of payment from a single source are to be met.

priority percentages. In relation to the earnings before interest and after tax of a company, figures that show, for each claim on those earnings, the percentage of those earnings payable to other claims having priority over that claim and the total percentage of those earnings payable to that claim and the claims having priority over it.

prior-period adjustment. Term used in America for 'prior-year adjustment'.

prior-period item. Term used in IAS 8 for 'prior-year adjustment'.

prior-year adjustment. An amount which is, or should be, reported specially in a financial statement to show that the amount reported in the preceding statement as retained earnings has been materially altered because of a change in accounting policies or the discovery of a fundamental error. See SSAP 6 and ED 36. In America, called 'prior-period adjustment'. In IAS 8, called 'prior-period item'.

private company. 1. Generally, a company that does not issue invitations to the general public to invest in it. A private company normally raises capital from its founder members, its employees and possibly a small number of other investors.

2. In British company law, any registered company that is not a public company. It is a criminal offence for a private company that is a limited company to invite the public generally to invest in it, though a private company that is an unlimited company may make such an invitation and a private company that is a company limited by guarantee may invite the public to lend it money.

private drawing. Another term for 'drawing'.

private ledger. Abbreviation: PL. In the accounts of a partnership or the business of a sole trader, either the general ledger as a whole, or the capital accounts alone.

private placement. Term used in America for 'private placing.'

private placing. A placing of redeemable securities in which the securities are taken by persons who intend to hold them until redemption so that no arrangements are made for the securities to be marketable. In America, called 'private placement'.

private practice. In Britain, the part of the accountancy profession in which each individual accountant or partnership of accountants offers to provide accountancy services to a number of clients as independent professional adviser and not as employee. In Britain, it is unnecessary to be professionally qualified in order to set up in private practice as an accountant; however, only professionally qualifed accountants (and authorised auditors) may audit the accounts of a registered company. In America, where private practice is called 'public practice' or 'public accounting', it is necessary to be licensed under state law which almost invariably requires a licensee to be a certified public accountant. Also called 'practice'.

private treaty. A contract for the sale of property arrived at by negotiation between the seller and buyer without competitive bidding (e.g., at an auction or sale by tender) from other potential buyers.

privileged will. A will that takes effect without any formal act of execution. In the law of England and Wales, a member of Her Majesty's Armed Forces on actual military service or a sailor or mariner at sea may make a privileged will.

processing unit. A part of a computer consisting of one or more processors and their internal stores. Also called 'central processing unit', 'central processor'.

processor. A part of a computer that interprets and executes instructions.

pro forma. 1. *Preposition phrase.* A representation of the layout or form of an account, calculation, etc.

2. *Preposition phrase.* A pro-forma invoice.

3. *Verb.* Written: pro-forma. To issue a pro-forma invoice to a potential customer.

pro-forma invoice. Also written: pro forma invoice. A document which shows, in respect of a proposed sale, what the invoice would be. Used to obtain payment in advance of a sale or to obtain permission for payment to be made for a sale under exchange control or when sending goods on consignment to an agent.

probability. The likelihood or relative frequency of occurrence of something; usually expressed as a number between 0 and 1 (or as a percentage).

probability density function. The derivative of the distribution function of a continuous random variable.

probability distribution. A function which gives for each value, or set of values, of a random variable the probability that it will take that value, or a value in that set of values.

probate. A certificate given by a court that a will has been proved and registered in the court and that administration of the estate has been granted to the executor who proved the will, a copy of which is attached to the certificate. In England and Wales, probate is granted by the Family Division of the High Court.

procedure. A description of a course of action undertaken for a particular purpose; a method of performing a task.

process costing. Another term for 'continuous-operation costing'.

procurement lead time. A period of time between the recognition that something must be purchased and the time when that thing is available for use.

produce advance. A merchandise advance made for the purchase of agricultural or horticultural produce. Also called 'produce loan'.

produce loan. Another term for 'produce advance'.

product. 1. A thing, or service, supplied by an organisational unit (an enterprise, a work station, a factory) and resulting from work performed within that unit.

2. In mathematics the result of carrying out the operation of multiplication.

product cost. The cost of a finished product calculated by adding together constituent labour costs, material costs and expenses.

product group. A number of products with one or more common characteristics which make it convenient to combine them for planning and control purposes (BS 5191 : 1975).

production control. Ensuring that planned quantities of products are produced according to a specified quality, and with planned costs.

production cost. Prime cost of a specified quantity of production plus absorbed overhead (excluding non-production overhead) of that production (ICMA official terminology).

production cost centre. American spelling: production cost center. A cost centre in which production is carried on. Also called 'direct cost centre'. Compare 'service cost centre'.

production cost of sales. The sum of direct production cost of sales for a period and fixed production overhead cost for that period. Also called 'cost of sales' (which is the term preferred in the ICMA official terminology), 'cost of goods sold', 'factory cost', 'manufacturing cost', 'manufacturing cost of goods produced'.

production cost variance. The difference between the total standard production cost of the quantity of product actually produced during a budget period and the actual production cost for that period.

production order. A document used in an organisation to initiate the manufacture of a product or the provision of a service, specifying such matters as quantity and delivery date. Also called 'factory order', 'manufacturing order', 'shop order', 'works order'.

production overhead. In calculating the cost of stocks and work in progress, defined in SSAP 9, para. 20, as an overhead incurred in respect of materials, labour or services for production, based on the normal level of activity, taking one year with another.

production overhead cost. A cost that is an indirect expense, indirect labour cost or indirect material cost, or an aggregate of such costs. Also called 'oncost', 'production overhead' or, in a manufacturing enterprise, 'factory overhead', 'factory overhead cost' or 'manufacturing overhead'. In the ICMA official terminology, production overhead cost is called 'overhead cost' and it may also be called 'overhead', but this may be ambiguous because 'overhead' usually refers to selling and administration costs as well as indirect production costs. In America, sometimes called 'burden' or 'factory burden'.

production planning. Analysis of the production methods and resources required to manufacture products and establishment of manufacturing programmes and plans.

production volume ratio. The ratio:

$$\frac{\text{standard hours of production during a budget period}}{\text{budgeted number of standard hours of production for the period}}$$

Also called 'activity ratio'.

productive stock. Another term for 'direct stock'.

productive work. Work that alters the physical or chemical nature of the product or makes a necessary contribution to its completion (BS 3138 : 1979).

product moment. Another term for 'covariance'.

product-moment coefficient of correlation. Another term for 'coefficient of correlation'. Deriving from the use of 'product moment' as an alternative term for 'covariance'.

profession. An occupation requiring predominantly intellectual skills acquired after lengthy training.

profit. An improvement in financial position as a result of one or more transactions, or as a result of the transactions and events accounted for during an accounting period.

Profit on an individual transaction is measured by subtracting from the proceeds of the transaction the expenses incurred to obtain those proceeds. Profit is often considered in terms of particular types of expense only so that only those expenses are deducted from proceeds to arrive at a figure for profit. For example, the profit on sale of goods may be calculated by deducting from the proceeds of sale only the cost of producing or acquiring the goods and not the costs of selling them or the administrative costs of the enterprise. A profit calculated without deducting all expenses is usually described as a 'gross profit' and a profit calculated by deducting all expenses is usually described as a 'net profit'.

Traditionally, the change in financial position over an accounting period was thought of as the aggregate of the profits and losses made on the individual transactions during that period, using accrual accounting to match revenues and expenses for the period, and ignoring new contributions of capital and distributions to owners. However, this method of measuring change in financial position may not show the change in value of the entity – either the value of its assets or the capacity of the entity to earn revenues – if only the historical costs of assets are considered. Depreciation accounting is used to ensure that the use of fixed assets and the need to replace them are reflected by a charge against revenue in computing profit. Current cost accounting may be used to compute profit after providing for the maintenance of the operating capability of the business of the accounting entity. Various forms of asset revaluation may be used, outside current cost accounting, to give a better measure of the value of the entity to its owners.

profitability index. The ratio of the total of the present values of amounts receivable in respect of something to the total of the present values of amounts payable in respect of the thing. Also called 'benefit-cost ratio'.

profit and loss account. Abbreviation: P and L account. 1. A financial statement summarising revenues and expenditures for a period and showing how the profit or loss for the period after payment of tax is computed, starting with turnover or net sales. If the accounting entity is not a business enterprise this account is called an 'income and expenditure account' or 'revenue account'. Sometimes the term 'profit and loss account' is used only for the section of this statement in which net profit is computed starting with gross profit, and the whole statement is then called a 'trading and profit and loss account'. A profit and loss account normally accompanies a balance sheet and deals with the period ending with the date of that balance sheet and beginning on the date of the preceding balance sheet. Schedule 4 to the Companies Act 1985 gives four alternative formats for the profit and loss account and requires every profit and loss account of a registered company to show the items listed in any one of those formats in the order and under the headings given in the format adopted. In America the term 'income statement' is used instead of 'profit and loss account' in this sense.

2. An item in a balance sheet which states the amount of retained profit of the accounting entity at the balance sheet date. In America the term 'retained earnings' or 'retained income' is used instead of 'profit and loss account' in this sense.

3. A ledger account recording gross profit or loss (when posted from the trading account) and the revenues and expenses which are used to compute profit or loss for an accounting period. Normally each revenue and expense transaction is entered initially in the relevant ledger account for that class of transaction. The profit and loss account is prepared by balancing those revenue and expense accounts periodically and posting the balances to the profit and loss account. In America it is not usual to keep a separate trading account or to calculate gross profit or loss separately, and there a profit and loss account includes all the items which in Britain would be entered in a trading account. In Britain a single account combining the trading account and profit and loss account is called a 'trading and profit and loss account'.

For an accounting entity that is not a business enterprise, an account similar to a trading and profit and loss account is kept which is called an 'income and expenditure account'.

profit margin. A ratio of profit measured in some way to turnover (or net sales). The simplest version is the ratio of net profit to turnover. Others are the contribution margin, gross margin and the profit-to-turnover ratio.

profit on manufacture. Another term for 'manufacturing profit'.

profits available for distribution. The profits of a registered company that may be distributed to its members, otherwise than on the winding up of the company, without offending against the law. A company's distributable profits are defined in s. 263(3) of the Companies Act 1985 as 'its accumulated, realised profits, so far as not previously utilised by distribution or capitalisation, less its accumulated, realised losses, so far as not previously written off in a reduction or reorganisation of capital duly made'. A public company is subject to a further restriction, contained in s. 264 of the Companies Act 1985, that its net assets must not be less than the aggregate of its called-up share capital and undistributable reserves at the time of or after a distribution.

profit-sharing ratio. The ratio of the shares of a partnership firm's profits that will be taken by the partners. The Partnership Act 1890, s. 24(1), provides that, unless otherwise agreed, all partners are entitled to share equally in profits. The profit-sharing ratio also determines the way in which any losses are to be borne.

profit-to-turnover ratio. Defined in the ICMA official terminology as the ratio of the profit before interest and tax for a period to the turnover for that period. If the ratio is expressed as a percentage then it is called 'percentage profit on turnover'.

profit variance. The difference between the total standard profit on the actual quantity of products sold during a budget period and the actual profit received during that period.

profit-volume chart. A graph plotting the profit from selling a product against the quantity sold. The quantity for which the profit is zero is the break-even point.

program. 1. *Noun.* Short form of the term 'computer program'.

    2. *Noun.* American spelling of 'programme'.

    3. *Verb.* To devise a computer program.

program evaluation and review technique. American spelling of 'programme evaluation and review technique'.

program flowchart. Also written: program flow chart. Another term for 'programming flowchart'.

program library. An organised collection of computer programs.

programme. American spelling: program. 1. A plan expressed in very general terms.

    2. A plan expressed in terms of the timing of events.

    3. A group of activities of an organisation directed towards a common purpose.

programme evaluation and review technique. American spelling: program evaluation and review technique. See the entry for 'PERT'.

programming flowchart. Also written: programming flow chart. A diagram representing the sequence of operations in a computer program. Also called 'flowchart', 'program flowchart'.

programming language. A system of characters, conventions and rules established for expressing computer programs. The short form 'language' is often used.

programming problem. In operational research, another term for 'allocation problem'.

program test time. Time during which a data processing system is used to test a user's computer program. It is part of system production time.

project network. Another term for 'network'.

project network analysis. Abbreviation: PNA. Analysis of interrelated activities by using a project network technique. Also called 'network analysis'.

project network technique. Abbreviaton: PNT. Any of a group of techniques that are used for describing, analysing, timing and controlling interrelated activities and which involve the use of networks.

promissory note. Defined in s. 83 of the Bills of Exchange Act 1882 as 'an unconditional promise in writing made by one person to another signed by the maker, engaging to pay, on demand or at a fixed or determinable future time, a sum certain in money, to, or to the order of, a specified person or to bearer'.

    If a promissory note names the person to whom payment is to be made then that person is called a 'payee'. A promissory note may simply be called a 'note'.

promotion expense. Term used in America for 'publicity cost'.

proof. A statement of claim made by a creditor in an insolvency. A written proof must be sent to the official receiver, liquidator or trustee in bankruptcy as appropriate, stating the date, nature and amount of the debt and whether any security has been given for it. It is no longer necessary for a proof to be supported by a statutory declaration unless this is insisted upon by the official receiver, liquidator or trustee in bankruptcy.

proper accounting records. Accounting records that are required to be kept by every British trade union and employers' association and which are such records as are necessary to give a true and fair view of the state of the affairs of the trade union or employers' association and to explain its transactions (Trade Union and Labour Relations Act 1974, s. 10).

property. 1. In law, a relationship between a person (called the 'owner') and a thing by which the owner is entitled to the benefits that may be derived from the thing and is entitled to compensation if any other person takes any of those benefits without the permission of the owner. The owner is said to have property 'in' the thing which is the subject-matter of the property. In the law of England and Wales, property is classified as either 'real' property or 'personal' property. The subject-matter of personal property may be either tangible (a 'thing in possession') or intangible (a 'thing in action').

2. In non-legal use, tangible objects owned by a person – especially land.

property, plant and equipment. Defined in IAS 16 as: tangible assets of an accounting entity that:

(a) are held by the entity for use in the production or supply of goods and services, for hire to others, or for administrative purposes;

(b) have been acquired or constructed with the intention of being used on a continuing basis; and

(c) are not intended for sale in the course of the entity's ordinary activities.

Items held for the maintenance or repair of property, plant and equipment may themselves be counted as property, plant and equipment. Items leased to the accounting entity may be counted as property, plant and equipment.

proportional consolidation. A method of preparing consolidated accounts for a holding company and a subsidiary that is not a wholly owned subsidiary in which a proportion of the subsidiary's results, corresponding to the proportion of ownership held by the holding company, is included in the consolidated accounts and there is no statement of minority interests in the consolidated accounts. Compare 'full consolidation'.

proprietor. 1. An owner of property.

2. An owner of a business enterprise.

3. Another term for 'sole trader'.

prospectus. Defined in the Companies Act 1985, s. 744, as 'any prospectus, notice, circular, advertisement, or other invitation, offering to the public for subscription or purchase any shares in or debentures of a company'. In this context, 'company' means a registered company.

protective trust. A trust that has one beneficiary (called the 'principal beneficiary') who is entitled to income from the trust property, but whose interest lasts only until something (e.g., bankruptcy) occurs which would deprive the principal beneficiary of the right to receive the income. A protective trust is normally created by directing that property is to be held on 'protective trusts for the benefit of' a person in accordance with s. 33 of the Trustee Act 1925.

protest. 1. *Noun.* A document given by a notary public and bearing the notary's seal attesting the fact that a bill of exchange has been dishonoured.

2. *Verb.* To make a protest (in sense 1).

prove. *Verb.* To make a statement of claim in an insolvency.

provision. 1. An amount, deducted from revenue for an accounting period in computing profit for that period, as depreciation of a fixed asset.

2. An amount credited to a liability account to represent an estimate of a liability whose extent and/or timing are uncertain.

provisional liquidator. 1. An individual appointed to act temporarily as liquidator of a company that has been ordered by the court to be wound up. After a short time the provisional liquidator is replaced by a liquidator appointed by the company's creditors, though in practice the individual who acts as provisional liquidator is usually appointed liquidator.

2. An individual appointed by a court to take charge of a company's affairs pending the hearing by the court of a petition for the compulsory winding up of the company.

provision for bad debts. Another term for 'provision for doubtful debts'.

provision for discounts allowable. A provision for cash discounts that, it is assumed, will be claimed by the debtors existing at a balance sheet date. In America, called 'allowance for sales discount'.

provision for doubtful debts. A provision made to allow for the possibility that some debts due for payment in the future may never be paid. If the provision is based on a listing of individual debts which are considered doubtful, it is called a 'specific' provision; if it is simply a percentage of total debtors, it is called a 'general' provision. In practice a provision is likely to be partially specific and partially general. Sometimes called 'provision for bad debts'. In America, called 'allowance for doubtful accounts', 'allowance for uncollectible accounts'.

proxy. 1. A person appointed to represent another person at a meeting.

2. A document appointing a person to represent another person at a meeting.

PRT. Abbreviation of 'petroleum revenue tax'.

prudence in accounting. Inclusion of revenue and profits in accounts only when they are realised and inclusion in profits of all known liabilities, whether their size and timing are known or can only be estimated. This is one of the four fundamental accounting concepts identified in SSAP 2 and is one of the accounting principles set out in the Companies Act 1985, Schedule 4. See also the entry for 'conservatism'.

In IAS 1, prudence is not regarded as a fundamental accounting assumption but as a consideration which should govern the selection and application of appropriate accounting policies.

pseudocode. A method of representing computer programs in which a program is represented in a form that requires translation before execution.

public accounting. Term used in America for 'private practice'.

Public Accounts Commission. A body of commissioners appointed by the House of Commons which supervises the National Audit Office.

Public Accounts Committee. Informal version of the title 'Committee of Public Accounts'.

public company. 1. Generally, a company that is permitted to invite the general public to invest in it, either by contributing capital to it or by lending money to it.

2. In British company law, a registered company that has registered, or re-registered, as a public company and so has a certificate of incorporation stating that it is a public company. A public company must be a limited company. There are several conditions for registration, or re-registration, as a public company, one of which is that the name of the company must end with the words 'public limited company' or the abbrevation 'plc' (or the Welsh equivalent 'cwmni cyfyngedig cyhoeddus' or 'ccc'). Another condition is that the memorandum of association of a public company must state that the company is to be a public company.

3. In the past, often used to mean 'listed company'.

publicity cost. A cost identified with advertising and sales promotion undertaken in order to increase sales of products or to enhance the reputation of the entity for which the cost is identified. In America, called 'promotion expense'.

public limited company. Abbreviation: plc. In British company law, a registered company that is a public company.

public practice. Another term for 'private practice'.

public-sector accounting. Accounting in central government, local authorities and public corporations.

Public Trustee. A public official appointed by the Lord Chancellor under the Public Trustee Act 1906, who may accept appointment as a trustee, or a custodian trustee, or as personal representative of a deceased individual and is usually appointed in circumstances in which it is inappropriate to appoint an accountant or solicitor in public practice, e.g., because the amount of property involved is small.

Public Works Loan Board. Abbreviation: PWLB. A body of commissioners, with a staff, which makes long-term loans to local authorities, using money from the National Loans Fund and charging interest at a rate determined by the Treasury. Payments of interest and repayments of principal are made to the National Loans Fund.

Public Works Loan Commissioner. A commissioner appointed by the Crown under the Public Works Loans Act 1875 as a member of the Public Works Loan Board.

pur autre vie. *Preposition phrase.* For the life of another – used to describe a property interest that a person has until another individual dies.

purchase. 1. *Noun.* In accounting, a business transaction in which an accounting entity receives goods or services from a supplier in exchange for money or some other benefit given or promised.

2. *Verb.* To enter into a business transaction with the object of acquiring goods or services in exchange for money or some other benefit given or promised.

3. *Noun.* Plural form (purchases). Goods bought for resale.

purchased goodwill. Goodwill of an incorporated company that is established as a result of purchasing a business where acquisition accounting is used. See SSAP 22.

purchased life annuity. 'A life annuity granted for consideration in money or money's worth in the ordinary course of a business of granting annuities on human life' (Income and Corporation Taxes Act 1970, s. 230(6)).

purchased parts stock. In stock control, stock that is in the same state as when purchased and has not been issued, i.e., stock held in the purchased parts store (BS 5191 : 1975).

purchase invoice. An invoice, from the purchaser's point of view.

purchase order. A document offering to purchase specified goods or services from a supplier (or accepting a supplier's offer to sell), usually setting out a full description of what is to be purchased, the price, delivery date and possibly other terms of the contract.

purchaser. A person who enters into a transaction to purchase something.

purchase requisition. A document used within an organisation to require the purchase of stated goods or services. A purchase requisition may have to be approved by a particular person in the organisation before it becomes effective.

purchases day book. Abbreviation: PDB. A record of purchases, apart from those recorded in the cash book, prepared from invoices received from suppliers, stating, for each transaction, the name of the supplier, the amount of the invoice and the reference number that has been given to the invoice by the accounting entity. Each transaction is posted to the credit of the supplier's account in the creditors ledger, if such accounts are kept, but only periodic totals need be posted to the debit of the purchases account in the ledger. If separate creditors' accounts are not kept then the credit entry in the ledger is made in the cash book on payment of invoices. Also called 'bought day book', 'purchases journal'.

purchases ledger. The creditors ledger of a trading enterprise.

purchases return. A thing that has been purchased but returned to the seller with the expectation that the invoiced charge will be cancelled – from the purchaser's point of view. Also called 'return outward'. From the seller's point of view this is a 'sales return' or 'return inward'.

purchases returns book. Abbreviation: PRB. A list of purchases returns, giving, for each return, the date, name of supplier, amount of invoiced charge to be cancelled, and, possibly, number of the accounting entity's debit note. Each return is debited to the supplier's account in the creditors ledger, if such accounts are kept, but only periodic totals need be credited to the purchases returns account. If separate creditors' accounts are not kept then the amounts of debit notes are offset against invoices when making payments, effectively giving a debit posting in the cash book. Also called 'returns outward book'.

purchasing lead time. The period of time between ordering something from a supplier and taking delivery of that thing.

purchasing power. The quantity of goods and services which may be purchased for a particular quantity of money. Usually measured, at a particular time, by an index number which gives the percentage, that can be purchased at that time, of a collection of goods that could be purchased with the same amount of money at the base date – which is the reciprocal of the index number for the prices of those goods and services.

pure binary numeration system. A positional representation system in which the ratio of the weight of any digit place to the weight of the digit place with the next lower weight is two, in which there is a digit place with weight one, and in which the digits used are 0 and 1.

pure research. See the entry for 'research and development expenditure'.
PV. Abbreviation of 'present value'.
PWLB. Abbreviation of 'Public Works Loan Board'.

Q

quadratic function. A function, associating two sets of numbers, in which the value of the dependent variable y may be computed from the independent variable x by the formula:

$$y = b_0 + b_1 x + b_2 x^2$$

where b_0, b_1 and b_2 are constants.

quadratic programming. Mathematical programming when the objective function is a quadratic function and all the constraints are linear functions.

qualified acceptance. An acceptance of a bill of exchange that expressly varies the effect of the bill as drawn (Bills of Exchange Act 1882, s. 19(2)). In particular, an acceptance is qualified which is:

(a) conditional, i.e., which makes payment by the acceptor dependent on the fulfilment of a condition therein stated;

(b) partial, i.e., an acceptance to pay part only of the amount for which the bill is drawn;

(c) local, i.e., an acceptance to pay only at a particular specified place (an acceptance to pay at a particular place is a general acceptance, unless it expressly states that the bill is to be paid there only and not elsewhere);

(d) qualified as to time;

(e) the acceptance of one or more of the drawees, but not of all.

qualified auditor's report. Another name for a 'qualified audit report'.

qualified audit report. An audit report in which the auditor directs attention to any important limitation attending the examination or to doubt or disagreement about any item reported or that the auditor is unable to form an opinion on whether the statements give a true and fair view. Also called 'qualified auditor's report'.

qualifying distribution. A payment of dividend, or other distribution of its assets, to a member of a company by the company on which advance corporation tax must be paid. See Finance Act 1972, s. 84.

quality cost variance. The difference between the budgeted cost of scrapping, rectifying or selling, at substandard prices, product that fails to conform to quality specification and the actual cost incurred.

quantile. Another term for 'fractile'.

quantity discount. A reduction in price of goods which a seller offers to any purchaser who takes more than a certain quantity. Also called 'volume discount'.

quantum meruit. An amount claimed as a reasonable payment for work done by one person for another when there was no agreement about how much was to be paid for the work. '*Quantum meruit*' is Latin for 'as much as he has earned'.

quartile. A fractile of order p where p is 0.25 (the 'first quartile'), 0.5 (the 'second quartile') or 0.75 (the 'third quartile').

quasi-loan. For the purposes of ss. 330 to 346 of the Companies Act 1985, defined in s. 331(3) of the Act as: 'a transaction under which one party ("the creditor") agrees to pay, or pays otherwise than in pursuance of an agreement, a sum for another ("the borrower") or agrees to reimburse, or reimburses otherwise than in pursuance of an agreement, expenditure incurred by another party for another ("the borrower"):

'(a) on terms that the borrower (or a person on his behalf) will reimburse the creditor; or

'(b) in circumstances giving rise to a liability on the borrower to reimburse the creditor'.

In summary, a quasi-loan is an arrangement between two persons A and B under which A agrees to meet some of B's financial obligations on the condition that B reimburses A.

quasi-reorganisation. In America, reduction of the amount recorded as contributed capital of an incorporated company in order to reflect a loss of capital. In Britain, an equivalent procedure is called 'reduction of capital' but it always requires court sanction which is not necessary in an American quasi-reorganisation.

queueing time. Alternative spelling of 'queuing time'.

queuing time. Alternative spelling: queueing time. 1. In queuing theory, the time spent waiting in a queue. Also called 'waiting time'.

2. In production planning, the period of time between the arrival of material at a work station and the start of work on it (BS 5191 : 1975, in which the spelling 'queueing' is used). In production planning, according to BS 5191 : 1975, the term 'waiting time' is not synonymous with 'queuing time'.

quick asset. A current asset that either is cash or can be converted into cash in a short time, usually taken to be a month or less, without loss of value. Examples include demand deposits at a bank, government stock, many trade debtors.

quick ratio. Another term for 'acid-test ratio'.

quick succession relief. A reduction in the capital transfer tax chargeable on the death of an individual where the tax is attributable to a chargeable transfer to that individual which occurred within five years before that individual's death (Capital Transfer Tax Act 1984, s. 141).

quid pro quo. One thing in return for another; consideration.

quorum. A fixed number of members of a committee, a meeting, etc., whose presence is necessary for the valid transaction of business.

quotation. 1. Statement of the price which a person is prepared to accept for something, such as: (a) the price for carrying out work specified by a potential customer, (b) the price for supplying goods or services specified by a potential customer.

2. Statement of the prices at which a dealer is prepared to buy something and to sell the same thing – given without knowing whether the person requesting the quotation intends to buy or sell.

A quotation in senses 1 or 2 is an offer which becomes a binding contract if accepted within a reasonable time.

3. Another term for 'listing'.

quoted. *Adjective.* Listed on a stock exchange. The term is used because dealers on a stock exchange quote buying and selling prices for securities that are listed on the exchange.

quotient. 1. In relation to a division operation in which the remainder is not to be treated as a separate part of the result, the result of the division.

2. In relation to the division of a number x by a number y, in which the remainder is to be treated as a separate part of the result, the integer N with the property that:

$$|x - Ny| < |y|$$

R

rack-rent. The maximum rent that can be obtained for a piece of land in normal market conditions at a particular time.

RAM. Acronym from 'random-access memory'. In data processing, a store with direct access to every location.

R and D expenditure. Abbreviation of 'research and development expenditure'.

random access. Another term for 'direct access' although its use is deprecated in BS 3527 : Part 12 : 1978.

random-access memory. See the entry for 'RAM'.

random numbers. A sequence of numbers produced in such a way that the number in a particular place in the sequence cannot be predicted by knowing the previous numbers in the sequence.

random sample. In statistics, a sample, containing a particular number of items, chosen from a population in such a way that any possible sample with that number of items could have been chosen with a known probability. The term usually refers to a 'simple random sample' – i.e., one in which any possible sample has an equal probability of being chosen.

random variable. A dependent variable for which a probability distribution has been defined. Also called 'variate'.

random walk. The path of an object that moves in steps, where the direction and/or magnitude of each step is determined by chance.

range. 1. In mathematics, the set of values that may be taken by a function.

  2. In statistics, the difference between the greatest and the smallest observed values of a quantitative characteristic.

rank. 1. *Verb.* To list or arrange things in order of importance (according to some concept of what makes them important) or in order of the degree to which they possess some specified attribute.

  2. *Noun.* A position in a series of things that have been ranked.

rate. 1. A charge or payment (e.g., of discount, interest or wages) expressed as an amount per unit of what is paid for.

  2. A tax levied on the occupation (or sometimes ownership) of land within a certain geographical area. In England and Wales the two principal rates that are levied are the general rate and rates for the supply of water.

rateable value. A monetary value that is assigned to an item of real property and which is the basis for calculating the general rate payable for occupation of the property. The rateable value of property is based on the annual rent that might reasonably be expected to be received for the property if it were let from year to year.

rate of return. 1. In portfolio theory, the income and capital gain to be obtained by buying an investment at one time and selling it at a later time (usually, one year later) expressed as a percentage of the purchase price.

2. In evaluating investments other than marketable securities, the average annual profit from the investment expressed as a percentage of the average amount of money invested. Profit is usually measured after tax and after allowing for depreciation.

rate of stock turn. Another term for 'stock turnover'.

ratio. The number (called the 'numerator') of units of one thing corresponding to a particular number (called the 'denominator') of units of another thing; the result of dividing one number by another.

ratio analysis. Assessment of the performance of an organisation by calculating ratios and noting how these alter over time or in comparing them with the same measures calculated for other organisations.

rational number. The product of an integer m and the reciprocal of a non-zero integer n, denoted by m/n, by mn^{-1} or by:

$$\frac{m}{n}$$

m is called the 'numerator' and n is called the 'denominator' of the rational number.

raw material. Material used as input to a production process resulting in finished products (BS 5191 : 1975).

raw materials stock. Stock of raw material that is not part of work in progress, i.e., stock held in the raw materials store (BS 5191 : 1975).

R/D. Abbreviation of 'refer to drawer'.

RDG. Abbreviation of 'regional development grant'.

read-only memory. See the entry for 'ROM'.

real account. A ledger account, the balance on which will not be transferred to profit and loss account (or income and expenditure account) but will be shown in the balance sheet.

real property. Property of the following kinds:

(a) freehold estates in land;

(b) some interests in land that will subsist for a period of time of uncertain duration;

(c) property in the deeds of title to land;

(d) property in peerages and baronetcies.

The term 'real property' derives from the Latin word *res*, 'thing'. The common-law rule was that a wrongful possessor of an item of real property would be ordered by a court to give up the thing, or *res*, and restore it to its rightful owner, whereas a wrongful possessor of an item of any other kind of property was required to pay monetary compensation to the rightful owner, but not to give up the property.

Also called 'realty'.

real-time. 1. *Adjective.* Used to describe the operation of a computer in accordance with time requirements imposed by events or processes taking place outside the computer, for example, operation in conversational mode or processing data relating to a physical process while that process is happening so that results of the computation can be used to affect the process.

2. *Adjective.* Used to describe data processing that can be influenced by human intervention while in progress.

3. *Noun phrase.* Written: real time. The actual time in which physical processes or events take place and within which a computer must process data to influence the processes or events.

realty. Another term for 'real property'.

receipt. 1. *Noun.* Action of taking delivery of something or state of having taken delivery.

2. *Noun.* Written acknowledgement of having taken delivery of goods or having received payment of money. The Cheques Act 1957, s. 3, provides: 'An unendorsed cheque which appears to have been paid by the banker on whom it is drawn is evidence of the receipt by the payee of the sum payable by the cheque'.

3. *Noun.* Plural form (receipts). Amount of money received in defined circumstances.

4. *Verb.* To write on an invoice an acknowledgement that the amount charged has been paid.

receipts after discontinuance. Another term for 'post-cessation receipts'.

receipts and payments account. A summary of cash transactions over a period, sometimes prepared as a financial statement for an accounting entity that is not a business enterprise. As it does not show prepayments and accruals, and does not separately identify capital expenditure, a receipts and payments account is unlikely to give a true and fair view of the financial position of the entity. This term is not in use in America.

receipts and payments basis. A principle, which may be used as a basis for the preparation of financial statements, that revenues and costs should be dealt with in the accounts for the period in which money was actually received or paid. Also called 'cash basis'.

receivable. Another term for 'account receivable'.

receiver. An individual appointed to collect a person's property and look after it either so that its fate can be determined by a court or so that it can be utilised for the benefit of a creditor.

receivership. 1. The office and duties of a receiver – especially, a receiver appointed, by the chargee under a floating charge created by a company, after the company has defaulted on the obligations secured by the charge.

2. In relation to a company that has given a floating charge over its assets and has defaulted on the obligations secured by the charge, in the state of being administered by a receiver appointed by the chargee under the floating charge.

receiving order. In the bankruptcy law of England and Wales, an order of a court appointing the official receiver as receiver of an individual's property pending the court's decision on whether to adjudge the individual bankrupt. The 1984 Insolvency Bill proposes the abolition of receiving orders.

reciprocal. In relation to a non-zero number a, the number b such that $ab = 1$. The reciprocal of a is denoted by $1/a$, by a^{-1} or by:

$$\frac{1}{a}$$

Zero does not have a reciprocal.

recognise. *Verb.* To take into consideration in accounts, especially, in a profit and loss account (or income and expenditure account).

recognised bank. A bank that has been granted recognition by the Bank of England under the Banking Act 1979. With some exceptions, only a recognised bank may represent itself to the general public in the UK as carrying on a banking business, and only a recognised bank may include the word 'bank' in its name.

recognised stock exchange. 1. In UK tax legislation:

(a) the Stock Exchange, and

(b) any such stock exchange outside the United Kingdom as is for the time being designated as a recognised stock exchange by order made by the Board of Inland Revenue.

See Income and Corporation Taxes Act 1970, s. 535. A large number of stock exchanges outside the UK have been designated by order of the Board.

2. For the purposes of the Companies Act 1985, the Stock Transfer Act 1963 and the Prevention of Fraud (Investments) Act 1958, the Stock Exchange is now the only 'recognised stock exchange'.

reconciliation. An analysis of the causes of difference between two amounts, accounts or balances, for example, a bank reconciliation.

reconstruction. In company law, transfer of one company's entire business and assets to a new company specially formed for the purpose whose shares are allotted to the members of the old company. The new company may, for example, have a different capital structure from that of the old, reflecting a loss of capital by the old company, or it may be incorporated in a different country. Sometimes called 'external reconstruction' when the term 'internal reconstruction' is used for reduction of capital without forming a new company.

record. In data processing, a group of related items of data that is treated as a separate item when it is one of a collection of similar groups of data regarded as a file.

record book. A book that a trustee in bankruptcy or a liquidator in a compulsory winding up is required to keep, recording minutes of proceedings and resolutions adopted at meetings of creditors and of a committee of inspection (if there is one). In a compulsory winding up, minutes of meetings of contributories must also be kept in the record book.

recourse. A right of a person who finances a transaction between two parties to resort to one of the parties for repayment of the finance if the other party fails to provide repayment.

recoverable ACT. Defined in SSAP 8, para. 20, as the amount of advance corporation tax paid or payable by a company on outgoing dividends paid and proposed which can be:

(a) set off against a corporation-tax liability on the profits of the period under review or of previous periods; or

(b) properly set off against a credit balance on deferred tax account; or

(c) expected to be recoverable taking into account expected profits and dividends – normally those for the next accounting period only.

recoverable amount. The greater of the net realisable value of an asset and, where applicable, the amount recoverable from its further use (SSAP 16, para. 43; ED 37, para. 13).

rectification note. 'A document which authorises additional operations to bring a substandard product up to specification' (BS 5191 : 1975). Also called 'rework note'.

red clause credit. A letter of credit under which the advising bank is authorised to make advances to the beneficiary for working capital before receiving the commercial documents stipulated in the credit. Traditionally the clause authorising advance payments is in red.

redeemable preference share. A redeemable share that is a preference share.

redeemable security. A security issued on condition that the issuer will buy it back at some time in the future.

redeemable share. A share in a company issued on condition that the company will buy it back and cancel it at some time in the future.

redemption. Release of property from temporary ownership by, or a charge in favour of, some other person, for example, when redeemable shares are bought by the issuing company or when the obligation secured by a charge on property is met so that the charge comes to an end.

redemption premium. An addition to the nominal value of debenture stock or a redeemable share or a similar security payable when the security is redeemed by its issuer. Also called 'premium on redemption'.

red herring. A preliminary prospectus for a new issue of securities, either in the USA or in the market for international bonds. In both of these markets the fact that a prospectus is preliminary is indicated by red printing. This use of 'red herring' is a presumably ironic adaptation of its use to mean a false trail.

red-lining. The policy of refusing to grant consumer credit to individuals who live in a particular locality.

reducing balance method. Another term for 'declining balance method'.

reducing instalment method. American spelling: reducing installment method. Another term for 'declining balance method'.

reduction of capital. In British company law, reduction of the nominal value of issued shares or even cancellation of issued shares and corresponding reduction of the amounts recorded in the share capital accounts to reflect, for example, a loss of capital or a return to members of capital no longer required. Sometimes called 'internal reconstruction'.

Redundancy Fund. A fund under the control and management of the Secretary of State, consisting of a proportion of secondary Class 1 social security contributions, from which redundancy rebates are paid. Any temporary deficit in the Fund is overcome by a loan from the National Loans Fund.

redundancy payment. A payment that an employer is required, by Part VI of the Employment Protection (Consolidation) Act 1978, to make to an employee who is dismissed because of redundancy.

redundancy rebate. A repayment to an employer of part of a redundancy payment that the employer was required to make under Part VI of the Employment Protection (Consolidation) Act 1978.

refer to drawer. *Verb, preposition and noun.* Abbreviation: R/D. A phrase traditionally written on a cheque when the bank on which it is drawn refuses to pay it. The phrase is generally taken to mean that there is insufficient money in the bank account on which the cheque was drawn to pay it, so if there is some other reason for refusing to pay the cheque that reason must be stated on the cheque. Reasons for refusing to pay cheques are traditionally written in red capital letters.

refinance. *Verb.* To provide new money for a particular purpose in place of money that was previously used for that purpose but is no longer available.

refinance credit. A method of financing an export sale in which the exporter is paid under a payment credit, but the advising bank of the credit, instead of calling for reimbursement from the issuing bank, accepts an accommodation bill drawn on it by the importer and payable to the issuing bank. The advising bank then sells (i.e., discounts) the accommodation bill on behalf of the issuing bank and uses the proceeds to offset the issuing bank's liability under the payment credit. When the accommodation bill matures, it is paid by the advising bank, which calls for reimbursement from the issuing bank which in turn obtains reimbursement from its customer, the importer, who has thus received a period of credit. Also called 'reimbursement credit'.

re-fund. Also written: refund. *Verb.* To use money borrowed on a newly created loan to repay money owed on an existing loan.

regional development grant. Abbreviation: RDG. A cash grant which may be given by the Secretary of State, under the Industrial Development Act 1982, to a person in respect of the carrying out of a project of investment in the productive capacity or productive processes of an undertaking in a development area.

register. 1. *Noun.* A file of data with common subject-matter, especially one prepared with special care to serve as a permanent record or prepared under a legal duty.

2. *Verb.* To record, in a register (in sense 1), data concerning something.

3. *Noun.* In a computer, a small store used for a special purpose. The storage capacity of a register may be as small as a bit, byte or word.

registered accountant. A member of the Society of Company and Commercial Accountants in public practice.

registered company. A company incorporated in England and Wales or in Scotland by registration with the Registrar of Companies in accordance with the Companies Act in force at the time of registration. A registered company is incorporated as from the first moment of the date on its certificate of incorporation. A registered company may be either a limited company or an unlimited company and may be either a public company (which must be a limited company) or a private company.

registered office. An address which a registered company must notify to the Registrar of Companies and must state on all its business letters. Any notice delivered or posted to the registered office is deemed to be served on the company.

registered security. A security that is issued on condition that the name of the holder must be recorded in a register kept by, or on behalf of, the issuer. Transfer of a registered security from one holder to another involves altering the details recorded in the register. Compare 'bearer security'.

register of interests in shares. A register which a British public company is required to maintain recording details of each member of the company who owns or controls more than 5% of the shares that carry a general right to vote at meetings of members of the company.

Registrar of Companies. An official appointed by the Secretary of State responsible for receiving and approving applications for the incorporation of new registered companies and for receiving, and making available to the public, annual reports and other information relating to companies. There are two Registrars: the Registrar of Companies in England and Wales, Companies Registration Office, Crown Way, Maindy, Cardiff CF4 3UZ, and the Registrar of Companies in Scotland, Exchequer Chambers, 102 George Street, Edinburgh EH2 3DJ.

regression analysis. The process of estimating the parameters of a regression equation, by using the method of least squares, and of carrying out statistical tests on the estimates of the parameters.

regression coefficient. A coefficient of an independent variable in a regression equation. Also called 'beta coefficient' because traditionally represented by the Greek letter beta (β).

regression equation. A linear function that is used as a symbolic model of the relationship between a dependent variable and one or more independent variables and which has parameters estimated by the method of least squares. If y is the independent variable and $x_1, \ldots, x_n$ are the independent variables then a regression equation states that the estimated value $\hat{y}$ of y is:

$$\hat{y} = \beta_0 + \beta_1 x_1 + \ldots + \beta_n x_n$$

where $\beta_0, \ldots, \beta_n$ are constants called 'regression parameters'. The regression parameters that are coefficients of the independent variables (e.g., $\beta_1, \ldots, \beta_n$ in the above equation) are called 'regression coefficients' or 'beta coefficients'.

regression parameter. A parameter of a regression equation.

regulated agreement. In the Consumer Credit Act 1974, a regulated consumer credit agreement or a regulated consumer hire agreement.

regulated consumer credit agreement. Any consumer credit agreement other than one which is exempt from the provisions of the Consumer Credit Act 1974 because it is specified in s. 16 of the Act or in an order made under s. 16. The Consumer Credit (Exempt Agreements) Order 1985 (SI 1985 No. 620) has been made under s. 16 to specify exempt agreements.

regulated consumer hire agreement. Any consumer hire agreement other than one which is exempt from the provisions of the Consumer Credit Act 1974 because it is specified in s. 16 of the Act or in an order made under s. 16. The Consumer Credit (Exempt Agreements) Order 1985 (SI 1985 No. 620) has been made under s. 16 to specify exempt agreements.

reimbursement credit. Another term for 'refinance credit'.

reject note. A document which states that an item of product does not conform to specification.

related company. For the purposes of Schedule 4 to the Companies Act 1985, a corporation is a related company of a company that is preparing accounts in accordance with the schedule if it is not in the same group as that company, but that company holds, on a long-term basis, a 'qualifying interest' in the corporation for the purpose of securing a contribution to its activities by the exercise of any control or influence arising from that interest. 'Qualifying interest' means an interest in equity shares in the corporation of a class carrying rights to vote in all circumstances at general meetings of the corporation. The definition is given in para. 92 of the schedule.

related party. In relation to an accounting entity, an individual, partnership firm or company with the ability to control the accounting entity or exercise significant influence over it in making financial and operating decisions (IAS 24, para. 4). In this context, 'control' means ownership, directly, or indirectly through subsidiaries, of more than one-half of the voting power of the entity, or a substantial interest in voting power and the power to direct, by statute or agreement, the financial and operating policies of the management of the entity. 'Significant influence' means participation in the financial and operating policy decisions of the entity, but not control of those policies.

related-party transaction. A transfer of resources or obligations between related parties, regardless of whether a price is charged (IAS 24, para. 4).

relative error. If a is an approximation to a quantity then the relative error of the approximation is the absolute error of the approximation divided by a.

release note. A document which states that a product conforms to specification and which authorises further operations or delivery to the customer.

relevant benefits. See the entry for 'retirement benefits scheme'.

relief. An exemption from a requirement to pay tax on an amount of income or capital gain. Also called 'tax relief'.

remainder. If a number x is divided by a number y and N is the integer with the property that:

$$|x - Ny| < |y|$$

then the remainder is:

$$x - Ny$$

remit. *Verb.* To send money from one place to another.

remittance. A sum of money sent from one place to another.

remittance advice. A note accompanying a remittance specifying the purpose of the payment (e.g., by giving the numbers of invoices being settled) and indicating how the amount paid was calculated. Also called 'remittance slip'.

remittance basis. A basis of assessment to UK income tax in which only sums received in the United Kingdom in a period are taken into account, and not sums received elsewhere.

remittance slip. Another term for 'remittance advice'.

remitting bank. The bank to which a principal has entrusted the collection of documents. See also the entry for 'collecting bank'.

reorder interval. See the entry for 'reorder-interval system'.

reorder-interval system. In stock control, a system for replenishing stock in which an order for fresh stock is placed after a predetermined period of time, called the 'reorder interval' or 'review period'. Also called 'periodic review system'.

reorder level. See the entry for 'reorder-level system'.

reorder-level system. In stock control, a system for replenishing stock in which an order for new stock is placed whenever the existing stock falls to a predetermined quantity, called the 'reorder level' or 'order point'. Sometimes the quantity representing the reorder level is kept physically separate from the rest of the stock to make clear when the reorder level is reached, and this is called a 'two-bin system' or 'last-bag system'.

repayment guarantee. An arrangement under which a guarantor promises to reimburse the buyer for any down payment or stage payments made for a contract if the contract is not properly performed.

replacement cost. The cost at which an identical asset could be purchased or manufactured.

replacement price. The price at which material identical to that which is to be replaced could be purchased at the date of valuation.

report form. A layout for a balance sheet in which items are shown in a single column stating assets first then liabilities and then owners' equity. Also called 'narrative form', 'statement form', 'vertical form'.

reporting currency. The currency in which amounts are expressed in the financial statements of an accounting entity.

reporting partner. The partner in a firm of auditors responsible for the conduct of a particular audit.

reproduction cost. Term used in America for 'replacement cost'.

reputed ownership. Apparent ownership, by an individual, in the course of a trade or business, of goods, giving an impression of wealth which may mislead creditors. Under the 'doctrine of reputed ownership' of the bankruptcy law of England and Wales, goods in the reputed ownership of an individual who is adjudicated bankrupt are vested in the trustee in bankruptcy to be used to benefit creditors generally and are lost by their true owner (Bankruptcy Act 1914, s. 38(c)). The provision is now of limited practical significance and the 1984 Insolvency Bill proposes that it should be abolished.

rerun time. Time during which a data processing system is used for reruns required because of faults or mistakes in operation. It is part of operating time.

resale. A sale of something after the seller has bought it from some other person.

rescind. *Verb.* To declare that a contract will be treated as having come to an end so that no further contractual promises need be fulfilled.

rescission. Treatment of a contract as having come to an end so that no further contractual promises have to be fulfilled. In some circumstances it is also necessary to return things already supplied by one party to the other under the contract.

research and development expenditure. Abbreviation: R and D expenditure. Defined in SSAP 13, para. 18, as 'expenditure falling into one or more of the following broad categories (except to the extent that it relates to locating or exploiting mineral deposits or is reimbursable by third parties either directly or under the terms of a firm contract to develop and manufacture at an agreed price which has been calculated to reimburse both elements of expenditure):

'(a) Pure (or basic) research: original investigation undertaken in order to gain new scientific or technical knowledge and understanding. Basic research is not primarily directed towards any specific practical aim or application.

'(b) Applied research: original investigation undertaken in order to gain new scientific or technical knowledge and directed towards a specific practical aim or objective.

'(c) Development: the use of scientific or technical knowledge in order to produce new or substantially improved materials, devices, products, processes, systems or services prior to commencement of commercial production.'

resell. *Verb.* To sell something after buying it from another person.

reseller. A person selling something after buying it from another person.

reservation of title. An arrangement under which a seller of goods retains the legal title to the goods until they are paid for.

reserve. 1. Plural form (reserves). Profits or surpluses of an accounting entity (including extraordinary items and after payment of taxes) not distributed to the owners of the entity. If the entity is a registered company then the reserves must always be accounted for separately from contributed capital, and share premium is considered to be part of the reserves. If the entity is a partnership firm or a sole proprietorship then the reserves may simply be added to the capital accounts of the owners. In America, called 'accumulated earnings', 'retained earnings', 'earnings retained for use in the business', 'retained income' or, in the past, 'earned surplus'.

2. Part of the reserves (in sense 1) of an accounting entity set aside for some particular purpose.

reserved stock. In stock control, 'material committed to specific orders, but not necessarily physically separated from other stock' (BS 5191 : 1975). Also called 'allocated stock', 'appropriated stock', 'assigned stock', 'earmarked stock'.

reserve liability. Contingent liability of the members of a limited company who hold partly paid shares to pay a portion of the nominal value of those shares which the members have resolved, by special resolution, shall not be called up unless the company is wound up.

reserve price. A price below which a seller is not prepared to sell or above which a buyer is not prepared to buy.

residual or scrap value. Term used in the Capital Gains Tax Act 1979 to mean the predictable value, if any, which a wasting asset will have at the end of its predictable life as estimated in accordance with s. 37 of the Act.

residual value. 1. The value of an asset at the end of its useful life. This may be called 'gross residual value' when 'net residual value' is used to mean the value of an asset at the end of its useful life less expenses of realising that value.

2. In ED 37, in relation to a depreciable asset, 'the realisable value of the asset at the end of its useful economic life, based on prices prevailing at the date of acquisition or revaluation, where this has taken place. Realisation

costs should be deducted in arriving at the residual value.' (ED 37, para. 12.) In other contexts this would be called 'net residual value'.

residue. The part of a testator's estate that remains after debts and taxes have been paid, funeral expenses have been met and gifts that are limited in some way (e.g., specific gifts or general gifts of specified amounts) have been made.

restricted-use credit. Defined in the Consumer Credit Act 1974, s. 11, as credit provided under a regulated consumer credit agreement:

(a) to finance a transaction between the debtor and the creditor, whether the transaction forms part of that agreement or not; or

(b) to finance a transaction between the debtor and a person (the 'supplier') other than the creditor; or

(c) to refinance any existing indebtedness of the debtor's, whether to the creditor or to another person.

restrictive endorsement. Alternative spelling: restrictive indorsement. An endorsement that prohibits the further negotiation of the endorsed instrument, or which expresses that it is a mere authority to deal with the instrument as directed by the endorsement and that it is not a transfer of the ownership of the instrument – see Bills of Exchange Act 1882, s. 35.

restrictive indorsement. Alternative spelling of 'restrictive endorsement'.

restrictive injunction. An injunction by which a person is required to refrain from doing a particular act or thing.

resulting trust. A trust that is either a presumed resulting trust or an automatic resulting trust.

retained earnings. Term used in America for 'reserves'.

retained income. Term used in America for 'reserves'.

retention money. A part of the charge for work done by a contractor that is not paid until some time after the work is completed so that deductions can be made if the work turns out to be faulty or as an incentive to the contractor to provide maintenance services.

retention of title. Retention, by a seller of goods, of legal title to the goods until the goods have been paid for, even though possession of the goods is given to the buyer before that time. Also called 'reservation of title', 'title retention'. See also the entry for 'Romalpa clause'.

retire. 1. *Verb.* To withdraw from circulation a bill of exchange, promissory note, or other financial document, or security, by purchasing, paying or redeeming it.

2. *Verb.* To repay a debt; to extinguish a liability.

3. *Verb.* To bring an end to the use of a fixed asset, e.g., by scrapping or selling it.

4. *Verb.* To cease performing a job or engaging in a profession or vocation.

retirement benefits scheme. Term used in the Finance Act 1970, Part II, chapter 2 (exemption from taxation of occupational pension schemes) to mean a scheme for the provision of 'relevant benefits', meaning any pension, lump sum, gratuity or other like benefit to be given on retirement or on death, or, in connection with past service, after retirement or death, or to be given in anticipation of or in connection with any change in the nature of the service of the employee in question; such benefits do not include any benefit which arises solely by reason of disablement by accident of a person occurring during his service or on death by accident so occurring, but do include benefits payable to the employee's wife or widow, children, dependants or personal representatives.

return. 1. The value that results from the use of something; the money received as a result of making an investment, often expressed as a percentage of the sum invested.

2. A return inward or return outward.

3. A formal or official report made in response to an authoritative order or legal requirement.

return inward. Another term for 'sales return'.

return on assets. Another term for 'return on capital employed'.

return on capital employed. Abbreviation: ROCE. The ratio of profit of an accounting entity for a period to capital employed in the accounting entity during that period. Various measures of profit and of capital employed may be used in calculating this ratio. Also called 'return on assets', 'return on investment'. The term 'return on capital employed' is used in the ICMA official terminology but is not used in America, where 'return on investment' is the usual term.

return on investment. Abbreviation: ROI. Another term for 'return on capital employed'.

return outward. Another term for 'purchases return'.

returns book. See the entries for 'purchases returns book' and 'sales returns book'.

returns inward book. Another term for 'sales returns book'.

returns outward book. Another term for 'purchases returns book'.

revaluation. Change in the amount stated in the accounting records as the value of assets following a valuation of those assets. In this context the valuation itself may be termed a 'revaluation'. The difference between the net book values before and after revaluation is credited or debited, as appropriate, to an account called 'revaluation reserve'. (In America, revaluation reserve is called 'appraisal-surplus account'.)

revenue. 1. An amount of money, or other valuable benefits, received or expected to be received by an accounting entity in connection with its ordinary activities – excluding contributions of capital and loans made to the entity. 'Revenue' is used to refer to a gross amount receivable without any deductions to represent any of the costs of obtaining the revenue.

FASB Statement of Financial Accounting Concepts No. 3 states: 'Revenues are inflows or other enhancements of assets of an entity or settlements of its liabilities (or a combination of both) during a period from delivering or producing goods, rendering services, or other activities that constitute the entity's ongoing major or central operations' (para. 63).

2. The receipts of a government or state.

3. (Usually spelled with capital R.) The department of a government responsible for collecting taxes.

revenue account. Another term for 'income and expenditure account'.

revenue expenditure. Expenditure expected to benefit only the current period of account and so treated as an expense in the profit and loss account of the period.

revenue reserve. A reserve of a registered company that may be distributed to the members of the company otherwise than on the winding up of the company. Compare 'capital reserve'.

reverse bid. An agreed take-over in which the offeror is a company, which is larger than the offeree company, and shareholders in the offeror agree to give up their shares in exchange for new shares in the offeree company. The result is that the offeror becomes a subsidiary of the offeree company, but the offeror's shareholders acquire a majority of the shares in the offeree company.

reverse Polish notation. Another term for 'postfix notation'.

reversing entry. An entry in a ledger account made at the beginning of a financial period which reverses the effect of an adjusting entry made at the end of the preceding period.

review period. See the entry for 'reorder-interval system'.

revision variance. The difference between an original and a revised standard cost.

revolving credit. 1. A facility granted to a person whereby the person may borrow money, or buy goods on credit, up to a known initial credit limit; when money is borrowed or goods are bought, the credit limit is reduced by the value of the transaction; the credit limit can be increased again by the amount of any money paid to the grantor of the facility, but never to more than the initial limit.

2. In international trade, a letter of credit for a certain maximum amount over a time period (e.g., a month) which is automatically renewed for the following time period, and so on. If any amount not utilised in one period can be carried over and used in a subsequent period then the revolving credit is said to be 'cumulative'. If any sum not utilised in one period ceases to be available then the revolving credit is said to be 'non-cumulative'.

rework note. Another term for 'rectification note'.

rights issue. An issue of shares in a company which are offered to existing members with each member being offered a number of shares which will (as far as practicable) maintain that member's proportionate holding in the company.

rigid budget. Another term for 'fixed budget'.

risk. 1. A probability of failure or loss associated with a particular course of action; the probability of an undesirable event.

2. An evaluation of an undesirable event taking into account the probability that it will occur and the magnitude of its effect if it should occur.

3. In portfolio theory, the variance of the probability distribution of the rate of return on an investment.

risk class. In portfolio theory, a class of investments that are all judged to have the same risk as measured by variance of rate of return.

risk-free. *Adjective.* Used to describe an investment (such as a government stock) when there is negligible risk that the return will be different from the expected return. Also used to describe the rate of interest payable, or the expected return, on such an investment. The adjective 'riskless' is used with the same meaning.

riskless. Another term for 'risk-free'.

risk premium. In portfolio theory, the difference between the expected rate of return on an investment of a particular type at a particular time and the risk-free rate of return at that time. Also called 'excess return', 'market risk premium'.

ROCE. Abbreviation of 'return on capital employed'.

ROI. Abbreviation of 'return on investment'.

rolling budget. A budget for a budget period that is moved forward at regular intervals. For example, a budget for a year in which, each month, the budget period is extended into the future by one month with a compensating deletion of the first month of the budget. Also called 'evolving budget'.

rollover relief. An allowance that capital gains tax will not be payable on a particular disposal of an asset but that the gain will be taxed on the occasion of a subsequent disposal (unless a further rollover can be claimed). In particular, where a business asset is sold at a profit but the proceeds are used to buy a replacement asset, the gain is not taxed until the replacement is sold. (See Capital Gains Tax Act 1979, s. 115.)

ROM. Acronym from 'read-only memory'. In data processing, a store containing data put in during manufacture and unalterable thereafter.

***Romalpa* case.** The case of *Aluminium Industrie Vaassen BV* v *Romalpa Aluminium Ltd* [1976] 1 WLR 676, which brought to the attention of the business community in England and Wales the practice of retention of title.

***Romalpa* clause.** A clause in a contract of sale of goods providing for retention of title by the seller until the goods are paid for. See the entry for '*Romalpa* case'.

round. *Verb.* In relation to a number represented in a positional representation system, to substitute zero for, or omit, any digit in a digit place with a weight less than a chosen weight, possibly adjusting the digits in the remaining digit places according to rules such as those stated in the entries for 'round off' and 'round up'. See also the entry for 'round down'.

round down. *Verb with particle.* To round a representation of a number without adjusting any of the digits not omitted or replaced by zero.

round off. 1. *Verb with particle.* To round a decimal numeral by substituting zero for, or omitting, all digits in digit places with weights less than a chosen weight, accompanied by adding 1 to the digit in the digit place with the chosen weight (and executing any necessary carries) if the digit replaced in, or omitted from, the following digit place is 5 or more. This is the rounding convention usually followed in computing. A similar convention may be followed in positional representation systems other than the decimal.

    2. *Verb with particle.* To round a decimal numeral by substituting zero for, or omitting, all digits in digit places with weights less than a chosen amount, accompanied by adding 1 to the digit in the digit place with the chosen weight (and executing any necessary carries) in any of the following circumstances:

    (a) Where the digit replaced in, or omitted from, the next digit place is 6 or more.

    (b) Where the digit replaced in, or omitted from, the next digit place is 5 and non-zero digits have been replaced in, or omitted from, any following digit places.

(c) Where the digit replaced in, or omitted from, the following digit place is 5, all digits in following digit places are zero, and the digit in the digit place with the chosen weight is odd.

This rounding convention minimises rounding errors when a large number of numerals are to be rounded. A similar convention may be followed in positional representation systems other than the decimal.

round up. *Verb with particle.* To round a representation of a number in a positional representation system by substituting zero for, or omitting, all digits in digit places with weights less than a chosen weight, accompanied by (unless all the digits in those digit places are zero) adding 1 to the digit in the digit place with the chosen weight and dealing with any resulting carry digit.

routine. 1. A course of action that is regularly repeated or is intended to be the standard method of carrying out some task.

2. A computer program or part of a computer program, used often or for a variety of purposes.

royalty. A payment made to a person for being permitted to benefit from exercising a right owned by that person and related to the benefits derived from that right. The most common rights that are exercised subject to royalty payments are rights to extract minerals and rights to use copyright material. The person to whom the royalty is paid is often called the 'landlord'.

rule of 78. If an asset is paid for by instalments paid at regular intervals over a period of time then, usually, part of the money so paid is payment of the value of the asset at the beginning of the period (called the 'capital value') and part is a charge for being allowed to spread payment over a period of time (called the 'finance charge' or 'charge for credit'). The 'rule of 78' is a method of dividing each instalment into capital and finance charge in such a way that the finance charge is reduced by an equal amount in each successive instalment (compare 'actuarial method'). If the finance charge is F and the number of instalments is T then the sums of the positive integers less than or equal to T is computed. It is:

$s = 1 + 2 + 3 + \ldots + T = \frac{1}{2} T (T + 1)$

Then in the nth instalment the finance charge is:

$F \times (T - n)/s$

If the number of instalments is 12 (as in the common case of 12 monthly payments) then $s = 78$. The principle is the same as in the sum of the years' digits method of calculating a depreciation charge.

rule of 72. The rule that if a sum of money is invested to earn compound interest at r per cent per time period then the amount of principal and interest will be twice the original amount invested after approximately $72/r$ time periods.

running-account credit. Defined in the Consumer Credit Act 1974, s. 10, as: 'a facility under a personal credit agreement whereby the debtor is enabled to receive from time to time (whether in his own person, or by another person) from the creditor or a third party cash, goods and services (or any of them) to an amount or value such that, taking into account payments made by or to the credit of the debtor, the credit limit (if any) is not at any time exceeded'. 'Credit limit' means, in respect of any period, the maximum debit balance which, under the personal credit agreement, is allowed to stand on the account during that period, disregarding any term of the agreement allowing that maximum to be exceeded merely temporarily.

S

s. Abbreviation of 'section'.

safety stock. In stock control, stock that is held in order to protect against unforeseen circumstances (such as increased usage, lengthened lead time etc.) and which is normally held in store (BS 5191 : 1975).

salaried partner. A partner in a partnership firm who receives a regular fixed remuneration or a senior employee of a partnership firm who is held out as being a partner.

salary. Monetary payment made regularly by an employer to an employee under a contract of employment. Usually used only for payments to employees engaged in non-manual work and payments made at intervals of a month or longer.

sale. 1. In accounting, a business transaction in which an accounting entity supplies its goods or services to a customer in exchange for money or some other benefit received or promised.

2. In law, a contract of sale of goods is called a 'sale' as from the time at which the property in the goods is transferred from the seller to the buyer in accordance with the contract. This may happen when the contract is made or at a certain time after the contract is made or after a condition has been fulfilled. See the entry for 'agreement to sell'. (Sale of Goods Act 1979, s. 2.)

3. An auction.

4. An offer by a retailer of reductions in the prices of many goods for a restricted period.

5. Plural form (sales). In America, in a financial statement, net sales for a period.

sale and leaseback. A sale of the property of one person to another on condition that the seller immediately becomes lessee of the property.

sale or return. Method of transacting business in which goods are supplied to a person for resale by that person on condition that any not resold may be returned to the supplier and will not be charged for.

sales credit note. A credit note sent to a customer because of the partial or total cancellation of a previously invoiced charge for goods or services supplied.

sales day book. Abbreviation: SDB. A record of sales, apart from those recorded in the cash book, giving, for each transaction, the name of the purchaser and the date, number and amount of the invoice. Each transaction is posted to the debit of the purchaser's account in the debtors ledger, but only periodic totals need be posted to the credit of the sales account. Also called 'sales journal', 'sold day book'.

sales invoice. An invoice, from the seller's point of view.

sales journal. Another term for 'sales day book'.

sales ledger. The debtors ledger of a trading enterprise.

sales mix. The quantities of different products sold by an enterprise.

sales mix profit variance. Where there is more than one product, the difference between the total standard profit to be received from the actual quantities of products sold during a budget period and the product of the total number of units sold and the average standard profit per unit.

sales return. 1. A thing that has been purchased but returned by the purchaser and for which the invoiced charge should be cancelled – from the seller's point of view. Also called 'return inward'. From the purchaser's point of view this is a 'purchases return' or 'return outward'.

2. A report of sales.

sales returns book. Abbreviation: SRB. A record of sales returns, giving, for each return, the name of the purchaser, date of the return, amount of invoiced charge to be cancelled, and, possibly, the number of the accounting entity's credit note. Each return is credited to the account of the purchaser in the debtors ledger but only periodic totals need be posted to the debit of the sales returns account. Also called 'returns inward book'.

sales revenue. Term used in America for 'turnover'.

sales value. The price at which something can be sold.

sales volume profit variance. Unit standard operating profit multiplied by the difference between the actual number of units sold during a budget period and the budgeted or standard number of units to be sold.

salvage note. A document which authorises the use of an item of product for a purpose for which it was not originally intended.

sample. 1. *Noun.* One or more items taken from a population in order to obtain a probable description of the whole population.

2. *Verb.* To choose one or more items from a population in order to obtain a probable description of the whole population. Sampling may be done either 'with replacement' – i.e., once an item has been chosen and measured it is returned to the population and it is possible for it to be chosen again – or 'without replacement' – i.e., any one item may be chosen only once.

3. *Noun.* A very small but representative portion which is extracted from a quantity of something offered for sale and which can be used by potential buyers to judge the quality, style or colour of the whole quantity.

4. *Noun.* A small amount of some product that is given free in order to introduce people to the product and persuade them to buy more.

5. *Verb.* To distribute small amounts of some product free of charge in order to introduce people to the product and persuade them to buy more.

samurai bond. An international bond originally issued in Japan on behalf of a borrower resident outside Japan.

Sandilands Report. The document, *Inflation Accounting. Report of the Inflation Accounting Committee*, Cmnd 6225 (London: HMSO, 1975), which was the report of a committee appointed by the then Chancellor of the Exchequer and the then Secretary of State for Trade and Industry on 21 January 1974 to consider whether, and if so how, company accounts should allow for changes in costs and prices. Named after the chairman of the committee, Francis Sandilands, then chairman of Commercial Union Assurance Co. Ltd.

SAS. Abbreviation of 'Statement on Auditing Standards'.

SAT. Designation of a Senior Accounting Technician – see the entry for 'Association of Accounting Technicians'.

satisficing. Achieving or attempting to achieve an outcome or state of affairs that satisfies known conditions without necessarily being an optimum.

savings-related share option scheme. A scheme established by an incorporated company which provides for the directors and employees of the company to obtain rights to acquire shares in the company paid for with money accruing to them from a certified contractual savings scheme. Approval of the scheme by the Board of Inland Revenue under the Finance Act 1980, s. 47 and Schedule 10, provides certain tax advantages.

scatter diagram. A graph of observed values of a dependent variable for various values of an independent variable in which observations are recorded as isolated points in the hope that they will show some pattern that will help to identify the form of the relationship between the variables.

schedule. 1. *Noun.* A statement of supplementary details appended to the main text of a document.

2. *Verb.* To give supplementary details in a statement appended to the main text of a document.

3. *Noun.* A plan expressed in terms of the timing of events.

4. *Verb.* To prepare a plan expressed in terms of the timing of events.

5. *Noun.* Usually spelled with capital S. One of the six categories of receipts of money by taxpayers on which UK income tax and corporation tax are charged. The Schedules are:

Schedule A: The rents or receipts to which the taxpayer becomes entitled in respect of land in the United Kingdom.

Schedule B: The value, to their occupier, of woodlands in the United Kingdom which are managed on a commercial basis.

Schedule C: Profits arising from certain United Kingdom and overseas public dividends.

Schedule D:

Case I: Profits of a trade.

Case II: Profits of a profession or vocation.

Case III: Income from interest, annuities, annual payments, or discounts.

Case IV: Income from foreign securities not charged under Schedule C.

Case V: Income arising from foreign possessions.

Case VI: Profits of an income nature not charged under any other Schedule or Case, and certain income that is specifically charged under this Case.

Schedule E: Income arising from offices, employments, and pensions, and certain income specifically charged under this Schedule.

Case I: Income from an office or employment held by a person who is both resident and ordinarily resident in the UK.

Case II: Income received in respect of duties performed in the UK by a person who is either not resident in the UK or, if resident, is not ordinarily resident in the UK.

Case III: Income received in the UK by a person resident in the UK, whether or not also ordinarily resident.

Schedule F: Dividends and other distributions of companies resident in the UK.

scheduled territories. The territories listed in the first schedule to the Exchange Control Act 1947 as amended from time to time. As from 1 January 1973 the scheduled territories are the Channel Islands, Gibraltar, the Republic of Ireland, the Isle of Man and the UK.

scheme of arrangement. A comprehensive scheme for the payment of the debts of an individual, which is proposed by that individual and which offers some advantage over the continuation of bankruptcy proceedings and which, if approved as required by law, terminates the bankruptcy proceedings. If the scheme of arrangement is accepted after adjudication of bankruptcy then the adjudication is annulled.

scorched-earth. *Adjective.* Used to describe a tactic employed by an offeree company, which is opposing a take-over bid, in which the offeree either sells assets that are believed to be particularly attractive to the bidder or purchases assets that are believed to be particularly unattractive to the bidder.

scrap. Something to be discarded as no longer suitable or usable in its present condition but which has some value either because it can be sold or because it can be put back into a process as a material. Compare 'waste'.

scrap note. A document which authorises the discard of a product as economically incapable of being rectified or salvaged.

scrap value. The value of something as scrap.

SDA. Abbreviation of 'special development area'.

SDB. Abbreviation of 'sales day book'.

SDR. Abbreviation of 'special drawing right'.

seal. A conventional symbol on a document by which a person signifies willingness to be bound by the statements made in the document. Also a device for putting such symbols on documents. Also the capacity to put such symbols on documents.

Nowadays the usual form of seal is a red disk of paper, called a 'wafer'. An incorporated company usually puts its seal on a document by using dies to impress a design on the document and a die used for this purpose is called a 'company seal'. In the past, pieces of wax or lead were used as seals. A statement in a document on which a seal has been placed is called a statement 'under seal'.

secondary auditor. An auditor of a subsidiary or associated company who is not also the primary auditor for the group of companies and is operationally distinct from the primary auditor.

secondary contributor. In British social security law, an employer of an individual who is gainfully employed in Great Britain under a contract of service. Such an employer is liable to pay secondary Class 1 social security contributions. Some other persons who pay earnings are also deemed to be secondary contributors even though the earnings are not paid under contracts of service.

second mortgage. A mortgage of property that is already mortgaged to another mortgagee.

secret reserves. See the entry for 'hidden reserves'.

secret trust. A gift of property made in the will of the donor without stating that the person who is to receive the gift is under an obligation to hold it in trust for some other person or charitable object. Called a 'fully secret trust' if it is to be distinguished from a 'half-secret trust', which is a gift made in a will mentioning that the recipient is to hold the property in trust but without naming the beneficiary of the trust.

section. Abbreviation: s. One of the consecutively numbered divisions of the text of an Act of Parliament, the number of which is the most commonly used means of identifying a particular provision within an Act and is printed in bold arabic numerals in copies of Acts published by authority.

secured creditor. A creditor of a person who has a charge or lien on property of the person. A creditor is a secured creditor only if the creditor has direct security, not collateral security.

securities broker. Term used in America for 'stockbroker'.

security. 1. An item of intangible property representing one interest in an investment (such as the capital of an enterprise or a loan raised for a person) which is the subject of many interests owned in common by many persons (or capable of being owned by many persons), and which is controlled and managed by a person (called the 'issuer' of the security) who pays to the owner of the security the returns offered by the investment.

2. A source of money from which a financial obligation, due in the future, may be met if the person who owes the obligation does not personally meet it. The commonest form of security is a charge on property. Security provided by the person from whom the obligation is due is called 'direct security'; security provided by a third party is called 'collateral security' or 'third-party security'. In America, any form of security is called 'collateral'.

security bill of sale. A bill of sale by which ownership, but not possession, of goods is given as security for meeting a financial obligation.

security market line. Abbreviation: SML. Another term for 'capital asset pricing model'.

segment. Activities of a business enterprise concerned with a separate major line of business or class of customer.

segment reporting. Showing separately in financial statements the financial position and results of a business enterprise attributable to different segments of the business.

self-investment. Defined in ED 32, para. 37, as the investment of all or part of a pension scheme's assets in the business of the employer company or that of a subsidiary or an associated company, by investing in any of the following:

(a) shares and securities of the company;

(b) loans secured by mortgages of real property owned by the company;

(c) freeholds and leaseholds owned by the scheme's trustees but leased to the company (excluding freeholds and leaseholds let or leased to another organisation and sublet by it to the company);

(d) secured or unsecured loans made to the company, including money due to the scheme but held by the company such as pension-fund contributions due but not yet paid over to the scheme.

sell. 1. *Verb.* To enter into a business transaction with the object of supplying goods or services in exchange for money or some other benefit given or promised.

2. *Verb.* To act as a sales representative.

seller. A person who enters into a business transaction to sell something. Also called 'vendor'.

selling cost. Cost incurred in securing orders for the products of an accounting entity, usually including the salaries, commissions and travelling expenses of sales representatives. Also called 'selling overhead'.

selling overhead. 1. Another term for 'selling cost'.

2. Another term for 'marketing cost'.

selling price variance. The difference between the actual average selling price per unit for a product during a budget period and the standard selling price per unit for that product multiplied by the actual quantity sold during that period.

semi-fixed cost. 1. Another term for 'stepped fixed cost'.

2. Another term for 'semi-variable cost'.

semi-variable cost. A cost containing both fixed and variable elements, which is therefore partly affected by changes in the level of activity. Stepped fixed costs may be regarded as a kind of semi-variable cost. Also called 'mixed cost', 'semi-fixed cost'.

senior. *Adjective.* In relation to securities, having a higher priority as a claim for payment than one or more other claims.

sensitivity analysis. Analysis of how errors in one or more estimates would affect the conclusion drawn from the estimates.

separable net assets. The total value of the assets of an accounting entity that can be identified and sold separately without necessarily disposing of the business or undertaking of the entity as a whole less the total value of the entity's liabilities that can be identified and discharged separately (SSAP 22, para. 22).

separable programming. Technique of mathematical programming that is used when a constraint is not a linear function but can be separated into pieces that are each nearly linear.

separate entity concept. The idea that financial transactions relating to an activity which has been identified as an accounting entity should be recorded separately from other financial transactions of the persons who carry on that activity. The term 'business entity concept' is used when the activity being considered is a business enterprise.

separate estate. The property of a partner in a partnership against which bankruptcy proceedings are being taken, as opposed to partnership property.

separation point. A point in manufacturing or processing after which one of a number of joint products, or a by-product, is operated on separately. In America, called 'splitoff point'.

sequestration. 1. In the law of England and Wales, proceedings for contempt of court in which property of the person who committed the contempt (who is called the 'contemnor') is seized by individuals called 'sequestrators' and held for disposal by the court against which the contempt was committed.

2. In the law of Scotland, legal proceedings under which the estate of an insolvent debtor is transferred to a trustee to be distributed among creditors – equivalent to bankruptcy proceedings in England and Wales.

sequestrator. An individual appointed in a writ of sequestration to seize property of a contemnor and hold it for disposal by the court against which the contempt was committed.

service centre. American spelling: service center. A cost centre which provides a service to other parts of the organisation.

service contract. Another term for 'contract of service'.

service cost centre. American spelling: service cost center. A cost centre for the provision of a service or services (for example, maintenance, purchasing, accounting) to other cost centres. Also called 'indirect cost centre'. In an organisation which provides services, rather than goods, a service cost centre may be called a 'support cost centre' or 'utility cost centre'. Compare 'production cost centre'.

service costing. 1. Costing a product that is a service.

2. Costing a service centre. Also called 'function costing'.

set. A collection, of things called 'elements' or 'members', that is defined by a rule that unambiguously determines whether or not a thing is included in the collection.

set off. *Verb with particle*. To reduce a debt owed by one person A to another person B by an amount owed by B to A.

settle. *Verb*. To arrange for some of one's property to be held in trust.

settled account. An account of transactions between two persons that has been agreed by them to be accurate. The term is usually used to imply that neither party may subsequently question the accuracy of the account.

settled property. 1. Property held in trust.

2. For the purposes of UK capital gains tax, property held in trust other than by a bare trustee (Capital Gains Tax Act 1979, s. 51).

settlement. 1. In relation to an invoice, bill, statement of account, or other statement of a debt owed, payment of the debt in question.

2. Ending of legal proceedings by agreement between the parties.

3. Creation of successive interests in property; creation of a trust whereby property is held by one person for a time and then by another. Also a document creating such a trust.

4. For the purposes of UK income tax, in chapter II (settlements on children) of Part XIV of the Income and Corporation Taxes Act 1970, ' "settlement" includes any disposition, trust, covenant, agreement, arrangement or transfer of assets' (s. 444(2) of the Act) but in chapter III (revocable settlements, etc.), ' "settlement" includes any disposition, trust, covenant, agreement or arrangement' (s. 454(3) of the Act). The courts have held that a settlement comes within the provisions of Part XVI of the Act only if there is an element of bounty – see *Commissioners of Inland Revenue* v *Plummer* [1980] AC 896 and *Commissioners of Inland Revenue* v *Levy* [1982] STC 442.

5. For the purposes of UK capital transfer tax, defined in the Capital Transfer Tax Act 1984, s. 43(2), as: 'any disposition or dispositions of property, whether effected by instrument, by parol or by operation of law,

or partly in one way and partly in another, whereby the property is for the time being:

'(a) held in trust for persons in succession or for any person subject to a contingency; or

'(b) held by trustees on trust to accumulate the whole or part of any income of the property or with power to make payments out of that income at the discretion of the trustees or some other person, with or without power to accumulate surplus income; or

'(c) charged or burdened (otherwise than for full consideration in money or money's worth paid for his own use or benefit to the person making the disposition) with the payment of any annuity or other periodical payment payable for a life or any other limited or terminable period;

'or would be so held or charged or burdened if the disposition or dispositions were regulated by the law of any part of the United Kingdom; or whereby, under the law of any other country, the administration of the property is for the time being governed by provisions equivalent in effect to those which would apply if the property were so held, charged or burdened'.

6. For the purposes of the Settled Land Act 1925, a detailed definition is given in s. 1(1) of the Act.

settlement day. Another term for 'account day'.

settlor. A person who has settled any property in trust. For the purposes of UK income tax, ' "settlor", in relation to a settlement, includes any person by whom the settlement was made or entered into directly or indirectly, and in particular (but without prejudice to the generality of the preceding words of this definition) includes any person who has provided or undertaken to provide funds directly or indirectly for the purpose of the settlement, or has made with any other person a reciprocal arrangement for that other person to make or enter into the settlement' (Income and Corporation Taxes Act 1970, s. 444(2), and see also s. 454(3)).

set-up time. In production planning, the time required to prepare a work station from a standard condition to readiness to commence a specified operation (BS 5191 : 1975).

75 per cent subsidiary. See the entry for 'subsidiary'.

several liability. Liability of two or more persons, each of whom is deemed to be individually responsible for the entire liability and may be sued individually for performance of it.

severally liable. *Adjective phrase.* Having several liability.

severance payment. A compensatory payment to an employee who has been dismissed.

shadow director. In relation to a company, a person in accordance with whose directions or instructions the directors of the company are accustomed to act (Companies Act 1985, s. 741).

share. A unit of measurement of interest in a company based on contribution of capital to the company. Instead of speaking of a 'share of interest' in a company, or a 'share of capital', it is usual to refer simply to a 'share in' the company.

A person may become a member of a company by promising to contribute capital to it. If different people contribute different amounts of capital, they expect to have different entitlements to dividends of the company's profits and votes at meetings of members. Entitlements to dividends, votes and other benefits may be calculated by reference to the number of shares held by each member. Each share has a 'nominal value', which is the minimum amount of capital that must be contributed for the share. Sometimes, the promise to contribute capital does not have to be fulfilled immediately and a member may be considered to be the holder of a share even though some or, rarely, all of the nominal value has not yet been contributed for it, and in such a case the share is said to be 'partly paid'. If all of the nominal value has been contributed for a share, then it is said to be 'fully paid'.

A member may be able to transfer some or all shares, acquired in exchange for a contribution of capital, to another person, who will thereby become a member without personally contributing capital to the company. If partly paid shares are transferred, then the transferee takes on the liability of contributing the part of the nominal value of the shares that has not yet been contributed. In practice, nowadays, almost all shares are fully paid. It is not possible for a member to transfer a fraction of a share.

share capital. Contributed capital of a company in which members' interests are measured in terms of shares. In the Companies Acts, 'share capital' without qualification means 'nominal share capital'.

share certificate. A document issued by a company to certify that a person named in the document is the owner of a specified number of shares in the company.

share-for-share offer. A take-over bid in which the offeror is a company, which offers its shares as the consideration for acquiring the shares in the offeree company. If the offer is successful, the pre-combination owners of the companies will continue to be the owners of the combined group.

shareholder. A member of a company in which members' interests are measured in terms of shares.

shareholders' equity. The equity of an incorporated company that would be distributed to shareholders if the company were wound up. Usually means 'ordinary shareholders' equity' – either because there is only one class of shareholders or because it is assumed that the claims of preference shareholders are treated as liabilities when calculating equity.

share incentive scheme. A scheme whereby a person acquires shares or an interest in shares in an incorporated company in pursuance of a right conferred on him or opportunity offered to him as a director or employee of that or any other incorporated company, and not in pursuance of an offer to the public (Finance Act 1972, s. 79(1)).

share option. An arrangement between a company and a person (called the 'option holder') under which the company may be required to allot one or more shares to the option holder at a time chosen by the option holder (possibly within defined limits) at a price fixed when the arrangement was made.

share premium. Capital which must be contributed to a company for a share in the company in addition to the capital representing the nominal value of the share.

share warrant. A bearer security which entitles its bearer to a number of shares in a company.

shop order. Another term for 'production order'.

shortage. In stock control, a required quantity that cannot be supplied from stock (see BS 5191 : 1975).

short bill. A bill of exchange that is due to mature in a short time (usually less than 10 days).

short interest. Interest for a period of less than one year.

short lease. In Schedule 4 to the Companies Act 1985, a lease that is not a long lease.

short-term obligation. Another term for 'current liability'.

short-term timing difference. An originating timing difference that arises from the use of the receipts and payments basis for tax purposes and the accruals basis in financial statements (SSAP 15, para. 21).

shrinkage. Decrease in quantity, measured by volume or by weight, of raw materials, work in progress or finished goods due to evaporation or other physical or chemical process inherent in the manufacturing, processing, storage or transportation operations used.

SI. Abbreviation of 'statutory instrument'.

sick pay. Payment by an employer to an employee who is unable to work because of illness.

sight bill. Another term for 'demand bill'.

sight draft. Another term for 'demand bill'.

sight note. A promissory note payable whenever it is presented for payment. Also called 'demand note'.

significance level. In relation to a statistical test, the maximum probability of rejecting the null hypothesis if the null hypothesis is true.

significant digit. In a numeral, a digit that is required for some purpose, especially for expressing a particular level of accuracy or precision.

significant result. In relation to a statistical test, a result that leads to the rejection of the null hypothesis.

simple contract. A contract not contained in a deed.

simple discount. A discount calculated by the formula:

$$Pti$$

where P is the amount from which the discount is to be deducted, i is the discount rate per unit of time and t is the number of units of time. Also called 'banker's discount' because it is the way a bank calculates discount when purchasing a bill of exchange.

simple interest. Interest calculated by the formula:

$$Pti$$

where P is the principal, t is the number of time periods and i is the interest rate per time period.

simple random sample. In statistics, a sample, containing a particular number of items, chosen from a population in such a way that any possible sample with that number of items could have been chosen with the same probability.

simple regression analysis. Regression analysis where there is only one independent variable.

simplex method. An algorithm for solving a linear programming problem by determining successive possible solutions and testing them for optimality. A graph of the linear constraints in a linear programming problem forms a geometrical figure called a 'simplex' and the simplex method involves testing the value of the objective function at successive vertices of the simplex.

simulation. Design and operation of a model of a system.

sinking fund. A fund of money that is set aside and invested to earn interest so that it can be used to 'sink' (i.e., pay off) a debt that is due for payment at a known time in the future.

16-bit. *Adjective.* Used to describe a computer or processor that is designed to deal principally with words that are 16 bits long and so, for example, has data buses with 16 parallel conductors and has arithmetic registers that store 16 bits.

size. In relation to a statistical test, another term for 'type I risk'.

sleeping partner. A partner in a firm who has contributed capital to the firm but takes no part in its business or professional activities. Such a partner nevertheless has unlimited liability for the debts of the partnership unless the partnership is registered as a limited partnership and the sleeping partner is named as a limited partner.

small companies rate. A reduced rate of corporation tax charged on the income of companies whose profits do not exceed a specified amount.

small company. In order to file modified accounts with the Registrar of Companies for a particular financial year, a private company is a small company if, in respect of that year and the preceding financial year (or that year alone if it is the company's first financial year), it satisfies any two or more of the following conditions (Companies Act 1985, ss. 248(1) and (5) and 249):

(a) its turnover does not exceed £1.4 million (or a proportionate amount if the financial year is not 12 months);

(b) its balance sheet total does not exceed £700,000;

(c) its weekly average number of employees during the financial year does not exceed 50.

small maintenance order. An order of a UK court under which small maintenance payments are made.

small maintenance payments. Defined in the Income and Corporation Taxes Act 1970, s. 65(1) as 'payments under an order made by a court in the United Kingdom:

'(a) by one of the parties to a marriage (including a marriage which has been dissolved or annulled) to or for the benefit of the other party to that marriage for that other party's maintenance;

'(b) to any person under 21 years of age for his own benefit, maintenance or education; or

'(c) to any person for the benefit, maintenance or education of a person under 21 years of age',

provided it is to be paid at a weekly or monthly rate not exceeding the financial limits currently in force for the purpose, which are revised, usually, annually. The court order under which small maintenance payments are made is called a 'small maintenance order'.

small workshop. An industrial building with a gross internal floor space of 2,500 square feet or less (Finance Act 1980, s. 75(2)). Special capital allowances are available for small workshops. See also the entry for 'very small workshop'.

SML. Abbreviation of 'security market line'.

smooth. *Verb.* To calculate, from an existing time series, a new time series which has less variability and, it is hoped, indicates an underlying trend.

social security contribution. An amount required to be paid under the Social Security Act 1975 to the Secretary of State by earners, employers and the self-employed in England and Wales, and Scotland, to pay for benefits payable from the National Insurance Fund, the Redundancy Fund and the Maternity Pay Fund, to contribute to the cost of the National Health Service and to pay for benefits payable under the Industrial Injuries and Diseases (Old Cases) Act 1975. There are four classes of contributions:

Class 1, earnings-related, payable where an individual is, or is deemed to be, gainfully employed in Great Britain under a contract of service, and consisting of:

(a) primary Class 1 contributions from employees, and

(b) secondary Class 1 contributions from employers.

Class 2, flat-rate, payable weekly by self-employed earners.

Class 3, payable by earners and others voluntarily with a view to providing entitlement to benefit, or making up entitlement.

Class 4, payable in respect of profits or gains of a trade, profession or vocation.

Society of Company and Commercial Accountants. A society of accountants in public practice, industry, commerce and a wide range of other organisations in which technical or managerial skills are required. The specialism of members of the society in public practice is the provision of accounting services to smaller businesses. Elsewhere, members hold accounting appointments or managerial positions at all levels of responsibility.

There are two grades of membership: Associate, designated ACSA, and Fellow, designated FSCA. Entrance to membership is by examination only. The professional examination consists of four parts, from the first three of which limited exemptions may be given on the basis of similarity of syllabus. Besides the examination requirement, candidates for associate-ship must have gained acceptable levels of relevant experience.

Members in public practice are styled 'registered accountants' and those elsewhere, 'incorporated company and commercial accountants'.

Address: 40 Tyndalls Park Road, Bristol BS8 1PL. Telephone: Bristol 738261.

Society of Investment Analysts. A society of individuals whose work is concerned with investment analysis and portfolio management. Members are to be found mainly in major investing institutions and in independent fund management companies and Stock Exchange firms. There are two grades of membership: Associate, designated ASIA, and Fellow, designated FSIA. An Associate must have passed the Associate examination of the Society, or obtained exemption from it, and must have been professionally engaged in investment analysis or portfolio management, or an activity deemed by the council of the Society to be equivalent, for a period of not less than two years. A Fellow must have been an Associate for at least five years and must either have passed the Fellowship examination or, in the opinion of the council of the Society, have contributed with distinction to the aims and objects of the Society.

Address: 211/213 High Street, Bromley, Kent BR1 1NY. Telephone: 01-464 0811.

software. The instructions for particular jobs, maintenance manuals, training manuals and other documentation concerned with the use of hardware. In particular, computer programs.

SOI. Abbreviation of 'Statement of Intent'.

sola. *Adjective.* Of a bill of exchange or bill of lading, issued without copies.

sold day book. Another term for 'sales day book'.

sold ledger. The debtors ledger of a trading enterprise.

sole practitioner. An individual who pursues a profession not in partnership with others and not as an employee of another person.

sole proprietor. Term used in America for 'sole trader'.

sole proprietorship. In America, a business enterprise operated by a sole proprietor.

sole trader. An individual who carries on a business enterprise without incorporating a company for that purpose and not in partnership with other persons. The individual may also be called the 'proprietor' of the business. In America, called 'sole proprietor'.

solvency. Ability of a person to pay debts as they fall due.

solvent. *Adjective.* Able to pay debts as they fall due.

SORP. Usually spoken as an acronym. Abbreviation of 'Statement of Recommended Practice'.

source and application of funds statement. Another term for 'statement of source and application of funds'.

source program. In relation to the translation of a computer program from one programming language into another, the program as expressed in the original language before translation.

SP. Abbreviation of 'space character'.

space. In data processing, another term for 'space character'.

space character. Abbreviation: SP. In data processing, a character that is usually represented by a blank site in a series of graphic symbols. Also called 'space'.

spares stock. In stock control, stock that is held available for maintenance purposes or for the replacement of defective parts. If spares stock is associated with a saleable product it is regarded as direct stock whereas if it is associated with fixed assets, it is regarded as indirect stock. See BS 5191 : 1975.

special category accounts. Accounts of a special category company, or of a holding company with a subsidiary that is a special category company, prepared under Chapter II of Part VII of the Companies Act 1985 showing less information than is required from other companies.

special category company. Defined in s. 257(1) of the Companies Act 1985 as a banking company, shipping company or insurance company where:

'(a) "banking company" means a company which is a recognised bank for the purposes of the Banking Act 1979 or is a licensed institution within that Act;

'(b) "insurance company" means an insurance company to which Part II of the Insurance Companies Act 1982 applies; and

'(c) "shipping company" means a company which, or a subsidiary of which, owns ships or includes among its activities the management or operation of ships and which satisfies the Secretary of State that it ought in the national interest to be treated under [Part VII of the Companies Act 1985] as a shipping company'.

special character. In data processing, a graphic character, in a character set, that is not a letter, digit or space character.

Special Commissioner. An individual appointed by the Treasury to judge appeals made by taxpayers against assessments to income tax. Special Commissioners are salaried officials who hear appeals which are more complex than those heard by General Commissioners, or involve legal rather than purely factual points. Also called 'Commissioner for the special purposes of the Income Tax Acts'.

special crossing. A crossing on a cheque or other financial document which specifies the bank to which the money must be paid.

special development area. Abbreviation: SDA. A part of a development area designated by the Secretary of State under the Industrial Development Act 1982, s. 1, for which special provision may be made in relation to regional development grants. As from 29 November 1984 there are no special development areas.

special drawing right. Abbreviation: SDR. A unit of account used by the International Monetary Fund. Its value is calculated daily as the US dollar equivalent of specified amounts of currencies that are widely used in international trade. The precise amounts and the currencies used are altered from time to time to reflect changing patterns of trade.

special endorsement. Alternative spelling: special indorsement. An endorsement in which an endorsee is named.

special indorsement. Alternative spelling of 'special endorsement'.

special manager. In insolvency law, a person appointed to manage the business of an insolvent individual while the official receiver is acting as receiver or trustee in bankruptcy, or of a company while the official receiver is acting as liquidator or provisional liquidator.

In relation to an insolvent individual the 1984 Insolvency Bill proposes that the circumstances in which a special manager may be appointed are when the official receiver is acting as interim receiver or anyone is acting as trustee. It also proposes that a special manager of a company may be appointed while anyone is acting as liquidator or provisional liquidator.

special notice. Notice of intention to propose the adoption of a resolution at a meeting of the members of a registered company given by the proposer to the company not less than 28 days before the meeting and given by the company to the members not less than 21 days before the meeting.

special resolution. In British company law, a resolution of the members of a company that is valid only if approved by three-quarters or more of the votes cast on it at a meeting of the members of which at least 21 days' notice was given specifying that the resolution was to be proposed as a special resolution. (The members may waive the requirement for 21 days' notice in some circumstances.) Compare 'ordinary resolution', 'extraordinary resolution'.

The term 'special resolution' is sometimes used in organisations other than registered companies for resolutions that are required to be passed by special procedure.

specialty contract. A contract embodied in a deed.

specific charge. Another term for 'fixed charge'.

specific gift. A gift in a will of a particular specified item of property. Compare 'general gift'.

specific identification. A method of valuing a class of stocks and work in progress where each article in the stock can be identified and its known purchase price, production cost or net realisable value is taken as its value.

specific-order costing. A costing method used to cost individual contracts, jobs or batches of product, rather than products that are produced continuously. Depending on the nature of the work to be costed, specific-order costing may be called 'batch costing', 'contract costing' or 'job costing'. Specific-order costing consists essentially of adding together all direct costs of the work and a proportion of production overhead cost and, sometimes, non-production overhead cost.

splitoff point. Term used in America for 'separation point'.

spoilage. The cost of units of production that become unsaleable during processing, manufacturing, storage or transportation because of accidental damage or defective working, machinery or packing, or because materials or components were defective. Spoiled units may have a scrap value or may be rectified by additional work or may be saleable as second-quality goods.

spot price. The price at which a person is willing to buy or sell something for immediate delivery.

spot rate. An exchange rate at which a person will buy or sell foreign currency for immediate delivery.

spreadsheet. A table showing, for each of a number of amounts, an analysis of the amount into component parts (the descriptions of the components being the same for each amount analysed) and the totals, for all the amounts, of each component.

square-root formula. The formula used to calculate an economic order quantity.

SRB. Abbreviation of 'sales returns book'.

SSP. Abbreviation of 'statutory sick pay'.

stag. A person who applies for a number of securities in a new issue with the intention of immediately selling them at a profit to persons who would have obtained them in the issue had the stag not got them first.

stale cheque. American spelling: stale check. A cheque presented for payment so long after its date that the bank on which it is drawn will refuse to pay it until it has been confirmed by the drawer. Most banks regard a cheque as stale if it is presented more than six months after its date. Also called 'out-of-date cheque'.

stamp duty. A tax, payable on documents of particular kinds, for which evidence of payment is given by a stamp on the document. In the UK, the stamp is now an impressed stamp put on the document by the government department that receives payment of the tax.

standard. An amount of expenditure, work, output etc., established as a measure of performance with which actual performance may be compared.

standard cost. An amount, which is determined, for the purposes of planning and control, as the amount which something should cost in operations in the future under specified conditions. Costs are usually described as 'standard costs' only if they have been established systematically for a wide range of operations within an organisation using reliable techniques based on measurement rather than estimation.

standard costing. 1. A costing technique in which the cost of a product is assessed as the sum of the standard costs of the materials, components and operations that go into making it.

2. A management technique in which standard costs and revenues and variance analysis are used to monitor the operation of an organisation.

standard deviation. In statistics and probability theory, the positive square root of variance.

standard direct labor cost. American spelling of 'standard direct labour cost'.

standard direct labor rate. American spelling of 'standard direct labour rate'.

standard direct labour cost. American spelling: standard direct labor cost. The standard cost of the direct labour which would be used, if standard performance were achieved, to produce a specified quantity of a product.

standard direct labour rate. American spelling: standard direct labor rate. A standard cost that represents the average wage rate (usually expressed as an amount per hour) paid to the workers whose earnings constitute the standard direct labour cost of a product.

standard direct material cost. The standard cost of the quantity of direct materials that would be used, if standard material usage were achieved, to produce a specified quantity of a product. Also called 'standard direct materials cost'.

standard direct materials cost. Another form of the term 'standard direct material cost'.

standard error. In statistics, the standard deviation of the probability distribution of an estimator.

standard fixed overhead cost. The standard cost of all items of expenses, labour and materials whose costs are included in fixed overhead expenditure for a specified period.

standard form. Another term for 'normalised form'.

standard hour. In work study, the amount of work which, if undertaken at standard performance, should take one hour to complete.

standardised distribution. The probability distribution of a standardised variate.

standardised normal distribution. The probability distribution of a standardised normal variate. Its probability density function is:

$$f(x) = \frac{1}{\sqrt{(2\pi)}} \exp(-\tfrac{1}{2}x^2)$$

Also called 'standard normal distribution' but the term 'standardised normal distribution' is used in BS 5532 : Part 1 : 1978.

standardised normal variate. The standardised variate corresponding to a normal variate.

standardised variate. If X is a random variable with expectation μ and standard deviation σ then the corresponding standardised variate is the random variable Y defined by:

$$Y = (X - \mu)/\sigma$$

A standardised variate has expectation 0 and standard deviation 1.

standard marginal costing. A standard costing system for planning and control in which attention is focused on a standard for contribution per unit of a product.

standard material usage. The quantity of material required as an average, under specified conditions, to produce a specified quantity of output. Also called 'standard materials usage'.

standard materials usage. Another form of the term 'standard material usage'.

standard minute. In work study, an amount of work which, if undertaken at standard performance, should take one minute to complete.

standard normal distribution. Another term for 'standardised normal distribution'.

standard operator performance. Another term for 'standard performance'.

standard overhead cost. The sum of standard fixed overhead cost for a specified period and standard variable overhead cost for a specified level of activity during that period.

standard performance. 1. In work measurement, the rate of output which 'qualified workers' will naturally achieve when performing a specified task without overexertion as an average over a working day or shift, provided they adhere to a specified method and are motivated to apply themselves to their work. A 'qualified worker' is one who is accepted as having the necessary physical attributes, who possesses the required intelligence and education and has acquired the necessary skill and knowledge to carry out the work to satisfactory standards of safety, quantity and quality. Also known as 'standard operator performance'. See also the entry for 'standard rating'.

2. The rate of output achievable by a machine as an average, under specified conditions over a given period of time.

standard price. A standard cost of a raw material or component. Also called 'standard purchase price'.

standard production cost. See the entries for 'total standard production cost' and 'unit standard production cost'.

standard purchase price. Another term for 'standard price'.

standard rating. The rating in numerical terms of the pace of working at a particular job which is the average at which 'qualified workers' (see the entry for 'standard performance') would naturally perform the job, provided they adhere to a specified method and are motivated to apply themselves to their work. On the rating scale defined in BS 3138 : 1979, standard rating is 100, and zero is the rating for no activity at all.

standard selling price. An estimate of the price at which a product should be sold, established for the purposes of planning and control by a systematic analysis of the costs of production and of the profit required. The price is usually referred to as a 'unit standard selling price', where the unit may be a single item of product or a batch of identical items or a batch of output from a process.

standard stock level. In stock control, the average level of stock measured over a period of time (BS 5191 : 1975).

standard time. In work measurement, the total time in which a task should be completed at standard performance.

standard unit of work. In work study, a standard minute or a standard hour of work.

standard variable overhead cost. The standard cost of all items of expenses, labour and materials whose costs are included in variable overhead expenditure per unit of the measure of activity used (for example, direct labour hour or number of units produced).

standby credit. A letter of credit used to guarantee repayment of a loan made to the applicant for the credit: the issuing bank promises to pay the amount of the loan on receipt of a certificate of default by the applicant.

statement. Another term for 'statement of account'.

statement form. Another term for 'report form'.

statement of account. A list, sent periodically to a customer of an accounting entity, of the customer's financial transactions with the entity and the balance owed by or to the customer. Also called 'statement'.

statement of affairs. A financial statement, in a prescribed form, which must be prepared by or on behalf of an insolvent individual during bankruptcy proceedings, or on behalf of a company when an administrative receiver or provisional liquidator is appointed.

statement of changes in financial position. Another term for 'statement of source and application of funds'.

Statement of Intent. Abbreviation: SOI. A statement by the Accounting Standards Committee indicating, at an early stage, how the Committee proposes to deal with a matter in the course of the process of setting standards.

statement of operations. Another term for 'income and expenditure account'.

Statement of Recommended Practice. Abbreviation: SORP, usually spoken as an acronym. A statement of rules which accountants are encouraged to follow when preparing financial statements but which are not concerned with matters of major and fundamental importance and so are not incorporated in Statements of Standard Accounting Practice.

statement of source and application of funds. A financial statement for an accounting entity showing how the operations of the entity have been financed and how its financial resources have been used during the period between two balance sheets. The statement provides a link between the balance sheet at the beginning of the period, the profit and loss account of the period and the balance sheet at the end of the period. SSAP 10 requires a statement of source and application of funds to show the profit or loss of the period together with the adjustments required for items which did not use, or provide, funds in the period, and:

(a) dividends paid;

(b) acquisitions and disposals of fixed and other non-current assets;

(c) funds raised by increasing, or expended in repaying or redeeming, medium-term or long-term loans, or contributed capital;

(d) increase or decrease in working capital subdivided into components, and movements in net liquid funds.

Also called 'statement of sources and applications of funds', 'funds statement', 'source and application of funds statement', 'statement of changes in financial position'.

statement of sources and applications of funds. Another form of the term 'statement of source and application of funds'.

Statement of Standard Accounting Practice. Abbreviation: SSAP, often spoken as an acronym. A statement made by the professional institutes represented on the Consultative Committee of Accountancy Bodies (CCAB) of rules which should be followed when preparing financial statements. SSAPs are prepared by the Accounting Standards Committee which consults many persons who will be affected by an SSAP before recommending a final version. SSAPs are issued only on matters of major and fundamental importance. In the opinion of the professional institutes represented on the CCAB, financial statements will not give a true and fair view unless they are prepared in accordance with SSAPs. An annual publication of the ICAEW gives the text of SSAPs.

statement of transactions. Another term for 'income and expenditure account'.

Statement on Auditing Standards. Abbreviation: SAS. A statement, issued by the Auditing Standards Board of the American Institute of Certified Public Accountants, interpreting and amplifying generally accepted auditing standards. Members of the Institute are required to justify, in their audit reports, any deviation from Statements on Auditing Standards.

static budget. Another term for 'fixed budget'.

statistic. 1. A number calculated from data acquired by observation, measurement or experiment and used to describe the data or to estimate population parameters of the population from which the data came.

2. Plural form (statistics). Numerical data acquired by observation, measurement or experiment.

3. Plural form (statistics). The part of mathematics that deals with methods of collecting, organising and analysing data, and obtaining probable information about a population from samples taken from the population.

statistical test. A procedure, for deciding – with a known maximum probability of making a wrong decision – whether to accept a hypothesis about the distribution of a population, which involves calculating a statistic from a sample from the population. The hypothesis to be tested is called the 'null hypothesis' which is contrasted with an 'alternative hypothesis'. The maximum probability of rejecting the null hypothesis if the null hypothesis is true (this is called making an 'error of the first kind') is called the 'significance level' of the test. Usually a low value, e.g., 5% or 1%, is chosen for the significance level.

It is also possible to accept the null hypothesis, as a result of carrying out a statistical test, even though the null hypothesis is not true. This is called making an 'error of the second kind' and the probability of not committing such an error is called the 'power' of the test.

status enquiry. An enquiry to a branch of a bank asking for information about a customer with an account at the branch.

statute-barred. *Adjective*. Unenforceable by legal action because the period fixed by statute during which legal proceedings must be commenced has expired.

statutory accountant. Another term for 'authorised auditor'.

statutory apportionment. Apportionment of rents, dividends and other periodical payments under the Apportionment Act 1870.

statutory audit. An audit carried out because it is required by statute.

statutory instrument. Abbreviation: SI. An order, a set of rules or regulations, or other subordinate legislation, made by the Privy Council or by a minister of the Crown in accordance with a procedure laid down in the Statutory Instruments Act 1946.

statutory legacy. A sum of money that must be given, from the estate of an individual who died intestate when domiciled in England or Wales, to that individual's surviving spouse. The size of the statutory legacy is fixed from time to time by the Lord Chancellor under the Family Provision Act 1966, s. 1. For deaths occurring after 28 February 1981 the amount is £40,000 if the intestate left issue but £85,000 if the intestate left no issue.

statutory sick pay. Abbreviation: SSP. A weekly payment, by an employer to an employee who is unable to work because of illness, that is required by Part I of the Social Security and Housing Benefits Act 1982 and which the employer may deduct from Class 1 social security contributions payable by the employer to the Secretary of State.

stepped cost. Another term for 'stepped fixed cost'.

stepped fixed cost. A cost that varies with the level of activity, but only has a small number of possible values, each of which applies over a fairly wide range of levels of activity. Also called 'stepped cost', 'semi-fixed cost'.

sterling. The legal tender of the United Kingdom.

stewardship. The duties and obligations of a person who manages something on behalf of other persons.

stochastic process. A set of random variables, each of which is associated with an element of another set T. If t is an element of T then the random variable associated with it may be denoted by X_t or $X(t)$ and the whole set of random variables making up the stochastic process may be denoted by $\{X_t\}$ or $\{X(t)\}$. Usually, T is a set of numbers representing time and $X(t)$ represents the state of a system at time t. The random variables are not required to be independent. In the stochastic processes usually studied the random variables are discrete and such processes may be called 'discrete-valued'. If T consists of isolated numbers (e.g., only integers) the process is described as 'discrete'. If T is a continuous set of all numbers in a particular interval then the process is described as 'continuous'.

stock. 1. A quantity of something that is kept or stored for use as the need arises, e.g., materials, supplies, work in progress or finished goods. Also called 'inventory'.

2. In BS 5191 : 1975, defined as 'all the tangible material assets of a company other than the fixed assets; comprising all the finished or saleable products, all the items to be incorporated into the finished products, and all the items to be consumed in the process of manufacturing the product [sic] or in the carrying out of the business'. Also called 'inventory'. In SSAP 9, the term 'stocks and work in progress' is used in this sense.

3. In the past, contributed capital of a business enterprise, either in the form of money to be used to purchase stocks of goods for sale, or in the form of goods to be used as the stock in trade of the business.

4. In Britain, one method of reckoning investors' investments in a marketable loan or in the contributed capital of a company. The extent of any particular investor's investment is measured by a monetary amount called the 'nominal value' of the investor's investment. The amount of interest or dividend payable to the investor is proportional to the nominal value as is the price at which the investment may be bought or sold. An investor may hold any amount of stock although with some securities there is a requirement that the nominal value of a holding must be an integral multiple of an amount called a 'stock unit'.

stock and work in progress. Alternative form of 'stocks and work in progress'.

stockbroker. A person who arranges the purchase and sale of securities on behalf of others. Also called 'broker'. In America called 'securities broker'.

stock certificate. A document certifying that a named person (or the bearer of the document) is the owner of a specified quantity of stock in a marketable loan or in the contributed capital of a company.

stock control. Defined in BS 5191 : 1975 as 'the systematic regulation of stock levels with respect to time and quantity'. Defined in the ICMA official terminology as 'the systematic regulation of stock levels with respect to quantity, cost and lead time'. In America called 'inventory control'.

stock cover. In stock control, the amount of stock physically on hand, less any reserved stock. See BS 5191 : 1975.

stock exhaust. Another term for 'stock-out'.

stockholding cost. The cost of keeping something in a store (e.g., of raw materials or purchased parts). Also called 'carrying cost'.

stockjobber. Another term for 'jobber'.

stock order. 'A production order to manufacture a product to replenish stock in a store' (BS 5191 : 1975). Also called 'stores order'.

stock-out. In stock control, the occurrence of a zero stock balance, not necessarily reflecting a shortage (BS 5191 : 1975). Also called 'stock exhaust'.

stock record. In stock control, a record of the quantity of stock for a single item, often containing a history of recent transactions and information for controlling the replenishment of stock (BS 5191 : 1975).

stocks and work in progress. Defined in SSAP 9 as comprising:
(a) goods or other assets purchased for resale;
(b) consumable stores;
(c) raw materials and components purchased for incorporation into products for sale;
(d) products and services in intermediate stages of completion;
(e) finished goods.

In America (and in IAS 2), called 'inventories'.

In BS 5191 : 1975, the terms 'stock' and 'inventory' are given virtually the same meaning as 'stocks and work in progress' is given in SSAP 9 and the term 'stocks' may be used in the same sense.

'Stock and work in progress' is an alternative form of 'stocks and work in progress'.

stock service level. In stock control, the number of demands for an item of stock met during a period expressed as a percentage of the number of demands made during that period.

stock-taking. Also written: stocktaking. Measurement of quantities of stocks and work in progress held. In America, called 'inventory'.

stock turnover. The number of times that an enterprise sells its stock of goods for sale during a period. In principle, measured by dividing cost of goods sold during the period by average value of stock of goods for sale held during the period. In practice, it is measured by dividing turnover for the period by the average value of stock of goods for sale held during the period. A high value of stock turnover is desirable but the value that can be achieved by any particular enterprise depends on the nature of the business that it conducts and comparison should only be made with enterprises in the same business. Also called 'rate of stock turn'. In America, called 'inventory turnover'.

stop order. An order of a court, made under the Charging Orders Act 1979, s. 5, prohibiting dealings in specified securities or funds in court.

storage. A store, or stores, in a computer.

storage capacity. In data processing, the amount of data that can be contained in a store.

storage device. In computing, another term for 'store'.

storage location. In data processing, another term for 'location'.

store. 1. *Noun.* A place where stocks of, e.g., raw materials or spares, are kept.

2. *Verb.* To put something aside for future use.

3. *Noun.* A part of a data processing device in which data may be retained for some time and from which data may be retrieved when required. Also called 'storage device'. Use of the alternative term 'memory' is deprecated by BS 3527 : Part 12 : 1978. However, in practice, 'memory' is used much more often than 'store'.

4. *Verb.* To put data into a store in a data processing device.

5. *Verb.* To retain data in a store in a data processing device.

6. *Noun.* An establishment where retail business is carried on, especially where a diverse selection of goods is offered for sale.

stores order. Another term for 'stock order'.

stores requisition. Another term for 'materials requisition'.

straight-line depreciation. A method of calculating depreciation of a fixed asset in which the same amount of depreciation D is provided for in each year of the useful life of the asset and D is equal to

$$(H - R)/L$$

where H is the historical cost of the asset, R is its estimated residual value and L is the number of years in its useful life. Also called 'equal-instalment depreciation'.

stratified sampling. In statistics, sampling from a population which has been divided into parts called 'strata' with specified proportions of each sample being chosen from each of the strata.

striking price. The price to be paid if an option is exercised. Also called 'exercise price'.

Student distribution. Another term for 't-distribution'.

Student's t-distribution. Another term for 't-test'.

Student test. Another term for 't-test'.

subcharge. A charge on the chargee's interest in a charge.

subconsolidation. Preparation of consolidated accounts for a subgroup.

subgroup. A group of companies consisting of a holding company and its subsidiaries where the holding company is itself a subsidiary of another corporation.

subject-to opinion. 1. In Britain and Ireland, a statement in an audit report by which the auditor effectively disclaims an opinion on a particular matter which is not considered fundamental.

2. In America, an audit report pointing out that there is a contingency whose outcome may affect whether the financial statements of an entity present fairly the financial position and results of the entity.

sublease. 1. *Noun.* A lease of a thing which the lessor leases from some other person.

2. *Verb.* (a) (Used actively.) To be a party to a sublease (in sense 1) of something.

(b) (Used passively.) To be the subject-matter of a sublease (in sense 1).

sublessee. The lessee under a lease which is a sublease.

sublessor. The lessor under a lease which is a sublease.

submartingale. A discrete stochastic process $\{X(t)\}$ with the property that for the random variable $X(t_{n+1})$ representing the state of the system at time t_{n+1}, the expectation of the conditional distribution of $X(t_{n+1})$ for given values of all the distributions relating to preceding times is not less than the value $x(t_n)$ of the distribution $X(t_n)$ for the immediately preceding time.

submortgage. A mortgage on the mortgagee's interest in a mortgage.

subpopulation. In statistics, a definite part of a population.

subrogation. Succession to the rights of another person, in particular, succession to the right to take legal proceedings to recover money owed to a person after paying the money to that person.

subroutine. A sequence of programming-language statements that occurs at several points within one computer program or in several different programs.

subroyalty. A royalty paid to a person for exercising a right for which that person in turn has to pay a royalty to another person.

subscription. 1. Acquisition of, or an offer to acquire, previously unissued shares or other securities from their issuer. Some authorities suggest that the term should only be used when the securities are, or are to be, acquired for cash.

2. A payment made regularly in advance for a service.

subsequent event. Term used in America for 'post balance sheet event'.

subsidiary. 1. In British company law, a corporation S is a subsidiary of a corporation H if H is a holding company of S.

2. In the Income and Corporation Taxes Act 1970, s. 532(1): 'for the purposes of the Tax Acts a body corporate shall be deemed to be:

'(a) a "51 per cent subsidiary" of another body corporate if and so long as more than 50 per cent of its ordinary share capital is owned directly or indirectly by that other body corporate;

'(b) a "75 per cent subsidiary" of another body corporate if and so long as not less than 75 per cent of its ordinary share capital is owned directly or indirectly by that other body corporate;

'(c) a "90 per cent subsidiary" of another body corporate if and so long as not less than 90 per cent of its ordinary share capital is directly owned by that other body corporate'.

Other subsections of s. 532 give elaborate rules for interpreting these definitions.

3. In non-legal use, one corporation is a subsidiary of another (which may be called the 'controlling company' or 'parent company') if the controlling company controls the majority of votes in the subsidiary. In IAS 3, a 'subsidiary' is 'a company which is controlled by another company (known as the "parent company")' where 'control' of a company means ownership, directly, or indirectly through subsidiaries, of more than one-half of the voting power of the company.

subsidiary account. An account, kept separately from the ledger, recording individual transactions of a particular type from which periodic totals are posted to a control account in the ledger. Also called 'detail account'.

subsidise. 1. *Verb.* To reduce the price of something by paying a subsidy.

2. *Verb.* To assist a producer or trader, or an industry, by paying subsidies.

subsidy. 1. A grant made by a government to a producer or trader so as to reduce prices charged by that producer or trader.

2. A grant made by a government to enable a producer or trader to continue in a business that might otherwise be unprofitable.

substantive test. A test of transactions or balances, or another procedure such as analytical review, that seeks to provide audit evidence of the completeness, accuracy and validity of the information contained in the accounting records or financial statements of the accounting entity being audited.

sub-subsidiary. A subsidiary of a subsidiary.

subsystem. A system that is part of a larger system.

subtotal. 1. *Noun.* The total of part of a set of numbers that are being totalled.

2. *Verb.* To compute the total of part of a set of numbers that are being totalled.

subtrahend. A number that is subtracted from another number (called the 'minuend').

suffix notation. Another term for 'postfix notation'.

sum. 1. *Noun.* The result of the addition of two or more numbers.

2. *Verb.* To carry out the addition of two or more more numbers.

3. *Noun.* A particular amount of money.

sum of the years' digits. A method of depreciation of a fixed asset over the *t* accounting periods (which are usually years) of its useful life in which the sum:

$$s = 1 + 2 + 3 + \ldots + t = \tfrac{1}{2}\, t(t + 1)$$

(i.e., the 'sum of the years' digits') is calculated and the depreciation for the *n*th period is:

$$(\text{historical cost}) \times (t - n)/s$$

sunk cost. A cost that was incurred in the past and which cannot be changed and so is not relevant for future decision-making.

supermicro. A microcomputer powerful enough to be used simultaneously by a small number of users with separate user terminals.

super-profit. Excess of the actual profit of an enterprise over the amount necessary to pay interest at a particular rate on the enterprise's contributed capital.

supervisor. 1. A manager whose job is mainly concerned with ensuring that tasks, specified by others, are performed correctly and efficiently by a group of people – especially when none of those people are themselves managers.

2. In data processing, another term for 'supervisory program'.

supervisory program. A computer program that controls the execution of other computer programs and regulates the flow of work in a data processing system. A supervisory program is normally part of an operating system. Also called 'executive program', 'supervisor'.

supply. 1. Plural form (supplies). Another term for 'consumables'.

2. Plural form (supplies). Materials used in production for which it is impossible or not worth while to determine the amount attributable to each unit of product (for example, cleaning materials, lubricating oil for machinery).

3. Written with capital S. Money to be supplied to the government out of the Consolidated Fund to pay for services specified in the Supply Estimates.

Supply Estimate. A statement, with supporting explanation, of the amount of money that the government asks Parliament to provide, from the Consolidated Fund, for expenditure by a government department on one of its functions, or by another body carrying out public functions, during a financial year. Also called 'vote'.

Supply service. A government expenditure that may be incurred in any year only if Parliament has voted its approval of the expenditure for that year.

support cost centre. American spelling: support cost center. A service cost centre in an organisation that supplies services.

surety. In the past, a person providing collateral (or third-party) security or an indemnity for the performance of an obligation. Used in the Consumer Credit Act 1974 to mean any person who has provided security, whether direct or collateral, or an indemnity for the performance of an obligation (s. 189(1) of the Act).

surplus. Amount by which income is greater than expenditure in an income and expenditure account.

surplus advance corporation tax. Advance corporation tax paid by a company which cannot be set against the company's liability to corporation tax for an accounting period (see Finance Act 1972, s. 85(3)).

surplus of franked investment income. The amount by which the franked investment income received by a company in an accounting period exceeds the amount of the franked payments made by it in that period (Finance Act 1972, s. 89(6)).

suspense account. A ledger account in which entries are made temporarily, for example, because the ledger account to which they should be posted cannot be identified, or because they represent errors which have been found, but not yet corrected. In banking, an account to which a deposit of money is credited when it is not possible to identify the customer whose account should be credited with the money.

SYD. Abbreviation of 'sum of the years' digits'.

symbolic model. A model in which the variables of a system are represented by symbols and the relationships between the variables are represented by mathematical relationships between the symbols.

system. A collection of component items that are interdependent and may be identified and treated as a whole.

system flowchart. Also written: system flow chart. Another term for 'data flowchart'.

system production time. The time during which a data processing system is actually used by some user. It is part of operating time.

system test time. Time during which a data processing system is tested for proper operation. It is part of operating time.

T

T/A. Abbreviation of 'trading as'.

Table A. A model set of articles of association for a company limited by shares provided by British Companies Acts since the Companies Act 1862 and now prescribed by regulations made by the Secretary of State under the Companies Act 1985, s. 8. See the Companies (Alteration of Table A etc.) Regulations 1984 (SI 1984 No. 1717).

T account. A written accounting record of transactions of an accounting entity of a particular type (for example, transactions with a particular person or transactions concerning a particular type of asset) which is laid out with a single horizontal rule at the top and a single vertical rule separating debit and credit entries, the rules forming the shape of the letter 'T'. This layout is used for illustrating accounting techniques, e.g., in teaching where it is unnecessary to have additional ruled columns for such details as the number of the folio on which the corresponding double entry appears.

take-over. Also written: takeover. The combining of two business enterprises in such a way that the owners of one of the enterprises give up their interest in exchange for consideration given by the other enterprise. Also called 'acquisition'.

take-over bid. Also written: takeover bid. An offer made to the holders of all shares in a company, or all shares of a particular class in a company, to purchase those shares with a view to obtaining at least sufficient shares to give the maker of the offer (called the 'offeror') enough votes to control the company. The company whose shares are the subject-matter of the bid is called the 'offeree company'. The phrase 'take-over offer for a company', defined in the Company Securities (Insider Dealing) Act 1985, s. 14, has the same meaning.

take-over offer for a company. Also written: takeover offer for a company. Phrase used in the Company Securities (Insider Dealing) Act 1985 with the meaning of 'take-over bid'.

tangible asset. An asset that is tangible property.

tangible asset value. In relation to a registered company, balance sheet asset value less net intangible assets expressed as an amount per ordinary share.

tangible personal property. Property in things in possession.

tangible property. Property in land or a thing in possession. The subject-matter of the property is a physical object which is tangible (i.e., capable of being touched) rather than an enforceable right to be paid money or to receive some other benefit.

target program. In relation to the translation of a computer program from one programming language into another, the translated program.

task. 1. In work measurement, an identifiable part of a job. A task may consist of a number of operations, which are the smallest units of work used for the purposes of planning and control. See BS 3138 : 1979.

2. In multiprogramming or multiprocessing, one or more sequences of instructions treated by a control program as an element of work to be accomplished by the computer.

taxable income. The amount of income of an accounting entity for a period, determined in accordance with the rules governing taxation of the entity, on which taxation for the period will be charged. See IAS 12.

taxable person. For the purposes of UK value added tax, a person who makes or who intends to make taxable supplies and who is registered or is required to be registered under the Value Added Tax Act 1983 (see s. 2(2) of the Act). A person who makes taxable supplies but is not registered is liable to be registered if the value of that person's taxable supplies exceeds a limit which is specified in Schedule 1 to the Value Added Tax Act 1983 and is altered from time to time to reflect changes in the value of money.

taxable supply. For the purposes of UK value added tax, a supply of goods or services made in the United Kingdom other than an exempt supply (Value Added Tax Act 1983, s. 2(2)).

tax accountant. Term used in the Taxes Management Act 1970 to mean a person who assists any other person in the preparation of returns or accounts to be made or delivered by the other person for any purpose of income tax, capital gains tax or corporation tax. The persons assisted are described as 'clients' of the tax accountant.

Tax Acts. When used in an Act of Parliament passed on or after 12 March 1970, defined in the Interpretation Act 1979, Schedule 1, as: 'the Income and Corporation Taxes Act 1970 and all other provisions of the Income Tax Acts and the Corporation Tax Acts'. The same definition applies to subordinate legislation made after 1 January 1979 and Northern Ireland legislation passed on or after 12 March 1970. Compare 'Taxes Acts'.

tax advantage. For the purposes of the Income and Corporation Taxes Act 1970, Part XVII, chapter I (cancellation of tax advantages from certain transactions in securities), defined as 'a relief or increased relief from, or repayment or increased repayment of, tax, or the avoidance or reduction of a charge to tax or an assessment to tax or the avoidance of a possible assessment thereto, whether the avoidance or reduction is effected by receipts accruing in such a way that the recipient does not pay or bear tax on them, or by a deduction in computing profits or gains' (Income and Corporation Taxes Act 1970, s. 466(1)).

tax avoidance. Another term for 'tax planning'.

tax credit. In UK taxation, when a company resident in the United Kingdom makes a qualifying distribution which is received by a person resident in the United Kingdom, an amount equal to the advance corporation tax paid on the distribution which may be set against the income tax chargeable on the recipient's income. If the tax credit exceeds the income tax chargeable on the recipient's income then the excess will be paid to the recipient by the Inland Revenue. See Finance Act 1972, s. 86.

tax-deductible. *Adjective.* Allowed to be deducted from total income before arriving at the amount of income on which tax must be paid.

Taxes Acts. Defined in the Taxes Management Act 1970 (which was passed on 12 March 1970), s. 118(1) as amended, to mean: the Taxes Management Act 1970 and:

'(a) the Tax Acts; and

'(b) the Capital Gains Tax Act 1979 and all other enactments relating to capital gains tax; and

'(c) the Development Land Tax Act 1976 and any other enactment relating to development land tax'.

Taxes Management Act 1970. Abbreviation: TMA 1970. A UK statute that consolidates the law relating to the administration and collection of income tax, capital gains tax, corporation tax and development land tax.

tax evasion. Illegal failure to pay taxes, for example, by not correctly declaring liability.

tax-free. *Adjective.* Used to describe an amount of money on which no tax is payable.

tax haven. A territory in which low taxes are levied on income and capital gains, and to which persons divert money of theirs from places where it would suffer taxation at higher rates.

tax holiday. A period during which an enterprise is exempt from tax on its profits – allowed as an incentive to the establishment of new enterprises.

tax invoice. An invoice prepared in accordance with regulations made by the Commissioners of Customs and Excise when a taxable supply is made providing information about the charging of UK value added tax.

tax loss. The amount of loss of an accounting entity for a period, determined in accordance with the rules governing taxation of the entity, from which the amount of tax recoverable by the entity may be calculated. See IAS 12.

taxman. Personification of the Inland Revenue.

tax planning. Arrangement of financial transactions so as to reduce the tax chargeable so far as this can be done without breaking the law. Also called 'tax avoidance'. Compare 'tax evasion'.

tax point. The time at which UK value added tax on a supply is chargeable. In the legislation the term 'time of supply' is used.

tax relief. An exemption from a requirement to pay tax on an amount of income or capital gain. The shortened form 'relief' is also used.

tax return. A return giving information that will provide the basis for an assessment to tax.

tax shield. A decrease, in the amount that has to be earned in order to make a payment, which arises because the payment is tax deductible.

tax week. One of the successive periods within a tax year beginning on 6 April and on every seventh day thereafter. At the end of each tax year there is a tax week of either one day (5 April) or, in a leap year, two days.

tax year. A period of 12 months, commencing on 6 April in one calendar year and ending on 5 April in the next calendar year, over which an individual's income is measured in order to calculate UK income tax. Also called 'fiscal year', 'year of assessment'.

t-distribution. The probability distribution of a random variable $T = U/\sqrt{(X^2/\nu)}$, where U and $\sqrt{(X^2/\nu)}$ are independent random variables, U is a standardised normal variate and X^2 is a random variable with a chi-squared distribution with ν degrees of freedom. The *t*-distribution is also said to have ν degrees of freedom.

Also called 'Student distribution' or 'Student's *t*-distribution' because it was described by an English statistician, William Sealy Gosset (1876–1937), who used the pen name 'Student'.

technical analysis. In investment analysis, assessment of whether to buy or sell a security or other investment based on consideration of the pattern of the variations over time in market prices for the investment. Compare 'fundamental analysis'.

teeming and lading. Concealing cash misappropriations by falsifying accounting records.

temporal method. When consolidating the accounts of an entity with transactions in one currency with the accounts of an entity with transactions in a foreign currency, a method of translating the foreign currency accounts in which each transaction in the foreign currency is translated at the exchange rate for the day of the transaction. Compare 'closing rate/net investment method'.

temporary account. Another term for 'nominal account'.

temporary investment. An investment in marketable securities which the investor does not intend to retain and which are not used by the investor to obtain a significant influence over the investee.

tender bond. An arrangement under which a guarantor promises that if a particular tenderer for a contract is awarded the contract but fails to take it up then the guarantor will pay compensation to the buyer. Also called 'bid bond', 'tender guarantee'.

tender guaranteee. Another term for 'tender bond'.

tenor. The length of time between acceptance and due date for payment of a bill of exchange.

term. 1. A definite period of time.

2. An interest in real property subsisting for a definite period of time.

3. The obligations of the parties to a contract in respect of one particular aspect of the performance of the contract.

4. 'A word or expression that has a precise meaning in some uses or is peculiar to a science, art, profession, or subject' (*Webster's Ninth New Collegiate Dictionary*, 1983).

term bill. Another term for 'time bill'.

terminal. Short form of the term 'user terminal'.

terminal value. The result of investing an amount of principal P to earn compound interest at a rate of interest i per unit of time for t time periods. If t is a positive integer, the terminal value is:

$$P(1 + i)^t$$

If $0 < t \leqslant 1$ then the terminal value is:

$$P(1 + it)$$

If $t > 1$ and t is not an integer, and $[t]$ is the largest integer less than t then the terminal value is:

$$P(1 + i)^{[t]} \left\{ 1 + (t - [t])i \right\} - P$$

Also called 'future amount'.

term loan. A loan of money for a fixed period of time.

term of years absolute. A right to hold real property for a fixed period of certain maximum duration. Such a right is a legal estate if it complies with the technical definition given in the Law of Property Act 1925, s. 205(1)(xxvii). Commonly called 'leasehold'.

terotechnology. Practical techniques for optimising the costs of ownership of physical assets, especially maintenance costs, including design of equipment for reliability and maintainability, and installation, commissioning, operation, modification and replacement of physical assets.

testament. See the entry for 'will'.

testament-dative. In Scotland, confirmation in favour of an executor dative.

testament-testamentar. In Scotland, confirmation in favour of an executor nominate.

testator. The maker of a will. A female testator is sometimes called a 'testatrix'.

testatrix. Term sometimes used for a female testator.

test statistic. A statistic calculated from a sample from a population in order to carry out a statistical test of a hypothesis about the distribution of the population.

theoretical ex-rights price. An estimate of what the market price of a company's shares of a particular class will be after a rights issue of shares of the same class, assuming that if the rights issue were not made the market price of the company's shares would stay the same and assuming that the whole rights issue is taken up at the offer price. If the price of a share before the rights issue is p, and n shares have been issued, and if the rights issue is to be of m shares at a price r then the theoretical ex-rights price is:

$$\frac{pn + rm}{n + m}$$

or:

$$\frac{p(n/m) + r}{(n/m) + 1}$$

Usually the ratio n/m of number of existing shares to number of rights shares is known and so the second version of the formula is easier to use.

theory of games. Another term for 'game theory'.

thin-film store. Shortened form of the term 'magnetic thin-film store'.

thing in action. Property in a right to be paid money or receive some benefit enforceable by legal action but which is not primarily a right to possession of a physical object. A debt, a policy of insurance, and a copyright, are examples of things in action. There may be some documentary evidence of the existence of the property – an invoice in the case of a debt, a policy document in the case of an insurance – but possession of such a document is not normally considered to be the most important benefit conferred by having property in the debt or in the insurance policy, etc.: the most important benefit is the right to be paid the debt, the right to be paid the insurance money, etc. Also called 'chose in action'.

thing in possession. Property in a physical object (other than land). Possession of the object is regarded as the principal benefit conferred by having the property. Also called 'chose in possession'.

third-party security. Another term for 'collateral security'.

three-column cash book. A cash book in which notes are made of discounts allowed and received so that only periodic totals need be posted to the discounts allowed and discounts received accounts.

till float. Another term for 'cash float'.

time bill. A bill of exchange that is to be paid a specified time after it has been accepted, or (nowadays rarely) after it was drawn. Also called a 'term bill' or 'draft at a tenor', the 'tenor' being the length of time between acceptance and due date for payment.

timekeeping. Recording of the time spent by workers at work or on individual jobs.

time of supply. Term used in legislation for 'tax point'.

time-period concept. Another term for 'periodicity concept'.

time-period principle. Another term for 'periodicity concept'.

time rate. A rate of payment for an individual's work per unit of time spent at work. Also called a 'day rate', 'timework rate'.

time series. A sequence of values of a quantitative characteristic observed at various times (usually at regular intervals).

time sheet. A document recording, for an individual employee, times spent at work and times spent on individual jobs.

times interest covered. Another term for 'interest cover'.

timework. Work that is paid for by a time rate. Also called 'daywork'.

timework rate. Another term for 'time rate'.

timing difference. A difference between profits as computed for taxation purposes and profits as stated in financial statements, resulting from the inclusion of items of income and expenditure in taxation computations in periods different from those in which they are included in financial statements (SSAP 15, para. 19; ED 33, para. 18).

title retention. Another term for 'retention of title'.

TMA 1970. Abbreviation of 'Taxes Management Act 1970'.

tooling requisition. A document used within an organisation to request the supply of tools, jigs or fixtures which may be returned to stores after use (BS 5191 : 1975).

tort. A wrong done to a person causing injury or loss for which proceedings may be taken under English common law for the recovery of unliquidated damages where the wrong is an act, statement or omission in breach of a duty or in contravention of a right imposed or conferred by law rather than by agreement.

tortious. *Adjective.* Of, or relating to, tort.

total account. Another term for 'control account'.

total charge for credit. A charge for credit provided under a consumer credit agreement calculated according to regulations made under s. 20 of the Consumer Credit Act 1974. The regulations currently in force are the Consumer Credit (Total Charge for Credit) Regulations 1977 (SI 1977 No. 327).

total income. In UK revenue law, the total income of a person from all sources estimated in accordance with the provisions of the Income Tax Acts (Income and Corporation Taxes Act 1970, s. 528(1)).

total standard production cost. The total of the standard costs of all items of labour, materials and expenses with costs that make up the product cost for a specified quantity of a product. It may be calculated on the principle of absorption costing or the principle of marginal costing.

total standard profit. A standard for the profit that will be derived from selling specified quantities of products at standard selling prices. It may be a standard for net profit on ordinary activities, gross profit or contribution.

track. In data processing, the path followed by a single reading or writing component on a data medium as the medium moves past the component.

trade. 1. *Noun.* Business involving buying and selling goods.

2. *Verb.* To engage in business involving buying and selling goods.

3. *Noun.* An occupation requiring the exercise of manual or mechanical skills.

trade acceptance. A bill of exchange that has been accepted by the drawee and which has been drawn to pay the price of goods purchased by the drawee from the drawer.

trade bill. A bill of exchange that has been drawn to pay the price of goods purchased by the drawee from the drawer.

trade bill payable. A bill payable that is a trade bill.

trade bill receivable. A bill receivable that is a trade bill.

trade creditor. 1. A creditor of a business enterprise whose debt arose in the normal course of the ordinary activities of the enterprise.

2. An amount owed to a creditor of a business enterprise whose debt arose in the normal course of the ordinary activities of the enterprise. In America, called 'trade payable'.

trade debt. A debt owed to a creditor arising from a transaction in the course of the ordinary business activities of the creditor.

trade debtor. 1. A debtor of a business enterprise whose debt arose in the normal course of the ordinary activities of the enterprise.

2. An amount owed by a debtor of a business enterprise whose debt arose in the normal course of the ordinary activities of the enterprise. In America, called 'trade receivable'.

trade discount. An amount which a seller of goods deducts from a standard price for the goods to arrive at the price to be charged to a particular customer. Unlike a cash discount, a trade discount is only a means of computing an invoice charge and does not have to be accounted for in the seller's ledger.

traded options. Options to buy securities – with standardised expiry dates, exercise prices and other conditions – designed so that large quantities can be marketed on a stock exchange.

trade investment. An interest of an investing group or company in an associated company.

trade payable. Term used in America for 'trade creditor'.

trade receivable. Term used in America for 'trade debtor'.

trade reference. A statement of the creditworthiness of a business enterprise given by another business enterprise that has traded with it.

trade terms. 1. The terms of a contract of sale of goods that deal with the transport of the goods from seller to buyer and insurance of the goods while in transit.

2. The terms (concerning, especially, trade discount and period of credit) that a business enterprise usually incorporates in contracts of sale of goods when selling to other enterprises in its trade.

trading account. 1. A section of a financial statement showing the amount of gross profit or gross loss and how it is computed from turnover or net sales. The term is not commonly used in America.

2. A ledger account of all the revenues and expenses from which gross profit is calculated. Normally each revenue and expense transaction is entered initially in a relevant ledger account for that class of transaction: the trading account is prepared by balancing those revenue and expense accounts periodically and posting the balances to the trading account. The balance on the trading account is the gross profit if it is a credit balance or the gross loss if it is a debit balance, and is posted to the profit and loss account. In America it is not usual to keep a separate trading account; the items are entered directly in the profit and loss account.

trading and profit and loss account. 1. Term sometimes used for a financial statement summarising revenues and expenditures for a period and showing how the profit or loss for the period after payment of tax is computed, starting with turnover or net sales. Nowadays, more usually called 'profit and loss account'.

2. A ledger account combining the functions of a trading account and a profit and loss account.

trading as. Abbreviation: T/A. *Participle with preposition.* Used to connect the name of a person with a business name used by the person.

trading on the equity. Term used in America for 'gearing'.

trading profit. Gross profit for a period on the ordinary activities of a trading enterprise.

training levy. A levy imposed by an industrial training board on employers in the industry that it covers. The funds raised by the levy are paid out as grants to employers in the industry to reimburse them for expenditure on training employees. An employer may apply to its training board for exemption from paying the levy on the ground that its own training schemes are adequate.

tranche. A slice; the portion of an amount between two limits.

transaction. A transfer of something of value between two or more accounting entities. A transaction may be an 'exchange' in which each participant both receives and gives value, as in purchases or sales of goods or services; or a transaction may be a unilateral transfer in which one entity incurs a liability or transfers an asset to another entity (or receives an asset or cancellation of a liability) without directly receiving (or giving) value in exchange.

transfer. 1. *Verb.* To put one person (called the 'transferee') in place of another (called the 'transferor') as owner of an item of property.

2. *Noun.* An instance of putting one person in place of another as an owner of an item of property.

3. *Noun.* A document by which one person is put in place of another as the owner of an item of property.

transferee. The person who becomes an owner of something as a result of a transfer.

transfer of value. For the purposes of capital transfer tax, a disposition made by a person (called the 'transferor') as a result of which the value of the transferor's estate immediately after the disposition is less than it would be but for the disposition; and the amount by which it is less is the 'value transferred' by the transfer (Capital Transfer Tax Act 1984, s. 3(1)). No account shall be taken of the value of excluded property which ceases to form part of a person's estate as a result of a disposition (Capital Transfer Tax Act 1984, s. 3(3)). The word 'disposition' is not defined in the Capital Transfer Tax Act apart from a provision that it includes a disposition effected by associated operations (Capital Transfer Tax Act 1984, s. 272).

transferor. The person who gives ownership of something by a transfer.

transfer price. A price charged by one department of an organisation to another, or by one company in a group to another company in the group, for supplying goods or services.

transfer risk. The risk, when selling something on credit to a buyer in another country, that exchange-control regulations will be altered so as to prevent or delay payment.

transit time. In production planning, the period of time between the completion of an operation and availability of the material at the succeeding work station, not including inspection or other ancillary operation times (BS 5191 : 1975).

transition matrix. A matrix of all the transition probabilities between all pairs of states of the system in a Markov chain with stationary transition probabilities.

transition probability. In relation to a discrete-valued stochastic process representing the state of a system at various times, the conditional probability that the system will be in state T at time t given that it is in state S at time s.

translate. *Verb.* To carry out translation.

translation. 1. Expression of financial data in terms of a different currency from the one in which they were stated.

2. In data processing, representation of data in a different form without significantly changing the meaning of the data.

transportation in. Term used in America for 'carriage inward'.

transportation problem. In operational research, an allocation problem in which divisible stocks of a commodity at various points are to be moved with minimum costs to satisfy demands at other points.

transposition. Erroneously recording a number by reversing the order of two of its digits.

travelling-salesman problem. American spelling: traveling-salesman problem. The problem of finding an itinerary for a sales representative which will minimise the total distance that the representative has to travel in going from a starting place to visit n other places exactly once each and return to the starting place. Many other problems of operational research are of the same form, and may be solved in the same way, as the travelling-salesman problem.

treasurership. The position of, or work usually undertaken by, an individual who is responsible for the treasury function in an organisation.

treasury function. The activities in an organisation that are concerned with the provision of finance for the organisation and with the ways in which the organisation uses its finance.

trial balance. A list of all the balances on the ledger accounts before posting them to the trading account and profit and loss account (or income and expenditure account) for a period. The totals of credit and debit balances should be the same.

true and fair view. The view of the financial position of a company which must be presented by the financial statements presented each year by the company's directors to its members. A legal obligation to present a true and fair view is imposed throughout the European Community. In Britain, the balance sheet which directors must prepare under s. 227(4) of the Companies Act 1985 must give a true and fair view of the state of affairs of the company as at the end of its financial year and the profit and loss account (or income and expenditure account) which directors must prepare under s. 227(1) of the Companies Act 1985 must give a true and fair view of the profit or loss of the company for the financial year (Companies Act 1985, s. 228). The meaning of the phrase 'true and fair' is considered in detail in an opinion from counsel obtained by the Accounting Standards Committee and published in *Accountng Standards 1984/85* (London: Institute of Chartered Accountants in England and Wales, 1984), pp. 178-85.

true discount. Another term for 'compound discount'.

truncation. In banking, simplification of the procedure for collecting payment of cheques, especially by sending only a description of the cheque to the paying bank and not the cheque itself.

trust. 1. An enforceable obligation binding a person who has control over property to deal with that property for the benefit of particular persons or for the advancement of a charitable object. The person who is under the obligation is called the 'trustee' and a person who will benefit from it is called a 'beneficiary' or 'cestui que trust'. It is possible for the trustee of a trust to be also a beneficiary under the trust.

2. In relation to a particular trust (in sense 1), a rule, established when setting up the trust, that prescribes what is to be done with the trust property.

3. Plural form (trusts). In relation to a charity, 'the provisions establishing it as a charity and regulating its purposes and administration, whether those provisions take effect by way of trust or not' (Charities Act 1960, s. 46).

4. A monopoly, especially one that arises because previously independent enterprises come under common control. In the USA in the 19th century, a monopoly of this kind could be created by the owners of

enterprises giving their stock to a board of trustees in exchange for trust certificates, the trustees being required to exercise the voting rights carried by their stock so as to manage the businesses in the best interests of the holders of trust certificates and to distribute dividends to those holders. A trust of this kind is also called a 'business trust' – the first was the Standard Oil Trust formed in 1879.

trust corporation. A corporation qualified, in accordance with statutory rules, to act as a personal representative of deceased individuals and, in certain circumstances, to act as a sole trustee. The rules currently in force are the Public Trustee Rules 1912 (SR&O 1912 No. 348) as amended by SI 1975 No. 1189, SI 1976 No. 836, SI 1981 No. 358, SI 1984 No. 109 and SI 1985 No. 132.

trust deed. A deed that sets out the terms of a trust.

trustee. A person who has control over property, but is under an enforceable obligation to deal with that property for the benefit of particular persons or for the advancement of a charitable object under the terms of a trust. The major duties of a trustee are:

(a) not to profit from the trust;

(b) not to delegate the trust except as allowed by the terms of the trust or by statute;

(c) not to deviate from the terms of the trust;

(d) to act impartially between beneficiaries if there is more than one;

(e) to distribute trust property only to those properly entitled;

(f) to invest trust money prudently.

trustee in bankruptcy. An individual appointed to administer the property of a bankrupt. In general, the duties of a trustee in bankruptcy are:

(a) To take control of the bankrupt's property and convert it into money as advantageously as possible.

(b) To distribute the money raised from the bankrupt's property to creditors as quickly as possible in accordance with their rights.

(c) To make no profit in any way except from the remuneration properly due.

(d) To have regard to the resolutions of the creditors and to the orders of the Department of Trade and Industry.

trustee investment. An investment identified by law as one which any trustee may make using trust money without being in breach of trust. In the law of England and Wales and Scotland, trustee investments are defined in the Trustee Investments Act 1961.

t-**test.** A statistical test that depends on the value of a statistic that has a *t*-distribution. A *t*-test is used, for example, to test whether the mean of a population is equal to a specified value, given the mean of a sample from the population and using the sample standard deviation as an estimate of the population standard deviation. Also called 'Student test'.

turnover. 1. Defined in the Companies Act 1985, Schedule 4, para. 95, as the amounts derived from the provision of goods and services falling within a company's ordinary activities, after deduction of: (a) trade discounts; (b) value added tax; and (c) any other taxes based on the amounts so derived. Every company must state its turnover for the financial year being reported on in a profit and loss account prepared in accordance with this schedule. A company must also show, for each substantially different class of its business, the turnover attributable to that class, and, for each substantially different geographical market, the turnover attributable to that market. In practice, value added tax and trade discounts are not normally included in accounts as part of the value of sales. See also the entries for 'gross turnover', 'net turnover'. In America, called 'gross sales' or 'sales revenue'. (In practice, in Britain, the amount reported as turnover may actually be net sales.)

2. A turnover ratio.

turnover ratio. The ratio of turnover (or net sales) for a period to the average value of a class of the entity's assets during that period. See, e.g., the entry for 'fixed assets turnover ratio'. The word 'ratio' is often omitted as in 'stock turnover'.

two-bin system. A form of reorder-level system for replenishing stock in which the quantity representing the reorder level is kept physically separate from the rest of the stock. Also called 'last-bag system'.

two-column cash book. A cash book in which no note is made of discounts allowed and received.

two-sided confidence interval. See the entry for 'confidence interval'.

two-sided test. See the entry for 'critical region'.

type I risk. In a statistical test, the probability of committing an error of the first kind. The maximum value of the type I risk is the significance level of the test. Also called 'size' of the test. Also called 'alpha risk'.

type II risk. In a statistical test, the probability of committing an error of the second kind. Also called 'beta risk'.

U

U. Abbreviation of 'unfavourable variance'.

ULS. Abbreviation of 'unsecured loan stock'.

ultimate holding company. In British company law, in relation to a corporation A, a corporation which is a holding company of A but which is not itself a subsidiary of another corporation.

ultimate parent company. In relation to a company A, another company B is A's ultimate parent company if B is not itself under the control of another company but there is a sequence of companies starting with B and ending with A such that each company in the sequence controls the next one. The term 'ultimate holding company' is used in Britain with a precise statutory definition.

ultra vires. Preposition phrase. Latin for 'beyond power'. Used to describe something done without legal authority and outside the powers or competence of the person purporting to do it.

ultra vires **doctrine.** A doctrine of British company law that a registered company can be put into legal relationships only for the purpose of pursuing the objects set out in the objects clause of its memorandum of association and that an attempt to put the company into legal relationships for any other purpose would be *ultra vires* and of no effect.

unadjusted trial balance. A trial balance taken from a ledger before adjusting entries have been posted.

unamortised cost. The difference between the historical cost of a fixed asset and the total amount provided for depreciation of the asset up to a particular time, or the difference between the value of a fixed asset that is included in accounts following revaluation of the asset and the total provided for depreciation of the asset since that revaluation.

unary operation. Another term for 'monadic operation'.

unbanked. *Adjective.* Not having a bank account.

uncalled share capital. In relation to a registered company, nominal share capital minus called-up share capital.

uncleared effects. In banking, financial documents that have been lodged by a customer of a bank for collection by the bank in respect of which the collection process is not yet complete.

unconsolidated subsidiary. A company, in a group of companies, whose financial position is not considered in consolidated accounts prepared for the group.

uncontrollable cost. A cost that is not a controllable cost.

uncontrollable variable. In operational research, a variable, in a system, that is not under the control of the managers of the system.

under-absorbed overhead. Actual overhead (usually, production overhead costs) for a period minus absorbed overhead for the period when absorbed overhead is the lesser amount. In America, called 'under-applied overhead'.

under-applied overhead. Term used in America for 'under-absorbed overhead'.

undercapitalised. *Adjective.* Having less contributed capital and/or reserves than is necessary for the scale of operations being undertaken.

undercast. *Verb.* To record an erroneous total that is smaller than the true total.

undisclosed principal. A principal on whose behalf a person transacts business as agent without disclosing the existence of the agency so that those with whom the business is transacted believe themselves to be dealing with the person alone and not as an agent.

undistributable reserves. For the purposes of s. 264 of the Companies Act 1985, the undistributable reserves of a company are:
  (a) the share premium account;
  (b) the capital redemption reserve;
  (c) the amount by which the company's accumulated, unrealised profits, so far as not previously utilised by any capitalisation (except a transfer of any profits of the company to its capital redemption reserve on or after 22 December 1980), exceed its accumulated, unrealised losses, so far as not previously written off in a reduction or reorganisation of capital duly made; and
  (d) any other reserve which the company is prohibited from distributing by any enactment (other than Part VIII of the Companies Act 1985) or by its memorandum or articles.

undivided shares. See the entry for 'joint'.

unearned income. For the purposes of UK income tax, any income which is not 'earned income'. Also called 'investment income'.

unearned revenue. Another term for 'deferred revenue'.

unfavourable variance. American spelling: unfavorable variance. Abbreviation: U. Another term for 'adverse variance'.

uniform accounting. Accounting for different accounting entities using the same accounting policies and generally treating similar transactions and events in the same way so as to facilitate comparison.

uniform costing. The use by several enterprises of the same costing systems, i.e., the same costing methods, costing principles and costing techniques.

unilateral relief. Double taxation relief given in the UK for tax paid to the authorities of another country even though there is no treaty between the UK and that country concerning double taxation. See Income and Corporation Taxes Act 1970, s. 498.

unimodal. *Adjective.* In probability theory and statistics, having only one mode.

unincorporate. *Adjective.* Not incorporated.

unincorporated association. An association of persons that is not a corporation. Sometimes the term is used to refer only to associations whose membership is likely to change from time to time, as opposed to partnerships.

unissued share capital. Nominal share capital less allotted share capital of a company.

unit. A security representing an interest in a unit trust.

unit cost. The cost of one unit of measurement of something.

United Kingdom 7-bit data code. Another term for 'ISO-7-UK'.

unitholder. A person who owns one or more units of a unit trust.

uniting of interests. The combining of two or more business enterprises in such a way that substantially all the owners of the separate enterprises continue as owners of the combined enterprise. Also called 'amalgamation', 'consolidation', 'fusion', 'merger'.

unit investment trust. In the USA, another term for 'unit trust' in the sense in which that term is used in the USA.

unit of account. A unit used for measuring monetary values. Usually, a unit of currency of a country is used as the unit of account in that country; for many international purposes there are artificial units of account, such as the European currency unit and the special drawing right.

unit price. The price charged for something expressed as a price per unit of measurement of the thing.

unit pricing. Stating unit prices.

unit standard operating profit. A standard for the profit to be received from the sale of one unit of a product at its standard selling price.

unit standard production cost. The total of the standard costs of all items of labour, materials and expenses with costs that make up the product cost for a unit of output of a product. It may be computed on the principle of absorption costing or the principle of marginal costing.

unit standard selling price. See the entry for 'standard selling price'.

unit trust. 1. In Britain, a scheme under which persons (called 'unitholders') supply capital in exchange for securities (called 'units') and an organisation (called the 'manager' of the unit trust) invests the capital in securities and/or other investments, income from which may be distributed to unitholders. The investments purchased by the manager are held by a separate organisation called the 'trustee' which controls the work of the manager for the benefit of the unitholders and acts as guardian of their interests. Most modern unit trusts are 'open-ended' – i.e., the manager promises to buy back units from unitholders at any time and can also sell new units at any time to obtain more capital. Units are bought from and sold to the manager only – at prices fixed by a definite method based on the value of the assets of the unit trust. The manager receives an initial service charge, which is a percentage of the selling price of each unit, plus a half-yearly management fee which is a percentage of the total assets held by the unit trust. See also the entry for 'mutual fund'.

2. In the USA, a scheme in which investors buy securities called 'redeemable trust certificates' and their money is invested in a fixed collection of securities, typically bonds held until maturity. Trustees of the scheme periodically distribute the returns from the securities to the holders of the certificates and will buy back certificates from holders. Usually the investments held for the scheme are not altered during the existence of the scheme and the number of certificates is never increased. Also called 'unit investment trust'.

unlimited company. A British registered company that is not a limited company. A company is an unlimited company if there is no reference to members having limited liability in its memorandum of association. In an unlimited company all members have unlimited liability for the company's debts although the only circumstance in which they can be called upon to pay is if the company is wound up and is insolvent.

unlimited liability. Liability of a person to pay all the debts of a business enterprise carried on by the person, there being no separation of the person's business and personal affairs. Unlimited liability is incurred by carrying on a business or profession in partnership or as a sole trader or practitioner.

unliquidated damages. Damages that can be quantified only by obtaining the opinion of an authority such as a court.

unlisted company. A company that has not issued any securities that are listed on any stock exchange. Also called 'unquoted company'.

unpublished price-sensitive information. In relation to securities of a company, defined in s. 10 of the Company Securities (Insider Dealing) Act 1985 as: 'information which:

'(a) relates to specific matters relating or of concern (directly or indirectly) to that company, that is to say, is not of a general nature relating or of concern to that company, and

'(b) is not generally known to those persons who are accustomed or would be likely to deal in those securities but which would if it were generally known to them be likely materially to affect the price of those securities'.

unquoted company. Another term for 'unlisted company'.

unrealised revenue. Another term for 'deferred revenue'.

unregistered company. In British company law, a corporation (other than a corporation sole or a Scottish firm) incorporated in and having a principal place of business in Great Britain, apart from:

(a) a registered company or any corporation incorporated by or registered under any public general Act of Parliament;

(b) any corporation not formed for the purpose of carrying on a business which has for its object the acquisition of gain by the corporation or by the members;

(c) any corporation for the time being exempted by direction of the Secretary of State for Trade and Industry.

See Companies Act 1985, s. 718 and Companies (Unregistered Companies) Regulations 1985 (SI 1985 No. 680).

unrestricted-use credit. Credit provided under a regulated consumer credit agreement which is not restricted-use credit.

unsecured creditor. A person who is owed money but has not arranged any direct security for the payment of the money, especially where the debtor has become insolvent.

unsecured loan stock. Abbreviation: ULS. Stock relating to a marketable loan where there is no security for payment of interest or repayment of principal.

unusual item. Defined in IAS 8 as a gain or loss of an accounting entity deriving from an event or transaction distinct from the ordinary activities of the entity and therefore not expected to recur frequently or regularly. Equivalent to 'extraordinary item' as defined in SSAP 6.

up time. Also written: uptime. Time during which a machine or device or production facility is in a condition to perform its intended function. Also called 'operable time'.

usage rate. In stock control, the rate of consumption of stock (BS 5191 : 1975).

usance. In the past, a customary time between the date on which a bill of exchange was drawn and the date on which it would be due for payment. The usance of a bill depended on where it was drawn and where it was payable.

useful economic life. 1. In relation to purchased goodwill, the best estimate of the life of the goodwill at the date of purchase (SSAP 22, para. 26).

2. In relation to a depreciable asset of an accounting entity, 'the period over which the present owner will derive economic benefits from its use' (ED 37, para. 11).

useful life. In relation to a depreciable asset of an accounting entity, either:

(a) the period over which the asset is expected to be used by the entity; or

(b) the number of production or similar units expected to be obtained from the asset by the entity.

See IAS 4. Compare 'useful economic life'.

user terminal. An input-output unit by which a user of a data processing system may communicate with the system. The short form 'terminal' is often used.

usury. Charging of an excessive rate of interest for lending money. In the UK, there is no legal limit to the rate of interest that may be charged, but a court may regard a credit bargain which requires the debtor to make grossly exorbitant payments as an extortionate credit bargain which it may reopen so as to do justice between the parties under the Consumer Credit Act 1974, ss. 137 to 140.

utility cost centre. American spelling: utility cost center. A service cost centre in an organisation that supplies services.

V

valuation. 1. Statement of an opinion of the value of something.
2. The amount which is stated as an opinion of the value something.
3. The process of forming an opinion of the value of something.
In America the term 'appraisal' is used instead of 'valuation'.

valuation account. A ledger account recording amounts that will eventually be deducted from amounts in other ledger accounts. For example, a reserve for depreciation, which contains amounts that will eventually be deducted from amounts in fixed asset accounts. Also called 'absorption account', 'offset account'.

value. 1. *Noun.* A monetary amount associated with an asset, liability, transaction or event for the purposes of accounting, and usually reflecting the amount of money for which the thing could be exchanged.
2. *Verb.* To associate with an asset, liability, transaction or event a monetary amount for the purposes of accounting, usually reflecting the amount for which the thing could be exchanged.
3. *Noun.* A number, symbol or other item substituted for a variable in a generalised symbolic statement so as to produce a particular instance of that statement.
4. *Noun.* The number that is associated by a function with a particular argument.
5. *Noun.* The amount of a quantitative attribute on some particular occasion.

value added. The difference between the turnover of an enterprise for a period and the amount it has paid during that period, other than to employees and providers of finance, for materials, goods and services used in its ordinary activities. Also called 'added value'.

value added statement. A report of the amount of an enterprise's value added during a period with an analysis of its distribution among: (a) employees, (b) dividends on shares and interest on loans, (c) taxation of income, (d) depreciation and retained earnings (usually described as 'provision for maintenance and expansion of assets'). Also called 'added value statement'.

value added tax. Abbreviation: VAT. A tax charged on the value added by an enterprise over a period. In the UK the tax is charged on the supply of goods or services by enterprises, apart from certain supplies (e.g., of insurance and education) that are exempt. When an enterprise supplies goods or services it requires value added tax to be paid by the customer and this is known as 'output tax' of the enterprise. The value added tax that an enterprise pays when buying goods or services for use in its business is called its 'input tax'. At regular intervals, an enterprise pays, to the Commissioners of Customs and Excise, the difference between the total output tax received and the total input tax paid by the enterprise. If an enterprise's input tax exceeds the output tax then the difference is refunded. Enterprises with only a small turnover are not required to charge value added tax (see the entry for 'taxable person').

value received. A phrase traditionally put on a bill of exchange to show that it is drawn to pay a debt of the drawee and not as an accommodation bill.

value shifting. Term used in the Capital Gains Tax Act 1979 for a scheme whereby the value of an asset is materially reduced and a tax-free benefit is conferred on the person disposing of the asset, or a person with whom the disposer is connected, or on any other person (unless it is shown that avoidance of tax was not the main purpose or one of the main purposes of the scheme). A benefit is conferred on a person if that person becomes entitled to any money or money's worth or if the value of any asset in which the person has an interest is increased or the person is wholly or partly relieved from any liability. The benefit is tax-free if no tax is payable on it.

value to the business. In relation to an asset of an accounting entity, defined in SSAP 16, para. 42, as:

(a) the net current replacement cost of an asset; or, if a permanent diminution to below net current replacement cost has been recognised,

(b) recoverable amount.

Also called 'current cost'.

value transferred. In capital transfer tax, the amount by which the transferor's estate immediately after a transfer of value is less than it would be but for the transfer (Capital Transfer Tax Act 1984, s. 3(1)).

variable. 1. In a symbolic (e.g., mathematical) statement that is made about all elements of a particular set (e.g., all numbers in a particular set of numbers), a symbol for an unspecified representative element of that set, used in such a way that substituting one particular element of the set for the symbol consistently throughout the statement will produce a version of the statement specific to that element. For example, 'x' is a variable in the statement '$x - x = 0$', which may be made about any element in the set of all numbers, and substituting the particular number '5' consistently for 'x' produces '$5 - 5 = 0$', which is the version of the statement specific to '5'.

2. A quantitative or qualitative characteristic that is, or may be, represented by a variable (in sense 1).

variable cost. A cost which tends to vary as the level of activity varies, at least in the short term.

variable overhead cost. Term used in the ICMA official terminology for 'variable production overhead cost'.

variable production overhead. Another term for 'variable production overhead cost'.

variable production overhead cost. A production overhead cost that is a variable cost, or an aggregate of such costs. Called 'variable overhead cost' in the ICMA official terminology. Sometimes called 'variable production overhead'.

variables sampling. In auditing, taking a sample from the records of transactions or events of a particular kind and measuring some quantitative characteristic of each item in the sample (usually, the size of any error).

variance. 1. In management accounting, the difference between planned, budgeted or standard cost and actual cost; the difference between planned, budgeted or standard revenue and actual revenue. If the difference results in increased profit, the variance is said to be 'favourable' (abbreviation: F); if the variance results in a reduction of profit, it is said to be 'adverse' (abbreviation: A) or 'unfavourable' (abbreviation: U).

2. In statistics, a measure of the dispersion of observed values based on the mean squared deviation from their arithmetic mean. If there are n observations $x_1, x_2, \ldots, x_n$ with mean $\bar{x}$, then either of the following may be used as the variance:

$$\Sigma(x_i - \bar{x})^2/n$$

$$\Sigma(x_i - \bar{x})^2/(n - 1)$$

If n is large (in practice, greater than 30), the difference between these two formulae is negligible. The first is more memorable, but the second usually gives a more useful result.

3. In probability theory, in relation to a random variable or a probability distribution, a measure of the extent to which the random variable is dispersed about its mean. If X is the random variable and μ is its mean, then its variance is:

$$E((X - \mu)^2)$$

or, in words, the expectation of the square of the centred random variable.

variance accounting. A technique of management accounting in which the planned activities of an undertaking are quantified in budgets, standard costs, standard selling prices and standard profit margins, and the differences between these budgets and standards and the actual results are analysed.

variance analysis. Analysis – of the variance between a planned, budgeted or standard cost, revenue or profit and the actual result – into the variances of two or more components of the cost, profit or revenue. Usually, each component may be further analysed, and so on.

The similar term 'analysis of variance' is used for a completely different procedure in statistics.

variate. Another term for 'random variable'.

VAT. Abbreviation of 'value added tax'.

vatman. Personification of the bureaucracy that administers value added tax.

vector. A matrix that consists of only one row or only one column.

vendor. Another term for 'seller'.

Venn diagram. A diagram in which sets are represented by regions drawn on a surface. Named after John Venn (1834-1923), an English logician who explained and systematically developed diagrammatic representation in logic, especially in his book, *Symbolic Logic*, published in 1881.

venture capital. 1. Capital contributed to an enterprise, especially capital contributed at an early stage in the development of a new enterprise which may have a significant chance of failure but also a significant chance of providing above-average returns, and especially where the provider of the capital expects to have some influence on the direction of the enterprise.

2. Money available for use as venture capital (in sense 1).

vertical form. Another term for 'report form'.

very small workshop. An industrial building with a gross internal floor space of 1,250 square feet or less (Finance Act 1982, s. 73(2)). Special capital allowances are available for very small workshops.

vested interest. An interest, in property, that is not a contingent interest. An interest may be described as 'vested' even if it does not exist until a future time, provided it is certain to come into being at that future time and does not depend on the occurrence of a contingency.

vocation. An occupation that an individual has chosen to follow for most of his or her life, especially one to which the individual is deeply committed.

voidable contract. A contract that one party is entitled to rescind but which is valid and enforceable if that party does not rescind it.

volenti non fit injuria. Latin sentence meaning 'to a willing person no injury is done'. A maxim expressing the legal principle that a person who freely and voluntarily does something knowing that there is a risk of being injured by doing it has no right to claim damages for any injuries actually incurred by doing it.

volume discount. Another term for 'quantity discount'.

voluntary liquidation. Another term for 'voluntary winding up'.

voluntary winding up. A winding up of a registered company initiated by a resolution of the members of the company. If, within the five weeks preceding the adoption of the resolution to wind up, a majority of the directors of the company make, at a board meeting, a statutory declaration of the company's solvency (see the entry for 'declaration of solvency') then the winding up is a 'members' voluntary winding up'; otherwise it is a 'creditors' voluntary winding up'. The directors' declaration may be made on the same day as the members' meeting provided it is made before the meeting. Also called 'voluntary liquidation'.

vote. In UK government finance, another term for 'Supply Estimate'.

voucher. 1. A document that corroborates or explains an entry in accounting records, especially a document that explains why a payment was made.

2. A token given by a finance house to a consumer for the price of an item the consumer wishes to purchase which can be presented to a nominated retailer in exchange for the item. The consumer makes regular fixed payments to the finance house to repay the nominal value of vouchers the consumer has obtained.

voucher trading. System of retail credit trading involving the use of vouchers.

W

wage. Monetary payment made regularly by an employer to an employee under a contract of employment. Usually used for payment in cash for manual work paid at weekly intervals. The plural form 'wages' and the singular form are used interchangeably.

wages account. A special bank account opened by a bank for a customer that is a registered company in financial difficulties so as to record all loans made by the bank to the customer for the purpose of paying wages of employees of the customer. Within limits, these loans will be preferential debts if the company is wound up or if a receiver is appointed under a floating charge. Also called 'wages and salaries account'.

wages and salaries account. Another term for 'wages account'.

waiting time. 1. In queuing theory, another term for 'queuing time'.

2. In production planning, time during which an individual worker is available for work, but is prevented from working by, for example, shortage of material, machine breakdown etc. (BS 5191 : 1975). In production planning, according to BS 5191 : 1975, the term 'queuing time' is not synonymous with 'waiting time'.

warehouse stock. Finished goods stock held at a warehouse (BS 5191 : 1975).

warrant. 1. *Verb.* To give a warranty.

2. *Noun.* A security issued by a company giving a holder the right to be allotted ordinary shares in the company on terms fixed on the issue of the warrant. Usually the holder cannot require allotment until a year or more after issue of the warrant.

warranty. 1. In the law of contract, a promise made by one party to a contract, which is subsidiary, or additional, to the main purpose of the contract. Compare 'condition'.

2. In the law of insurance, a promise given by the assured in a contract of insurance, which the assured must comply with in order to make a claim.

3. In trading, a guarantee given by a manufacturer of a product of the quality of the product with a promise to repair or make good defects.

waste. Material that is discarded as unusable or of no further use and which cannot be sold. Compare 'scrap'.

wasting asset. For UK tax purposes, an asset with a predictable, useful life not exceeding 50 years. More detailed definitions for particular purposes are given in the Capital Gains Tax Act 1979, s. 37, and the Capital Transfer Tax Act 1984, s. 132.

waybill. Another term for 'consignment note'.

WDA. Abbreviation of 'writing-down allowance'.

WDV. Abbreviation of 'written-down value'.

weight. 1. Another term for 'weighting factor'.

2. In a positional representation system, the factor by which a digit in a particular digit place must be multiplied in order to calculate the number that it represents.

weighted arithmetic mean. Another term for 'weighted average'.

weighted average. The weighted average of n numbers $x_1, x_2, \ldots, x_n$ is:

$$\Sigma w_i x_i / \Sigma w_i$$

where $w_1, \ldots, w_n$ are non-negative numbers (called 'weights' or 'weighting factors') that represent the relative significance or importance of the xs and which are not all zero. Also called 'arithmetic weighted average', 'weighted arithmetic mean', 'weighted mean'.

weighted average cost of capital. A weighted average of the costs of each type of capital in the capital structure of an accounting entity weighted according to the importance of each type in the structure.

weighted mean. Another term for 'weighted average'.

weighting factor. A number by which another number (such as a measurement, estimate or observation) is multiplied and which represents the significance, reliance or importance attached to the measurement, etc., compared to others which are given different weighting factors. Also called 'weight'. See also the entry for 'weighted average'.

white knight. Informal. A person who makes an agreed bid for a company in order to prevent an opposed bid from succeeding.

wholly owned subsidiary. Also written: wholly-owned subsidiary. One corporation S is a wholly owned subsidiary of another corporation H if its only members are H and one or more nominees of H, or other wholly owned subsidiaries of H or nominees of wholly owned subsidiaries of H (Companies Act 1985, s. 736(5)(b); Friendly and Industrial and Provident Societies Act 1968, s. 14(4)).

will. A statement made by an individual of the gifts of that individual's property to be made after the individual's death. A will may also exercise a power of appointment by which the individual makes a gift of some other person's property. Also called 'testament' or 'will and testament' (in the past the words 'will' and 'testament' were thought to refer to statements disposing of different types of property, but there is no agreement on which types of property the two words referred to).

winding up. The process of bringing an end to a company (either incorporated or unincorporated) or a non-profit-making association or any scheme for which financial transactions have occurred. The process involves settling all claims against the entity being wound up, which usually involves converting its assets into money, and paying contributed capital and any surplus assets to the owners or beneficiaries of the entity. Also called 'liquidation'. See the entries for 'compulsory winding up' and 'voluntary winding up'.

winding-up order. An order of a British court which commences the compulsory winding up of a company under the Companies Act 1985.

winding up subject to the supervision of the court. The voluntary winding up of a registered company in which a court order has been made under the Companies Act 1985, s. 606, requiring the liquidator to act in accordance with directions of the court and submit accounts to the court. Also called 'winding up under supervision'. The 1984 Insolvency Bill proposes the abolition of the procedure.

winding up under supervision. Another term for 'winding up subject to the supervision of the court'.

windmill. Colloquial. Another term for 'accommodation bill'.

window-dressing. Carrying out artificial transactions which will later have to be reversed, in order to improve temporarily the financial position shown by financial statements, without disclosing that the position will later be reversed.

wind up. *Verb with particle.* To bring the affairs of an accounting entity to an end by settling its liabilities, as far as possible, and distributing any surplus assets to whoever is entitled to them.

WIP. 1. Abbreviation of 'work in process'.
   2. Abbreviation of 'work in progress'.

withholding tax. An amount withheld from a payment to serve as advance settlement of the tax liability of the recipient of the payment. See the entry for 'deduction at source'.

with-the-exception-of opinion. In America, another term for 'except-for opinion'.

word. In data processing, a string of characters which it is convenient to regard as a unit.

work centre. American spelling: work center. 'A set of work stations grouped for convenience of planning or work flow' (BS 5191 : 1975).

working. A statement of how a particular item in a solution to, or report on, a problem has been computed. The working is stated so that anyone reading the solution or report may check the calculation, but it is not essential to an understanding of the solution or report. Also sometimes called 'working paper'.

working capital. The money and other assets available for conducting the day-to-day operations of an accounting entity; normally, the amount by which current assets exceed current liabilities. Also called 'funds'. The term 'net working capital' is sometimes used for the excess of current assets over current liabilities if the term 'gross working capital' is used for the total value of current assets.

working capital adjustment. The increase in working capital required during the period covered by a current cost profit and loss account in order to maintain the operating capability of the net operating assets of the entity. It comprises two elements: a cost of sales adjustment and a monetary working capital adjustment. If current costs are falling, the working capital adjustment is the decrease possible in working capital during the period of the profit and loss account.

working capital ratio. Another term for 'current ratio'.

working capital turnover. The ratio:

$$\frac{\text{turnover}}{\text{working capital}}$$

working paper. 1. Another term for 'working'.

2. Plural form (working papers). An auditor's notes, memoranda, calculations and other data collected while making an audit examination.

work in process. Abbreviation: WIP. Uncompleted products held at any time which will be completed by further work in the future. Sometimes also called 'work in progress': the term 'work in process' seems more appropriate where the products result from a sequence of repetitive processes or operations.

work in progress. Abbreviation: WIP. Uncompleted products held at any time, and uncompleted contracts, which will be completed by further work in the future. Sometimes also called 'work in process'. In America, sometimes called 'goods in process'.

works order. Another term for 'production order'.

work station. Also written: workstation. A set of resources forming a productive unit at a particular location which is the smallest such unit for the purposes of planning and control.

work ticket. Another term for 'operation card'.

write down. 1. *Verb with particle*. To make a provision for depreciation of an asset.

2. *Verb with particle*. To alter the gross carrying amount of an asset to a lower value and transfer the difference to an expense account or to profit and loss account.

write off. *Verb with particle*. To credit an asset account and debit a liabilities account or profit and loss account (or income and expenditure account) so as to recognise a loss in value of assets. The writing off is said to be 'to' the account that is debited.

write up. 1. *Verb with particle*. To make entries in accounting records in their final form from temporary notes, subsidiary accounts or other documents; to make entries in ledger accounts from subsidiary accounts or from journals.

2. *Verb with particle*. To replace the gross carrying amount of an asset with a higher amount, e.g., on revaluation.

writing-down allowance. Abbreviation: WDA. A capital allowance that may be made in certain circumstances to represent depreciation.

writ of execution. A writ directing a public officer or some other person to take action to enforce a court judgment or order.

written-down value. Abbreviation: WDV. Another term for 'net book value'.

Y

yard. 1. Colloquial. In Britain, one thousand millions (from 'milliard').
   2. Colloquial. In America, one hundred dollars.

year of assessment. A period of 12 months commencing on 6 April in one calendar year and ending on 5 April in the next calendar year over which an individual's income is measured in order to calculate UK income tax. Also called 'fiscal year', 'tax year'.

Yellow Book. The publication, *Admission of Securities to Listing*, issued by authority of the Council of the Stock Exchange, which traditionally has a yellow cover.

yield to maturity. Term used in America for 'maturity yield'.

Z

Z chart. A graph displaying a number of successive observations of a time series. If n observations are to be shown then for each of the times at which the observations were taken, three points are plotted:

(a) the observed value at that time;

(b) the cumulative total of observations since the start of the period shown;

(c) the total of the n observations preceding and including the one for that time.

All the points of type (a) are joined by one line; all the points of type (b) by a second line; and all the points of type (c) by a third. The three lines form a shape like a capital Z.

zero-base budgeting. A method of drawing up budgets in which each budgeted expenditure must be justified for each budget period without reference to the fact that there was a similar expenditure in the previous period.

zero-coupon. *Adjective.* Used to describe a marketable loan for which no interest payments will be made. Either the securities are issued at a deep discount or a very large premium is payable on redemption.

zerofill. *Verb.* Another term for 'zeroise'.

zeroise. *Verb.* In data processing, to ensure that the only characters stored in a register or in a location in a store are zeros. The verb 'zerofill' has the same meaning.

zero-rating. A provision that a supply of goods or services by a taxable person is a taxable supply, but that no tax shall be charged on it, i.e., that the rate at which tax is treated as charged on the supply is nil. See Value Added Tax Act 1983, s. 16. A supply of goods or services is zero-rated if the goods or services are of a description for the time being specified in Schedule 5 to the Value Added Tax Act 1983.

zero suppression. Deletion from a numeral of zeros whose presence or absence does not affect the value of the numeral.